The Most Fundamental Right

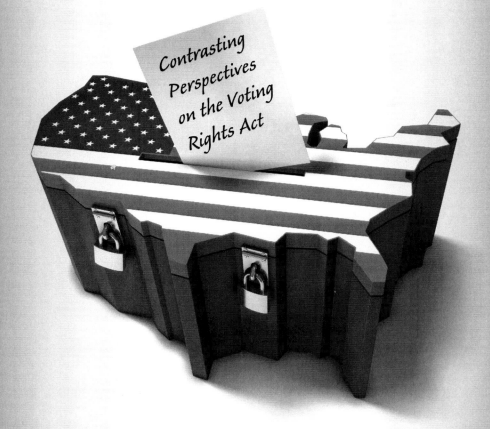

Contrasting
Perspectives
on the Voting
Rights Act

EDITED BY Daniel McCool

INDIANA UNIVERSITY PRESS   *Bloomington & Indianapolis*

This book is a publication of

INDIANA UNIVERSITY PRESS
601 North Morton Street
Bloomington, Indiana 47404–3797 USA

iupress.indiana.edu

Telephone orders 800–842–6796
Fax orders 812–855–7931

© 2012 by Indiana University Press

Manufactured in the United States of America

Library of Congress Cataloging-in-Publication Data

Cataloging information is available from the Library of Congress.
ISBN 978-0-253-00192-4 (cloth : alk paper)
ISBN 978-0-253-00194-8 (pbk : alk paper)
ISBN 978-0-253-00710-0 (ebook)

1 2 3 4 5   17 16 15 14 13 12

THIS BOOK IS DEDICATED TO THE AMERICAN VOTER.

AMENDMENT XV

Section 1.

The right of citizens of the United States to vote shall not be denied or abridged by the United States or by any state on account of race, color, or previous condition of servitude.

Section 2.

The Congress shall have power to enforce this article by appropriate legislation.

Contents

Preface

The initial impetus for this book was a forum on voting rights at the University of Utah in 2006, sponsored by Rocco Siciliano. Mr. Siciliano has more than a passing interest in voting rights and minority issues. As an advisor to President Eisenhower, Rocco set up a meeting in 1958 between the president and civil rights leaders, including Martin Luther King, Jr. It was an auspicious moment. One of the topics they discussed was voting rights, according to Siciliano's autobiography, *Walking on Sand.* We are indebted to Rocco for his many years of public service and for his sponsorship of the Siciliano Forum. We also want to thank the College of Social and Behavioral Science at the University of Utah, a cosponsor of the Siciliano Forum on Voting Rights.

This book presents a lively debate among leading experts on the Voting Rights Act. It is important to note that all the authors are in agreement on one central idea: that elections should be free and fair to all people, regardless of race or ethnicity. Indeed, the reason why these authors became involved in the debate over the Voting Rights Act is because they care passionately about our elections and how to achieve that sometimes elusive goal of fairness. There are few if any fair-minded people today who are opposed to the original 1965 Voting Rights Act; we all understand that it was desperately needed at that time. The different perspectives presented here concern the contemporary application and enforcement of that act and its future directions. This is especially true of the "renewable" sections of the act, which continue to engender debate and litigation.

The book is divided into three sections. The first section provides an overview of the historical, legal, and political context of the Voting

Rights Act (the VRA). In the first chapter I describe the basic outlines of the VRA and its development over time. Peyton McCrary explains the significance of "preclearance" in chapter 2, and Richard Engstrom describes the role of "influence districts" in the implementation of the VRA in chapter 3. In the second section the chapters are presented in pairs; each pair includes contrasting perspectives on a particular aspect of the VRA. Laughlin McDonald and Abigail Thernstrom present contrasting perspectives on the contemporary VRA in chapters 4 and 5. The following two chapters are concerned with the voting rights of American Indians, with a focus on South Dakota, which has seen the most litigation. Bryan Sells, in chapter 6, presents the view of a litigator who has represented tribal members in numerous cases; Chris Nelson presents a view from the state of South Dakota. The final pairing focuses on the language provisions in the VRA. James Tucker argues in favor of the language provisions in chapter 8, and Roger Clegg takes an opposing stance in chapter 9. The final section of the book provides an overview of the debate over the VRA and its potential future impact from two very different perspectives; Edward Blum in chapter 10 and Debo Adegbile in chapter 11.

It is customary to dedicate a book to a specific individual, usually a family member, a mentor, or another author. But we want to dedicate this book to the icon of all free peoples, "the voter." May we continue to work for the perfect vehicle that expresses their political preferences.

D. C. M.
Salt Lake City

The Most Fundamental Right

PART ONE

The Political and Legal Context of the Voting Rights Act

ONE

Meaningful Votes

DANIEL MCCOOL

A BRIEF HISTORY

The debate over minority voting rights began in earnest the night of April 11, 1865. General Robert E. Lee had surrendered the Army of Northern Virginia two days earlier, and the end of the Civil War was in sight. Washington, D. C., was in a state of exultation, and a boisterous crowd of citizens gathered below a window of the White House, demanding that the president say a few words. Lincoln came to the window and, reading by candlelight, explained his vision for a postwar nation. Among his ideas was a proposal to give some blacks, especially those who had fought in the war, the right to vote. Among the listeners in the crowd was John Wilkes Booth. He muttered to his friend, "That means nigger citizenship. That's the last speech he'll ever make."[1]

In the aftermath of the Civil War and Lincoln's assassination, the Thirteenth, Fourteenth and Fifteenth Amendments to the Constitution were adopted. The Fifteenth Amendment, which became part of the Constitution in 1870, reads, "The right of citizens of the United States to vote shall not be denied or abridged by the United States or by any State on account of race, color, or previous condition of servitude. The Congress shall have power to enforce this article by appropriate legislation." The debate over the Fifteenth Amendment was contentious; southern states argued that it interfered with states rights. But after the amendment was adopted, the *New York Times* editorialized that the amendment would "put an end to further agitation of the subject."[2]

The *Times* was wrong; bills to give teeth to the Fifteenth Amendment were introduced repeatedly in the U.S. Congress in the latter half of the nineteenth century. The most innovative bill, the Federal Elections bill of 1891, failed to become law due to opposition from southern Democrats. At that point, the Congress gave up on passing a meaningful voting rights bill.[3] It was not until 1965, one hundred years and three months after Lincoln's window speech, that Congress passed the Voting Rights Act (VRA). The Congress was responding to President Johnson's demand that in the wake of "Bloody Sunday" at the Edmund Pettus Bridge in Selma, Alabama, Congress pass the "goddamnest toughest" voting bill possible.[4] The act was passed with broad bipartisan support, but there was stiff opposition from southerners who claimed the act was a "yoke of shame," "very unjust," and an "extreme measure."[5]

Thus began the long odyssey of the Voting Rights Act, amended and renewed four times, most recently in 2006, making it what one congressman called "arguably the most carefully reviewed civil rights measure in our Nation's history."[6] The adoption and the extensions of the VRA have always passed with support from both parties, in spite of opposition, and all the extensions were signed into law by Republican presidents.

Although there is currently a lively debate, featured in this book, over the merits of the current law, nearly everyone describes the original VRA in superlatives:

· "Many characterize the Voting Rights Act as the most important and effective civil rights legislation Congress ever adopted."[7]
· The VRA is "the crowning achievement of social justice and equality for all Americans."[8]
· "The Act is rightly lauded as the crown jewel of our civil rights laws."[9]
· "The Voting Rights Act can be characterized accurately as one of the most successful pieces of civil rights legislation ever adopted by the Congress."[10]
· "The Voting Rights Act of 1965 has arguably been the most successful legislation to have come out of the Great Society reforms of the 1960s."[11]

- "The Voting Rights Act is a sacred symbol of American Democracy."[12]
- "The Voting Rights Act of 1965 has been widely hailed as the single most important achievement of our civil rights laws."[13]
- "The historic accomplishments of the Voting Rights Act are undeniable."[14]

The VRA is a unique piece of legislation, divided into permanent and temporary sections. Section 2 is permanent, i.e., it does not sunset on a specific date. It outlaws election procedures that "result in the denial or abridgment of the right of any citizen of the U.S. to vote on account of race or color." The act also permanently outlaws literacy and moral requirements and other such "test or device" that denies or abridges the voting rights of racial minorities.[15]

Sections 4 through 9 and 203 are temporary, and thus have to be periodically renewed. Of these, Section 5 requires "preclearance" of all changes in voting laws or procedures in certain states and political subdivisions – "covered jurisdictions" – that meet criteria specified in Section 4 (see chapter 2). The objective of Section 5 was, in the words of the U.S. Supreme Court, to "shift the benefit of time and inertia from the perpetrators of evil to the victim."[16] Sections 6 through 9 authorize the U.S. government to deploy federal examiners to oversee voter registration and federal observers to oversee polling places.[17] Another temporary provision, Section 203, was added in 1975. It requires that voting materials be provided in languages other than English and assistance be provided to individuals with limited English proficiency in certain areas of the country.[18]

The 1965 act only authorized the temporary provisions for five years, so the first reauthorization was in 1970, which reauthorized the provisions for another five years, extended the coverage of Section 5, and made the prohibition of tests and devices applicable to the entire nation. The next reauthorization, in 1975, renewed the provisions for seven years, added Section 203, and made the ban on tests and devices permanent. In 1982, Congress once again renewed the expiring provisions, this time for twenty-five years. Congress also amended Section 2 in response to an adverse Supreme Court ruling.[19] The new language prohibited voting practices that *result* in discrimination, and made it unnecessary to prove discriminatory *intent,* which is very difficult to document. The Congress also changed the "bailout" procedure – the process by which political jurisdictions covered under Sections 4 and 5 can remove themselves from coverage.[20]

Each of the four reauthorizations has provided an opportunity to expand the law's coverage against what supporters describe as "the great degree of human ingenuity that has gone into devising methods to abridge or deny" the rights of minority voters.[21] Conversely, each renewal has presented opportunities for opponents of the VRA to terminate or modify the renewable sections. Media attention has tended to focus on the bipartisan support for the act and has often downplayed the opposition. But in fact there has always been resistance, especially to the renewable sections. When the act was up for renewal in 1970, Governor Lester Maddox of Georgia declared that the law was "illegal, unconstitutional and ungodly and un-American and wrong against the good people of this country."[22] President Nixon expressed opposition to the renewal of Section 5, but signed the reauthorization anyway.[23]

In 1975, there were again voices of opposition, especially against the new language provisions.[24] A group of southern senators argued that "the Southern States covered by the 1965 act have made significant gains that deserve recognition and encouragement rather than 10 more years of punitive sanctions. More minority citizens are registered, voting, and holding office in these States than at any time in American history. Congress should recognize this. . . . Sections 4 and 5 should be allowed to expire."[25]

By 1982 the opposition was much more diverse. Many of the old southern segregationists were gone, and new opposition arose from conservative legislators from other parts of the country. Senator Orrin Hatch of Utah was a critic of Section 2.[26] Congressman Henry Hyde of Illinois argued that the South had "been in the penalty box long enough," and should not be subject to Section 5.[27] One of the witnesses, a Texas lawyer, who appeared before the House committee proposed amending Section 2 to outlaw voting discrimination unless it was "reasonably necessary to protect a legitimate and concrete public interest."[28] The attorney general for the state of South Carolina argued that "[t]he Voting Rights Act has, in my opinion, served its purpose and it should be allowed to expire.... It is now time to remove the state of South Carolina from its state of vassalage."[29] Some people within the Reagan administration resisted renewal, and some opposed the Section 2 results test, but in the end President Reagan chose to sign the bill.[30] And in another sign of changing political realities, Senator Strom Thurmond of South Carolina – once a symbol of ardent segregation – voted in favor of the extension.[31] In short, the politics of the VRA were getting much more complicated.

The most recent authorization also encountered significant opposition. Although it passed both houses by huge margins, it did not "sail through Congress... without any major turbulence."[32] Rather, there was a spirited contest between differing visions of the renewable sections of the act and its role in American democracy. This lively debate, and the larger issue of the future impact of the entirety of the VRA, are the focus of this book.

IMPACT

The statistics regarding increases in minority voting and political participation since the first VRA was passed are stunning. Many of them occurred within the first five years after the act's passage in 1965.[33] According to one study, "there was a substantial jump in black voter registration in a relatively short period" following the passage of the VRA.[34] Other data support this. African American voter registration in the eleven states of the former Confederacy increased from 43.1 percent in 1964 to 62 percent in 1968. In Mississippi, the gap between white and black voter registration rates went from 63.2 percent in 1965 to 6.3 percent in 1988.[35] Of course, not all of these increases are wholly attributable to the VRA, but the act is clearly responsible for an "immediate and breathtaking transformation."[36]

As a result, the forty years following the passage of the act have been "marked by major gains in minority office holding."[37] By 2002, an impressive 9,430 African Americans held elective office; there were only 1,469 in 1970.[38] By 2004, 43 African Americans were serving in Congress, and more than 482 African Americans were in state legislatures. The number of Latino registered voters grew from 7.6 million in 2000 to 9 million in 2004.[39] By 2000 there were 5,205 Hispanic elected officials in the nation.[40] There have also been dramatic increases in Native American voting and political participation (see chapters 6 and 7).[41] By 2005 there were 37 American Indians serving in state legislatures, and seven Native Alaskans serving in that state's legislature.[42] The number of Asian Americans holding elective office increased from 120 in 1978 to 346 in 2004.[43]

Another measure of the V R A's impact is the amount of litigation and legal actions taken under the act. Much of this litigation has occurred under Section 2 – one of the permanent sections of the act. Since the 1982 reauthorization, there have been 331 reported cases, encompassing 763 decisions, filed under Section 2. Plaintiffs prevailed in 123 of these cases.[44] In addition, there may be more than a thousand Section 2 cases that went unreported.[45]

There have also been numerous cases filed under Section 5. The Department of Justice and private parties have filed 107 enforcement actions in court in an effort to force political jurisdictions to abide by the "preclearance" requirement.[46] The U.S. Justice Department has the obligation to review all preclearance requests, which can be quite numerous. The preclearance requests submitted to the Department of Justice have averaged between 4,000 and 6,000 annually from covered jurisdictions.[47] In 2004, for example, the Department reviewed 5,211 submissions.[48]

Another measure of Section 5 activity is the number of objections filed by the U.S. Justice Department in response to the preclearance requests.[49] A study of objection letters from 1965 to 1999 found that 996 letters had been sent, affecting 1,074 jurisdictions.[50] Another 47 objection letters were sent from 2000 to 2008.[51] According to the National Commission study, about half of the objection letters were filed after the 1982 reauthorization.[52] In response to these objection letters, covered jurisdictions withdrew 205 proposed voting law changes between 1982 and 2003.[53]

Section 203, which covers thirty-one states in whole or in part, has also generated litigation. Since 1965 the Justice Department has filed forty cases to force compliance with the language provisions in the VRA.[54] In addition, the 505 political subdivisions covered by Section 203 or the language-assistance provision in Section 4 have provided language assistance to thousands of voters.[55]

Another kind of legal action under the VRA is the deployment of federal observers. Since 1965, more than 22,000 federal observers have been assigned to political jurisdictions; in 2004 alone more than 1,400 observers were deployed to 105 jurisdictions in 29 states.[56]

These impressive data have given rise to two contradictory arguments. From one perspective, these gains are potent evidence that the VRA is absolutely essential and the renewable provisions must continue for, at a minimum, the twenty-five years that was just authorized by Congress in the 2006. But to others, these data strongly indicate that the act, especially its renewable sections, is no longer necessary, that it is an anachronism left over from an era that no longer exists. Both of these perspectives were very much in evidence during the debate over reauthorization in 2006, and both are fully represented in the following chapters.

Although nearly all parties agree that the VRA was a necessary step in 1965, there is widespread disagreement over the current and future impact and need for the VRA. The opinions can be quite divergent. On the floor of the House, Congresswoman Sheila Jackson Lee of Texas described the VRA as "no ordinary piece of legislation. For millions of Americans, and many of us on this Committee, the Voting Rights Act of 1965 is a sacred treasure, earned by the sweat and toil and tears and blood of ordinary Americans who showed the world it was possible to accomplish extraordinary things."[57] A very different perspective was presented by Congressman Lynn Westmoreland of Georgia:

> [T]he bill we have before us is fatally flawed. This rewrite is outdated, unfair, and unconstitutional. [It] treats Georgia as if nothing has changed in the past 41 years. In other words, this rewrite is based on the assumption that the Voting Rights Act hasn't worked.[58]

It was clear, even before the debate in Congress began, that there would be considerable conflict over reauthorization. Both sides prepared for the coming battle.

PREPARING FOR REAUTHORIZATION

The struggle to pass a VRA reauthorization bill started long before the 2007 expiration of the temporary provisions. Both sides had a considerable body of research upon which to base their arguments in Congress. For proponents, the first step was to prepare a detailed record that documented continuing discrimination, which in turn justified extending the renewable sections. This not only made good politics, it also reduced the probability of a successful constitutional challenge; earlier Supreme Court decisions had made it clear that such a record was necessary so that the remedy offered by the act was "proportional and congruent" with the perceived problem.[59]

Responding to this need, the Lawyers' Committee for Civil Rights Under Law teamed up with eighteen cosponsors to form the National Commission on the Voting Rights Act. Their mission was to conduct hearings across America, especially in the covered jurisdictions, and produce a report based on those hearings and other sources describing the continuing need for the VRA's temporary provisions. The commission held ten hearings and heard testimony from more than a hundred witnesses. The commission staff, led by Chandler Davidson, wrote a 168-page report to support their claim that the VRA "cannot simply be dismissed as a relic of our past. Its protections are still needed. The promise of our constitution is still a work in progress."[60]

The Voting Rights Project of the American Civil Liberties Union also had an active role in preparing for the reauthorization. It produced a series of publications, including "Remembering Bloody Sunday," "The Voting Rights Act: What It Has Meant and What Is at Stake," and "The Voting Rights Act of 1965: What Expires in 2007 and What Does Not." The Voting Rights Project also produced numerous press releases and ran a daily media update on its website.[61] The executive director, Laughlin McDonald, and Daniel Levitas, also of the Voting Rights Project, prepared an 885-page report, titled "Vote: The Case for Extending and Amending the Voting Rights Project," that summarized the 293 VRA cases in which the Voting Rights Project had had a role since the last reauthorization in 1982.[62]

A corresponding effort was made by the Leadership Conference on Civil Rights, an umbrella group that works with 192 civil rights organizations. Of those 192 groups, a number of them played a dominant role in preparing for, and supporting, VRA reauthorization, including the NAACP Legal Defense Fund, the National Congress of American Indians, the Native American Rights Fund, the Asian-American Justice Center, the Mexican-American Legal Defense and Education Fund, and the National Council of La Raza.[63]

The opposition to the VRA was also quite busy in the years and months preceding the 2007 renewal deadline. In years past, most of the criticism of the VRA had come from disgruntled southern segregationists, but after the 1982 reauthorization a growing number of academics and think-tank researchers were voicing either criticisms of the act or concerns about its impact and effectiveness (see chapters 5, 7, 9, and 10). These criticisms and concerns consist of four major arguments.

First, opponents argue that the VRA, as presently constituted, creates an unfair partisan advantage and has morphed into a law that effectively guarantees proportional representation for minorities. According to this viewpoint, the VRA is an affirmative action program applied to voting law. Abigail Thernstrom argues that the VRA has strayed far beyond its original goal of minority enfranchisement and has "shaded into a belief in the entitlement of black and Hispanic candidates everywhere to extraordinary protection from white competition."[64] Columnist George Will called the VRA "antiquarian nonsense" that provides "a few government-favored groups entitlements to elective office."[65] Edward Blum of the American Enterprise Institute described Section 5 as an "unworkable, unfair, and unconstitutional mandate that is bad for our two political parties, bad for race relations, and bad for our body politic."[66]

A second argument, also made by opponents, is that the very success of the Voting Rights Act has rendered it unnecessary. Abigail Thernstrom writes, "In 1965, sections 4 and 5 of the Voting Rights Act were designed to deal with a world that by now has virtually disappeared."[67] This perspective was suggested in a recent report by the U.S. Commission on Civil Rights. The commission pointed to dramatic gains in minority voting and a marked reduction in the number of objections filed by the Department of Justice in response to submissions from covered jurisdictions, and then asked rhetorically, "With this progress and the passage of time, the concern about Section 5's encroachment on state authority will loom larger. . . . Should Section 5 be extended?"[68] Political scientists Charles Bullock and Ronald Keith Gaddie examined the progress of minority enfranchisement in Georgia and found that "the disparity in black and white registration rates had largely been eliminated" and that "the politics of Georgia have undergone a dramatic transformation."[69]

Third, some legal scholars have argued that the act as presently constituted no longer meets constitutional standards. Samuel Issacharoff asks, "[H]ave the altered political environment and the compromised administrability of section 5 done more than call into question its constitutional moorings?"[70] Richard Hasen makes a related argument that because of the absence of overt segregationists, it is more difficult to justify Section 5 and thus meet constitutional requirements. He calls this the "Bull Connor is Dead problem," arguing "there is not much of a record of recent state-driven discrimination Congress could point to [to] support renewal."[71]

A fourth argument, made by academics, is that the "majority-minority" districts drawn in response to VRA requirements are actually detrimental to the public policy interests of minorities, who tend to favor Democratic candidates.[72] Thus, according to this view, "Republicans benefit politically from the VRA's mandate to create safe minority election districts."[73] Crucial to this perspective is a distinction between "descriptive representation" and "substantive representation."[74] The former is representation based on race, ethnicity, or some other demographic feature. The latter is based on the ability to influence policy to the benefit of one's policy preferences.[75] Epstein and O'Halloran argue that "recent increases in the number of blacks elected to Congress have come at the cost of substantive representation."[76] In a study of the U.S. House of Representatives, David Lublin found that "[r]acial redistricting paradoxically worked to vastly undercut the influence of minority representatives by contributing to the election of greater numbers of Republicans."[77]

The debate over these four arguments is much in evidence in subsequent chapters. And all of them played a prominent role in the debate

over reauthorization in 2006. When the reauthorization bill was introduced, it began with a statement of purpose: "The purpose of this Act
is to ensure that the right of all citizens to vote, including the right to
register to vote and cast meaningful votes, is preserved and protected as
guaranteed by the Constitution."[78] The phrase "meaningful votes" was
not included in the original 1965 Act. To some, this simply meant that the
efficacy and power of the act had been improved over the years. To critics, this introduced a troubling and potentially discriminating facet to
the VRA: "Now there were 'meaningful' and 'meaningless' votes – votes
that 'counted' and those that did not."[79]

THE VRA RETURNS TO CONGRESS

Even though the temporary sections of the VRA did not expire until 2007,
proponents of the act wanted to begin the legislative process early and
pass a bill in 2006. This was because Congressman James Sensenbrenner,
Jr., was chair of the House Judiciary Committee. He had a played a role
in the 1982 reauthorization and had clearly stated he favored reauthorization in 2006.[80] But Sensenbrenner was scheduled to step down as committee chair in 2007 and was set to be replaced by a congressman much
less supportive of the VRA, so the proponents of the bill wanted to make
sure the legislative action took place under Sensenbrenner's leadership.[81]
This created an unusual opportunity; it meant that Democrats who favored the VRA had a strong ally in a conservative Republican who was
serving in a crucial leadership position.

   On the Democratic side, pro-VRA legislators coalesced around the
leadership of Congressman Melvin Watt of North Carolina, who had just
been elected chair of the Congressional Black Caucus and served on the
Judiciary Committee. Although Watt and Sensenbrenner disagreed on
many major issues, they came together in the belief that the Voting Rights
Act should be reauthorized. Congressman Watt described their alliance:

> We had an admiration for each other's willingness to fight for what we believed
> in. So if we believed in the same thing we could build a relationship of trust. We
> thought we could fight off the people coming at us from all directions. We cut a
> deal that I would get my people to not ask for more, and he could get his people
> to settle for that and not ask for less.[82]

In the ensuing debate, this deal became a crucial element in the politics of the VRA; both Watt and Sensenbrenner had to oppose people in their respective parties who wanted either a stronger bill or a weaker bill. As a VRA activist put it, they had to "elbow away the extremes of both parties."[83]

Prior to introducing the bill in the House, the Judiciary Committee's Subcommittee on the Constitution held ten oversight hearings, heard from forty-six witnesses "representing a spectrum of interests,"[84] received written testimony from the U.S. Department of Justice and sixty other interested parties, and ultimately produced twelve thousand pages of testimony and evidence (critic Abigail Thernstrom characterized it as a "blizzard of anecdotes").[85] The committee also incorporated into the record the report of the National Commission on the Voting Rights Act, the report from the ACLU's Voting Rights Project, and eleven reports from sixteen of the states covered by Section 5. House staff prepared a hundred-plus-page report detailing the justifications for renewing the expiring provisions of the act.[86] The entire house record was then entered in full into the Senate record, and House members appeared before the Senate Judiciary Committee to encourage them to support the bill. The Senate Judiciary Committee and its subcommittees held nine hearings and heard from forty-two witnesses.[87] The extensive hearings and substantial written record buttressed the evidentiary record already compiled to justify extension of the expiring provisions. House Judiciary Committee chairman Sensenbrenner called it "one of the most extensive considerations of any piece of legislation that the United States had dealt with" during his twenty-seven years in the House.[88]

With the formidable Sensenbrenner/Watt partnership in place in the House, proponents of the VRA introduced their bill, HR 9, in the House on May 2, 2006, and named the bill after three icons of the civil rights movement: "The Fannie Lou Hamer, Rosa Parks, and Coretta Scott King Voting Rights Act Reauthorization and Amendments Act of 2006."[89] The Senate immediately followed suit with an identical bill, S. 2703. The original 25 House cosponsors grew to 153 by June 29. Of those 153 legislators, 46 were from the South, 39 from the East, 33 from the Midwest, and 35 from the West. In the Senate, 49 cosponsors had signed on by June 29; 7 from the South, 16 from the East, 16 from the Midwest, and 10 from the West. Congressman Sensenbrenner opened the debate with a clear and succinct statement as to why he believed the V R A should be reauthorized:

> [H]istory reveals that certain States and localities have not always been faithful to the rights and protections guaranteed by the Constitution, and some have tried to disenfranchise African American and other minority voters through means ranging from violence and intimidation to subtle changes in voting rules. As a result, many minorities were unable to fully participate in the political process for nearly a century after the end of the Civil War.[90]

The opponents of the V R A's renewable sections knew from the beginning that they were fighting an icon. Congressman Westmoreland realized this when he visited Congressman Sensenbrenner's office "and there was a hand-written note in a shadow box from Ronald Reagan and his pen from the 1982 renewal signing."[91] Included among the sponsors was Congressman John Lewis, who had been one of the civil rights marchers who was beaten on the Edmund Pettus Bridge. The opponents had to figure out how to amend the law while still honoring the memory and moral authority of the civil rights movement – not an easy challenge. Congressman Charles Norwood of Georgia succinctly described the conundrum faced by those legislators who wanted to significantly amend the V R A but knew they were fighting history. His floor speech is worth quoting at length because it captures both the iconic nature of the V R A and the struggle that led to its passage, as well as the frustrations felt by opponents of the renewable provisions:

> Mr. Chairman, today we battle a phantom that has haunted this Chamber since the day, probably, it was first built. It has stalked us since before we were a Nation. It poured the curse of slavery on our infant Republic. It fed the flames or regional conflict until we suffered the most devastating war in our history. It gave birth to segregation, poll taxes, and literacy tests. Our forebears, in spite of their many blessings that they left us, failed this challenge. They had a chance with Dred Scott and instead decided that slaves were not human beings. They had a chance with Jim Crow, but instead built a segregated society. Today, we have a rare chance, and I mean rare, to revisit the fundamental issue, discrimination, that our predecessors avoided dealing with.... [But] I do not understand how you can go home and you can say you are all for equal rights, fair rights, protections for voters in Georgia, but it is not all right to have those same protections in Tennessee or in Arkansas or in Wisconsin or Ohio.[92]

To Congressman Norwood, Section 5's limited coverage was a form of discrimination; to others, it was an important remedy to discrimination. The opponents charged that the "civil rights card" was being used to unfairly label them. Roger Clegg, president of the Center for Equal Opportunity, made this claim: "What I am afraid has happened is that Democratic Representatives are afraid in this area to do anything that might offend some minority incumbents and some of their minority constituents; their Republican counterparts are afraid to be called racist by various demagogues and interest groups."[93]

Opponents also mounted a fight against Section 203, arguing that it "encourages the balkanization of our country . . . facilitates voter fraud . . . [and] wastes the taxpayers' money."[94] More than fifty members of Congress signed a letter to Congressman Sensenbrenner asking him to oppose Section 203, arguing that bilingual ballots "encourage the linguistic division of our nation" and discourage immigrants from learning English.[95] During the floor debates, Section 203 got caught up in the concurrent debates over immigration and English-only legislation.[96]

But proponents argued that the VRA was an effective counter to racism and still necessary to ensure electoral fairness. Governor Timothy Kaine of Virginia expressed this view in a letter that was entered into the House record during the debate: "Unfortunately, the Voting Rights Act is as necessary today as it was when Congress enacted it. The VRA continues today to serve to protect and guard against discriminatory practices in elections and protects the rights of minority voters. While the nation has dramatically changed over the years, instances of discrimination still exist."[97] Congressman John Conyers of Michigan, an African American who was in Congress at the time of the 1965 VRA, tied past problems with the present: "[W]e have to remember one historical fact. For 400 years, we have been dealing with the problem of discrimination and racism in America. I think it would be simplistic in Congress that we would think, after 40 years, we do not need to worry about it that much anymore."[98]

One of the interesting side debates during the reauthorization hearings focused attention on this question of whether the nation had changed sufficiently to render the VRA unnecessary, or still needed the act as both a remedy and a deterrent against unfair voting practices. Opponents of Section 5 repeatedly cited a statement made by Congressman John Lewis in the case of *Georgia v. Ashcroft:* "There has been a transformation. It's a different State, it's a different world we live in. We've come a great distance. It's not just in Georgia, but in the American South, I think people are preparing to lay down the burden of race." Congressman Westmoreland, a leader of the VRA opponents, read this statement on the floor of the House.[99] This elicited a strong response from Congressman Lewis: "[I]t is true that years ago I said that we are in the process of laying down the burden of race. But it is not down yet and we are not asleep yet. The Voting Rights Act was good and necessary in 1965 and it is still good and necessary today. So don't misquote me. Don't take my words out of context."[100]

It was clear that despite the alliance forged by Sensenbrenner and Watt, there was going to be a fight over the Voting Rights Act reauthorization. And it was not entirely clear where the president stood; his record of support of the renewable sections was inconsistent.[101] But in June 2006, he indicated his support for reauthorization, displaying his usual rhetorical encumbrance: "I am working very carefully with members of Congress to implement that which I said when I signed the proclamation for Rosa Parks, is, 'I want this Voting Rights Act extended.'"[102] There were some Republicans in the Congress that disagreed outright with him, and there were others who opposed the renewable provisions but felt they could not afford to publicly come out against the act due to the political repercussions. This mix of attitudes guaranteed that passage of the bill would entail consider political wrangling.

CHANGES IN THE LAW

The debate over the 2006 reauthorization turned on a number of issues, but both sides had a very specific agenda: The proponents wanted to reauthorize all the renewable provisions (except for federal examiners, which were no longer needed) and, perhaps just as important, they also wanted to amend the law to compensate for what they viewed as damage done by three Supreme Court cases. The opponents were against these "fixes," but they also wanted to significantly amend Section 5 and either amend or abolish Section 203. They introduced four major amendments to the bill in the House. These issues are debated at length in the ensuing chapters, so only a brief introduction is necessary here.

In the forty-seven years since its enactment, the VRA has been the subject of numerous Supreme Court tests. Two of these cases, in the eyes of the act's supporters, "significantly weakened Section 5's effectiveness as a tool to protect minority voters.[103] A third case prevented private plaintiffs from seeking reimbursement for expert witnesses. Reauthorization presented an opportunity to enter language into the act to effectively overturn these three cases.

The first case, *Reno v. Bossier Parish School Board* (known as *Bossier II* because it was the second Supreme Court case in this jurisdiction), concerned Section 5's requirement that covered jurisdictions preclear any changes to voting laws.[104] The standard, until *Bossier II*, was that any changes that had a discriminatory purpose or intent would not be approved. But the high court in *Bossier II* ruled that Section 5 only outlawed "retrogressive dilution," that is, voting law changes that made things worse for minority voters. Thus, under the *Bossier II* standard, Section 5 "does not prohibit preclearance of a redistricting plan enacted with a discriminatory but nonretrogressive purpose."[105]

This new standard fundamentally changed the enforcement of Section 5.[106] Proponents felt that it rendered it virtually ineffective, "a parody of what the Voting Rights Act stands for."[107] The Senate report referred to *Bossier II* as a "strange loophole in the law" that would allow unconstitutional voter discrimination to be approved.[108] HR 9 overturned *Bossier II* by making three changes in Section 5. First, it replaced the phrase "does not have the purpose and will not have the effect" with "neither has the purpose nor will have the effect." Second, it added a subsection that prohibited clearance of any voting change "that has the purpose or will have the effect" of discrimination. And third, just to make sure the courts got the message, the bill defined the word "purpose" to include "any discriminatory purpose."[109] The new language effectively rendered the death knell to *Bossier II*.

The second Supreme Court case that became the target of HR 9 was *Georgia v. Ashcroft*, decided in 2003 (see chapter 3).[110] Prior to this decision, the standard for Section 5 approval was whether an election procedure had the potential to dilute minority voting strength.[111] But the *Georgia* decision lowered this standard by permitting approval of voting changes that merely give minorities the ability to influence elections, even if they are not able to elect candidates of their choice. Opponents of Section 5 called the new standard "a more nuanced assessment of the on-the-ground political realities of a jurisdiction."[112] But proponents argued that the new standard "may allow states to turn black and other minority voters into second class voters, who can 'influence' the election of white candidates but cannot elect candidates of their choice or of their own race."[113] The House report stated that if the *Georgia* standard "remains uncorrected," it would endanger the gains made by minorities because it "permits a jurisdiction to choose among different theories of representation, introduces a substantial uncertainty for minority communities into a statute that was specifically intended to block persistent and shifting efforts to limit the effectiveness of minority political participation."[114] HR 9 remedied this by adding language to Section 5 that specifies that the purpose of the section was to protect the ability of minority citizens to "elect their preferred candidates of choice."[115]

To proponents of the VRA in Congress, overturning these two cases was critical because they were "inconsistent with the congressional intent and purpose of the Voting Rights Act.[116] Opponents had a very different take on the matter: "This bill is bad for everyone, because it perpetuates the racial gerrymandering and racial segregation that is now an inextricable by-product of the Section 5 preclearance process. In fact, it makes that process worse by overturning *Bossier Parish* and *Georgia v. Ashcroft.*"[117]

The third case that was overturned in HR 9 dealt with expert witness fees. In voting rights cases, especially Section 2 cases, plaintiffs and defendants must hire expert witnesses to help them make their case.[118] In Section 2 cases, the burden of proof is on the plaintiffs; they must prove that they meet three conditions established in *Thornburg v. Gingles* and a host of "Senate factors" that were identified at the time of the 1982 reauthorization.[119] This is a tough hurdle to jump, and private Section 2 suits can be very complex and very expensive.[120] Section 14 of the VRA allowed private parties that prevailed in court to recover attorney's fees, but in 1991 the Supreme Court limited Section 14 to legal fees not including expert witness fees.[121] HR 9 resolved that problem by adding language that inserted "reasonable expert fees" into the act.

All of these changes – overturning three Supreme Court cases – were written into HR 9, which was introduced on May 2, 2006. Rather than attempt to stop the bill altogether or have the "fixes" removed from the bill, the opponents focused on introducing a set of amendments that would make the final bill more palatable to their interests. Although several amendments were offered by both opponents and proponents, four in particular were pushed hard by those who wanted to fundamentally change Sections 4, 5, and 203 of the Voting Rights Act.

Two of these proposed amendments dealt with the coverage formula set out in Section 4 that determines which jurisdictions are covered by the Section 5 preclearance requirements. Congressman Charles Norwood introduced an amendment to base coverage on voter registration and turnout levels for the three most recent election cycles; any jurisdiction where registration and voting fell below 50 percent would be covered. This formula would not take into account past discrimination or evidence of current discrimination. Rather, Norwood argued, it would apply Section 5 to the entire nation: "Under this amendment, minority voters nationwide will have access to the same Section 5 protections, if there has been a violation of their rights. At the same time, all voters across America will be treated the same if there has been no violation in the last 12 years."[122]

The rationale for changing the Section 4 formula was that covered states have made substantial progress and are now no different than noncovered jurisdictions and thus should not be singled out. Congressman Nathan Deal of Georgia made that argument, noting that more successful Section 2 lawsuits had been filed in noncovered jurisdictions than in covered ones. He then presented data showing how much progress had been made in his home state: "In Georgia, 66.3 percent of eligible blacks were registered to vote. Only 59.3 percent of whites were registered to vote, a 7 percent plus on those who are black. On voter turnout in Georgia in that election cycle, 51.6 percent of black voters voted; only 48.3 percent of white voters voted. So, we have made substantial progress."[123]

Congressman Westmoreland also argued that Georgia no longer deserved to be singled out by Section 5:

There is no question that the Voting Rights Act was needed in 1965. Georgia had a terrible record and merited the drastic remedy imposed on it by preclearance and Section 5. The thrilling thing is, it worked: Georgia is not the same place it was. Today, we have more than 600 elected black officials; nine of the 34 statewide officeholders are minorities, and black voter turnout in the 2000 election exceeded white voter turnout. Georgia is a changed State, changed for the better because of the Voting Rights Act.[124]

The highlight of the debate over the Norwood Amendment was a direct exchange between Norwood and Sensenbrenner. Norwood argued that his proposed formula would bring 1,010 jurisdictions, scattered all across America, under Section 5 coverage, and thus eliminate "default amnesty for modern violations."[125] This provoked a lively reply from Sensenbrenner:

> [T]his amendment guts the Voting Rights Act, and let's make no bones about it . . . there is not a single State, except Hawaii, with voter registration and turnout below the 50 percent level required by this amendment. That means that only the State of Hawaii in its entirety would be covered, along with random scattershot jurisdictions across the country that do not have the century-long history of discrimination that the covered States do. . . . To give you a sense of the absurdity of this amendment, let's take the example of Montana. . . . The amendment . . . would not cover Blaine County, where just a few years ago a Federal District Court and a U.S. Court of Appeals found widespread evidence of discrimination against American Indians. . . . By radically altering the coverage formula of the Voting Rights Act in a way that severs its connection to jurisdictions with proven discriminatory histories, this amendment will render HR 9 unconstitutional.[126]

The House rejected the Norwood amendment, 318 to 96.

The second proposed amendment to Section 5 was introduced by Congressman Lynn Westmoreland. His amendment would have required the U.S. Justice Department to review, on an annual basis, all covered jurisdictions to assess whether they were eligible for bailout (i.e., would no longer have to submit voting changes for preclearance). If the attorney general decided that a jurisdiction was indeed eligible, he or she would consent to a declaratory judgment that would automatically bail out that jurisdiction. Congressman Westmoreland explained that his amendment was designed to "help save the Voting Rights Act" by allowing numerous jurisdictions with "clean records" to easily bail out.[127]

Again Congressman Sensenbrenner provided the rejoinder, arguing that the Westmoreland amendment "would turn the Voting Rights Act on its head by requiring the Voting Section of the Department of Justice to conduct an annual, once a year, review of nearly 900 jurisdictions, and thus, drain all of its resources away from preventing voting discrimination. . . . It does everything to make the Voting Rights Act hopelessly incapable of effective administration."[128] Sensenbrenner also argued that the amendment gave too much power to the Justice Department's Voting Section: "That is an unprecedented voting rights policy that places far too much power in a single Federal executive agency, giving it the unfettered authority to remove entire States from coverage."[129] The Westmoreland amendment was defeated, 302 to 118.

A third amendment, introduced by Congressman Steve King, would have repealed Section 203. This amendment became embroiled in the ongoing immigration debate and reignited arguments regarding "English only" proposals. Congressman King argued that Section 203 "contradicts our immigration law, because knowledge of English is a condition for naturalization."[130] Congressman John Hostettler of Indiana spoke in favor of the King amendment: "[I]t is a tremendous prize [for new citizens] to be able to go into the polling place and use that English language, the de facto new native tongue in the process of exercising that very blessed right, and that is the right to vote. . . . [English] is what we have determined over many years in this country to be the native tongue, and I believe that it is time for this particular provision to be sunsetted and to be eliminated."[131] The King amendment was defeated in the House Judiciary Committee, 26 to 9.[132] King then proposed another amendment that would reauthorize Section 203 for just six years rather than the twenty-five years proposed in HR 9, arguing that a twenty-five-year extension would "institutionalize multilingual balance."[133] This second King amendment was also defeated in committee, 24 to 10.[134] King was the only member of the Judiciary Committee to vote against reporting out HR 9. King then managed to get 79 of his House colleagues to sign a letter to Sensenbrenner stating that they would not support the VRA unless the language provision was removed.[135] In response, Sensenbrenner allowed the King amendment to be resurrected and voted on by the full House; it was rejected 238 to 185.[136]

And finally, Congressman Louis Gohmert of Texas introduced an amendment to reduce the extension from the twenty-five years in H R 9 to ten years, arguing that ". . . we need to review this act again sooner than 2032 to be sure that the voting rights of all individuals are being protected and if the formula needs to be readjusted in 2016 so that areas experiencing racial disparities in voting can fix those problems."[137] Again, Sensenbrenner offered the retort: "[T]o protect minority voting rights for decades to come, to prevent tying Congress's hands in 10 years by denying it the sufficient record on which to decide future renewals as required by the Supreme Court, and prevent nullifying the current Voting Rights Act's incentive to maintain clean voting records for 10 years, this amendment should be soundly defeated." It was, 288 to 134.[138]

The debate over these amendments was heated, and it was not entirely evident that H R 9 would survive the conflict. Supporters of H R 9 referred to the four amendments as "poison pills"[139] and "mean-spirited."[140] Supporters of the amendments called them "sensible changes" that would help the V R A survive Supreme Court scrutiny,[141] and "fair commonsense amendments" that prepare the V R A for the twenty-first century.[142] Despite these disparate views of the V R A, the coalition put together by Sensenbrenner and Watt held together and fought off various amendments of all stripes, and when the final vote came in the House on July 13, H R 9 prevailed by a vote of 390 to 33.[143] Congressman Westmoreland, alluding to the expected constitutional test, remarked, "We needed 218 votes in the House but we'll only need five votes on the Supreme Court."[144]

In the Senate, the debate over the V R A happened to coincide with President Bush's appearance at the N A A C P convention. In his speech, the president talked about a "new founding" for African Americans that began with the civil rights movement and the Voting Rights Act. He thanked the House of Representatives for passing the V R A, and then spoke directly about the impending vote in the Senate: "Soon the Senate will take up the legislation. I look forward to the Senate passing this bill promptly, without amendment, so I can sign it into law."[145] Later that day, the Senate passed the legislation, which was followed by a statement by the president that he "would be pleased to sign The Voting Rights Act into law."[146]

The congressional conflict over the VRA reauthorization was over. But there was one more act in the drama. When the Senate was considering the bill, a number of senators indicated that they either were not in favor of passage or supported the amendments proposed in the House. But Arlen Specter, chairman of the Senate Judiciary Committee, favored reauthorization, and he began the Senate debate by describing it as:

> a historic day for the Senate and really a historic day for America as we move forward with Senate action to reauthorize the Voting Rights Act.... In an era where many have challenged the ability of the Congress to function in the public interests and in an era where there is so much partisan disagreement, it is good to see the two parties in the House and the Senate coming together to reauthorize this very important legislation.[147]

For those in the Senate who were not enthusiastic about passing the VRA, there was a sense that the debate was rushed and something of a foregone conclusion. However, no one wanted to publicly come out against the popular bill. As a result, much of the opposition occurred behind the scenes, according to one of the people involved in the legislation.[148] Nevertheless, the Senate passed the legislation unanimously.

After the law had been passed by both houses, the Senate Judiciary Committee took the unusual step of producing a post hoc report giving the dissenters an opportunity to voice their concerns about the VRA. In a section of the report titled "Additional Views of Mr. Cornyn and Mr. Coburn," the two senators complained that although "each hearing had a very balanced panel and many amendment ideas were offered by witnesses, it was clear that no amendment would be given serious consideration because of the political nature of the bill and the expedited, rushed process." They concluded with a strongly worded assessment: "We cannot help but fear that the driving force behind this rushed reauthorization process was the reality that the Voting Rights Act has evolved into a tool for political and racial gerrymandering."[149] This prompted eight senators to write a rejoinder, stating they did not subscribe to the Senate report and noting that a "post-passage legislative history is a contradiction in terms. Any after-the-fact attempts to re-characterize the legislation's language and effects should not be credited."[150]

The day after the Senate report was published, President Bush held a signing ceremony for the newly reauthorized VRA. He promised to "vigorously enforce" the act that had "helped bring a community on the margins into the life of American democracy."[151]

CONCLUSION

After the debate over the VRA, Congressman Melvin Watt made it a point to remind his colleagues of the history of his state's delegation to Congress:

> When U.S. Representative George H. White of North Carolina rose to address the House on January 29, 1901, he was the last African American remaining in Congress following Reconstruction. By then, all other African American members had been defeated by the systematic removal of Black voters from the voting roles or by the refusal to allow Black citizens to register using such means as poll taxes, literacy tests, fraud, intimidation or other tactics. . . . As I stood behind President Bush at the White House when he signed the [VRA of 2006] into law, I couldn't help feeling a touch of vindication for the many Black voters who had been deprived of their most basic right.[152]

For most members of Congress, the 2006 reauthorization of the VRA was yet another milestone on the road to political equality. But a significant number of legislators felt that the supporters of the act relied too heavily on history and not enough on current political reality:

> The Voting Rights Act in the 109th Congress was an example of putting politics above principle, and power above people. The basis for the VRA was to encourage and enable everyone to participate in the election process. It was never intended to manipulate the political system. It has turned into an instrument of political manipulation and an invitation for partisan lawsuits as long as this country is in existence.[153]

The constitutional test of Section 5 of the new act, promised by its opponents, was quick to materialize. The test case came out of a small utility district near Austin, Texas. Gregory Coleman, the attorney for the utility district, announced the case with a reference to the newly elected president: "The America that has elected Barack Obama as its first African-American president is far different than when Section 5 was first enacted in 1965."[154] The High Court, under the leadership of Chief Justice John Roberts, was viewed as potentially hostile to Section 5, and there was considerable speculation that they would rule against the act.[155] But instead, the Court chose an indecisive posture.

In *Northwest Austin Municipal Utility District Number One v. Holder,* the Court upheld, by a 7-1 vote, the Voting Rights Act, deferring a decision on its constitutionality: "Whether such conditions continue to justify such legislation is a difficult constitutional question we do not answer today."[156] However, the Court issued an open invitation for further court challenges: "The evil that Section 5 is meant to address may no longer be concentrated in the jurisdiction singled out for preclearance. . . . There is considerable evidence that it fails to account for current political conditions."[157] One commentator interpreted that language to mean that "the Justices are prepared to invalidate the statute as it stands."[158] Another simply saw it as a way to avoid the "symbolically monumental" decision to strike down an iconic law.[159] A third commentator concisely noted that the Court "punted" but that "it's hard to read this decision and think that Section 5 is going to have an easy time for it the next time it is challenged in this Court."[160]

Without a doubt, the VRA will see continued challenges. The ink was barely dry on the *Northwest Austin* case when Shelby County, Alabama, filed a lawsuit seeking to invalidate Section 5.[161] Edward Blum, the director of the Project on Fair Representation, characterized it as a "perfect case" to "say that Congress didn't do its job [in 2006] because it failed to properly analyze the extent that purposeful racial discrimination exists in voting."[162] However, Section 5 was upheld by both district and appellate courts; Shelby County promised to appeal to the Supreme Court.[163] Two other VRA cases, *Laroque v. Holder* and *State of Arizona v. Holder,* are also currently in the courts.[164] In addition, the redistricting that followed the 2010 census will most likely provoke additional cases.

The chapters in this book make it clear that the controversies over the VRA will continue. The long-term objective of the act was laid out succinctly by former justice Sandra Day O'Connor: "[T]he Voting Rights Act, as properly interpreted, should encourage the transition to a society where race no longer matters; a society where integration and color-blindness are not just qualities to be proud of, but are simple facts of life."[165] Assessments as to whether the current VRA adds to, or detracts from, that objective varied dramatically when the VRA reauthorization was debated in the Congress in 2006. Is it an act that needs to be "modernized?"[166] Should it be characterized as a "Voting Discrimination Act"?[167] Or conversely, is it true that "the Voting Rights Act was not and never will be about special rights – it is about equal rights."[168] Is it correct that "any diminishment of the Voting Rights Act is a diminishment of our democracy"?[169] Perhaps the most evocative statement made during the debate came from Congressman John Lewis, a living symbol of the civil rights movement who shed his blood many years ago on a bridge that, as it turns out, was a bridge from the past to the future. On the floor of the House, Lewis said, "When historians pick up their pens and write about this period, let it be said that those of us in the Congress in 2006, we did the right thing, and our forefathers and our foremothers would be very proud of us."[170] This book is very much an attempt to make that assessment: did they do the right thing?

NOTES

1. Ronald White, *The Eloquent President* (New York: Random House, 2005), pp. 305–6; David Herbert Donald, *Lincoln* (New York: Simon & Schuster, 1995), p. 588; Doris Kearns Goodwin, *Team of Rivals* (New York: Simon & Schuster, 2005), p. 728.

2. Alexander Keyssar, *The Right to Vote* (New York: Basic Books, 2000), p. 103.

3. Ibid., pp. 106–11.

4. "Protecting Minority Voters: The Voting Rights Act at Work, 1982–2005," report by the National Commission on the Voting Rights Act, February 2006, p. 11.

5. Laughlin McDonald, *A Voting Rights Odyssey* (New York: Cambridge University Press, 2003), p. 11.

6. Providing for Consideration of HR 9, Fannie Lou Hamer, Rosa Parks, Coretta Scott King Voting Rights Act, July 13, 2006, U.S. House of Representatives, 109th Cong., 2nd sess. *Congressional Record*, H5148. Quoting Congressman Melvin Watt.

7. U.S. Commission on Civil Rights, "Voting Rights Enforcement and Reau-

thorization: The Department of Justice's Record of Enforcing the Temporary Voting Rights Act Provisions." Published by the U.S. Commission on Civil Rights, U.S. Department of Justice, Washington, D.C., May 2006.

8. African American Ministers in Action to the Honorable Lynn Westmoreland, June 29, 2006, on file with the ACLU Voting Rights Project.

9. U.S. Senate, Committee on the Judiciary, 109th Cong., 2d sess. Report, "Fannie Lou Hamer, Rosa Parks, Coretta Scott King, and Cesar E. Chavez Voting Rights Act," 109–295, Calendar No. 523, July 26, 2006 (hereafter "Senate Report"), p. 1.

10. Statement of Bradley J. Schlozman, acting assistant attorney general, Civil Rights Division, Department of Justice, October 25, 2005, p. 7. Transcript in possession of the author.

11. Bruce MacLaury, "Foreword," in *Controversies in Minority Voting*, ed. Bernard Grofman and Chandler Davidson, p. vii (Washington, D.C.: The Brookings Institution, 1992).

12. Richard Pildes, "Introduction," in *The Future of the Voting Rights Act,* ed. David Epstein, Richard Pildes, Rodolfo de la Garza, and Sharyn O'Halloran, p. xi (New York: Russell Sage Foundation, 2006).

13. House Concurrent Resolution 216, House Calendar No. 72, 109th Cong., 1st sess. Report No. 109-195.

14. *Northwest Austin Municipal Utility District Number One v. Holder.* No. 08-322 (June 22, 2009): 6.

15. 42 USC 1973. The latest Supreme Court case regarding Section 2 is *Bartlett v. Strickland,* No. 07-689, 556 U.S. (2009).

16. *South Carolina v. Katzenbach,* 383 U.S. 301, 309 (1966).

17. The authorization for federal examiners was eliminated in the 2006 reauthorization; federal observers are still covered by the law.

18. See Angelo Ancheta, "Language Accommodation and the Voting Rights Act," in *Voting Rights Act Reauthorization of 2006,* ed. Ana Henderson, pp. 293–325 (Berkeley, Calif.: Berkeley Public Policy Press, 2007); Joycelyn Benson, "Language Protection for All? Extending and Expanding the Language Protections of the Voting Rights Act," in *Voting Rights Act Reauthorization of 2006,* ed. Ana Henderson, pp. 327–74 (Berkeley, Calif.: Berkeley Public Policy Press, 2007).

19. *City of Mobile v. Bolden,* 446 U.S. 55 (1980).

20. House Report on HR 109, Fannie Lou Hamer, Rosa Parks, Coretta Scott King, and Cesar E. Chavez Voting Rights Act, 109th Cong., 2nd. sess., May 22, 2006 (hereafter "House Report"), pp. 5–6; McDonald, *A Voting Rights Odyssey,* ch. 10–13; Chandler Davidson, "The Voting Rights Act: A Brief History," in *Controversies in Minority Voting,* ed. Bernard Grofman and Chandler Davidson, pp. 24–42 (Washington, D.C.: The Brookings Institution, 1992).

21. "Protecting Minority Voters," p. 15. Section 203 required a separate reauthorization in 1992. That legislation, called the Voting Rights Language Assistance Act, enlarged the coverage and extended it for fifteen years so that its next renewal would coincide with the other renewable provisions. Public Law 102-344. See U.S. Congress, House of Representatives, 102nd Cong., 2nd. sess. HR Report No. 102-655, reprinted in 1992 USCCAN 766.

22. Quoted in McDonald, *A Voting Rights Odyssey,* p. 140.

23. Steven F. Lawson, *In Pursuit of Power* (New York: Columbia University Press, 1987), p. 301.

24. David Hunter, "The 1975 Voting Rights Act and Language Minorities," *Catholic University Law Review* 25 (1976): pp. 250–70.

25. U.S. Congress, Senate, 94th Cong., 1st sess., Senate Report No. 94-295, pp. 73–74. Reprinted in 1975 USCCAN 822–23.

26. Abigail Thernstrom, *Whose Votes Count? Affirmative Action and Minority Voting Rights* (Cambridge, Mass.: Harvard University Press, 1987), pp. 106–8.

27. Hyde later changed his mind and voted for the reauthorization.

28. *Hearings before the Subcommittee on Civil and Constitutional Rights of the Committee on the Judiciary,* U.S. House of Representatives, 97th Cong., 1st. sess. May, June, July 1981. Serial No. 24, p. 924. Testimony of William White.

29. Ibid., pp. 1464–65.

30. Ibid., pp. 893–95.

31. U.S. Congress, Senate, 97th Cong., 2nd sess. Senate Report No. 97-417, 1982, p. 88.

32. Katherine Tate, "Black Politics, the GOP Southern Strategy, and the Reauthorization of the Voting Rights Act," *The Forum* 4, no. 2 (2006): p. 1.

33. Thernstrom, *Whose Votes Count?* pp. 11–18. Also see Frank Parker, *Black Votes Count* (Chapel Hill: University of North Carolina Press, 1990). Also see "Protecting Minority Voters," pp. 98–99.

34. Ronald Waters, "The Partisan Landscape: How Blacks Became the Indispensable Democrats," in *The Unfinished Agenda of the Selma-Montgomery Voting Rights March,* ed. Dara Byrne, pp. 45–54 (New York: John Wiley and Sons, 2005).

35. "Protecting Minority Voters," p. 37. Also see Lisa Handley and Bernard Grofman, "The Impact of the Voting Rights Act on Minority Representation: Black Officeholders in Southern State Legislatures and Congressional Delegations," in *Quiet Revolution in the South,* ed. Chandler Davidson and Bernard Grofman, pp. 335–50 (Princeton, N.J.: Princeton University Press, 1994).

36. Senate Report, p. 6.

37. Zoltan Hajnal and Jessica Troustine, "Transforming Votes into Victories: Turnout, Institutional Context, and Minority Representation in Local Politics," in *Voting Rights Act Reauthorization of 2006,* ed. Ana Henderson, pp. 83–106 (Berkeley, Calif.: Berkeley Public Policy Press, 2007).

38. Abigail Thernstrom, *Voting Rights – and Wrongs: The Elusive Quest for Racially Fair Elections* (Washington, D.C.: American Enterprise Institute Press, 2009), p. 193.

39. House Report, May 22, 2006, pp. 9–10. Also see Rudolfo de la Garza and Louis DeSipio, "Reshaping the Tub: The Limits of the VRA for Latino Electoral Politics," in *The Future of the Voting Rights Act,* ed. David Epstein, Richard Pildes, Rodolfo de la Garza, and Sharyn O'Halloran, pp. 139–62 (New York: Russell Sage Foundation, 2006).

40. "Protecting Minority Voters," p. 41.

41. See Daniel McCool, Susan Olson, and Jennifer Robinson, *Native Vote* (New York: Cambridge University Press, 2007). Also see Laughlin McDonald, *American Indians and the Fight for Equal Voting Rights* (Norman: University of Oklahoma Press, 2011); Laughlin McDonald, "Expanding Coverage of Section 5 in Indian Country," in *The Future of the Voting Rights*

Act, ed. David Epstein, Richard Pildes, Rodolfo de la Garza, and Sharyn O'Halloran, pp. 163–222 (New York: Russell Sage Foundation, 2006).

42. "Protecting Minority Voters," p. 45. See also: McCool, Olson, and Robinson, *Native Vote,* pp. 187–88.

43. "Protecting Minority Voters," p. 47.

44. See Ellen Katz, "Not Like the South? Regional Variation and Political Participation through the Lens of Section 2," in *Voting Rights Act Reauthorization of 2006,* ed. Ana Henderson, pp. 183–221 (Berkeley, Calif.: Berkeley Public Policy Press, 2007); Ellen Katz, "Documenting Discrimination in Voting: Judicial Findings Under Section 2 of the Voting Rights Act Since 1982," *Michigan Journal of Law Reform* 39 (Summer 2006): pp. 643–772. Also see www.votingreport.org.

45. "Protecting Minority Voters," pp. 85–88.

46. Ibid., p. 101.

47. House Report, p. 10.

48. Bradley Schlozman statement, p. 4.

49. See Peyton McCrary, Christopher Seaman, and Richard Valelly, "The Law of Preclearance: Enforcing Section 5," in *The Future of the Voting Rights Act,* ed. David Epstein, Richard Pildes, Rodolfo de la Garza, and Sharyn O'Halloran, pp. 29–37 (New York: Russell Sage Foundation, 2006).

50. Peyton McCrary, Christopher Seaman, and Richard Valelly, "The End of Preclearance as We Knew It: How the Supreme Court Transformed Section 5 of the Voting Rights Act," *Michigan Journal of Race and Law* 11 (Spring 2006): pp. 292–313.

51. Ibid., p. 278. For data on objections between 2004 and 2008 see www.usdoj .gov/crt/voting/sec_5/obj_activ.htm

52. "Protecting Minority Voters," 52. The Senate report states that 754 objections have been filed since 1982. See Senate Report, p. 8. The ACLU report states that

more than a thousand have been filed since 1982. See Laughlin McDonald and Daniel Levitas, "The Case for Extending and Amending the Voting Rights Act: Voting Rights Litigation, 1982–2006," report of the Voting Rights Project of the American Civil Liberties Union, www.votingrights .org (March 2006).

53. "Protecting Minority Voters," p. 58. Critics of Section 5 note that the Department of Justice objection letters have declined steadily over the last forty years and have "virtually disappeared" in the last decade. See 2006 U.S. Commission on Civil Rights, "Voting Rights Enforcement and Reauthorization," p. x.

54. www.usdoj.gov/crt/voting/sec_ 203.

55. James Thomas Tucker and Rodolfo Espino, "Government Effectiveness and Efficiency? The Minority Language Assistance Provisions of the VRA," *Texas Journal on Civil Liberties and Civil Rights* 12, no. 2 (2007): pp. 163–232. Also see U.S. General Accounting Office, "Bilingual Voting Assistance," Report No. GAO-08-182 (January 2008).

56. House Report, p. 20. Also see James Thomas Tucker, "The Power of Observation: The Role of Federal Observers under the Voting Rights Act," *Michigan Journal of Race and Law* 13 (Fall 2007): pp. 227–76. "Protecting Minority Voters," p. 32, estimates the number of observers at twenty-five thousand.

57. Providing for Consideration of HR 9, Fannie Lou Hamer, Rosa Parks, Coretta Scott King Voting Rights Act, July 13, 2006, U.S. House of Representatives, 109th Cong., 2nd sess. *Congressional Record*, H5158. Quoting Congresswoman Sheila Jackson Lee.

58. Ibid., p. 5150, quoting Congressman Lynn Westmoreland.

59. *City of Boerne v. Flores* 521 U.S. 507 (1997). Also see *Board of Trustee v. Garrett* 531 U.S. 356 (2001); House Report, p. 28.

60. Barbara Arnwine, executive director of the Lawyers' Committee for Civil Rights Under Law, in the foreword to "Protecting Minority Voters," p. vi.

61. www.aclu.org/Votingrights/ Votingrights.cfm.

62. McDonald and Levitas, "The Case for Extending."

63. Julie Fernandez, senior counsel, Leadership Conference on Civil Rights, in-person interview, Washington, D.C., February 8, 2007.

64. Thernstrom, *Whose Votes Count?* p. 235. Also see Abigail Thernstrom, "Concurring Statement of Commissioner Abigail Thernstrom," in U.S. Commission on Civil Rights, "Voting Rights Enforcement and Reauthorization: The Department of Justice's Record of Enforcing the Temporary Provisions." Published by the U.S. Commission on Civil Rights, U.S. Department of Justice, Washington, D. C. May 2006; Thernstrom, *Voting Rights – and Wrongs*.

65. George Will, "VRA: All of It, Forever?" *Newsweek*, October 10, 2005, p. 70.

66. *House Judiciary Committee's Subcommittee on the Constitution, Oversight Hearings on the Voting Rights Act,* 109th Cong. 2nd sess., October 25, 2005. Testimony of Edward Blum.

67. Thernstrom, *Voting Rights – and Wrongs,* p. 202.

68. U.S. Commission on Civil Rights, "Voting Rights Enforcement and Reauthorization," p. 13.

69. Charles Bullock and Ronald Gaddie, "An Assessment of Voting Rights Progress in Georgia Prepared for the Project on Fair Representation, American Enterprise Institute Policy Series." October 5, 2005. Published by the American Enterprise Institute.

70. Samuel Issacharoff, "Does Section 5 of the Voting Rights Act Still Work?" in *The Future of the Voting Rights Act,* ed. David Epstein, Richard Pildes, Rodolfo de la

Garza, and Sharyn O'Halloran, p. 118 (New York: Russell Sage Foundation, 2006).

71. Richard Hasen, "Congressional Power to Renew Preclearance Provisions," in *The Future of the Voting Rights Act*, ed. David Epstein, Richard Pildes, Rodolfo de la Garza, and Sharyn O'Halloran, p. 82 (New York: Russell Sage Foundation, 2006).

72. Much of this literature was summarized by Justice O'Connor in *Georgia v. Ashcroft*, 539 U.S. 482–83 (2003).

73. Richard Pildes, "Political Competition and the Modern V R A," in *The Future of the Voting Rights Act*, ed. David Epstein, Richard Pildes, Rodolfo de la Garza, and Sharyn O'Halloran, p. 11 (New York: Russell Sage Foundation, 2006).

74. Lani Guinier, "Voting Rights and Democratic Theory: Where Do We Go from Here?" in *Controversies in Minority Voting*, ed. Bernard and Chandler Davidson, pp. 283–92 (Washington, D. C.: The Brookings Institution, 1992).

75. See Carol Swain, *Black Faces, Black Interests: The Representation of African-Americans in Congress* (Cambridge, Mass.: Harvard University Press, 1993); Charles Cameron, David Epstein, and Sharyn O'Halloran, "Do Majority-Minority Districts Maximize Substantive Black Representation in Congress?" *American Political Science Review* 90 (Dec. 1996): pp. 794–812. For a contrasting view, see Vincent Hutchings and Nicholas Valentino, "The Centrality of Race in American Politics," *Annual Review of Political Science* 7 (2004): 383–408, especially pp. 396–97.

76. David Epstein and Sharyn O'Halloran, "Trends in Minority Representation, 1974–2000." In *The Future of the Voting Rights Act*, ed. David Epstein, Richard Pildes, Rodolfo de la Garza, and Sharyn O'Halloran, p. 63 (New York: Russell Sage Foundation, 2006).

77. David Lublin, *The Paradox of Representation* (Princeton, N.J.: Princeton University Press, 1997), p. 124. For a very different interpretation, see David Canon, *Race, Redistricting, and Representation* (Chicago: University of Chicago Press, 1999).

78. Sec. 2(a), as reported in the House Report, p. 1.

79. Thernstrom, *Whose Votes Count?* p. 4.

80. See House Concurrent Resolution 216, U.S. House of Representatives, 109th Cong., 1st sess., 2005.

81. James Thomas Tucker, "The Politics of Persuasion: Passage of the Voting Rights Act Reauthorization Act of 2006." *Journal of Legislation* 33, no. 2 (2007): pp. 212–215.

82. Congressman Melvin Watt, U.S. House of Representatives, in-person interview, February 9, 2007.

83. Julie Fernandes, interview, February 8, 2007.

84. This quote is from the House Report, p. 7. Congressman Charles Norwood, who opposed Section 5, would probably disagree with that statement. During the floor debate he said, "43 of the people you had testify were 43 people who came in to justify what you had done in H R 9." Providing for Consideration of H R 9, Fannie Lou Hamer, Rosa Parks, Coretta Scott King Voting Rights Act, July 13, 2006, U.S. House of Representatives, 109th Cong., 2nd sess. *Congressional Record*, H5183. Quoting Congressman Charles Norwood.

85. Thernstrom, *Voting Rights and Wrongs*, 2009, p. 173. For a critique of her book, see Richard Engstrom, "Thernstrom v. the Voting Rights Act: Round Two." *Election Law Journal* 9, no. 3 (2010): pp. 203–10.

86. House Report, pp. 3–4, 7.

87. There are forty-three names on the witness list; Abigail Thernstrom appeared twice. Some of the Senate witnesses, such as Laughlin McDonald, also appeared as witnesses before the House Committee. Senate Report, pp. 2–3.

88. Providing for Consideration of HR 9, Fannie Lou Hamer, Rosa Parks, Coretta Scott King Voting Rights Act, July 13, 2006, U.S. House of Representatives, 109th Cong., 2nd sess. *Congressional Record*, H5143. Quoting Congressman James Sensenbrenner, Jr.

89. HR 9, introduced May 2, 2006. Fannie Lou Hamer was the leader of the Mississippi Freedom Democratic Party at the 1964 Democratic Convention. See Kay Mills, *This Little Light of Mine* (Lexington: University of Kentucky Press, 2007).

90. Providing for Consideration of HR 9, Fannie Lou Hamer, Rosa Parks, Coretta Scott King Voting Rights Act, July 13, 2006, U.S. House of Representatives, 109th Cong., 2nd sess. *Congressional Record*, H5143. Quoting Congressman James Sensenbrenner, Jr.

91. Congressman Lynn Westmoreland, U.S. House of Representative, in-person interview, February 9, 2007.

92. Providing for Consideration of HR 9, Fannie Lou Hamer, Rosa Parks, Coretta Scott King Voting Rights Act, July 13, 2006, U.S. House of Representatives, 109th Cong., 2nd sess. *Congressional Record*, H5152. Quoting Congressman Charles Norwood. Congressman Norwood passed away in February 2007.

93. Senate Committee on the Judiciary, Providing for Consideration of S 2703, Fannie Lou Hamer, Rosa Parks, Coretta Scott King Voting Rights Act, 109th Cong., 2nd sess., July 13, 2006, p. 4. Testimony of Roger Clegg, president, Center for Equal Opportunity.

94. *Senate Committee on the Judiciary's Subcommittee on the Constitution, Providing for consideration of S 2703, Fannie Lou Hamer, Rosa Parks, Coretta Scott King Voting Rights Act*, 109th Cong., 2nd sess., June 13, 2006, p. 3. Testimony of Linda Chavez, president, One Nation Indivisible.

95. Leslie Fulbright, "Campaign Begins on Voting Rights Act." *San Francisco Chronicle,* April 7, 2006, p. 2.

96. See Terry M. Ao, "When the Voting Rights Act Became Un-American: The Misguided Vilification of the Section 203," *Alabama Law Review* 58, no. 2 (2006): pp. 377–97.

97. Providing for Consideration of HR 9, Fannie Lou Hamer, Rosa Parks, Coretta Scott King Voting Rights Act, July 13, 2006, U.S. House of Representatives, 109th Cong., 2nd sess., *Congressional Record* H5143. Quote is from a letter from Governor Timothy Kaine to Representative Tom Davis, dated July 12, 2006.

98. Providing for Consideration of HR 9, Fannie Lou Hamer, Rosa Parks, Coretta Scott King Voting Rights Act, July 13, 2006, U.S. House of Representatives, 109th Cong., 2nd sess. *Congressional Record,* H5189. Quoting Congressman John Conyers.

99. Providing for Consideration of HR 9, Fannie Lou Hamer, Rosa Parks, Coretta Scott King Voting Rights Act, July 13, 2006, U.S. House of Representatives, 109th Cong., 2nd sess. *Congressional Record,* H5150. Quoting Congressman Lynn Westmoreland. The Lewis quote was also read by Roger Clegg in his testimony before the Senate Judiciary Committee, cited above.

100. Ibid.

101. See Tucker, "Politics of Persuasion," pp. 4–6.

102. The White House, press conference, June 26, 2006.

103. House Report, p. 31.

104. 528 U.S. 320 (2000).

105. Ibid., pp. 328, 341.

106. See McCrary, Seaman, and Valelly, "The Law of Preclearance," pp. 20–21.

107. McDonald and Levitas, "The Case for Extending," p. 29.

108. Senate Report, p. 10.

109. See the House Report, pp. 3, 31, 41. Also see Tucker, "The Politics of Persuasion," pp. 13–16.

110. 539 U.S. 461 (2003).

111. *Beer v. U.S.* 425 U.S. 130 (1976).

112. Issacharoff, "Does Section 5 of the Voting Rights Act Still Work?" p. 112.

113. McDonald and Levitas, "The Case for Extending," p. 32.

114. House Report, p. 34.

115. HR 9, Section 5(d).

116. Providing for Consideration of HR 9, Fannie Lou Hamer, Rosa Parks, Coretta Scott King Voting Rights Act, July 13, 2006, U.S. House of Representatives, 109th Cong., 2nd sess. *Congressional Record,* H5136. Quoting Congressman Steve Chabot.

117. Senate Judiciary Committee, testimony of Roger Clegg, p. 4. Also see Roger Clegg and Linda Chavez, "An Analysis of the Reauthorized Sections 5 and 203 of the Voting Rights Act of 1965: Bad Policy and Unconstitutional," *The Georgetown Journal of Law and Public Policy* 5 (2007): pp. 561–82.

118. Bernard Grofman, "Expert Witness Testimony and the Evolution of Voting Rights Case Law," in *Controversies in Minority Voting,* ed. Bernard Grofman and Chandler Davidson, pp. 197–229 (Washington, D.C.: The Brookings Institution, 1992).

119. *Thornburg v. Gingles,* 478 U.S. 30 (1986). The Senate factors are listed in Grofman, "Expert Witness Testimony," pp. 200–1.

120. McDonald and Levitas, "The Case for Extending," pp. 36–37.

121. *West Virginia University Hospitals, Inc. v. Casey,* 499 U.S. 83 (1991).

122. Providing for Consideration of HR 9, Fannie Lou Hamer, Rosa Parks, Coretta Scott King Voting Rights Act, July 13, 2006, U.S. House of Representatives, 109th Cong., 2nd sess. *Congressional Record,* H5153. Quoting Congressman Charles Norwood.

123. Providing for Consideration of HR 9, Fannie Lou Hamer, Rosa Parks, Coretta Scott King Voting Rights Act, July 13, 2006, U.S. House of Representatives, 109th Cong., 2nd sess. *Congressional Record,* H5161. Quoting Congressman Nathan Deal.

124. Providing for Consideration of HR 9, Fannie Lou Hamer, Rosa Parks, Coretta Scott King Voting Rights Act, July 13, 2006, U.S. House of Representatives, 109th Cong., 2nd sess. *Congressional Record,* H5182. Quoting Congressman Lynn Westmoreland.

125. Providing for Consideration of HR 9, Fannie Lou Hamer, Rosa Parks, Coretta Scott King Voting Rights Act, July 13, 2006, U.S. House of Representatives, 109th Cong., 2nd sess. *Congressional Record,* H5181. Quoting Congressman Charles Norwood.

126. Providing for Consideration of HR 9, Fannie Lou Hamer, Rosa Parks, Coretta Scott King Voting Rights Act, July 13, 2006, U.S. House of Representatives, 109th Cong., 2nd sess. *Congressional Record,* H5181–82. Quoting Congressman James Sensenbrenner. The Montana case to which he refers is *U.S. v. Blaine County,* 363 F.3d 897 (9th Cir. 2004).

127. Providing for Consideration of HR 9, Fannie Lou Hamer, Rosa Parks, Coretta Scott King Voting Rights Act, July 13, 2006, U.S. House of Representatives, 109th Cong., 2nd sess. *Congressional Record,* H5198. Quoting Congressman Lynn Westmoreland.

128. Providing for Consideration of HR 9, Fannie Lou Hamer, Rosa Parks, Coretta Scott King Voting Rights Act, July 13, 2006, U.S. House of Representatives, 109th Cong., 2nd sess. *Congressional Record,* H5200. Quoting Congressman James Sensenbrenner.

129. Ibid., p. H5199.

130. House of Representatives, Committee on the Judiciary, 109th Cong., 2nd

sess. Business Meeting, May 10, 2006. *Congressional Record,* p. 5. Quoting Congressman Steve King.

131. Ibid., p. 8. Quoting Congressman John Hostettler.

132. House of Representatives, Committee on the Judiciary, 109th Cong., 2nd sess. Business Meeting. May 10, 2006, *Congressional Record,* p. 13.

133. Ibid., p. 20. Quoting Congressman Steve King.

134. Ibid., p. 23.

135. For an incisive description of the politics of the King amendments see Tucker, "The Politics of Persuasion," pp. 27–33.

136. Providing for Consideration of HR 9, Fannie Lou Hamer, Rosa Parks, Coretta Scott King Voting Rights Act, July 13, 2006, U.S. House of Representatives, 109th Cong., 2nd sess. *Congressional Record,* H5206.

137. Providing for Consideration of HR 9, Fannie Lou Hamer, Rosa Parks, Coretta Scott King Voting Rights Act, July 13, 2006, U.S. House of Representatives, 109th Cong., 2nd sess. *Congressional Record,* H5186. Quoting Congressman Louis Gohmert.

138. Providing for Consideration of HR 9, Fannie Lou Hamer, Rosa Parks, Coretta Scott King Voting Rights Act, July 13, 2006, U.S. House of Representatives, 109th Cong., 2nd sess. *Congressional Record,* H5205.

139. Providing for Consideration of HR 9, Fannie Lou Hamer, Rosa Parks, Coretta Scott King Voting Rights Act, July 13, 2006, U.S. House of Representatives, 109th Cong., 2nd sess. *Congressional Record,* H5167. Quoting Congressman Elijah Cummings.

140. Providing for Consideration of HR 9, Fannie Lou Hamer, Rosa Parks, Coretta Scott King Voting Rights Act, July 13, 2006, U.S. House of Representatives, 109th Cong., 2nd sess. *Congressional Record,* H5176. Quoting Congressman Joe Crowley.

141. Providing for Consideration of HR 9, Fannie Lou Hamer, Rosa Parks, Coretta Scott King Voting Rights Act, July 13, 2006, U.S. House of Representatives, 109th Cong., 2nd sess. *Congressional Record,* H5200. Quoting Congressman Charles Norwood.

142. Providing for Consideration of HR 9, Fannie Lou Hamer, Rosa Parks, Coretta Scott King Voting Rights Act, July 13, 2006, U.S. House of Representatives, 109th Cong., 2nd sess. *Congressional Record,* H5135. Quoting Congressman Phillip Gingrey.

143. Ibid., H5207.

144. Office of Congressman Lynn Westmoreland, "Westmoreland Statement on the House Passage of the Voting Rights Act," press release, July 13, 2006.

145. Presidential Documents, Administration of George W. Bush (Washington, D.C.: U.S. Government Printing Office, July 20, 2006), p. 1371.

146. Ibid.

147. U.S. Senate, 109th Cong., 1st. sess., HR 9 Fannie Lou Hamer, Rosa Parks, and Coretta Scott King Voting Rights Act Reauthorization and Amendments Act of 2006, July 20, 2006, *Congressional Record* S7949.

148. Anonymous interview, Washington, D.C. Also see U.S. Senate, 109th Cong., 1st. sess., HR 9 Fannie Lou Hamer, Rosa Parks, and Coretta Scott King Voting Rights Act Reauthorization and Amendments Act of 2006, July 20, 2006, *Congressional Record* S7978–S7981.

149. Senate Report, p. 20.

150. Ibid., p. 43. This section was written by Senators Leahy, Kennedy, Biden, Kohl, Feinstein, Schumer, Feingold, and Durbin.

151. The White House, Office of the Press Secretary, "President Bush Signs Voting Rights Act Reauthorization and Amendments Act of 2006," July 27, 2006.

152. "The Prophesy of George H. White." n.d., mimeograph provided by the office of Congressman Melvin Watt.

153. Congressman Lynn Westmoreland, in-person interview, Washington, D. C., February 9, 2007.

154. Quoted in Robert Barnes, "Justices Will Hear Challenge to Voting Rights Act," *The Washington Post,* January 10, 2009, A02. In regard to race and Obama's election, see Charles Bullock III and Ronald Keith Gaddie, *The Triumph of Voting Rights in the South* (Norman: University of Oklahoma Press, 2009); Baodong Liu, *The Election of Barack Obama: How He Won* (New York: Palgrave-Macmillan, 2010); Richard Engstrom, "Race and Southern Politics," *Election Law Journal* 10, no. 1 (2011): pp. 53–61.

155. See Richard Hasen, "Will the Supreme Court Kill the Voting Rights Act?" *Slate,* April 27, 2009; The Editors, "A Turning Point for Voting Rights Law," *The New York Times,* April 29, 2009.

156. *Northwest Austin Municipal Utility District Number One v. Holder.* No. 08-322 (June 22, 2009): p. 16.

157. Ibid., p. 8.

158. Tom Goldstein, "Analysis: Supreme Court Invalidates Section 5's Coverage Scheme," SCOTUSblog, June 22, 2009, www.scotusblog.com/wp/analysis supreme-court-invalidates'section-5-5% e2%80%99s-scheme-2.

159. Rick Hasen, "Initial Thoughts on NAMUDNO," Election Law Blog, June 22, 2009, www.electionlawblog.org.

160. Heather Gerken, "The Supreme Court Punts on Section 5." Balkinization, June 22, 2009, www.balkin.blogspot.com.

161. *Shelby County, Alabama v. Holder,* Civ. Action No. 10-0651 (Dist. Ct. D.C.).

162. Quoted in Mary Orndorff, "Shelby County Voting Rights Case to Go before D. C. Judge," *The Birmingham News,* September 9, 2010.

163. *Shelby County, Ala. v. Holder* 2012 WL 1759997 (C.A.D.C.). May 18, 2012; Joan Biskupic, "Insight: From Alabama, an Epic Challenge to Voting Rights." Reuters, June 4, 2012.

164. *Laroque v. Holder* (Civil Action 10-5433), decided July 8, 2011; *State of Arizona v. Holder* (Case No. 1: 2011: cv 01599), filed August 30, 2011.

165. *Georgia v. Ashcroft,* 539 U.S. 461 (2003).

166. Providing for Consideration of HR 9, Fannie Lou Hamer, Rosa Parks, Coretta Scott King Voting Rights Act, July 13, 2006, U.S. House of Representatives, 109th Cong., 2nd sess. *Congressional Record,* H5150. Quoting Congressman Lynn Westmoreland.

167. Providing for Consideration of HR 9, Fannie Lou Hamer, Rosa Parks, Coretta Scott King Voting Rights Act, July 13, 2006, U.S. House of Representatives, 109th Cong., 2nd sess. *Congressional Record,* H5172. Quoting Congressman Tom Price.

168. Providing for Consideration of HR 9, Fannie Lou Hamer, Rosa Parks, Coretta Scott King Voting Rights Act, July 13, 2006, U.S. House of Representatives, 109th Cong., 2nd sess. *Congressional Record,* H5161. Quoting Congresswoman Eddie Bernice Johnson.

169. Providing for Consideration of HR 9, Fannie Lou Hamer, Rosa Parks, Coretta Scott King Voting Rights Act, July 13, 2006, U.S. House of Representatives, 109th Cong., 2nd sess. *Congressional Record,* H5162. Quoting Congresswoman Nancy Pelosi.

170. Providing for Consideration of HR 9, Fannie Lou Hamer, Rosa Parks, Coretta Scott King Voting Rights Act, July 13, 2006, U.S. House of Representatives, 109th Cong., 2nd sess. *Congressional Record,* H5164. Quoting Congressman John Lewis.

TWO

The Constitutional Foundations of the "Preclearance" Process: How Section 5 of the Voting Rights Act Was Enforced, 1965–2005

PEYTON MCCRARY

In July 2006, Congress adopted a revision of the 1965 Voting Rights Act that reauthorized the "preclearance" requirements set forth in Section 5 for another twenty-five years and amended the legal standards to be applied in its enforcement, restoring the standards for assessing the purpose and effect of voting changes that had been altered by two recent Supreme Court decisions.[1] Section 5 is often regarded as one of the act's two most powerful provisions.[2] In the preclearance process jurisdictions covered by Section 5, for the most part states of the former Confederacy, must obtain federal approval of voting changes, either from a three-judge panel in the District of Columbia or from the Department of Justice, before these changes become legally enforceable. Approval requires proof by the jurisdiction that the change "does not have the purpose and will not have the effect of denying or abridging the right to vote on account of race or color."[3] Shortly after its adoption the Supreme Court ruled that Section 5, like the rest of the act, was constitutional. "Congress concluded that the unsuccessful remedies which it had prescribed in the past would have to be replaced by sterner and more elaborate measures," wrote Chief Justice Earl Warren.[4] Twice since then the Court has upheld the constitutionality of Section 5, as amended.[5]

Less than a month after passage of the 2006 reauthorization act, however, a predominantly white jurisdiction in Texas filed a lawsuit seeking to "bail out" of Section 5 coverage or, in the alternative, a ruling that the revised preclearance provision was unconstitutional.[6] This constitutional challenge relied on the conviction that the extension and revision of Section 5 goes beyond the legal authority of Congress, under the "congruence and proportionality" test enunciated by the Supreme Court in a series of recent decisions striking down federal legislation.[7] A three-judge court determined that the jurisdiction, a municipal utility district in Austin, Texas, was not entitled to bail out and that Section 5, as revised and reauthorized in 2006, remained constitutional.[8] The Supreme Court reversed the trial court and ruled that the jurisdiction was entitled to escape Section 5 coverage. As a result, the Court did not have to decide the constitutional challenge.[9] The majority opinion made it clear that five of the nine justices had serious concerns about the constitutionality of amended Section 5. The principal concern expressed in the majority opinion by Chief Justice John Roberts, however, was the coverage formula that determined which jurisdictions are covered by Section 5 – *not* the changes made by the Congress to the standards for assessing purpose and effect.[10]

The purpose of this chapter is to explore the evolution of the standards employed in deciding whether voting changes are entitled to preclearance since the inception of the Voting Rights Act and, in particular, to compare the purpose and effect prongs of Section 5 with the standards employed in enforcing the Fourteenth and Fifteenth Amendments. This entails a close examination of both decisions by the federal courts and administrative enforcement of Section 5 by the United States Department of Justice in the four decades after 1965.[11] Such a historical account of how preclearance review actually worked offers an essential starting point for any informed analysis of the degree to which amended Section 5 is constitutional.[12]

THE CONGRUENCE BETWEEN SECTION 5 AND THE
RECONSTRUCTION AMENDMENTS, 1965–1969

The preclearance provision enacted by Congress in 1965, as well as the act's suspension of literacy tests, applied to covered states and counties the "freezing principle" recently adopted by the federal courts in Fifteenth Amendment cases as a way of coping with the constantly chang-

ing discriminatory devices used by southern registrars and election officials.[13] The courts had "frozen" state laws in the sense that registrars
were prohibited from applying registration requirements against African
Americans differently from the way requirements had been applied to
whites over the years.[14] As they had before 1965 – and as Congress had anticipated in adopting Section 5 – southern legislators took steps to minimize the electoral impact of black voters newly enfranchised by the act.
A mere two weeks after passage of the act, for example, Alabama passed
special legislation extending the term of office for county commissioners
in black-majority Bullock County from four to six years, thus postponing
new elections for two years.[15] On behalf of local black plaintiffs, veteran
civil rights lawyer Fred Gray of Montgomery challenged this action as a
violation of the Fifteenth Amendment. The Department of Justice filed
its own suit, alleging that the change was not only unconstitutional but
also prohibited by the preclearance requirements set forth in Section 5
of the act.[16] A three-judge court found that the extension of commissioners' terms in April of 1966 "freezes into office for an additional two years
persons who were elected when Negroes were being illegally deprived
of the right to vote," and that is, "in effect, to freeze Negroes out of the
electorate." Such a result, declared the court, "is forbidden by the Fifteenth Amendment."[17]

Appeals court judge Richard Rives agreed with the Justice Department that the Bullock County change was "in conflict with Section 5 of
the Voting Rights Act." Judge Rives conceded that it was a "close call" as
to whether an extension of officeholders' terms is covered by the phrase
"any voting qualifications or prerequisite to voting, or standard, practice, or procedure with respect to voting" (the language by which the
act identifies the type of voting changes requiring preclearance), but he
concluded that "the legislative history shows that the present language
was meant to broaden the section and to make it inclusive of any kind of
practice."[18] Judge Rives did not have a second vote for that view, however.
One judge would have approved the change. The third member of the
panel, district judge Frank Johnson agreed with Rives that the change
should be struck down but did not "find it necessary to reach the question of the applicability of Section 5 of the Voting Rights Act" because
he found the change unconstitutional.[19]

In 1966, the Democratic Executive Committee of Barbour County – Alabama governor George Wallace's home county – switched from electing its members from single-member districts to electing them at large. Both plaintiffs' attorney Fred Gray and the Department of Justice challenged this change as well. Judge Johnson found it racially motivated and also discriminatory in effect: "predominantly Negro beats now have their representatives determined for them by the predominantly white voters in the county as a whole."[20] The county executive committee again tried to switch to at-large elections in 1968, in order "to keep the Democratic Committee on an at-large basis," according to the local paper, and "free from federal intervention."[21] The Department of Justice argued that the change was not only unconstitutional but also violated the preclearance requirement of the Voting Rights Act.[22] Judge Johnson found that the adoption of at-large elections was "purposeful discrimination against Negroes in violation of [both] the Fourteenth and Fifteenth Amendments," but did not rule on the Section 5 claim.[23] When a new election was held on a single-member district basis, four blacks were elected to the Barbour County Democratic Executive Committee because African Americans voted cohesively for candidates of their choosing.[24]

The standard of proof under the Fourteenth and Fifteenth Amendments was not burdensome in the hands of a judge like Frank Johnson, but he was poles apart from the sort of federal judges who heard the first challenges to at-large elections in Mississippi. At the other extreme was Judge Harold Cox of the Southern District of Mississippi, an avowed white supremacist.[25] Congress designed Section 5 to take decisions about voting rights out of the hands of judges like Cox and instead to entrust preclearance decisions to federal authorities less hostile to minority voting rights.

Black voters in Adams and Forrest Counties, represented by attorneys with the Lawyers' Committee for Civil Rights Under Law, used Section 5 to challenge the adoption of at-large elections under a 1966 Mississippi statute that could, before a judge like Frank Johnson, have been attacked under the constitutional intent standard.[26] Under the terms of this statute any county could eliminate the system of single-member district elections used in Mississippi for almost a century in favor of at-large elections. During the debates over this bill, legislative sponsors often claimed that at-large elections were designed merely to satisfy the "one-person, one-vote" principle, but Senator Ben Hilbun was, like others, more blunt about the racial purpose of the statute: "the countywide balloting will safeguard 'a white board and preserve our way of doing business.'"[27]

Rather than put together a full-fledged challenge to the constitutionality of this statute, attorneys for African American plaintiffs took to court the easier-to-prove claim that such changes – as well as the voting changes attacked in two related Mississippi lawsuits – were subject to preclearance review under Section 5, potentially a quicker and cheaper way of attacking discriminatory legislation.[28] The district courts in each case decided that the statutes at issue were not subject to Section 5, which in their view only applied to changes regarding voter registration and the casting of individual ballots.[29]

There was little support for this narrow view, however, when the Mississippi cases reached the Supreme Court on appeal.[30] In oral argument before the Supreme Court, Elliott Lichtman of the Lawyers' Committee naturally took issue with Mississippi's stunted view of the preclearance requirement: "Congress intended once and for all to make the Fifteenth Amendment effective," and to that end "any new statute relating to the effectiveness of the right to vote" – and this language would include each of the changes at issue in these four consolidated cases – "must be scrutinized by the Attorney General before it becomes effective."[31] Stephen Pollack, the assistant attorney general for civil rights who argued the case for the United States, dismissed Mississippi's position – "that the statute reaches only the qualifications for registration" – as having "little support" in either the language or the legislative history of the act.[32]

The standard for assessing the purpose or effect of a voting change was not among the questions before the Court, but the issue arose during oral argument. Lawyers for both minority voters and the Department of Justice took the position that voting changes should be assessed by the same standard as in a constitutional challenge, except, of course, that the submitting authority bore the burden of proof. Armand Derfner of the Lawyers' Constitutional Defense Committee said regarding his own case, "I don't think we would be here if we did not believe that this was a statute that violates the 15th Amendment."[33] Pollack – whose office would have to make the actual preclearance decisions on behalf of the attorney general – emphasized that both three-judge courts in the District of Columbia and the Department of Justice "should apply Fifteenth Amendment standards" in enforcing Section 5.[34]

The Supreme Court agreed in its landmark decision *Allen v. State Board of Elections*,[35] taking an expansive view of the type of voting changes covered by the preclearance requirement and linking the enforcement of Section 5 with enforcement of the Reconstruction Amendments. The majority opinion, authored by Chief Justice Earl Warren, declared emphatically that Section 5 required jurisdictions in states covered by the Voting Rights Act to submit for preclearance "*any* state enactment" that changed the existing electoral practices "in even a minor way" – including *each* of the changes before the Court.[36] To the Court the words "any" and "all" in the text of Section 5 were not limited to changes affecting registration, the procedures for casting ballots, or other changes with the potential of denying the right to vote, but would apply also to procedures that would dilute minority voting strength.[37]

In regard to the 1966 Mississippi statute authorizing at-large elections, the Court expressly ruled that "a change from district to at-large voting for county supervisors" could have a discriminatory impact. "Voters who are members of a racial minority might well be in the majority in one district, but in a decided minority in the county as a whole," noted the Court. Thus at-large elections could "nullify their ability to elect the candidate of their choice just as would prohibiting some of them from voting."[38] The Court based its ruling on the principle set forth in the Alabama one-person, one-vote decision in *Reynolds v. Sims* – a Fourteenth Amendment case: "the right to vote can be affected by a dilution of voting power as well as by an absolute prohibition on casting a ballot."[39]

Justice John M. Harlan disputed the majority's view that Congress in 1965 had intended Section 5 to cover electoral practices that dilute minority voting strength – a view for which he found no evidence in the legislative history.[40] Justice Harlan was correct that the right to register and cast a ballot was, quite naturally, the first concern of Congress in 1965. He did not, however, take account of the fact that in discussing the range of voting changes Section 5 was designed to cover, the House

Judiciary Committee cited an early example of vote dilution – the racial gerrymander which removed virtually all the black residents from
the city of Tuskegee, Alabama, which the Supreme Court struck down
in *Gomillion v. Lightfoot*.[41] Thus changes that diluted minority voting
strength were among the discriminatory changes enumerated in the 1965
legislative record, which, as the Chief Justice put it, documented in great
detail "the history some States had of simply enacting new and slightly
different requirements with the same discriminatory effect" whenever a
court struck down a discriminatory practice. As the Court saw it, Congress was acting within its authority when it designed Section 5 as a way
of countering "the ingenuity of those bent on preventing Negroes from
voting."[42]

CONGRESS ENDORSES THE COURT'S
INTERPRETATION OF SECTION 5

When Congress voted to extend the Voting Rights in 1970, members
unhesitatingly confirmed their intention that Section 5 should require
preclearance of changes that might dilute minority voting strength.[43] Republican William McCulloch, who had been among his party's key supporters of the 1965 enactment in the House, emphasized that the majority
opinion in *Allen* correctly described the intended scope of the Section 5
preclearance requirement when it was adopted. Southern white resistance
had simply proved stronger than anticipated in 1965, McCulloch said.

> Boundary lines have been gerrymandered, elections have been switched to
> an at-large basis, counties have been consolidated, elective offices have been
> abolished where blacks had a chance of winning, the appointive process has
> been substituted for the elective process, election officials have withheld the
> necessary information for voting or running for office, and both physical and
> economic intimidation have been employed.[44]

Newly elected Republican president Richard Nixon had a different view, however. When Congress took up the first proposal to extend
Section 5 in 1969, the Nixon administration sponsored amendments
that would have eliminated the preclearance requirement from the act
entirely, relying instead on filing affirmative lawsuits to challenge each
discriminatory change.[45] Opponents of this draconian change pointed

out that eliminating preclearance and relying only on litigation would require a great deal more staff resources in the Civil Rights Division and would consume large amounts of additional court time when the workload of the federal courts was already great. In addition, the burden of proof would shift from submitting jurisdictions under the present system to the Department of Justice under the new approach, making the achievement of minority voting rights more difficult.

Civil rights supporters saw this proposal, and other aspects of the administration's bill, as designed to gut effective enforcement of voting rights in the South, and thus opposed it in favor of a simple five-year extension of the 1965 act. The administration bill passed the House in 1969, but, after a substantial struggle in the Senate, voting rights advocates defeated this version and extended the preclearance requirement for another five years.[46]

The Justice Department defines its role in preclearance reviews as serving as a "surrogate" for the District of Columbia trial courts.[47] The vast majority of voting changes come to the department rather than to the courts, because jurisdictions prefer the greater speed and convenience of administrative review. Because the Supreme Court has agreed to hear arguments and issue opinions in only a few cases, however, the District of Columbia trial courts have played a major role in shaping Section 5 case law. Often the Supreme Court has declined to hear oral argument and summarily affirmed the trial court's decision. Although a summary affirmance simply endorses the lower court's decision and not necessarily its reasoning, it serves as a binding precedent for the lower courts and the Department of Justice until contradicted by a future Supreme Court decision.[48]

The attorney general has from the start delegated responsibility for preclearance decisions to the assistant attorney general (AAG) who heads the Civil Rights Division. Administrative reorganization in 1969 produced a separate section within the Civil Rights Division specializing in voting rights. The newly created Voting Section then provided the factual investigation for preclearance reviews and made detailed recommendations to the AAG for civil rights. Prodded by congressional subcommittees with oversight responsibility, the department developed detailed guidelines for enforcing Section 5 that were, in turn, endorsed by the Supreme Court.[49] In 1975, after extensive hearings providing substantial evidence of the continuing need for the preclearance process, Congress extended the life of Section 5 and other special provisions for another seven years.[50] The Supreme Court subsequently found the 1975 extension of the preclearance requirement constitutional in *City of Rome v. United States*.[51]

The legal standard for determining whether voting changes were entitled to preclearance in those years was the same legal standard for assessing the intent and effect of election laws employed by the courts in Fourteenth or Fifteenth Amendment cases. As the Supreme Court put it in a 1971 decision, in adopting Section 5 "Congress intended to adopt the concept of voting articulated in *Reynolds v. Sims*," in order to "protect Negroes against a dilution of their voting power."[52] In a 1975 decision the Court equated the purpose requirement of Section 5 with the constitutional intent standard: "An official action . . . taken for the purpose of discriminating against Negroes on account of their race has no legitimacy at all under our Constitution or under the statute."[53] That was the standard Congress necessarily had in mind when reauthorizing Section 5 in 1975.

BIFURCATION OF THE CONSTITUTIONAL AND SECTION 5 EFFECT STANDARDS IN *BEER V. UNITED STATES*

The congruence between the constitutional and statutory standards for assessing the *effect* of voting changes was, however, brought to an abrupt halt in 1976 by the Supreme Court. The city of New Orleans sought a declaratory judgment preclearing its redistricting plan following the 1970 census in a case ultimately decided in 1976 in *Beer v. United States*.[54] The three-judge trial court refused to preclear the plan on the grounds that it had the effect of diluting minority voting strength as defined by the Supreme Court in the landmark Fourteenth Amendment case of *White v. Regester*.[55] The Supreme Court majority in *Beer* reversed the trial court, however, ruling that the term "effect" has a different meaning under Section 5 than under the Constitution. It determined that in the preclearance context, discriminatory effect was to be defined as "retrogression," a newly minted term that described changes that place minority voters in a *worse* position than under the status quo.[56] As a result of *Beer*, changes that do not make matters worse for minority voters are entitled to preclearance under the effect prong of Section 5, even where the new method of election appears likely to dilute minority voting strength or otherwise discriminate (as in voting changes affecting registration or casting a ballot).

"The Court's conclusion," wrote Justice Thurgood Marshall in dissent, "is simply wrong; it finds no support in the language of the statute and disserves the legislative purposes behind it."[57] The Supreme Court's interpretation of the text of Section 5 hinges upon a word – retrogression – that does not appear in the text of the statute at all. The Court's assessment of congressional intent in adopting Section 5 relied entirely on a passage from the House Report on the 1975 act – but neither House or Senate in that year undertook an analysis of congressional intent in either 1965 or 1970.[58] The idea that the 1965 Congress saw the preclearance requirement as limited to retrogression seems, in fact, thoroughly counter-intuitive. Justice Marshall cited documents from the legislative history of the act demonstrating that Section 5 "was designed to preclude new districting plans that 'perpetuate discrimination.'"[59] As Justice Stephen Breyer pointed out a quarter-century later, there were some jurisdictions in the Deep South in 1965 where "historical discrimination had left the number of black voters at close to zero," and as a result "retrogression would have proved virtually impossible where § 5 was needed most."[60]

Whether or not the *purpose* of the change was racially discriminatory was not among the questions before the Court in *Beer*.[61] The majority opinion appeared, however, to leave the purpose prong of Section 5 intact: "We conclude, therefore, that such an ameliorative new legislative apportionment cannot violate § 5 *unless* the new apportionment itself so discriminates on the basis of race or color *as to violate the Constitution*."[62] To most commentators the Court's wording appears understandable only as a reference to the purpose test in Fourteenth or Fifteenth Amendment cases.[63] Even Justice William Rehnquist, who opposed a strong Voting Rights Act, seemed to agree. "It is clear that if the proposed changes would violate the Constitution, Congress could certainly prohibit their implementation."[64] Moreover, that is the interpretation placed upon this wording by numerous federal courts, includ-

ing the Supreme Court, in applying a constitutional "purpose" test in
preclearance cases.[65]

APPLYING THE CONSTITUTIONAL PURPOSE
STANDARD UNDER SECTION 5

For a quarter-century after *Beer*, assessing the purpose of a voting change
under Section 5 followed the constitutional intent standard codified by
the Supreme Court in the *Arlington Heights* decision, a housing discrimination case.[66] An early illustration of how the Section 5 purpose
standard was to be applied is the decision – summarily affirmed by the
Supreme Court – in *Wilkes County v. United States*.[67] The case involved
a change from single-member districts to an at-large plan in 1972 for
both the county commission and school board in a Georgia plantation
county. The evidence showed that voting patterns were racially polarized and that, as a result, no black candidates had been elected to either
governing body, even though African Americans made up 43 percent of
the population. Under the constitutional purpose standard the starting
point for the trial court's analysis was the fact that the change to at-large
elections followed a substantial increase in minority voter registration
following adoption of the Voting Rights Act, thus making it possible
for black voters to elect a candidate of their choice under a fairly drawn
single-member district plan. The county claimed that the purpose of
the switch to at-large elections was solely to satisfy the one-person, one-
vote requirement, but the court found that argument a mere pretext; the
districts could simply have been equalized in population after the 1970
census instead of shifting to at-large elections. At the time of the change
no African Americans had been elected to office, served as Democratic
party officials in the one-party county, or been appointed to fill vacancies
for elected offices. Nor had any black citizens been consulted about the
decision to adopt an at-large plan. Thus in the court's view the county's
at-large plan failed to satisfy the purpose requirement of Section 5 and
was not entitled to preclearance.[68]

Another influential trial court decision applying the Section 5 purpose standard – also summarily affirmed by the Supreme Court – was
the Georgia congressional redistricting case of *Busbee v. Smith*.[69] The

case turned on the facts surrounding the fifth congressional district, centered in the capital city of Atlanta. Because of sufficient white cross-over voting, black civil rights leader Andrew Young had represented the district during the mid-1970s, even though whites were a majority of its voting-age population. When Young left to head the United Nations delegation in 1977, the district elected a moderate white Democrat, Wyche Fowler. After the 1980 census the legislature increased the black population percentage in the fifth district to 57 percent, but whites were still 54 percent of the registered voters. Voting patterns had become more racially polarized since Young's victories, and most observers believed that the black concentration in the newly configured district was not great enough to provide African American voters an equal opportunity to elect a candidate of their choice.[70]

The trial court found abundant evidence, both direct and circumstantial, that "[t]he Fifth District was drawn with the goal of diluting black voting strength."[71] A key player in the legislative decision-making process was Joe Mack Wilson, chairman of the House Reapportionment Committee, who complained to fellow legislators that "the Justice Department is trying to make us draw nigger districts and I don't want to draw nigger districts."[72] The trial court also found that Speaker Tom Murphy "purposefully discriminated on the basis of race in selecting the House members of the conference committee where the final redistricting plan was determined" by selecting white legislators "he knew would adamantly oppose the creation of a congressional district in which black voters would be able to elect a candidate of their choice," and by refusing to appoint any black members to the conference committee.[73] The redistricting plan was not entitled to preclearance, even though it was ameliorative rather than retrogressive in effect: "the State must also demonstrate the absence of discriminatory purpose." The court found the plan objectionable because it was "designed to minimize black voting strength."[74]

THE ISSUE OF RETROGRESSIVE INTENT

The restrictive interpretation of the Section 5 purpose prong adopted by the Supreme Court in its 2000 decision in *Reno v. Bossier Parish School Board* (hereafter *Bossier II*)[75] was first advanced by the state of Georgia when seeking preclearance of this racially motivated 1981 congressional redistricting plan (see preceding paragraph). On appeal to the Supreme Court in *Busbee,* the state sought unsuccessfully to reduce the purpose prong of Section 5 to something very different from the constitutional intent standard – whether a redistricting plan "that does not have the purpose of diminishing the level of black voting strength" is objectionable.[76] Because the Supreme Court summarily affirmed the decision of the trial court, observers had every reason to believe that the purpose prong of Section 5 was *not* limited to retrogressive intent but was instead as broad as the constitutional purpose standard.[77]

In 1987, the Supreme Court agreed to hear a case, the *City of Pleasant Grove* case, where a covered jurisdiction presented an "intent to retrogress" theory. The factual context in this case was unusual. Pleasant Grove, Alabama, a virtually all-white city near Birmingham in heavily industrial Jefferson County, sought preclearance of a series of annexations. Its refusal to annex nearby black population concentrations was part of what the trial court called "an astounding pattern of racial exclusion and discrimination in all phases of Pleasant Grove life," and as a result, the city had remained an "all-white enclave in an otherwise racially mixed area of Alabama."[78] The evidence of intentional discrimination was so strong, noted the Supreme Court, that "even if the burden of proving discrimination was on the United States, the [trial] court 'would have had no difficulty in finding that the annexation policy of Pleasant Grove is, by design, racially discriminatory in violation of the Voting Rights Act.'"[79] The city claimed as well that there could be no retrogressive effect to the annexations because there were no black people in the city and thus no one whose voting strength could be worsened.[80] The *Pleasant Grove* majority rejected this view: "Section 5 looks not only to the present effects of changes, but to their future effects as well," adding that the purpose requirement also applied to "anticipated as well as present circumstances."[81]

Pleasant Grove also argued, as had Georgia some years earlier, that the purpose requirement of Section 5 was limited to retrogressive intent. This time Justice Lewis Powell, joined by Chief Justice William Rehnquist and Justice Sandra Day O'Connor, agreed with the theory: "[F]or a city to have a discriminatory purpose within the meaning of the Voting Rights Act, it must intend its action to have a retrogressive effect on the voting rights of blacks."[82] The majority, however, observed that it had rejected such reasoning since the *City of Richmond* case in 1975, quoting its earlier ruling that a change motivated by a racially discriminatory purpose "has no legitimacy under our Constitution or under the statute . . . *whatever its actual effect may have been or may be.*"[83]

THE COURTS TURN AGAINST SECTION 5

In a series of redistricting decisions, beginning with a 1993 case, *Shaw v. Reno,*[84] a new 5-4 conservative majority on the U.S. Supreme Court invalidated majority-black or majority-Hispanic congressional districts in several southern states under a new constitutional standard that has been applied only to the creation of majority-minority districts.[85] Although these were not Section 5 cases, the Court took pains to criticize the Justice Department's implementation of the preclearance requirements of the act and, in particular, its view of the Section 5 purpose prong. In striking down a Georgia congressional redistricting plan, the Court found that race had been "the predominant factor motivating the legislature" in drawing district lines.[86] As the Court saw it, Georgia had succumbed to improper pressure from the Department of Justice, which, in reviewing redistricting plans in the 1990s, had converted the Section 5 purpose standard into a policy of requiring covered jurisdictions to "maximize" minority voting strength by creating as many majority-minority districts as possible, no matter what the cost to traditional districting principles.[87] The Court reiterated this view a year later in its decision striking down North Carolina's congressional redistricting plan.[88]

Also in the mid-1990s, trial courts in Section 5 declaratory judgment actions overturned prior objections by the Justice Department to the addition of judicial posts – based on evidence of discriminatory purpose in expanding the use of numbered place and majority vote requirements to new judgeships.[89] In the 1980s, guided by court decisions regarding judicial elections, the department had begun objecting to numerous additional judicial posts created to deal with expanding case loads but employing election procedures that were recognized as having the potential for diluting minority voting strength.[90] By 1995, however, the courts rejected this reasoning, based in part on criticism of the way the department interpreted factual evidence when applying the purpose standard.[91]

The litigation used by the Supreme Court to overturn the accepted interpretation of the Section 5 purpose standard arose from the Department's objection to a school board redistricting plan in Bossier Parish,
Louisiana. In that state, parishes elect their governing bodies (called
police juries), and their parish school boards as well, by districts rather
than at large.[92] In the 1980s Bossier Parish used different election plans
for police jury and school board; neither had a single black-majority district. Although blacks made up 20 percent of the parish population and 18
percent of its voting age population, the school board had never elected
an African American.[93] After the 1990 census, both bodies displayed
wide population disparities among their twelve single-member districts
and thus required redistricting. The police jury quickly redistricted and
secured preclearance of its plan. Although the new plan had no black-
majority districts, neither had the police jury plan in the 1980s and the
change was thus not retrogressive.[94]

The school board refused initially to adopt the police jury's plan,
which was drawn to protect police jury incumbents, in part because
it would have pitted two sets of school board incumbents against one
another.[95] The police jury plan also had an unusually high deviation
from population equality, and, as the dissenting justices later pointed
out, four districts "failed the standard measure of compactness used by
the [School] Board's own cartographer."[96] The school board engaged the
same consultant to draw a separate plan, but after local black leaders proposed an alternative plan with two black-majority districts, the school
board put aside its reservations and adopted the police jury plan, which
it submitted for preclearance. After reviewing the sequence of events
leading to the school board's decision, interpreted by Voting Section
lawyers as evidence under the *Arlington Heights* standard that the plan
was adopted with a discriminatory purpose, the Department of Justice
objected to the plan.[97]

The school board then filed a Section 5 declaratory judgment action in the District of Columbia.[98] The three-judge panel precleared the plan by a 2-1 majority, on the theory that the Justice Department was trying to use Section 5 to maximize black voting strength.[99] Judge Gladys Kessler dissented vigorously, asserting that under *Arlington Heights* the evidence in the case "demonstrates convincingly that the Bossier School Board acted with discriminatory purpose."[100] The United States appealed the case to the Supreme Court, even though it knew that the conservative majority already took a dim view of the department's Section 5 policy.[101]

Although a majority on the Supreme Court substantially agreed with the lower court's view of the evidence, it nevertheless vacated the lower court decision and remanded the case for reconsideration.[102] Writing for a 5-4 majority, Justice Sandra Day O'Connor instructed the trial court to consider a theory not previously advanced by the school board – and not, for that reason, considered by the trial court – that under Section 5 a purpose inquiry is restricted to the question of retrogressive intent, that is, whether the change was designed not merely to discriminate against minority voters but to make matters worse for them.[103] At oral argument in *Bossier I* the school board's attorney, Michael Carvin – who knew the case law well – explicitly rejected the suggestion that, as one justice put it, "the only purpose that is relevant under Section 5 is purpose to cause retrogression, as distinct from purpose to discriminate by effecting a purposeful dilution." Carvin's response was, "Oh, no. No, not at all. I think that . . . the Court's decision in *Richmond* and *Pleasant Grove* has already decided that issue."[104]

When the Supreme Court ultimately decided the Bossier Parish case in January 2000, with Justice Antonin Scalia writing for the majority, it overturned the precedents of the last quarter-century, holding that "§ 5 does not prohibit preclearance of a redistricting plan enacted with a discriminatory but nonretrogressive purpose."[105] The key to *Bossier II* lies in the Court's fealty to the *Beer* precedent.[106] If the term "effect" in Section 5 means retrogression, as the *Beer* majority had decided in 1976, then in Justice Scalia's view the term "purpose" must also be tied to the concept of retrogression because "we refuse to adopt a construction that would attribute different meanings to the same phrase ["denying or abridging"] in the same sentence, depending on which object it is modifying."[107] Of course, the word "retrogression" does not appear in the text of the statute at all, but was coined by the *Beer* majority based on its strained reading of a congressional committee report.[108]

Under the Court's new definition of the Section 5 purpose prong, the Department of Justice would have to preclear even so flagrantly discriminatory a change as the Georgia congressional redistricting struck down in *Busbee v. Smith*.[109] Justice Scalia readily admitted that, as appellants had contended, "our reading of § 5 would require the District Court or Attorney General to preclear proposed voting changes with a discriminatory effect or purpose, or even with both." He saw no problem with preclearing racially motivated changes: "That strikes appellants as an inconceivable prospect only because they refuse to accept the limited meaning that we have said preclearance has in the vote-dilution context." Once precleared, he pointed out, racially motivated changes can be challenged under Section 2.[110]

Most troubling was Justice Scalia's warning that to give the purpose prong the expansive reading advocated by the United States would raise "concerns about § 5's constitutionality" because it would "exacerbate the 'substantial' federalism costs that the preclearance procedure already exacts."[111] The most *substantial* "federalism costs" of Section 5 have always been the requirement that *all* voting changes must secure federal approval before being enforced, together with the fact that in a preclearance review the burden of proof shifts to the submitting jurisdiction. The Supreme Court determined in 1966 and again in 1980 that these federalism costs were justified by the substantial record of racial discrimination placed before the Congress when it adopted the Voting Rights Act.[112] Why defining the statutory meaning of purpose as identical to its meaning under the Fourteenth or Fifteenth Amendments would risk a finding that Section 5 is unconstitutional is unclear.

CONGRESS RESTORES THE TRADITIONAL
SECTION 5 STANDARD

To understand the significance of the Court's emasculation of the Section 5 intent standard in *Bossier II*, it is necessary to understand the evolution of the legal basis of objections to voting changes interposed by the Department of Justice over the years.[113] During the 1970s the department rarely cited discriminatory intent when objecting to voting changes. Before *Beer* it usually referred to the likely discriminatory effect of the change, citing the effect standard in constitutional cases; after *Beer* it characterized the change as retrogressive. In the 1980s only 44 percent of the objections were based on retrogression alone; 25 percent were based on a finding of discriminatory purpose, and another 22 percent on both purpose and retrogressive effect. By the 1990s, the department based a surprising 43 percent of its objections on purpose and only 21 percent on retrogression; 19 percent were based on both purpose and effect.[114] Objections declined dramatically and purpose-based objections all but disappeared after *Bossier II*. Between the Court's decision on January 24, 2000, and June 25, 2004, the department interposed only 41 objections, as compared with 250 objections during a comparable period a decade earlier.[115] Moreover, virtually all these objections were based on a finding of retrogressive effect; at most two of the 41 objections were based entirely on the elusive concept of retrogressive intent.[116]

The Supreme Court further complicated the enforcement of Section 5 with its 2003 decision in the redistricting case of *Georgia v. Ashcroft*.[117] Before this decision, written by Justice O'Connor for a five-person majority, the effect of a redistricting plan was assessed as to its impact on the opportunity of minority voters to elect their preferred candidates.[118] In the *Georgia* case, however, Justice O'Connor emphasized that "a court should not focus solely on the comparative ability of a minority group to elect a candidate of its choice."[119] In this new scheme of things, states were permitted to choose varying combinations of (1) the traditional "safe" majority-minority districts, (2) what Justice O'Connor called "coalitional" districts, or (3) nebulously defined "influence" districts.

The first option was the traditional majority-minority district, in which "it is highly likely that minority voters will be able to elect the candidate of their choice." Under the second option, coalition districts, minority voters combine to form a functional majority with "white voters who are willing to form interracial political coalitions in support of minority candidates." By spreading minority voters across a larger number of districts, coalition districts offer the possibility of greater substantive representation – the election of a larger number of representatives who are responsive to the views of minority voters. By increasing the need for crossover votes, however, that approach also carries an increased "risk that the minority group's preferred candidate might lose," Justice O'Connor conceded. Despite that risk, all nine justices agreed that co-alition districts provided an acceptable alternative to majority-minority districts, where justified by the observed level of crossover voting.[120] The third choice, "influence" districts, would not permit minority voters to elect candidates of their choice but as Justice O'Connor saw it they could "play a substantial, if not decisive, role in the electoral process."[121] Unlike a coalition district, neither courts nor political scientists have developed clear measures of what constitutes an influence district.[122]

When Congress, beginning in the fall of 2005, reviewed the history of Section 5 court decisions in considering whether to reauthorize the preclearance requirement of the act, it decided to revise the language of Section 5. Concerned that *Georgia v. Ashcroft* was ambiguous and would permit covered jurisdictions to use the influence district concept to "ef-fectively shut minority voters out of the political process," the House Judiciary Committee restored the effect standard of Section 5 as it had operated before the *Georgia* decision – the "ability to elect" standard, as it is known – and its new language was adopted by the full House and by the Senate.[123] More importantly, Congress revised the language of Section 5 so as to restore the purpose standard as it had operated before *Bossier II*.[124]

CONCLUSION

From its inception in 1965, as we have seen, the standard for evaluating the purpose and effect of voting changes in jurisdictions covered by Section 5 was the same as the standard for enforcing the Reconstruc-tion Amendments, except that the burden of proof was on the covered jurisdictions. In 1976, however, the Supreme Court created a separate standard for addressing the effect of a voting change – the retrogression test – in *Beer v. United States*.[125] Even so, the purpose prong of Section 5 remained the same as the constitutional standard for proving discrimi-natory intent until 2000, when the Supreme Court once again created a new statutory standard in *Reno v. Bossier Parish School Board*.[126] In practice, *Beer* proved to be an effects test minority voters could live with, but redefining the purpose prong of Section 5 in *Bossier II* virtually eliminated objections based on purpose.

The constitutional challenge filed shortly after the 2006 reauthorization of Section 5 did not list the revision of the standard for evaluating voting changes in its complaint, nor was revision of the standard addressed by the Supreme Court in listing its concerns about the constitutionality of Section 5 in 2009,[127] nor is restoration of the pre-2000 standard for evaluating voting changes an issue raised in subsequent challenges to the constitutionality of Section 5.[128] Instead the focus of these constitutional challenges has been the coverage formula that determines which jurisdictions are covered by Section 5, the degree to which sufficient evidence of *intentional* discrimination exists for covered jurisdictions to justify federal oversight of voting changes, and other issues. If the Supreme Court ultimately finds Section 5 of the Voting Rights Act unconstitutional, in short, it is unlikely to be as a result of congressional revision of the standards for evaluating voting changes in covered jurisdictions. As we enter the redistricting cycle following the 2010 census, the federal courts and the Department of Justice are to evaluate voting changes in jurisdictions covered by Section 5 according to the standards that guided preclearance review from 1976 to 2000 – and were historically rooted in the case law for enforcing the Reconstruction Amendments.

NOTES

The author is a historian in the Civil Rights Division of the United States Department of Justice and an adjunct professor of law at the George Washington University. The views expressed in this essay may not necessarily reflect those of the Department of Justice. The research for this essay began in 1998–1999, when the author served as the Eugene Lang [Visiting] Professor, Department of Political Science, Swarthmore College. The financial assistance provided by the Lang professorship is acknowledged with appreciation.

1. Fannie Lou Hamer, Rosa Parks, and Coretta Scott King Voting Rights Act Reauthorization and Amendments Act of 2006, Pub. L. No. 109-246, §§ 4–5, 120 Stat. 577, 580–81 (to be codified at 42 USC §§ 1973b–1973c). The offending Supreme Court decisions were *Reno v. Bossier Parish School Board,* 528 U.S. 320 (2000), and *Georgia v. Ashcroft,* 539 U.S. 461 (2003). The statute amended a number of other provisions as well. See James T. Tucker, "The Politics of Persuasion: Passage of the Voting Rights Act Reauthorization Act

of 2006," *Journal of Legislation* 33, no. 2 (2007), 205–67.

2. See, e.g., Drew S. Days III, "Section 5 and the Role of the Justice Department," in *Controversies in Minority Voting: The Voting Rights Act in Perspective,* ed. Bernard Grofman and Chandler Davidson, 53 (Washington, D.C.: The Brookings Institution, 1992). Section 2 of the act was revised in 1982 to create a new "results test" for affirmative challenges to election practices, which has rivaled the preclearance process in effectuating minority voting rights. See generally Chandler Davidson and Bernard Grofman, eds., *Quiet Revolution in the South: The Impact of the Voting Rights Act, 1965–1990* (Princeton, N.J.: Princeton University Press, 1994).

3. Pub. L. 89-110, Sec. 5, 42 USC 1973. Note the different verb tenses in the wording of the statute: The purpose of a change is assessed by examining the past decision-making process that led to the change, but because the change has yet to be implemented only its potential effect can be estimated.

4. *South Carolina v. Katzenbach,* 383 U.S. 301, 309 (1966).

5. The Court upheld the constitutionality of Section 5, as amended in 1975, in *City of Rome v. United States,* 446 U.S. 156, 173–80 (1980), and in a more narrowly defined "as applied" constitutional challenge, *Lopez v. Monterey County,* 525 U.S. 266, 283–84 (1999).

6. Complaint at 1, *N. Austin Mun. Util. Dist. No. 1 v. Gonzalez,* No. 1:06-CV-1384 (D.D.C. Aug. 4, 2006). All challenges to the constitutionality of the Voting Rights Act must be filed in the U.S. District Court for the District of Columbia; because the utility district also sought to be removed from Section 5 coverage ("bailout"), the case had to be heard before a three-judge court, with a direct appeal to the Supreme Court. 42 USC §§ 1973(b)(c) (2000).

7. *City of Boerne v. Flores,* 521 U.S. 507 (1997); *Fla. Prepaid Postsecondary Educ. Expense Bd. v. Coll. Sav. Bank,* 527 U.S. 627 (1999); *Kimel v. Fla. Bd. Of Regents,* 528 U.S. 62 (2000); *United States v. Morrison,* 529 U.S. 598 (2000); *Bd. Of Trs. Of Univ. Of Ala. v. Garrett,* 531 U.S. 356 (2001).

8. *N. Austin Mun. Util. Dist. No. 1 v. Mukasey,* 573 F. Supp. 2d 221 (D.D.C. 2008).

9. *N. Austin Mun. Util. Dist. No. 1 v. Holder (NAMUDNO),* 129 S.Ct. 2504, 2508 (2009).

10. Ibid., 2512–13.

11. The following discussion draws on two earlier articles: Peyton McCrary, Christopher Seaman, and Richard Valelly, "The End of Preclearance As We Knew It: How the Supreme Court Transformed Section 5 of the Voting Rights Act," *Michigan Journal of Race & Law* 11 (Spring 2006), 275–323; and Peyton McCrary, "How the Voting Rights Act Works: Implementation of a Civil Rights Policy, 1965–2005," *South Carolina Law Review* 57 (Summer 2006), 785–825, reinforced by the independent analysis in Mark A. Posner, "The Real Story Behind the Justice Department's Implementation of Secton 5 of the VRA: Vigorous Enforcement, As Intended by Congress," *Duke Journal of Constitutional Law & Public Policy* 1 (2006), 1–81.

12. The first published analysis of the constitutionality of Section 5 after its extension in 2006 is Mark A. Posner, "Time Is Still on Its Side: Why Congressional Reauthorization of Section 5 of the Voting Rights Act Represents a Congruent and Proportional Response to Our Nation's History of Discrimination in Voting," *N.Y.U. Journal of Legislation & Public Policy* 10, no. 1 (2006–2007), 51–131. Nathaniel Persily, "The Promise and Pitfalls of the New Voting Rights Act," *Yale Law Journal* 117 (November 2007), 174–253, discusses both the legislative process underlying the 2006 reauthorization and the issue of its constitutionality.

13. Brian J. Landsberg, *Free At Last to Vote: Alabama Origins of the Voting Rights Act* (Lawrence: University Press of Kansas, 2007), 104–7, 154, 159–60, 162 (Table 7.1), 168–72, 188–89; Jack Bass, *Unlikely Heroes* (New York: Simon & Schuster, 1981), 271–72; Donald S. Strong, *Negroes, Ballots, and Judges: National Voting Rights Legislation in the Federal Courts* (Tuscaloosa: University of Alabama Press, 1968), 44, 49–52, 93.

14. Applications of the freezing principle began with *United States v. Alabama,* 192 F. Supp. 677 (M.D. Ala. 1961), aff'd, 304 F.2d 583 (5th Cir. 1961), aff'd, 371 U.S. 37 (1962); *United States v. Penton,* 212 F. Supp. 193 (M.D. Ala. 1962); and *United States v. Duke,* 332 F.2d 759 (5th Cir. 1964), and the freezing doctrine was adopted by the Supreme Court in *Louisiana v. United States,* 380 U.S. 145 (1965).

15. U.S. Commission on Civil Rights, *Political Participation* (Washington, D.C.: Government Printing Office, 1968), 41–42.

16. *Sellers v. Trussell* and *United States v. Crook,* 253 F. Supp. 915 (M.D. Ala. 1966).

17. 253 F. Supp. 915, 917 (M.D. Ala. 1966). The court relied on *Gomillion v. Lightfoot,* 364 U.S. 3329 (1960), a Fifteenth Amendment decision, and *Fortson v. Dorsey,* 379 U.S. 433, 436–38 (1965), which found racial vote dilution justiciable under the Fourteenth Amendment.

18. 253 F. Supp. 915, 917–18 (M.D. Ala. 1966).

19. Ibid. Judge Johnson sometimes reversed the usual practice of deciding a case on statutory rather than constitutional grounds wherever possible. See note 23 below.

20. *Smith v. Paris,* 257 F. Supp. 901, 904–05 (M.D. Ala. 1966), aff'd 386 F.2d 979 (5th Cir. 1967). Between the passage of the act and the switch to at-large elections in February 1966, black registered voters had increased from 723 to 3,100, approximately one-third of the county electorate, and were in the majority in four of the

sixteen districts. In the 1966 Democratic primary, black candidates won a majority in those four districts but lost countywide. Peyton McCrary, Jerome Gray, Edward Still, and Huey Perry, "Alabama," in *Quiet Revolution in the South: The Impact of the Voting Rights Act, 1965–1990,* ed. Chandler Davidson and Bernard Grofman, 39–41, 399–400 (Princeton, N.J.: Princeton University Press, 1994).

21. Ibid., 40–41.

22. Complaint, May 2, 1968, 5, *U.S. v. Democratic Executive Committee of Barbour County, Alabama,* No. 2685-N (M.D. Ala.).

23. "This Court does not reach that question," observed Judge Johnson, "since this case involves a clear violation of the Constitution, entitling plaintiff to full and prompt judicial relief." *U.S. v. Democratic Executive Committee of Barbour County, Alabama,* 288 F. Supp. 943, 945, 946, n. 3 (M.D. Ala. 1968).

24. McCrary et al., "Alabama," 41.

25. Bass, *Unlikely Heroes,* 164–68. Frank R. Parker, *Black Votes Count: Political Empowerment in Mississippi after 1965* (Chapel Hill: University of North Carolina Press, 1990), 84, cites an instance in a case challenging the use of the state's literacy test for voter registration in which Judge Cox took judicial notice that "the intelligence of the colored people don't [sic] compare ratio-wise to white people."

26. The plaintiffs initially charged that the adoption of at-large elections was unconstitutional as well as in violation of Section 5: Complaint, July 11, 1967, 8–10, *Marsaw v. Patterson,* C.A. No. 1201 (S.D. Miss.). *Marsaw* was consolidated with the Forrest County case, *Fairley v. Patterson,* 282 F. Supp. 164 (S.D. Miss. 1967).

27. Quoted in Peyton McCrary, "Bringing Equality to Power: How the Federal Courts Transformed the Electoral Structure of Southern Politics, 1960–1990," *University of Pennsylvania Journal of Constitutional Law* 5 (May 2003): 665, 689.

28. Ibid., 689; *Fairley v. Patterson,* 282 F. Supp. 164 (S.D. Miss. 1967). In *Whitley v. Johnson,* 260 F. Supp. 630 (S.D. Miss. 1967), black plaintiffs sought to overturn restrictions on qualification rules for independent political candidates. *Bunton v. Patterson,* 281 F. Supp. 918 (S.D. Miss. 1967), challenged a law authorizing certain counties to change from elected to appointed school superintendents.

29. *Whitley v. Johnson,* 260 F. Supp. 630 (S.D. Miss. 1967); *Bunton v. Patterson,* 281 F. Supp. 918 (S.D. Miss. 1967); *Fairley v. Patterson,* 282 F. Supp. 164 (S.D. Miss. 1967).

30. The act provides for direct appeal in Section 5 matters from three-judge panels to the Supreme Court. *Allen v. State Board of Elections,* 393 U.S. 544 (1969).

31. Transcript of Oral Argument, *Fairley v. Patterson,* Oct. 16, 1968, at p. 22, 28 (same), Papers of William J. Brennan, Library of Congress.

32. Ibid., 50. Chief Justice Earl Warren's law clerk urged that "a narrow reading to let the states get away with the sort of manipulative dilution of the Negro vote" involved in switching to at-large elections "is wholly at war with the Act's purpose to strike down legislative nullification of the Fifteenth Amendment." Under Section 5 courts reviewing a new practice are charged with determining "not merely whether it would deny the right to vote on racial grounds, but also whether it would *abridge* that right." Anticipating the position the Court would soon adopt, the clerk asserted that Section 5 "must be read broadly, or the gains in registration of Negroes will be offset by state devices to dilute the Negro vote." ECD, Memo, March 1, 1968, on *Fairley v. Patterson,* 5, 7, Earl Warren Papers, Library of Congress. As a subsequent law clerk put it, the Mississippi laws at issue in these cases "constitute the very type of indirect legislative manipulations that prompted Congress

to enact the extraordinary requirement of obtaining prior federal approval." PJM, Bench Memo, Oct. 10, 1968, at p. 24, Earl Warren Papers, Library of Congress.

33. Transcript, 8.

34. Ibid., 62. At that time the courts treated vote dilution as covered by the Fifteenth Amendment. See note 23 and related text above.

35. 393 U.S. 544 (1969).

36. 393 U.S. 544, 566 (1969) (emphasis added). Abigail Thernstrom, *Whose Votes Count?: Affirmative Action and Minority Voting Rights* (Cambridge, Mass.: Harvard University Press, 1987), 4, describes the Mississippi laws challenged in *Allen* as intentionally discriminatory: "by 1969 public officials in Mississippi and elsewhere had made all too plain their readiness to alter the electoral environment by instituting, for instance, county-wide voting, eliminating the single-member districts from which some blacks were likely to get elected." Yet she criticizes *Allen* as "the opening wedge in a profound transformation of the [Voting Rights] act," because under its terms Section 5 covered electoral procedures that abridge the suffrage through vote dilution. Thernstrom reiterates this view in *Voting Rights – and Wrongs: The Elusive Quest for Racially Fair Elections* (Washington, D.C., American Enterprise Institute Press, 2009), 32, writing that *Allen* "rewrote" the Voting Rights Act, "altering its core purpose" and (p. 34) set the federal courts on a "slippery slope" leading to "what were, in effect, reserved legislative seats." She adds (p. 36) that "it was inevitable that federal authorities would, in time, insist on districting maps drawn to maximize black officeholding." It should be clear that I disagree with this view.

37. The statute defined the term voting as including "all action necessary to make a vote effective." 393 U.S. 544, 572–74 (1969).

38. 393 U.S. 544, 569 (1969). The Mississippi laws eliminating the electorate's opportunity to vote for an important county official by making the post appointive, and placing obstacles in the path of citizens wishing to run as independent candidates, also struck the Court as changes requiring the scrutiny of the preclearance process, as did Virginia's restrictions on assistance to illiterate voters. Ibid., 570–71.

39. 393 U.S. 544, 569 (1969), citing *Reynolds v. Sims,* 377 U.S. 533, 555 (1964). In *Reynolds,* of course, the Court was specifically addressing the problem of *quantitative* vote dilution rather than racial vote dilution. But many of the cases the Court cited in support of its prohibition of population inequality were decisions outlawing racial discrimination under the Fifteenth Amendment, suggesting that the two concepts were closely related. 377 U.S. 533, 555, 557 (1964).

40. 393 U.S. 544, 583–91 (1969). Justice Harlan concurred, however, with the majority's ruling on the other three changes. 393 U.S. 544, 592–93. Justice Hugo Black, uncharacteristically reflecting the states-rights view of his native Alabama, dissented in all the cases and would have found Section 5 unconstitutional. Ibid., 595–97.

41. 364 U.S. 339 (1960); HR Rep. No. 439, 89th Cong., 1st sess., 8 (1965). See also the comments of attorney general Nicholas Katzenbach about the *Gomillion* case and of Congressman Don Edwards of California concerning the need for preclearance of redistricting plans, *Hearings Before Subcommittee No. 5 of the House Judiciary Committee on H.R. 6400 and Other Proposals to Enforce the Fifteenth Amendment,* 89th Cong., 1st sess., 15, 767 (1965). Most courts have interpreted *Gomillion* as a vote dilution case: see, e.g., *Gray v. Sanders,* 372 U.S. 368, 376 (1963), *Reynolds v. Sims,* 377 U.S. 533, 555 (1964), and *South Carolina v. Katzenbach,* 383 U.S.

30, 311 (1966). In a simultaneous debate over reapportionment, moreover, Senator Robert F. Kennedy of New York referred to the use of at-large elections as part of the effort of southern white legislators "to keep the Negro a political cripple indefinitely." Robert G. Dixon, Jr., *Democratic Representation: Reapportionment in Law and Politics* (New York: Oxford University Press, 1968), 408.

42. 393 U.S. 544, 548–49, 564–69 (1969).

43. Steven F. Lawson, *In Pursuit of Power: Southern Blacks and Electoral Politics, 1965–1982* (New York: Columbia University Press, 1985), 130–51, 154–57, 227–29, 236–53. As the Supreme Court put it later, "had Congress disagreed with the interpretations of Section 5 in *Allen,* it had ample opportunity to amend the statute." *Georgia v. United States,* 411 U.S. 526, 534 (1973).

44. *Voting Rights Act Extension: Hearings before Subcommittee No. 5 of the House Committee on the Judiciary,* 91st Cong., 1st sess., ser. 3 (1969), 3–4 (hereafter cited as *House Hearings* (1969)). Other 1965 framers who cited *Allen* favorably include Rep. Emanuel Celler, D-NY, chairman of the subcommittee, ibid., 1; Rep. William F. Ryan, D-NY, ibid., 184.

45. *House Hearings* (1969), 218, 226–27, 280–82, 297–98; *Amendments to the Voting Rights Act of 1965: Hearings before the Subcommittee on Constitutional Rights of the Senate Committee on the Judiciary,* 91st Cong., 1st and 2nd sess. (1969, 1970), 182, 189, 505–6, 517, 519 (hereafter cited as *Senate Hearings* (1969, 1970)). For a comprehensive account see Lawson, *In Pursuit of Power,* 134–37, 328.

46. Lawson, *In Pursuit of Power,* 137–57.

47. The responsibility to act as a surrogate for the D.C. court, 28 CFR § 51.52(a) (2004), was set forth in the department's original Section 5 guidelines. 28 CFR § 51.19 (1971).

48. See the court decisions cited in McCrary, Seaman, and Valelly, "The End of Preclearance As We Knew It," 281–82.

49. *Procedures for the Administration of Section 5 of the Voting Rights Act of 1965*, 28 Fed. Reg. 18, 186 (Sept. 10, 1971). The guidelines, revised several times over the years, are found at 28 CFR pt. 51 (2004). The Supreme Court has found the regulations "wholly reasonable and consistent with the Act." *Georgia v. United States*, 411 U.S. 526, 541 (1973). See as well *Lopez v. Monterey County*, 525 U.S. 266, 281 (1999). Later Supreme Court decisions expanded the scope of Section 5 and strengthened the department's enforcement powers. Drew S. Days III and Lani Guinier, "Enforcement of Section 5 of the Voting Rights Act," in *Minority Vote Dilution*, ed. Chandler Davidson, 164, 167–80 (Washington, D.C.: Howard University Press, 1984); John P. MacCoon, "The Enforcement of the Preclearance Requirement of Section 5 of the Voting Rights Act of 1965," *Catholic University Law Review*, 29 (1979): 107–27.

50. Lawson, *In Pursuit of Power*, 235–53, 348–50.

51. 446 U.S. 156 (1980).

52. *Perkins v. Matthews*, 400 U.S. 379, 390 (1971).

53. *City of Richmond v. United States*, 422 U.S. 358, 378 (1975).

54. 425 U.S. 130 (1976).

55. 412 U.S. 755 (1973). The trial court in *Beer* relied for its effect ruling on *White* and various lower court decisions in Fourteenth Amendment vote dilution cases. See *Beer v. United States*, 374 F. Supp. at 384, 387–90, 393–99, 401–2.

56. *Beer*, 425 U.S. at 141.

57. Ibid., 146.

58. H. Rep. No. 94-106, at 60 (1975). McCrary, Seaman, and Valelly, "The End of Preclearance," 305, demonstrates that the passage relied on by the *Beer* majority simply reprinted a characterization of Section 5 from a little-known 1972 oversight committee report evaluating the preclearance review of Mississippi's 1971 voter re-registration program – and *not* a review of the legislative history of the Voting Rights Act. *Enforcement of the Voting Rights Act of 1965 in Mississippi: Hearing Before the Civil Rights Oversight Subcomm. of the House Comm. on the Judiciary*, 92nd Cong. 14 (1972).

59. 425 U.S. 130, 151 (1976).

60. *Reno v. Bossier Parish School Board*, 528 U.S. 320, 374 (2000) (Breyer, J., dissenting).

61. Because the trial court decided the case on the grounds that the redistricting plan had a dilutive effect, it did not reach the issue of whether the change had a discriminatory purpose. *Beer*, 374 F. Supp. at 387.

62. *Beer*, 425 U.S. at 141 (emphasis added). The Court could hardly have intended its reference to a constitutional violation to mean that a voting change that was dilutive in effect under *White v. Regester* – but not retrogressive – would be objectionable under Section 5, because in announcing the retrogression test, the *Beer* majority made clear that the dilutive effect standard was inapplicable in the Section 5 context.

63. McCrary, Seaman, and Valelly, "The End of Preclearance," 284; Steve Bickerstaff, "Reapportionment by State Legislatures: A Guide for the 1980's," *Southwestern Law Journal* 34 (1980), 607, 669; James F. Blumstein, "Defining and Proving Race Discrimination: Perspectives on the Purpose vs. Results Approach from the Voting Rights Act," *Virginia Law Review* 69 (1983), 633, 661–63. See however the quite different interpretation by the Court in *Reno v. Bossier Parish School Board*, 528 U.S. 320, 337 (2000).

64. *City of Rome v. United States*, 446 U.S. 156, 210 (1980) (Rehnquist, J., dissenting).

65. *City of Pleasant Grove v. United States*, 479 U.S. 462, 469, 476 n. 11 (1987).

See as well *City of Port Arthur v. United States*, 459 U.S. 159, 168 (1982) (holding that even a nonretrogressive plan "would nevertheless be invalid if adopted for racially discriminatory purposes"); *Busbee v. Smith*, 549 F. Supp. 494, 516–17 (D.D.C. 1982), *aff'd mem.*, 459 U.S. 1166 (1983) ("Simply demonstrating that a plan increases black voting strength does not entitle the State to the declaratory relief it seeks; the State must also demonstrate the absence of discriminatory purpose."); *Mississippi v. United States*, 490 F. Supp. 569, 583 (D.D.C. 1979), *aff'd*, 440 U.S. 1050 (1980) ("The prohibited 'purpose' of section 5 may be described as the sort of invidious discriminatory purpose that would support a challenge to official action as an unconstitutional denial of equal protection."). See also Posner, "The Real Story," 65–67.

66. *Village of Arlington Heights v. Metropolitan Housing Development Corp.*, 429 U.S. 252, 265–66 (1977). The role of the *Arlington Heights* decision was clarified in the voting rights context by the decision in *City of Mobile v. Bolden*, 446 U.S. 55 (1980), a challenge to the city's at-large elections under the Reconstruction Amendments. Reversing the lower courts, the Supreme Court remanded the case, and a companion suit challenging at-large school board elections in Mobile County, for a new trial on the intent question. The plaintiffs prevailed under the intent standard after demonstrating that a racial purpose lay behind shifts to at-large elections in 1876 and 1911. *Bolden v. City of Mobile*, 542 F. Supp. 1050 (S.D. Ala. 1982); *Brown v. Bd. of Sch. Comm'rs*, 542 F. Supp. 1078 (S.D. Ala. 1982). Peyton McCrary, "History in the Courts: The Significance of City of Mobile v. Bolden," in *Minority Vote Dilution*, ed. Chandler Davidson, 47–63 (Washington, D.C.: Howard University Press, 1984), summarizes the testimony in both cases.

67. 450 F. Supp. 1171 (D.D.C. 1978), *aff'd mem.*, 439 U.S. 999 (1978). The trial court followed the guidelines for assessing circumstantial evidence of discriminatory intent set forth in the *Arlington Heights* decision, 429 U.S. 252, 265–66 (1977).

68. Ibid., 1174–78. The four single-member districts used in Wilkes County before 1972 were severely malapportioned: one district contained 47 percent of the county's population, more than double the remaining three. Two of the four had black population majorities, but the county claimed that the at-large system was not retrogressive because blacks did not form a majority of the registered voters in any of the old 1960s districts. *Wilkes County v. United States*, 439 U.S. 999 (1978) (No. 78–70). The trial court, noting that low black voter registration was itself a function of historical discrimination, found that even under the old malapportioned plan African Americans had *more* influence on the outcome of county elections than under the adopted at-large system. In the court's view the correct benchmark for measuring retrogression was a properly apportioned – and "fairly drawn" – system of single-member districts, and such a plan *could have* been drawn after the 1970 census to include a district with a population that was 71 percent black (giving black voters an equal opportunity to elect a candidate of their choice)." Based on this reasoning the court also decided that the effect of the change was retrogressive. *Wilkes County*, 450 F. Supp. at 1175–77. Thernstrom, *Whose Votes Count?*, 177, correctly points out that "these were very special circumstances" in that the old, malapportioned district alignment "was not a legitimate plan against which slippage could legitimately be measured."

69. 549 F. Supp. 494 (D.D.C. 1982), *aff'd mem.*, 459 U.S. 1166 (1983).

70. Ibid., 498. The district in which Young was elected in 1972, thanks in part

to an unusual 25 percent white crossover vote, was adopted following a Department of Justice objection to an earlier plan, drawn in 1971 with the goal of preventing the election of an African American to Congress. Laughlin McDonald, *A Voting Rights Odyssey: Black Enfranchisement in Georgia* (New York: Cambridge University Press, 2003), 149–50.

71. Ibid., 515. See McDonald, *A Voting Rights Odyssey,* 168–72.

72. 549 F. Supp. at 501. According to the trial court, "Wilson uses the term 'nigger' [routinely] to refer to black persons." Ibid., 500.

73. Ibid., 510. Murphy explained at trial that "I was concerned that . . . we were gerrymandering a district to create a black district where a black would certainly be elected." Ibid, 509–10.

74. Ibid., 516–18. Thernstrom, *Voting Rights – and Wrongs,* 124, charges (improbably) that in administering Section 5 in the 1980s, the Civil Rights Division under William Bradford Reynolds – who was in fact an opponent of affirmative action in voting – used the intent standard to "maximize" black officeholding; the division's lawyers "wanted the proportional representation standard for racial fairness that the Court had embraced in the annexation decisions to apply to districting cases as well." When Reynolds objected to voting changes on purpose grounds, however, he was merely applying the purpose standard affirmed in *Busbee,* typically citing the decision in the objection letter. Posner, "The Real Story," 44 n. 31, points out that Thernstrom criticizes *both* the courts *and* the Department of Justice for "stretching the purpose inquiry far beyond its proper scope." If the courts were applying the incorrect standard, he notes, then the department "was properly carrying out what Thernstrom argues is its role, a surrogate for the D.C. District Court."

75. 528 U.S. 320 (2000). There was an interim Supreme Court decision in this case in 1997 (hence the 2000 decision is known as *Bossier II*).

76. Jurisdictional Statement at 1, *Busbee v. Smith,* 459 U.S. 1166 (1983) (No. 82–857), quoted in McCrary, Seaman, and Valelly, "The End of Preclearance," 287, and Posner, "The Real Story," 65.

77. *Busbee* bound the Section 5 trial courts and the Department of Justice when dealing with comparable voting changes to reject the theory of retrogressive intent, because summary affirmances "prevent lower courts from coming to opposite conclusions on the precise issues presented and necessarily decided by those actions." *Mandel v. Bradley,* 432 U.S. 173, 176 (1977); McCrary, Seaman, and Valelly, "The End of Preclearance," 287, and Posner, "The Real Story," 65.

78. *City of Pleasant Grove v. United States,* 623 F. Supp. 782, 784, 787–88 (D.D.C. 1985), aff'd 479 U.S. 462 (1987), denied preclearance of the annexations.

79. *City of Pleasant Grove,* 479 U.S. at 467 (quoting 623 F. Supp. at 788 n. 30).

80. Ibid., 470–71. Thernstrom, *Whose Votes Count?,* 156, agrees with the city's view.

81. 479 U.S. at 471. The dissent by Justice Powell rejected this interpretation as "purely speculative." Ibid., 472 (Powell, J., dissenting).

82. Ibid., 474 (Powell, J., dissenting). His written opinions reflect that Justice Powell was consistently hostile to Section 5. His correspondence with colleagues on the Court was often even more expressive. See, e.g., Powell to Justice Potter Stewart regarding *Georgia v. United States:* "As I have stated on more than one occasion, I consider the Voting Rights Act of 1965 – limited as it is to a handful of states rather than applying to the entire country – to be discriminatory and indefen-

sible legislation," because it required that "states, hat in hand, obtain the consent of the Attorney General or run the gauntlet of the federal court here in the District before an act of the state legislature may go into effect." Justice Powell also believed that coverage should not extend to "apportionment and annexation." Powell to Stewart, March 30, 1973, Lewis F. Powell Papers, Washington & Lee University Law School, Box 155, *Georgia v. United States.*

83. 479 U.S. at 471, n. 11 (quoting *City of Richmond v. United States,* 422 U.S. 358, 378 (1975), emphasis added by the Court in *Pleasant Grove*). Note that Justice Antonin Scalia supported the majority's rejection of the retrogressive intent theory in this case, although in 2000, as we shall see, he took the opposite position in *Bossier II.*

84. 509 U.S. 630 (1993).

85. *Miller v. Johnson,* 515 U.S. 900 (1995) [Georgia]; *Vera v. Bush,* 517 U.S. 952 (1996) [Texas]; *Shaw v. Hunt,* 517 U.S. 899 (1996) [North Carolina]. The same conservative majority also upheld a court-drawn congressional plan in Georgia that decreased the number of black-majority districts from three to one: *Abrams v. Johnson,* 521 U.S. 74 (1997). The Court rejected white plaintiffs' "racial gerrymandering" claim and upheld one congressional plan in North Carolina, however, in *Easley v. Cromartie,* 532 U.S. 234 (2001). See Tinsley E. Yarbrough, *Race and Redistricting: The Shaw-Cromartie Cases* (Lawrence: University Press of Kansas, 2002).

86. *Miller,* 515 U.S. at 916 ("[T]he legislature subordinated traditional race-neutral districting principles . . . to racial considerations.").

87. Ibid., 924–25. As the Court saw it, "Instead of grounding its objections on evidence of a discriminatory purpose, it would appear the Government was driven by its policy of maximizing majority-black

districts." Ibid., 924–25. See Posner, "The Real Story," 38.

88. In *Shaw v. Hunt,* 517 U.S. 899, 913 (1996), the Court observed, "It appears that the Justice Department was pursuing in North Carolina the same policy of maximizing the number of majority-black districts that it pursued in Georgia." Posner, "Time Is Still On Its Side," 91–92, explains that this analysis was based only on the Court's assessment of the record in a handful of congressional redistricting cases and ignored the vast number of local and state redistricting plans reviewed by the department.

89. *Georgia v. Reno,* 881 F. Supp. 7, 10 (D.D.C. 1995); *Texas v. United States,* No. 94 C 5702, 1995 WL 769169 (D.D.C., July 10, 1995), an unreported two-page *per curiam* opinion. See McCrary, "How the Voting Rights Act Works," 815–18.

90. The department followed the reasoning in *Haith v. Martin,* 618 F. Supp. 410, 412–13 (E.D.N.C. 1985), aff'd, 477 U.S. 901 (1986). See also *Brooks v. State Bd. of Elections,* 775 F. Supp. 1470, 1475 (S.D.Ga. 1989) (three-judge court), aff'd mem., 498 U.S. 916 (1990): "The Supreme Court's summary affirmance of *Haith v. Martin* may well have settled this issue."

91. McCrary, "How the Voting Rights Act Works," 815–18; Posner, "The Real Story," 71.

92. A police jury is a unit of local Louisiana government similar to a county board of supervisors. In 1968, the Louisiana legislature authorized police juries and school boards to use at-large elections for the first time. Following *Allen v. State Board of Elections,* the Department of Justice objected to both enactments and to numerous efforts by particular parishes to adopt at-large elections. McCrary, Seaman, and Valelly, "The End of Preclearance," 299–300. McCrary, "Bringing Equality to Power," 671–73, provides

evidence that in the 1960s Louisiana
legislators saw at-large elections as a key
device for diluting African American voting strength.

93. *Bossier Parish Sch. Bd. v. Reno*, 907
F. Supp. 434, 437 (D.D.C. 1995).

94. Unlike the school board, the police jury had elected – and re-elected – a
black candidate under the existing plan.
907 F. Supp. 434, 437 (D.D.C. 1995). This
police jury district included an air force
base, whose largely white residents rarely
voted in local elections, so that blacks
approached parity with whites in voter
turnout. Ibid.

95. The police jury plan reflected that
body's functional concerns such as road
maintenance and drainage – considerations that had no relevance for school
board members. *Bossier II*, 528 U.S. at
346–47 (Souter, J., concurring in part and
dissenting in part). For the distinction
between *Bossier I* and *Bossier II*, see note
103 below.

96. *Bossier II*, 528 U.S. at 347.

97. McCrary, Seaman, and Valelly,
"The End of Preclearance," 300–1.

98. Black leaders from Bossier Parish,
represented by the Lawyers' Committee
for Civil Rights Under Law, intervened in
the lawsuit as defendants, siding with the
Department of Justice. *Bossier Parish Sch.
Bd. v. Reno*, 907 F. Supp. at 436.

99. Ibid., 450.

100. Ibid., 454 (Kessler, J., concurring
in part and dissenting in part). Judge Kessler's assessment was later echoed by the
dissenters on the Supreme Court. "There
is no reasonable doubt on this record that
the Board chose the Police Jury plan for
no other reason than to squelch requests
to adopt the NAACP plan or any other
plan reflecting minority voting strength,"
observed the dissenters, and under the
traditional Section 5 purpose analysis, the
evidence regarding the board's adoption of
the redistricting plan "disqualifies it from

§ 5 preclearance." *Bossier II*, 528 U.S. at
356–57 (Souter, J., dissenting).

101. See for example *Miller v. Johnson*,
515 U.S. 900 (1995).

102. *Reno v. Bossier Parish School Board*,
520 U.S. 471, 474 (1997) (*Bossier I*).

103. *Bossier I*, 520 U.S. 471, 479, 486. The
"retrogressive intent" argument that the
five-justice majority found so persuasive in
Bossier II was not advanced by the parish
but only in a petition to file a late amicus
curiae brief on behalf of several covered
counties in Texas in *Bossier I*. See McCrary,
Seaman, and Valelly, "The End of Preclearance," 302 n. 131.

104. Quoted in McCrary, Seaman, and
Valelly, "The End of Preclearance," 302.

105. *Reno v. Bossier Parish School Board*,
528 U.S. 320, 341 (2000).

106. *Beer v. United States*, 425 U.S. 130
(1976). In his dissent, Justice David Souter
flatly declared that "*Beer* was wrongly
decided." In his view the Court "was
mistaken in *Beer* when it restricted the
effect prong of § 5 to retrogression, and
the Court is even more wrong today when
it limits the clear text of § 5 to the corresponding retrogressive purpose." *Bossier II*
at 342. Justice Souter is a staunch advocate
of *stare decisis* in interpreting statutory
language – "when statutory language
is construed it should stay construed."
Ibid., 363 (Souter, J., dissenting): "But it
is another thing entirely to ignore error in
extending discredited reasoning to previously unspoiled statutory provisions . . .
[as] the Court does in extending *Beer* from
§ 5 effects to § 5 purpose."

107. 528 U.S. 320, 341 (2000). Under Section 5 a covered jurisdiction has the burden of proving that the proposed change
"does not have the purpose and will not
have the effect of denying or abridging the
right to vote on account of race or color."
Ibid., 328 (quoting 42 USC § 1973c). On
Justice Scalia's preoccupation with syntax
in statutes, see William D. Popkin, "An 'In-

ternal' Critique of Justice Scalia's Theory of Statutory Interpretation," *Minnesota Law Review* 76 (1992): 1133, 1143.

108. H. Rep. No. 94-106, at 60 (1975). See McCrary, Seaman, and Valelly, "The End of Preclearance," 305. Ordinarily Justice Scalia professes to disdain legislative history – and "object[s] to [its] use . . . on principle" – preferring to parse the words of the statute rather than rely on committee reports and the record of hearings. Antonin Scalia, "Common-Law Courts in a Civil-Law System: The Role of United States Federal Courts in Interpreting the Constitution and Laws," in *A Matter of Interpretation: Federal Courts and the Law,* ed. Amy Gutmann, 3, 31 (Princeton, N.J.: Princeton University Press, 1997). Yet by anchoring his analysis in the concept of retrogressive effect in *Beer,* Justice Scalia relied on an earlier decision applying legislative history in a manner that violates one of his most cherished principles of statutory construction. See also William N. Eskridge, Jr., "The New Textualism," UCLA *Law Review* 37 (1990): 621, 651 n.116.

109. 549 F. Supp. 494 (D.D.C. 1982), *aff'd mem.,* 459 U.S. 1166 (1983). See the discussion above (text associated with notes 69 through 74).

110. *Bossier II,* 528 U.S. at 335. Of course, in a Section 2 case the United States – or minority plaintiffs – would have the burden of proof, unlike in a Section 5 review.

111. Ibid., 336, quoting *Lopez v. Monterey County,* 525 U.S. 266, 282 (1999).

112. *South Carolina v. Katzenbach,* 383 U.S. 301 (1966); *City of Rome v. United States,* 446 U.S. 156 (1980).

113. The following analysis is based on the quantitative evidence presented in McCrary, Seaman, and Valelly, "The End of Preclearance," 275–323, and in a more abbreviated version, Peyton McCrary, Christopher Seaman, and Richard Valelly, "The Law of Preclearance: Enforcing Section 5," in *The Future of the Voting Rights Act,*

ed. David Epstein et al., 20–37 (New York: Russell Sage Foundation, 2006).

114. McCrary, Seaman, and Valelly, "The End of Preclearance," 297 (Table 2). A small number of objections fell into various other categories.

115. Ibid., 313. The authors of the study do not contend that it would be reasonable to expect as many objections in the redistricting cycle after the 2000 census as during a comparable period in the 1990s, due simply to the constriction of the purpose prong of Section 5. In fact, the number of objections decreased sharply after 1994, perhaps in part in reaction to the Supreme Court's criticisms of the department in the *Shaw* decisions, but also because the redistricting cycle was largely completed. In the 2000 round of redistricting, moreover, most covered jurisdictions appear to have been more careful to avoid drawing retrogressive plans. That said, the gap between 40 and 250 is substantial, and likely reflects the impact of *Bossier II.* Posner, "The Real Story," 30 n. 91, indicates that he independently examined the post-2000 objections and reached the same conclusion.

116. McCrary, Seaman, and Valelly, "The End of Preclearance," 314 (Table 4).

117. 539 U.S. 461 (2003). Pamela S. Karlan, "*Georgia v. Ashcroft* and the Retrogression of Retrogression," *Election Law Journal* 3 (2004), 21–36, provides the best analysis of the decision.

118. This focus stemmed from the command in *Allen v. State Board of Elections,* 393 U.S. 544, 569 (1969), to protect minority voters from changes with the potential to "nullify their ability to elect the candidate of their choice."

119. *Georgia v. Ashcroft,* 539 U.S. 461, 480 (2003).

120. Ibid., 480–81, 492.

121. Ibid., 482.

122. See Richard Pildes, "Is Voting Rights Law Now At War With Itself? Social Science and Voting Rights in the

2000s," *North Carolina Law Review* 80 (2002): 1522, 1539: "The concept of influence is nebulous and difficult to quantify." The Court also seems to have changed its understanding of the term "influence district." See *Voinovich v. Quilter,* 507 U.S. 146, 154 (1993), where the term "influence districts" refers to "districts in which black voters would not constitute a majority but in which they could, with the help of a predictable number of cross-over votes from white voters, elect their candidates of choice" – in other words, "coalitional" districts.

123. Congress added a subsection to Section 5 clarifying that the purpose of preclearance review "is to protect the ability of such citizens to elect candidates of their choice." Pub. L. No. 109-246 § 5, 120 Stat. 580–81 (2006). See Tucker, "The Politics of Persuasion," 221–22.

124. Congress replaced the phrase "does not have the purpose and will not have the effect" – the wording found problematic by the *Bossier II* majority – with "neither has the purpose nor will have the effect."

It then added a subsection clarifying that the term "purpose" includes "any discriminatory purpose." Pub. L. No. 109-246 § 5, 120 Stat. 580–81 (2006). See Tucker, "The Politics of Persuasion," 221–22.

125. 425 U.S. 130 (1976).

126. 528 U.S. 320 (2000).

127. Complaint, *N. Austin Mun. Util. Dist. No. 1 v. Gonzalez,* No. 1:06-CV-1384 (D.D.C. Aug. 4, 2006); *Northwest Austin Municipal Utility District No. 1 (NAMUDNO),* 129 S.Ct. 2504 (2009).

128. *Shelby County, Alabama v. Holder,* 2011 WL 4375001 (D.D.C.), Memorandum Opinion, Sept. 21, 2011 (granting summary judgment to the defendant United States as to the constitutionality of the reauthorized Section 5). In a second case the plaintiffs, who were private citizens in a covered jurisdiction, claim that the 2006 revision in the standard for enforcing Section 5 is unconstitutional, but that issue is still undecided; see *Laroque v. Holder,* 755 F. Supp. 2d 156 (D.D.C. 2010), *rev'd in part and remanded,* No. 10-5433 (D.C. Cir.), Opinion, July 8, 2011.

THREE

Influence District and the Courts:
A Concept in Need of Clarity

RICHARD L. ENGSTROM

The concept of "influence district" is referenced frequently in discussions of minority voting rights and representational districting. An influence district is said to be a district in which voters constituting a cohesive quantitative minority of voters cannot elect a representative of their choice if their choice is a member of their own group, but can still be expected, given their level of presence in the district, to influence the legislative behavior of the person who is elected to represent the district. Theoretically the presence of any group satisfying these criteria could be the basis for calling a district an influence district for that group, but in application the concept has been applied almost exclusively to districts in which the group is a minority group protected by the Voting Rights Act (VRA), in particular African Americans and Latinos.[1]

Influence districts are one of three types of districts recognized by the United States Supreme Court in which minority voters do not constitute a majority of the voting age population. The others are "coalition districts" and "crossover districts." In these types of districts, minority voters do have a reasonable opportunity to elect representatives from within their group based on predictable levels of support for those candidates from other voters. In the case of coalition districts, the other voters are members of other protected minorities; in the case of crossover districts they are typically white or Anglos voters.[2] Influence districts, however, are districts "in which minority candidates do not win, but minority voters can play a significant role in electing candidates who will be sympathetic to their interests."[3]

The presence of districts alleged to be minority influence districts has been touted as a positive feature of redistricting plans. Indeed, one federal judge has stated that influence districts "are to be prized as a means of encouraging both voters and candidates to dismantle the barriers that wall off racial groups and replace those barriers with voting coalitions" [*Vecinos de Barrio UNO v. City of Holyoke*, 72 F.3d 973, 991 (First Cir. 1995)]. It has been argued that the possibility of creating an influence district in a plan without one, or the possibility of creating more influence districts than contained in a plan, demonstrate that minority votes are being diluted by the plan. Claims that districts constitute influence districts therefore have played a role in dilution litigation based on Section 2 and in preclearance issues under Section 5 (see Posner 1998: 109) of the federal VRA.[4]

Influence districts also play a major role in a popular yet highly contested theory that minorities will have greater "substantive" representation by replacing majority-minority districts, which typically result in the election of members of the minority group, with a larger but unspecified number of influence districts, which result in the election of whites or Anglos (see, e.g., Cameron, Epstein, and O'Halloran 1996, Lublin 1997, Epstein and O'Halloran 1999, 2006). This theory is often referred to as the "perverse effects theory" (see, e.g., Shotts 2003a and 2003b, and Engstrom 2006). Despite the well-documented fact that the legislators most responsive to the issue and policy preferences of minority voters have been those from within their own group who are accountable to electorates in which the group constitutes the majority,[5] the theory maintains that the creation of majority-minority districts that result in the election of such people will be harmful to the overall representation of these groups.

Creating majority-minority districts, the theory holds, results in fewer minority voters in adjacent districts, "bleaching" those districts to a point where representatives elected in them will have no interest in responding to minority interests or concerns. Minorities, it is maintained, would be better off with fewer majority-minority districts, and fewer minority legislators, and more influence districts, in which the size of the minority population is large enough that the representatives chosen in them will be responsive to the interests and preferences of minority voters. The theory does not maintain that whites or Anglos, individually, will represent minority voters as well as minority representatives would, but that more influence districts will provide better representation for minorities *in the aggregate,* even if they come at the expense of majority-minority districts and a corresponding reduction in "descriptive representation," i.e., minority legislators.

This theory has considerable intuitive appeal, but the empirical evidence for it is contested (see, e.g., the critiques by Grofman 2006: 275–281, and Canon 2008) and serious contextual limitations to its application have been revealed (Shotts, 2002, 2003a, and 2003b, Lublin and Voss 2000, 2003, Engstrom 2006, and Lublin and Lampkin 2007). Not surprisingly, the beneficial effects for minorities of such tradeoffs are disputed.[6] The idea that white or Anglo representatives accountable to white or Anglo majority electorates can be counted on to be responsive to minority concerns is considered naive by many. As two political scientists have commented, "the history of white representation of minority interests in districts with significant minority populations is not cause for optimism" (McClain and Stewart 1995: 25). Another scholar has likewise argued that Latinos have been "poorly served" by influence districts and that they are, for that group, an "empty promise" (Bedoya 2006: 2132, 2138). Indeed, the tradeoff is hardly persuasive to anyone who thinks, like an African American state legislator in Texas, that so-called minority influence districts are "begging and pleading, step-and-fetch-it districts" (quoted in Clarke 2005: 239), or a Latino political scientist who states that such a tradeoff could be "a fool's bargain" (Segura and Woods 2007: 138 n. 6).

The theory seems to have a receptive audience within the American judiciary however. It certainly did with a majority of the United States Supreme Court in *Georgia v. Ashcroft* in 2003 (539 U.S. 461) (see below). But the judiciary's application of the influence district concept itself, let alone assessment of the tradeoff notion, leaves much to be desired. Judicial applications of the concept have generally simply assumed that a "substantial" minority presence in a district somehow equates to influence, without examining districts in detail to assess whether that is in fact the case or likely to be the case. It is as if the relationship is axiomatic: a substantial but less than majority presence in a district results in influence on the behavior of the district's representative. As expressed by one judge, "In such a district, no viable candidate can ignore minority interests, because of the minority's strong influence at the ballot box" [*Vecinos de Barrio UNO v. City of Holyoke*, 960 F. Supp. 515, 523 (D.C. Mass. 1997)]. Another court has gone even further. It declared that a district admittedly designed to continue the re-election of a Latino Republican whom Latino voters had voted *against* six straight times, most recently casting only 8 percent of their votes for him, to be a Latino "influence district" simply because the citizen voting age population (CVAP) in the district was 45.8 percent. The evidence of the incumbent's lack of Latino voter support was recited by the court, but simply ignored when the court made its influence district determination, based solely on the CVAP percentage [*Sessions v. Perry*, 298 F. Supp. 2d 451, 494 (E.D. Tex. 2004)].

It certainly is not axiomatic that the presence of a "substantial" minority in a representative's election district will compel the representative to behave in a way responsive to that group, especially when the majority in the district does not share that group's candidate preferences, political philosophy, or positions on issues. It is premature for courts to make decisions about alleged influence districts, let alone adopt a theory endorsing their substitution for "ability-to-elect" districts (Becker 2007: 235), without first clarifying what an influence district entails and how it should be measured. It is essential that there be a reasonable, empirically grounded expectation that minorities within such districts will actually have influence on the representatives elected in them before these districts serve as substitutes for districts in which minority voters are able to elect the representatives of their choice. An inference that such a change will be beneficial to the minority cannot be drawn without attention to the others voters in the district. A "substantial" presence in the district, without more, does not justify such an inference.

The following reviews the federal judiciary's application of the influence district concept in voting rights cases. It identifies a number of instances when it was done with little, if any, evidence that minority voter influence on the elected representatives could be expected to result from the creation or continuation of such districts. It also identifies definitional and empirical questions that need to be addressed in order to make more informed decisions about the presence of influence districts. And it offers a measure for identifying presumptive influence districts that can be used in both the legislative and the judicial processes.

JUDICIAL CONSIDERATION OF INFLUENCE DISTRICTS

It has been noted that "neither courts nor political scientists have developed clear measures of what constitutes an influence district" (McCrary, Seaman, and Valelly 2006: 317; see also Note 2008: 504). The concept, in its present state, is viewed as "extremely vague" (ibid., 317), "murky" (Grofman, Handley, and Niemi 1992: 117; Karlan 2004: 259), "nebulous" (Pildes 2002: 1539; McCrary, Seaman, and Valelly, 2006: 316), "amorphous" (Chang 2005: 239), "opaque" (Note 2004: 2611), "ambiguous" (Thernstrom 2009: 181), and "difficult to quantify" (Pildes 2002: 1539). Its application has been called "paternalistic" (Grofman, Handley, and Niemi 1992: 117; Reeves 1997: 105) and "racially selective" (Engstrom and Kirksey 1998: 262–63).

The identification of influence districts can also be politically sensitive. When the election context is partisan, influence districts have also been viewed, not surprisingly given the partisan preferences of minority voters (see, e.g., Frymer 1999; Ardoin and Vogel 2006; and Fauntroy 2007), as favoring Democratic candidates over Republicans. The whites or Anglos elected in them are usually expected to be Democrats. One federal judge has even described an influence district as a "safe Democratic district" [*Turner v. Arkansas*, 784 F. Supp. 553, 563 (E.D. Ark. 1991); see also *Colleton County Council v. McConnell*, 201 F. Supp. 2d 616, 659 (D.C. S.C. 2002)]. One commentator has stated that they would "be more accurately described as Democratic Party gerrymanders" (Thernstrom 2009: 181). Indeed, Grofman has suggested that, in the Deep South at least, any district that elects a Republican should not be considered an influence district (2006: 263; see also Kousser concerning California, 1998: 172–73, and Canon concerning Georgia, 2008: 15). He also warns that Republicans can be expected to defend their preferred plans "by claiming that the districts . . . with significant black populations are minority influence districts even when, in fact, such districts have substantial probabilities of electing Republicans" (ibid., 262). Both parties of course will label districts as influence districts if that serves their overall political goals.

Litigation has done nothing to clarify the concept or its operationalization; it has instead contributed to the confusion. It is extremely important that clarity be provided so that there will be some constraint on using the expression as a rationalization for dilutive districting arrangements. Otherwise the political thicket of districting will be even more entangled than it has been, leaving players in the process with more discretion over where to place district lines, which can lead to the implementation and rationalization of political goals adverse to minority voters (see Engstrom 2002).

The application of the concept by courts and others has been very simplistic. It typically consists, as already noted, of identifying the percentage of a district that a protected minority constitutes, usually a percentage of the voting age population (VAP). Rarely is any attention given to the other voters within the district. The same applies to the application of the concept by political and other social scientists, although they are more likely, at least in their comparative studies of redistricting plans, to identify thresholds and ranges that supposedly capture minority influence districts. There is, however, no consensus as to what these thresholds or ranges should be (Canon 2008: 10).[7] The degree of responsiveness of a legislator to minority interests and concerns may vary, of course, with the extent to which minority interests are viewed as conflicting with those of other members of the representative's constituency, especially his or her re-election or core constituency (see Fenno 1978: 8, and LeVeaux and Garand 2003: 34), as well as the elected representative's perceived need for their future support.

The concept is premised, it must be remembered, on a conclusion that minority voters cannot elect the representative of their choice in the district. This is because voting preferences tend to be divided along group lines, often strongly so. These divisions may result from racial feelings directly, or from contrasting policy preferences between groups, which are in turn typically related to race. If this were not the case and the other voters found minority candidates just as impressive as other candidates, or minority policy preferences consistent with their own, there would be no need to be concerned about influence districts, or even majority-minority districts. The concept itself, in short, is premised on group divisions in the district electorates, divisions that have been well-documented in litigation concerning many areas across the United States (see Engstrom 2005b, 2005c).

The application of the concept almost invariably ignores this complexity, however. It consists of simply declaring a district, based solely on its minority percentage, to be an "influence district." Sometimes a percentage threshold is picked at which minority voters are assumed to possess such influence in districts, and all districts at or above that threshold, up to 50 percent, are called "influence districts," regardless of potentially important differences among them. But more often the percentage that a minority comprises in a particular district is cited, and nothing more. It is also assumed that influence on the elected representatives increases as minority presence increases, regardless of other characteristics of the districts. This determination is made without empirical evidence for the threshold, whether implicit or explicit, and without reference to evidence demonstrating that the alleged influence on the representative can reasonably be expected to follow.

EMPIRICAL RESEARCH ON RACE AND REPRESENTATION

The preference of minority voters protected by the VRA for representatives from within their own group has been clear through their voting behavior. It has also been documented, for African Americans, in Katherine Tate's survey-based findings concerning within-group representation for African Americans in the U.S. House, findings that are no doubt generalizable to many other legislative contexts. She concludes:

> Race matters to Black constituents. All things being equal, Black constituents believe that they are better represented in Congress when their representative is Black. Black constituents recognize that Black members strive to represent the interests of Blacks more so than White members do. They, therefore, credit Black members with doing more for them because of their race than legislators who represent them solely on the basis of their political party (2003: 155–156).

Empirical studies of legislative voting behavior indicate that the perceptions of African Americans Tate reports are firmly grounded. Almost all the recent studies of the relationship between race and legislative

voting focus on the U.S. House. This work consistently concludes that
African Americans are the legislators most responsive to African American interests. This conclusion holds across numerous indices of support. Kenny J. Whitby, for example, after examining roll call votes in the
House, concluded that "there is no cohort in Congress that represents
the views, values, or interests of the black community better than black
members of Congress" (1997: 141; see also Grose 2005: 438–39; Haynie
2005: 395, 405–7).[8] Similar results have been reported concerning the
linkage between the Latino members of the House and support for Latino interests (Casellas 2007: 226–29; Huerta and Santos 2006: 120–21;
Kerr and Miller 1997: 1071; see also, concerning school board members
elected by wards, Meier et al. 2005).

Research by political scientists on the relationship between the minority percentages of constituents and the responsiveness of white legislators to minority interests creates doubts about using these percentages, by themselves, as the basis for identifying influence districts. As a
student of congressional politics has noted, "Inferences about potential
legislative support [for black-oriented initiatives] based on statistical
analyses of the proportion of blacks in a district are extremely hazard-
ous" (Singh 1998: 149). The reason for this is that the level of influence
minorities might have on a representative varies not just with their relative presence in the district, but also with the types of other voters in the
district. Representatives that have a core or re-election constituency that
provides them with electoral security without relying on minority support may feel no need to be responsive to minorities. And even when they
are insecure, minorities can expect to have little influence if support for
their interests is seen by the representative to conflict with the interests
of the other voters. As Singh explains:

> The political environments of districts vary substantially and drawing conclu-
> sions about them from demographic statistics alone frequently fails to afford
> accurate assessments of the concrete political circumstances of individual
> legislators (1998: 157).

Research also has shown that there is considerable variation in the
responsiveness to minority concerns among white or Anglo representatives who have a substantial minority presence in their districts. The
party affiliation of the representatives and whether their districts are in

the South have been two glaring sources of variation. Party is, according to Whitby, "the key variable" generally in explaining differences in support in the House for the policy preferences of African Americans (1997: 104). David Canon likewise identifies party as "the most striking variable" accounting for such differences (1999: 179; see also Whitby and Krause 2001: 563–64, 567–68; Overby and Cosgrove 1996: 545–47; Grose 2005: 438–39; and for Latinos, Kerr and Miller 1997: 1069). Christine LeVeaux and James C. Garand even report that, for Republicans, the relationship between support for African American interests by representatives of majority-white districts is *inversely* related to the racial composition of their districts. They find that "[w]hen Republican incumbents are confronted with substantial African American populations in their districts, they appear to target their representational behavior toward their (presumably) more conservative white constituents than toward their African-American constituents" (2003: 40; see also Grofman 2006: 261).[9]

A recent study of a state legislative body, the Louisiana House of Representatives, reports similar findings. The study focused on efforts to facilitate access to the ballot for voters displaced by Hurricane Katrina and the subsequent flood in the New Orleans area, a group that was disproportionately African American. Facilitating access to the ballot in the forthcoming New Orleans mayoral election by these displaced voters was an issue with serious racial consequences because voting in that city, including its mayoral elections, had typically been strongly divided along racial lines (Liu and Vanderleeuw, 2007). Only African American legislators introduced bills to facilitate voting by displaced people. African Americans legislators were almost unanimous in their support for these measures, while white legislators never cast a majority of their votes for any of them. Support for these measures among white legislators ranged from 21 percent to 48 percent. The support of the white legislators was itself strongly divided along party lines. The white Democrats' support for these measures ranged from 66 percent to 94 percent. The support of Republicans, all of whom were white, ranged from 0 percent to 41 percent. Among the white Louisiana legislators representing majority-white districts, the relationship between the BVAP percentage in their districts and their support for these measures was not significant among either Democratic or Republican legislators (Hoston 2007: 92–102).[10]

White or Anglo U.S. House members representing districts in the South have also been found to be less supportive of African American interests than their white non-southern colleagues (see, e.g., Whitby 1997: 93–99, 104–9; Whitby and Krause 2001: 563–65, 567–68; and Canon 1999: 178–79). Together these two variables, party and region, have an important impact on support levels, with southern Republicans consistently being the least supportive group and white southern Democrats being less reliable supporters than their non-southern colleagues (Hutchings, McClerking, and Charles 2004: 465–66; LeVeaux and Garand 2003: 41; Canon 1999: 145–46, 151; Hutchings 1998: 527, 545; and Overby and Cosgrove 1996: 547). As reported in one study, "some southern Democrats with large African American constituencies are remarkably responsive to these voters whereas others frequently neglect their interests" (Hutchings, McClerking, and Charles 2004: 451; see also Whitby 1997: 124; and Whitby and Krause 2001: 563–64).[11]

GEORGIA V. ASHCROFT

The Supreme Court had little to say about the concept of influence districts until 2003, when it decided *Georgia v. Ashcroft*, a case concerning the preclearance, under Section 5 of the VRA, of the State of Georgia's 2001 state senate redistricting plan.[12] Under this provision, Georgia had the burden of proving that its new plan would not cause a retrogression in African American voting strength when compared to the previous plan (*Beer v. United States*, 425 U.S. 130, 141). At trial, the preclearance issue focused on three districts that the Department of Justice had concluded caused retrogression in the state's plan. Prior to the redistricting, the African American percentages of the VAP in these districts, numbered 2, 12, and 26, were reported by the state to be 60.4, 55.4, and 66.4 respectively. In its 2001 plan, the state shaved these percentages to below 51 percent, 50.3, 50.7, and 50.8.[13] The state made no claim that the reduced opportunity to elect representatives of their choice in these districts had been offset by new opportunities to elect such representatives created in other districts in the plan. It maintained instead that these districts, with their reduced VAP percentages, provided African American voters an "equal opportunity" to elect representatives of their choice *within* each of these districts.[14] The three-judge district court held, by a 2-1 vote, that these districts did indeed result in retrogression and denied preclearance to the plan [*Georgia v. Ashcroft*, 195 F. Supp. 2d 25 (2002)].

This decision was vacated by the Supreme Court when it held, in a 5-4 decision, that the trial court's review had been too narrow. The Court remanded the case with instructions to the trial court to determine whether possible influence and "coalitional districts" within the plan would offset the dilutive effect found within the three districts (*Georgia*, at 482).[15]

The precedential value of this Supreme Court decision was itself negated, however, when Congress, in extending and amending provisions of the VRA in 2006, held that the Court had "misconstrued Congress' original intention" in enacting the VRA and "narrowed the protections afforded by section 5."[16] Congress placed a provision in the act, widely referred to as the *Georgia v. Ashcroft* "fix" (see e.g., Tucker 2007: passim; Harris and Hardy 2007; and Canon 2007: 267, 2008: 4), declaring that the purpose of Section 5 is to protect the ability of minorities covered by the act "to elect their preferred candidates of choice."[17]

THE *GEORGIA V. ASHCROFT* APPROACH

Although the interpretation of the retrogression standard of Section 5 in *Georgia v. Ashcroft* is no longer controlling, it is still instructive to see what the Court had to say about influence districts in this decision,[18] even though it did little to clarify the meaning or measurement of that concept. Indeed, it might have muddied the waters even further.[19]

JUSTICE O'CONNOR'S OPINION FOR THE MAJORITY

Justice O'Connor's opinion for the Court majority relied, at least conceptually, on the perverse effects theory. Although she did not hold that influence and coalition districts must be included in the retrogression determination, she said that they could be. A jurisdiction could reduce the number of majority-minority districts, or "shave" them to a point

where they would be "toss up" districts, as Georgia claimed it had done
in the districts at issue (Becker 2007: 236 n. 60, 251), provided they com-
pensated for that by adding coalition or influence districts to the plan.
O'Connor's discussion of the theory was entirely in the abstract. None
of the studies referenced in the section above on race and representation
that were published prior to the decision, which was most of them, were
referenced by Justice O'Connor in her recitation of the perverse effects
thesis (482–483). Indeed Grofman, who did have an article cited in that
portion of O'Connor's opinion, has written, "The empirical evidence
is clear that the factual claim espoused by Justice O'Connor that the
greater the black, or other minority, voting strength in a district, the
more will the representative of that district respond positively to the concerns of minority voters is *fundamentally wrong*" (Grofman and Brunell
2006: 318, emphasis added).

The state had not identified any districts as being coalition or influence districts, let alone any criteria for such identifications. The state
framed the issue before the Court as:

  I. Whether Section 5 of the Voting Rights Act Requires the
     Drawing of Safe Majority-Minority Districts with Super-
     Majority Minority Populations, Rather than Districts that
     Afford Minorities Equal Opportunities at Success?

 II. Whether Section 5 can be Constitutionally Construed to
     Require the Drawing of Supermajority Minority Legislative
     Districts in Order to Create Safe Seats, Rather than Seats that
     Afford Minorities Equal Opportunities at Success?[20]

The state did not express the issue in terms of any substitution of influence or coalition districts for fewer majority-minority districts, or for
weaker majority-minority districts. At oral argument before the Court,
the state's attorney reiterated, "The only question in this Court – in this
case is where do you draw the line? Safe or equal seats?"[21]

The state's evidence matched its version of the issue. Not a single
influence district or coalition district that resulted from shaving majority–African American districts to just above 50 percent in African
American VAP was identified. The notion of going from "safe" districts
to the district-specific application of "equal opportunity" in return for

influence districts, or even coalition districts, was not part of the state's evidence.

There appears to be a widely held but mistaken view that the Supreme Court *upheld* the state's 2001 senate plan in *Georgia v. Ashcroft*.[22] It did not. The decision of the district court was not reversed, but rather vacated and the case remanded to the trial court to consider the evidence in light of its new decision rule. Justice O'Connor did state, however, that "we find that Georgia likely met its burden of showing nonretrogression," stating that "Georgia's strategy of 'unpacking' minority voters in some districts to create more influence and coalition districts is *apparent*" (487, emphasis added). The only thing Justice O'Connor identified as making this strategy apparent, however, was an increase of two districts having an African American VAP between 30 percent and 50 percent, and two more between 25 percent and 30 percent (487).[23] Nothing else was referenced concerning any of these districts other than these VAP percentages, and no evidence was recited, no doubt because none had been provided, that demonstrated the shaving of the African American percentage in the three districts at issue had made it possible for these other VAP percentages to be attained. But the Court made it very clear: "We leave it for the District Court to determine whether Georgia has indeed met its burden of proof" (490).[24]

GEORGIA V. ASHCROFT ON REMAND

Justice O'Connor's opinion in *Georgia v. Ashcroft* was "highly theorized" (Karlan 2004: 35), and it could have been expected that, on remand, the theory would be subjected to empirical evidence. Although Justice O'Connor relied on VAP percentages herself to suggest the appearance of additional influence districts, she also provided some guidance on the identification of such districts for the litigants and the district court. She defined an influence district as one in which "minority voters may not be able to elect a candidate of choice but can play a substantial, if not decisive, role in the electoral process" (482). She made it clear that influence districts are expected to result in "representatives sympathetic to the interests of minority voters" (483). She stated, "In assessing the comparative weight of these influence districts, it is important to consider 'the likelihood that candidates elected without decisive minority support would be willing to take the minority's interests into account'" (482, quoting her concurrence in *Thornburg v. Gingles*, 1986, 100). She also added, "And it is of course true that evidence of racial polarization is one of the many factors relevant in assessing whether a minority group is able to elect a candidate of choice or to exert a significant influence in a particular district" (485). Although she had relied on VAP percentages in stating that the state had likely met its burden, the ultimate assessment of whether the plan was retrogressive was, in contrast, to be a "fact-intensive" inquiry assessing the "totality of circumstances" (484).

Georgia had offered no evidence about racial polarization in any particular district, as the United States had concerning Senate Districts 2, 12, and 26,[25] or about the likelihood that those elected in so-called influence districts would take the minority's interests into account. Georgia, in short, had not provided a fact-intensive inquiry of the totality of circumstances that O'Connor said was necessary.[26] In light of this, O'Connor's dictum about the state likely meeting its burden on remand aside, there was no reason to think that empirically demonstrating the absence of retrogression would be a slam dunk for the state.

EVIDENCE ON REMAND

Only after the case was remanded did the state identify any specific influence districts in its plan. It never identified any coalition districts. The identifications of the so-called influence districts were not based, however, on any "fact-intensive" inquiry that would provide the additional evidence that O'Connor said would be necessary. The identification was based instead only on O'Connor's use of a 25 to 50 percent VAP range to identify apparent influence districts. The state, no doubt encouraged by Justice O'Connor's dictum that it had already "likely met its burden," even objected to the introduction on remand of any additional evidence that would be needed for such an inquiry.[27]

Georgia's senate districts never became the subject of such an inquiry by the district court. Although the court had decided to hear additional evidence, a trial on remand was never held. After the district court denied preclearance to Georgia's plan in 2002, the state had adopted an interim plan for the elections to be held later that year. This plan increased the African American VAP percentages in the three senate districts at issue to 54.50, 55.04, and 55.45, respectively. This plan was not opposed by the Justice Department and was precleared by the District Court.[28] Prior to a trial, however, this plan, found by the district court to be "largely similar" to the 2001 plan (15), was declared to be unconstitutional by a federal district court in Georgia because it violated the "one person, one vote" rule [*Larios v. Cox*, 300 F. Supp. 2d 1320 (N.D. Ga. 2004)].[29] Given the similarity in the plans, this effectively mooted the *Georgia v. Ashcroft* case, and it was therefore dismissed. The 2004 senate elections were held under a plan adopted by the district court in Georgia.

THE 2002 ELECTIONS

If there had been a trial, the Department of Justice planned to introduce evidence from the 2002 election that would have contradicted Justice O'Connor's theory.[30] The 2002 election revealed that the 25 percent threshold for identifying influence districts would have resulted in numerous errors of inclusion. As noted above, this threshold approach is a poor measure of influence districts, at least by itself. It in no way indicates that a protected minority has a reasonable opportunity to determine which of the candidates in a district will be the one chosen, nor does it alone provide a good basis for predicting responsiveness by the elected representative.

Districts in which the African American percentages fall at or above the thresholds identified by Justice O'Connor can vary greatly in the types of non–African American voters within them. Such districts could be safe Democratic districts in which African Americans will not be viewed as likely to cast a critical vote. Although less likely empirically, they could be safe Republican seats, in which African American voters are not likely to have any impact on the election outcome. As Justice Souter pointed out in his dissent, when it comes to influence districts, "percentages tell us nothing in isolation" (505).

The overinclusive nature of Justice O'Connor's and the state's 25 percent threshold, at least for Georgia's senate districts, is illustrated by an analysis of the 2002 elections. As noted above, the interim plan used

TABLE 3.1 ESTIMATED RACIAL DIVISIONS IN
CANDIDATE PREFERENCES

2002 GENERAL ELECTION

District	African American VAP %	Party of Winning Candidate/% of Votes for Winning Candidate		% African American Voters for Democratic Candidate	% Non-African Voters for Democratic Candidate
3	33.7	Democratic	53.3	95.7	37.4
4	25.8	Democratic*	55.9	98.5	47.2
5	25.3	Democratic	57.9	98.6	37.7
6	28.4	Republican	52.1	98.5	31.4
11	30.3	Republican	50.1	98.5	38.0
13	26.7	Democratic*	52.3	99.0	42.3
14	36.7	Democratic	65.4	95.2	51.0
18	31.1	Republican	51.2	98.1	35.1
20	32.6	Democratic	66.0	99.4	56.5
25	37.8	Democratic	55.1	98.8	39.2
40	29.7	Democratic	54.2	96.1	42.6
41	37.6	Democratic	59.1	93.6	17.9
44	34.7	Democratic	79.8#	94.2	69.6

* = Winner switched to Republican after election.

= Opponent was an Independent candidate.

in 2002 was similar overall to the 2001 plan (15).[31] An analysis has been performed on the thirteen apparent "influence districts" (over 25 percent and under 50 percent in African American VAP) for which contested elections were held in the 2002 general election. This analysis utilizes precinct-level data recording the total number of people receiving ballots in each precinct in the respective district, the total number of them that was African American, and the numbers of votes cast in each precinct for the various candidates. Estimates of the percentage of African American voters and the percentage of the non–African American voters supporting the Democratic candidates in these elections, derived through Gary King's ecological inference procedure (EI) (see King 1996), are reported in Table 1.[32]

African American support for the Democratic candidates is estimated to have been over 90 percent in each of these elections. Despite
this high level of support, the winner of the election in three of these
districts, 6, 11, and 18, was a Republican. These Republicans won despite
their support among African American voters being estimated at 1.5, 1.5,
and 1.9 percent respectively.[33] Indeed, one African American state senator testified that "it's clear that Republicans are absolutely not going to
be concerned about the essential issues that I'm concerned about and
that the majority of my constituents are concerned about."[34] In addition, in two more of these contested districts, 4 and 13, a Democrat won
with 98.5 percent and 99.0 percent support from the African Americans.
This support was decisive in the election of both of these Democrats,
as their vote among the non–African Americans is estimated to have
been 47.2 and 42.3 percent. But following the election, and before the
next session of the senate was convened, those senators switched from
the Democratic to the Republican Party. They were joined in the switch
by two other Democrats that had been elected in so-called influence
districts, 23 and 29, in which they ran unopposed. In short, by the time
the legislative session began, seven of the senators from the seventeen so-
called influence districts, 41.2 percent, were Republicans![35] These seven
Republicans were essential to changing the majority party in the senate
from Democratic to Republican, which was the very outcome that the influence districts were supposed to help preclude, according to the state.

Another interesting feature of the state's interim plan is that it demonstrated that there was no need to shave the three majority–African
American districts that the Department of Justice objected to, and the
district court found to cause retrogression, to less than 51 percent African American VAP in order to create a new influence district adjacent
to any of them. In the state's first plan, that of 2001, there were five districts adjacent to any of these districts that would qualify as influence
districts under the state's definition. They ranged from 27.9 percent to
35.8 percent in African American VAP. After the three districts were
increased to around 55 percent in VAP, there were still five so-called
influence districts adjacent to them, ranging from 26.6 to 36.7 percent in
African American VAP.[36]

LEGISLATIVE BEHAVIOR

Justice O'Connor had stated in her *Georgia v. Ashcroft* opinion that influence districts are expected to result in "representatives sympathetic to the interests of minority voters" and that it is important to consider "the likelihood that candidates elected without decisive minority support would be willing to take the minority's interests into account" (482–83). In response to this, the Department of Justice also planned to introduce evidence comparing the legislative behavior of Georgia state senators to the racial composition of their districts. Results from this study, by David T. Canon, have been published (2008: 4 n. 7). Canon reports, based on an examination of numerous bills, resolutions, and votes in the state senate from 1999 through January 13, 2004, that shaving majority–African American districts down to less than 51 percent African American in BVAP, and thereby putting the ability of African Americans to elect representatives of their choice in these districts at risk, and adopting more so-called influence districts, as the state did, would result in a "net loss" in the substantive representation received by African Americans in that chamber (4, 23).[37]

Canon compared contested roll call votes on amendments to and the final passage of bills that concerned African American interests during the 2001 and 2002 legislative sessions, those preceding the 2002 senate election. He reports that African American senators, all of whom were Democrats, voted in a way responsive to African American interests on these measures almost unanimously. Among the white senators, support for African American interests dropped only slightly, albeit statistically significantly, among the Democrats, but a "huge gulf," around 20 percentage points, separated them from the support levels of the Republicans. Canon further used the 25 percent African American VAP threshold for identifying influence districts, as had the state. The Democrats in these so-called influence districts were found to be slightly *less* supportive of African American interests than those Democrats in districts that were less than 25 percent (13, 15). There were no influence districts, so defined, represented by Republicans at that time.

Canon also examined roll call votes in the session following the election held in the new districts, the 2003 session, on what he describes as "the most highly-charged racial issue in the past several years [in Georgia]: changing the Georgia state flag" (15). The issue concerned whether to adopt a new flag that would not contain the Confederate battle flag within it. All the African American legislators were again Democrats, and they supported the position of their caucus on 88.6 percent of the votes they cast on this issue. The white Democrats in the so-called influence districts supported that position on 72.2 percent of their votes. This was higher, although not statistically significantly higher, than the rate for the white Democrats in districts that were less than 25 percent BVAP, which was 57.3. Among the Republicans in the apparent influence districts, all of whom were white, support dropped to 26.9 percent, only 5.8 percentage points above that for those representing districts less than 25 percent in BVAP, which was 21.1 percent (Canon 2008: 15–17).[38]

Pronounced differences also were found in the two other forms of legislative behavior Canon examined, the sponsorship and cosponsorship of bills and resolutions addressing African American interests. These analyses reviewed data reflecting behavior both before and after the 2002 election, from 1999 to January 13, 2004. He reports another "huge gap" in legislative behavior (19), this time in the racial content of bills introduced or cosponsored by African Americans and whites:

> African American Democrats average about 40% of their bills with [at least] some racial content, Republicans average 3%, while white Democrats have a much broader range from a little over 5% to about 19% in the different sessions (20).

The study further reveals that the 25 percent threshold does a poor job of distinguishing the behavior of white senators in alleged influence districts from those in districts with less African American presence. The data for 2003–2004 reveal that 17.3 percent of the bills sponsored by white Democrats with more than 25 percent BVAP in their districts had at least some racial content, compared to 21.3 percent sponsored by those in districts with less than 25 percent. Among the Republicans, these figures were 6.4 percent and 5.0 percent. The sponsorship and cosponsorship of resolutions also revealed a significant racial difference among the senators, with little sponsorship activity by white senators of either party or by those with constituencies with BVAP above or below the 25 percent threshold (17–18).

Canon concludes that "many politicians in influence districts are not responsive to the interests of their minority constituents" (23). He notes that there is great variation in the responsive behavior of white Democrats in alleged influence districts (15, 17, 23), and that all such districts held by Republicans were not, given the behavior of their senators, "performing" influence districts (11, 15).[39]

The perverse effects thesis that African Americans in Georgia would be better represented by eliminating, or in this case shaving, majority–African American districts might not have survived, on remand, the "fact-intensive" inquiry that Justice O'Connor stated would be necessary.

LOWER COURT DECISIONS

A number of lower federal courts have identified particular districts as "influence districts" based solely on the minority percentage of the VAP within them.[40] The most attention given to the concept by a lower court has been in *Rural West Tennessee African-American Affairs Council v. McWherter*, 877 F. Supp. 1096 (W.D. Tenn. 1995), which adopted a 25 percent VAP threshold prior to *Georgia v. Ashcroft*.

The *McWherter* case concerned a challenge under Section 2 of the VRA to state senate districts in west Tennessee. In the first decision in this case, in 1993, a three-judge district court ruled in favor of the plaintiffs and ordered the state to create an additional majority–African American senate district in west Tennessee [*Rural West Tennessee African-American Affairs Council v. McWherter*, 836 F. Supp. 453, 454, 467 (W.D. Tenn. 1993)]. The court explicitly rejected an argument by the state that it would be better for African American voters to be dispersed across districts rather than constitute the majority in another district. The court concluded that voting was racially polarized in Tennessee, that the state had a history of official racial discrimination, and that African Americans in west Tennessee continued to suffer from the lingering effects of that discrimination. The court held that in these circumstances Section 2 "strongly favor[s] the creation of majority black districts with visible black representation, instead of 'influence' districts" (465–66).

The following year the Supreme Court highlighted the importance of the "totality of circumstances" decisional standard for Section 2 cases in *Johnson v. De Grandy* (512 U.S. 997) and vacated the *McWherter* decision and remanded it to the district court (512 U.S. 1248). On remand the trial court in 1995 concluded that under that standard, "the degree to which minority voters can claim strong or weak influence in districts other than majority-minority districts certainly should be included in the calculus" (*Rural West Tennessee African-American Affairs Council v. McWherter*, 1102).[41] It explicitly rejected a fact-intensive, district-by-district determination of influence districts, favoring instead "a standard rule" (1104). The rule adopted was that "an influence district exists when members of a minority group compose 25% or more of the voting-age population of a district" (1101). The court also stated that "[i]n some cases, an influence district may also exist when a minority group consists of less than 25% of the voting-age population of a district" (ibid.). It never stated, however, how one would distinguish which of the districts under 25 percent were influence districts and which were not.

The court articulated a theory of sorts to justify the 25 percent threshold. By the time the case was remanded, two elections had been held under the senate plan, with some districts up for election in 1992 and the others in 1994. The court stated:

> In the 1992 and 1994 elections combined there were twenty-one contested senate races. In every contested race, if 25% of those who voted had changed their votes from the winning candidate to the losing candidate, they would have reversed the results of the election. Furthermore, in fifteen of the twenty-one contested races, if 25% of those who voted and also cast ballots for the winning candidate withdrew their support and did not vote at all, they would have changed the outcome of the election. Realities such as these are difficult for candidates to ignore (1105).

These so-called "realities" that candidates ignore at their peril are of course "what if" statements that would constitute extremely unusual vote or turnout swings in American elections. Any incumbent would no doubt be apoplectic if there were a reasonable likelihood of losing that much of his or her electoral support, but these types of swings simply do not happen often to incumbents in American elections. The threat is far more hypothetical than real. This in effect says that a candidate who wins a two-candidate election with 75 percent of the votes, a "landslide" by anyone's definition, will feel so electorally insecure that he or she

will seriously worry about such a massive defection among their supporters. Likewise, a candidate that wins 62.5 percent of the votes in a
two-candidate contest, a landslide margin by conventional standards,
is also expected to feel so electorally insecure that he or she will actually worry about such a large group of supporters voting en masse with
their feet. And these scenarios do not account for the possibility that
in some districts, the policy preferences of the 25 percent may often be
in conflict with the preferences of the other voters, including those in
the incumbent's core or re-election constituency. The three so-called
influence districts in the Tennessee plan were hardly marginal districts,
according to the 2002 election results. Democratic candidates won two
of them with 62.8 percent and 67.8 percent of the votes, while in the third
the Democratic candidate was not even opposed (1111).

The court, it must be noted, did provide a reference for its statement
that "realities such as these are difficult for candidates to ignore." The
reference is "See Abigail Thernstrom, Whose Votes Count? Affirmative
Action and Minority Voting Rights 109 (1987) (discussing influence of
black voters on U.S. Senator Strom Thurmond)" (1105). South Carolina's
Strom Thurmond may strike many as a surprising choice for a poster
boy for minority influence districts. The following is the entire and only
paragraph on p. 109 of Thernstrom's book that mentions Thurmond:

> There was perhaps no greater testimony to the potency of the new black vote
> than the changing response of southern white congressmen to the question
> of extension [in 1981–82 of the special provisions, including the preclearance
> requirement, of the VRA]. When the act first came up for renewal in 1970,
> southern opposition to its extension was loud and clear. By 1981, however, even
> Senator Thurmond – who in 1957 had filibustered for twenty-four hours against a
> civil rights bill – was close to silent. In the intervening years blacks had become
> one-third of his constituency; he had put blacks on his Senate staff; and he had
> worked to secure the appointment of a black federal judge in South Carolina.
> In the spring of 1981 Thurmond had stated that "after 17 years, the states ought
> to be given a chance to get out from the act." Yet, in fact, even in the Republican
> Senate Thurmond was no more free to ignore the black vote than were the
> seventy-one southern representatives who voted for the House bill (1987: 109).

Thurmond's near silence in 1981 may not be much of a recommendation for districts at or above 25 percent African American in VAP, or
even at or above 30 percent, if the rest of the electorate in a district is

similar to the white voters in South Carolina at that time. His votes on the V R A, when it was before the Senate in 1982, were not mentioned by Thernstrom. But when they are examined, it is clear that Thurmond did indeed feel quite free to ignore the preferences of his African American constituents, at least when it came to their voting rights. He voted to delete the "results" test from the amended Section 2, which provided that electoral arrangements that resulted in the dilution of a protected minority's voting strength would violate the act, regardless of what the intent behind their adoption or continued use might have been. He voted to allow southern federal district court judges to make preclearance de-terminations rather than have judges in Washington, D.C., do it. He also voted twice to make it easier for covered jurisdictions to "bail out" from complying with the special provisions, and he sponsored and voted for the "Thurmond Amendment," which would have shortened the length of time of the extension.[42] While Thurmond did vote for final passage of the bill, his efforts to weaken it certainly did not reflect great sensitivity to his African American constituents.[43]

The district court also referenced the testimony of two white in-cumbent senators to support its 25 percent threshold. One represented a district that was 21 percent African American in VA P, the other a district that was 33 percent. While the expressed sentiments of "incumbents who might run in the new districts" (*Georgia*, 495, Souter, dissenting) could well be self-serving, the court found these witnesses to be convincing. The court's recitation of their responsive behavior toward their African American constituents is typical of the type of testimony often provided by incumbent politicians. These senators stated that they campaigned in African American neighborhoods and sponsored "particular projects" of interest to their African American constituents. But when it came to specific legislation they had supported, the testimony was apparently limited to support for making Martin Luther King's birthday a state holiday and "other issues of interest to the black community . . . [i]n par-ticular, a gambling bill and several funding bills of particular concern" to their district (*Rural West Tennessee African-American Affairs Council v. McWherter*, 1105–6). Services and favors tend to be the evidence of responsiveness by white legislators, not bills introduced, amendments offered, or votes cast on proposed legislation.[44]

The *McWherter* court's theory and evidence for a 25 percent threshold left a lot to be desired, but at least the court made an effort to identify why it placed the threshold where it did. The decision was summarily affirmed by the Supreme Court in 1995 (*Rural West Tennessee African-American Affairs Council v. Sundquist*, 516 U.S. 801). It was not relied upon, however, by the Court's majority in *Georgia v. Ashcroft*. Indeed, there was no reference to the decision at all.

RACIAL STEREOTYPING AND A DOUBLE STANDARD

The *McWherter* decision was relied upon, however, by another three-judge district court the following year in *Hays v. Louisiana*, 936 F. Supp. 360 (1996), and the Supreme Court did reference a particularly disturbing passage from this decision in *Georgia v. Ashcroft*. The *Hays* case concerned Louisiana's congressional districts. The Court expressly adopted the 25 percent African American VAP threshold, citing the *McWherter* decision and the Supreme Court's affirmance of it (364 n. 17). Relying on *Shaw v. Reno*, 509 U.S. 630 (1993), the *Hays* court had held that the state's plan for U.S. House districts contained a majority–African American district that was a "racial gerrymander" in violation of the Equal Protection Clause of the Fourteenth Amendment. The court, in the remedial plan it created and ordered implemented, employed the 25 percent threshold to identify three of its districts as "influence districts" (352 n. 17). The court did not reference the rationale behind this threshold expressed in *McWherter*, nor did it offer one of its own. The three districts that the court called influence districts were Districts 4, 5, and 6, which were 29.3 percent, 27.8 percent, and 29.4 percent in African American VAP respectively. These three influence districts, according to the court, would empower the state's African Americans more than the majority–African American district it had dismantled in its plan, which had already elected an African American to represent it in the House (364 n. 17).

As noted, the *Hays* court did not provide any rationale for the 25 percent threshold. It cited no evidence demonstrating that African American voters could be expected to determine which of the various white candidates in these districts would be elected. There was no evidence that the non–African American voters in any of these districts, almost all of whom were white, would be so predictably divided in their choice of candidates that African American voters could have a reasonable chance of casting a decisive vote. While these districts did have increased percentages of African Americans in them compared to the corresponding districts in place at the time, these increases would not likely cause any great electoral insecurity for the Republican incumbents in them, at least from the prospect of Democratic challengers, given the other voters in the district.

One of these districts, District 5, was an exceptionally peculiar example of an African American influence district. The self-identified "racialist" David Duke, a former Grand Wizard of the Ku Klux Klan who had carried the majority of the white vote in two Louisiana statewide elections, the 1990 election for a U.S. Senate seat, and the 1991 runoff election for governor,[45] had won a majority of the total vote in both of those elections in the area encompassed by this new District 5 (Engstrom and Kirksey 1998: 262; Chervenak 1998: 217).[46] Duke, not surprisingly, had even announced that he was thinking about running for the U.S. House in that district (Chervenak 1998: 217 n. 19; see also Reeves 1997: 105). Noting that none of these districts could seriously be considered African American influence districts, one student of Louisiana politics commented that rather than enhancing the voting strength of African Americans, the court's plan instead "transported Louisiana back in time to an era in which the political system regularly subsumed black voters in majority white districts in order to dilute their political strength" (Chervenak 1998: 231).

Nor did the court recite any evidence indicating that districts in Louisiana in which African Americans were a minority but constituted at least 25 percent in VAP could be expected to elect representatives that would be responsive to African American interests. In fact the court, without explanation, completely ignored evidence to the contrary. Under the districting plan in place from 1982 through 1990 in Louisiana, the district with the largest percentage of African Americans in it, with the exception of the one majority–African American district, was the Eighth. This district was 36 percent African American in VAP according to both the 1980 and 1990 censuses. Voter registration in the district was

36.3 percent African American by 1992. The incumbent in that district at the time of redistricting, Republican Clyde Holloway, had never received as much as 10 percent of the votes cast by African Americans. Expert witnesses for both the plaintiffs and the defendants had testified, in a 1992 hearing, that Holloway's voting behavior in Congress had not been responsive to the concerns of African American voters. Further evidence introduced at a 1994 hearing revealed that from 1987 through 1990, Holloway had voted in favor of civil rights measures endorsed by the Leadership Conference on Civil Rights only 6 percent of the time. He had opposed, for example, both the House and the conference committee versions of the Civil Rights Act in 1990, and was even one of the few Republicans to oppose the bipartisan compromise that resulted in the Civil Rights Act of 1991 (Engstrom and Kirksey 1998: 261–62).

The so-called influence districts in Louisiana never performed as such. All three of the districts elected conservative Republicans in the three elections held while they were in place, generally by very comfortable margins. If the court's plan had in fact "empowered black voters in Louisiana" more than the plan it replaced, as the court claimed it would (364 n. 17), one would have to believe that these three "influence districts" provided African Americans with better representation than would an African American representative elected from a majority–African American district. The African Americans in these districts would more accurately be described as "filler people" (Aleinikoff and Issacharoff 1993) rather than as voters with much influence.

But the most disturbing part of the *Hays* court's treatment of the influence district concept was the racially selective nature of its application. Anyone who wants to know why they hear or read about minority influence districts, but rarely if ever "white influence districts," need only read footnote 17 in the *Hays* opinion, the only part of the opinion cited by the Supreme Court in *Georgia v. Ashcroft* (482). The majority–African American district dismantled by the court in its remedial plan was District 4, a district that was *44.7 percent white* in VAP. The majority-white districts in the state's plan, none of which had as much as 25 percent African American VAP, were described by the court as "bleached" (364 n. 17). The influence of the white minority in District 4, however, was equated with the influence of the African Americans in the bleached districts. The court announced that "[o]ffice holders and office seekers no longer need to heed the voices of the minority residents of their districts – here, *the whites of District Four,* the blacks of the other, 'bleached' districts" (364 n. 17, emphasis added).

It was never explained by the court why an African American representative in a district in which more than 44 percent of the VAP is white can be expected to be as insensitive to his or her white constituents as a white representative will be to his or her African American constituents when they constitute less than 25 of the VAP. Nor did the court explain why a white representative with a constituency in which the VAP is 25 percent or more African American will be a racially sensitive representative, while an African American with 44.7 percent white VAP in his or her constituency will be a *racial partisan.* Absolutely no evidence was provided for this racial distinction.[47] The representational consequences of these districts might, in fact, be the reverse. David Canon, for example, in his study of racial representation in the U.S. House, concludes just the opposite. He reports:

> Most white representatives from black influence districts do not spend much time representing their black constituents, while most black members of Congress spend a substantial portion of their time representing white constituents (Canon 1999: 91).[48]

The African American that had been elected in District 4 in Louisiana, Cleo Fields, was even identified by Canon as a representative who stressed racial commonality over difference while he served in Congress (1999: 42, 95, 96, and 140). Carol Swain, in her study of race and representation in the U.S. House, likewise concluded that white voters in districts in which African Americans constituted a majority of the VAP, but less than 65 percent, were "courted assiduously" by the African American representatives because they constituted "swing voters" in these districts (1993: 74). Her case studies of two such districts, District 2 in Mississippi, represented by Mike Espy, and District 5 in Georgia, represented by John Lewis, illustrated, according to her, "the enormous power of white voters in districts in which black candidates compete either with each other or against less attractive white candidates" (ibid.).

The *Hays* court, however, concluded that the voices of whites in District 4, for some unstated reason, would no longer need to be heeded, just as would those of African American voters in the now bleached white (Republican) districts.

The *Hays* court was hardly unique in being racially selective in its application of the concept of influence districts. It simply articulated the double standard in an explicit way. This selectivity needs to be exposed and challenged. The idea that only white representatives will be sensitive to other race voters in their district reveals a racial stereotype for which no foundation has been identified.[49]

If influence districts are supposed to be included in "totality of circumstances" determinations, whether they concern retrogression or dilution, then a fair assessment of relative opportunities needs to entail *all* influence districts. These include those districts in which electoral realities indicate that a representative whose race or ethnicity is that of a protected minority can be expected to be sensitive to their Anglo and other minority constituents, and in which representatives not part of a protected minority can be expected to be sensitive to their constituents who are part of a protected minority.[50] If the concept of influence district is going to continue to be applied in a racially selective manner, it should be incumbent on those who do so to identify, with evidence, why this is appropriate.

THE WORST APPLICATION OF THE CONCEPT

The leading candidate for the most inappropriate application of the "influence district" label occurred after the Supreme Court's decision in *Georgia v. Ashcroft*. It serves as an excellent illustration of how even a relatively high VAP percentage for a district, in this instance almost 46 percent CVAP, can be a poor indicator, by itself, of an influence district.

The case involved the 2003 "re-redistricting" of U.S. House districts in Texas.[51] A federal court in Texas, in *Sessions v. Perry*, 298 F. Supp. 2d 451 (2004), concluded that a district in which 45.8 percent of the CVAP was Hispanic and 44 percent of the registered voters had Spanish surnames, was a "Hispanic influence district" (489). The district had been created, however, for the explicit purpose of protecting a Republican incumbent, in this instance a Hispanic, from electoral defeat at the hands of Hispanic voters.

The district, District 23, had been majority-Hispanic. The previous version of it was 57.5 percent Hispanic in CVAP, with 55.3 percent of the registered voters within it having Spanish surnames. The incumbent in District 23 was Henry Bonilla, the only Hispanic elected to Congress as a Republican in Texas. Bonilla had never been the representative of choice of the Hispanic voters in the district, and his support among Hispanics dropped in all six of his successive elections, in each of which he faced a Hispanic Democratic. In 2002 he attracted an estimated 8 percent of the Hispanic vote in the district and won with an overall vote of only 51.5 percent (488).

The drop to 45.8 percent in CVAP and 44 percent in Spanish-surnamed registered voters was accomplished by removing roughly 100,000 Hispanics, largely Democratic voters, from the district and replacing them with about 100,000 Anglos, largely Republican voters. As for the reason for this change, the court noted, "The record presents undisputed evidence that the Legislature desired to increase the number of Republican votes cast in Congressional District 23 to shore up Bonilla's base and assist in his reelection" (488). Indeed, the state explicitly argued that the revision in the district was driven by partisan considerations, which it argued put it on safer legal ground than if it had been driven by race or ethnicity.

There was no explanation by the court for the influence district label being attached to the revised district other than its being 45.8 percent Hispanic in CVAP. This CVAP figure, according to the court, made the Hispanic presence in the district "large enough to constitute an influence district" (494). That this district was designed to provide for the re-election of Mr. Bonilla, against the wishes of his Hispanic constituents, was acknowledged by the court at least *five times* in its opinion (488, 490, 496, and 511). The court never explained how the Hispanic voters in this district would supposedly have influence over Bonilla, who was dependent on the Anglo Republican vote for his re-election. Evidence indicating that Hispanic voters could expect to have very little impact on the election outcome, in terms of the choice of the representative, and likewise on the subsequent legislative behavior of that person, was ignored.

The dissenting judge in *Sessions* noted that "[a]n influence district is a district in which the minority population carries enough political weight potentially to be the swing vote in the election and command the attention of the representative" (519). Given the reason for and the manner in which this district had been created, he not surprisingly found the majority's identification of this district as a Hispanic influence district to be an error. He found that Hispanics were virtually guaranteed to lose every general election in the district (519), a forecast with which the majority agreed (504). The district was designed, as he stated, to ensure "a lack of competitiveness and a corresponding lack of responsiveness" (519).

The Supreme Court, in *League of Latin American Citizens v. Perry* (26 S.Ct. 2594, 2006), reversed the district court's decision on District 23. It held, in a 5-4 decision in which the four justices widely referred to as the "liberal bloc" joined this part of Justice Anthony Kennedy's opinion, that the previous majority-Hispanic district provided Hispanic voters with an opportunity to elect a candidate of their choice, Bonilla's narrow win in 2002 notwithstanding, and the substitute version did not. It was therefore a violation of Section 2 of the VRA. Kennedy also concluded that the revised version of District 23 was motivated by the Republicans' desire to gain seats and to protect Mr. Bonilla (2613). The lower court's declaration that the revised version was a "Hispanic influence district" was completely ignored by the Supreme Court; no justice referred to it as such, although Justice Kennedy did state that "the Latinos' diminishing electoral support for Bonilla indicates their belief that he was 'unresponsive to the particularized needs of the members of the minority group'" (2622).[52]

The district court, on remand, revised District 23 to bring it back to a majority-Hispanic district again. The new district was 57.4 Hispanic in CVAP based on the 2000 census [*League of United Latin American Citizens v. Perry* (E.D. Tex. 2006), slip op. at 6] and 54.1 percent of the registered voters in it had Spanish surnames at the time of the 2006 special election to fill the seat.[53] In that election a Hispanic Democrat, Ciro D. Rodriguez, defeated Bonilla in a runoff election by a vote of 54.3 percent to 45.7 percent.[54]

A BETTER APPROACH

Percentage thresholds, whether implicit or explicit, are by themselves poor measures of influence districts because they ignore the variation in the overall political characteristics of districts. They therefore are likely to result in errors of inclusion and exclusion in their identifications. Yet they remain the dominant approach to identifying influence districts by the courts and by state and local governments claiming that such districts are present within their plans.

Some judges, however, realizing the inadequacy of this approach, have called for more intensive analyses of districts in order to make this determination. One of the judges on the *McWherter* panel clearly recognized the need for such analyses in a subsequent case involving state house districts in Tennessee, *Rural West Tennessee African-American Affairs Council v. Sundquist,* 29 F. Supp. 2d 448 (1998). After stating that he was bound by the circuit court decision in *McWherter* approving the 25 percent threshold, he acknowledged the most serious flaw in that approach:

> Without a particularized, and no doubt unwieldy, inquiry into the ability of rural west Tennessee black voters to actually "influence" the political process in the region's specific districts . . . it is extremely difficult to determine at what point the presence of these districts with sufficient minority populations to be labeled an "influence district" truly begin to demonstrate political equality, rather than unlawful minority vote fragmentation (462).

The judge found, however, that even counting the four majority-white districts with at least 25 percent African American VAP as influence districts, their presence did not justify the absence of any majority–African American district in the area at issue. The plan, he concluded, therefore violated Section 2.

On appeal, a panel of the Sixth Circuit affirmed the decision, with one judge concluding, in a concurring opinion, that it was an error to follow the *McWherter* definition. He stated that "the realities of white bloc voting command that we apply a more flexible standard in assessing the extent to which purported influence districts provide minorities with an equal opportunity to elect representatives of choice. . . . The bright-line 25% rule obscures the realities of white bloc voting, and implies 'influence' that may not in fact exist" [*Rural West Tennessee African-American Affairs Council v. Sundquist*, 209 F. 3d 835, 847 (2000) (Jones, J., concurring)].

The *McWherter* approach has been specifically rejected by a panel of the First Circuit in *Vecinos de Barrio Uno v. City of Holyoke*, 72 F. 3d 973 (1995). It noted that an influence district claim needed to be addressed in a Section 2 dilution case because "the voting strength of a minority group . . . extends to every district in which its members are sufficiently numerous to have a significant impact at the ballot box most of the time" (991). The court was concerned about the city's claim that a district 28 percent Hispanic in VAP was an influence district. It rejected the idea that a "numerical floor" could identify such districts (991), requiring instead that "the evidence must reveal that minority voters in the district have in fact joined with other voters to elect representatives of their choice. Moreover, the record must show that elected representatives from such a district serve, at least in part, the interest of the minority community and vie for its support" (991 n. 13). This decision rejecting the simple threshold approach was not referenced by the Supreme Court in *Georgia v. Ashcroft*.[55]

There is clearly a need to improve the identification of influence districts. As Justice Souter stated in his dissenting opinion in *Georgia v. Ashcroft*, "percentages tell us nothing in isolation" (505). This need for more information is especially important given that "it is all too easy to undermine the legitimate claims of minority communities for effective political participation by suggesting that minority voters should be satisfied with 'influencing' who is elected rather than seeking to control the election" (Earls 2006: 5).

Given the great differences in minority representation provided by legislators from within their own group accountable to majority-minority electorates, and that provided by white or Anglo legislators elected from so-called minority influence districts, substituting the latter for the former should not be easy to justify. The evidence for the alleged advantages of such tradeoffs needs to satisfy a serious burden. One important constraint should be improved criteria for identifying when a district deserves the influence district label. Criteria need to be established that will minimize, if not preclude, errors of inclusion and exclusion. Allowing influence districts to be determined by nothing but the relative presence of minority voters in a district is an invitation to abuse the concept, as the federal district court in Texas did in its ruling on U.S. House District 23 in *Sessions,* and the federal court in Louisiana did when justifying its remedial plan for congressional districts in the *Hays* case.

DEFINITION AND MEASUREMENT ISSUES

If the percentage of the VAP or CVAP that a minority group constitutes in a district, by itself, "tell[s] us nothing," then what else needs to be assessed? Justice O'Connor's majority opinion in *Georgia v. Ashcroft* may be a good place to begin. Although Justice O'Connor did rely solely on the relative presence of African Americans within districts to provide a count of *apparent* influence districts in the Georgia senate plan, she did provide some comments that are relevant to a more serious effort at identifying such districts.

Although influence districts are not the source of minority representatives, they are expected to result in responsive representatives from outside the group. This expectation is based on the representative's feeling electorally accountable to minority voters in the district. These voters are expected to be politically cohesive, which makes their vote important, not only to the initial election of that representative but also to his or her re-election. As expressed by Grofman, "unless a legislator has real potential *electoral consequences* to face if s/he fails to vote in accord with a group's wishes/interests, we cannot say that the group has electoral influence with the legislator" (2006, 260, emphasis in original).

Abigail Thernstrom, one of the earliest advocates of the perverse effects thesis, identifies the critical tradeoff issue in that thesis as "Are minorities sometimes better off with fewer seats but more diffused influence – a smaller number of blacks in office, but a greater number of representatives who *owe their election* to black constituents?" (1987: 7, emphasis added). But must a representative owe his or her election to an identifiable minority within a district in order for that district to be classified as an influence district for that group? The concept of electoral accountability does not require that the group be pivotal, and according to Justice O'Connor this may be too demanding a criterion. She identifies, as noted above, an influence district as one in which minority voters "can play a substantial, if not decisive, role in the electoral process" (*Georgia*, 482).

"Decisive" has a clear referent in this context – it means the winning candidate would have lost or would be projected to lose if the votes cast by minority voters had not been or would not be counted. In other words, the minority vote is, or is viewed as likely to be, pivotal to the outcome of elections in the district. Other voters in the district must be sufficiently divided in their candidate preferences so that the minority vote determines, or is expected to determine, who wins. When the minority voters are decisive, the representative can be considered as "owing" his or her election to them. Such a role for minority voters in a district, according to O'Connor, may be a sufficient, but not a necessary, condition for the district to be considered an influence district.

Justice O'Connor states that a "substantial role" in the election outcome is also sufficient.[56] Unlike a decisive role, a "substantial" role does not have a clear referent, and O'Connor does not provide any indication of what it must entail or how large it has to be. She does state however that "[i]n assessing the comparative weight of these influence districts, it is important to consider 'the likelihood that candidates elected without decisive support would be willing to take the minority's interests into account'" (*Georgia*, 482, quoting her concurrence in *Thornburg v. Gingles*, 1986, at 100).

One interpretation of substantial is that the minority vote must help Democrats to be elected. Pam Karlan has written, for example:

> What the Court seems to have meant by "significant – but not decisive" is that the district would likely elect a Democratic candidate in the general election, although not necessarily the Democratic candidate preferred by black voters in the nomination process (2004, 26).

In other words, if the candidate preferred by minority voters in the district loses the party nomination, that does not preclude classifying the district as an influence district, as long as the Democratic nominee, presumably favored by minority voters in the subsequent general election, wins the position. This would make the party identification of the candidate winning the office the decisive criterion.

This position is consistent with the argument that the relative presence of minority voters in a district is insufficient, by itself, to identify influence districts because it ignores the political preferences of the other voters. These other voters are not just "filler people," as they are often alleged to be in majority-minority districts, but rather the majority of voters. Unless they have divided political preferences, minority voters cannot expect to have much impact on the election outcome. It has been suggested, therefore, that districts won by Republicans, at least in the Deep South, should not be considered African American influence districts regardless of the relative presence of potential African Americans voters in them. African American voters rarely, as a group, support Republican candidates, and therefore few Republican elected officials are expected to perceive negative electoral consequences associated with being unresponsive to their interests and preferences. Districts in which Republicans are elected therefore are not good candidates for the minority influence districts (see Grofman 2006, 263; Canon 2008, 15; Grofman and Brunell 2007, 318; Kousser 1998, 172–173). Indeed, when it comes to minority influence districts, Grofman and Thomas Brunell are emphatic – "Party matters!" (2006, 318).

But as Canon's analysis of the Georgia state senate demonstrates, "Clearly some white Democrats in influence districts [based on a 25 percent African American VAP threshold] are not very responsive to black interests" (2008, 23). A substantial role therefore presumably should be based on something other than simply the election of Democrats.

Grofman has suggested that the standard should be based on the share of the winning candidate's vote that is attributable to minority voters. He states:

> Because the nature of electoral influence is strongly influenced by who a legislator's actual supporters are ... minority influence can be better examined by looking at the proportion of the legislator's voting support (i.e., his or her electoral constituency) that comes from minority and nonminority voters than by simply looking at the minority proportion in the legislator's district (i.e., in his/her geographic constituency)" (2006, 260).

He then states:

ceteris paribus, when it comes to racial minorities, if minority voters are not a *substantial part of* the support coalition of a winning legislator they cannot, in general, expect to have much influence with that legislator (ibid., at 261, emphasis in original).

This likewise would preclude almost all districts represented by Republicans from being classified as influence districts. It would also preclude attaching this label to safe Democratic districts in which minority voters are a small part of the electorate. But Grofman, like O'Connor, does not provide any greater specificity as to what "substantial," in this context, entails except to note that the role is not "substantial," whatever the share might be, if more minority voters support the losing rather than the winning candidate (ibid.).

Simply looking at the proportion of support a group provides to the electoral constituency of a winning candidate may not be enough, however. The electoral significance of this share can vary greatly depending on the margin of votes by which a candidate wins. A decisive vote, for example, need not be a substantial vote, at least in a quantitative sense. A group can be a small part of the electoral constituency yet be very important to the election prospects of a candidate or re-election prospects of a representative, depending on how the other voters divide. Perhaps the size of the group's vote for the candidate should be compared to the size of the candidate's margin of victory. A district in which a small but fully cohesive group constitutes 15 percent of a winning candidate's vote, and at least half of the candidate's victory margin (without which the candidate would not receive 50 percent of the total vote), might play a substantial role in the election and be considered an influence district under O'Connor's standard. In short, the importance of a group's vote to a candidate or representative can vary greatly depending on how electorally secure he or she feels in the district.[57]

PROPOSED MEASURE FOR PRESUMPTIVE
INFLUENCE DISTRICTS

A judicially manageable approach to classifying a district as a "minority influence district," or at least a reasonable presumption for such, consistent with O'Connor's standard, would be:

An influence district is a district in which minority voters, unable to elect a representative of their choice, including one from within their own group if that is their preference, casts either a decisive vote, or can be expected to cast such a vote, for their choice among the candidates contesting the seat; *or* casts a vote, or can be expected to cast a vote, for their choice among the candidates, that constitutes at least half of the margin of votes by which that candidate wins.

This definition takes into account the voting preferences of not only the minority voters in the district, but also the preferences of the other voters. It is manageable because it provides an empirically based standard for determining when a district is or is not a presumptive influence district – when the minority voters in it have or can be expected to have a decisive impact on the election of their choice among the candidates, or at least a substantial impact on the election of that candidate in that their support accounts for at least half of the vote margin by which that candidate wins.

The definition specifies no partisan affiliation for that candidate. He or she is simply the protected group's preference, as expressed through their voting behavior. It also does not contain a predetermined minimum threshold or range for the minority's relative presence in a district because such cutoffs may exclude potential influence districts. A district with a very small minority presence in it, however, is not likely to satisfy either the decisive or substantial standard to achieve presumptive influence district status, and even if it does it is still subject to challenge through rebuttal evidence.

This decision rule would not be definitive, but presumptive. If either of the criteria is satisfied, the burden of proof on the classification issue would switch to those challenging the classification. The same decision rule could be employed during the legislative process as well as the judicial, to both alternative districts as well as those adopted. This would also allow a comparative assessment of not only the number of influence districts in a plan, but their strength as well. Districts in which the minority vote is, or is expected to be, decisive are more likely to provide the "effective electoral carrot" and "effective electoral stick" (Grofman 2006: 260) needed to stimulate responsiveness. Likewise, the differences in the relative percentage of the marginal vote that can be attributed to minority voters in districts could be used to distinguish between or among the likelihood of representatives being responsive in their interests.

Determining whether minority voters were decisive, or cast at least half of a winning candidate's margin, in past elections does not require courts to be presented with new statistical or otherwise quantitative methodologies. These questions can be addressed by employing the same methods already widely used to assess racially polarized voting in voting rights cases. Particular applications of these procedures are of course open to challenge during the legislative and judicial process (see Engstrom 2005b).

Challenging or defending a district's status as an influence district could entail other information as well. District-specific factors, concerning intent as well as effect, could impact the ultimate decision. For example, the fact that a district was admittedly designed to re-elect a particular candidate who was never the choice of minority voters, such as Congressman Henry Bonilla in Texas, by reducing the percentage of minority voters in his or her district, could be important contextual information. And the past responsiveness of incumbents in presumptive influence districts to minority concerns and preferences could also be considered.[58]

This proposed measure is simply an initial effort to go beyond just the relative presence of minority voters in a district and take into account the preferences of the other voters in the district as well. Conceptual improvements are welcome, as are modifications based on lessons learned from actual applications of it. At this point, however, an initial validity test of the measure can be provided by some previous real-world applications of the concept. Congressional District 23 in Texas, designated as a Latino "influence district" by the federal court in *Sessions*, and Districts 4, 5, and 6 in Louisiana, designated as African American "influence districts" by the federal court in *Hays*, would no doubt have failed this test of presumptive influence districts.

CONCLUSION

In an area as politically sensitive as redistricting, the greater the clarity in concepts, the less judges are likely to be entangled in political thickets.

The "totality of circumstances" test that ultimately governs the determination of vote dilution under Section 2 and retrogression under Section 5 of the Voting Rights Act already leaves judges with enormous discretion in their decisions. A lack of clarity on the components of that test enhances this discretion even more.

"Influence district" is a concept that purportedly will enhance the representation of minority voters. As such, it will continue to be used to claim that one district is better than another, or that an entire set of districts is superior to another set. The concept, however, is in great need of explication. As currently used, by judges, lawyers, legislators, and social scientists, it can have the opposite effect. If it continues to refer, in application, to a relative presence of minority voters in a district without regard to the rest of the electorate within that district, as is now so often the case, then it will not only result in good faith errors in identification but will also be used as a justification for the intentional manipulation of district lines designed to achieve other, contrary purposes.

The judiciary's application of the concept has been reviewed above, and the need for further attention to it has been identified. This attention is especially needed in the post-2010 round of redistricting so that influence district claims during that round will be subjected to greater justification than they have been in previous rounds. A proposed measure for a presumptive influence district is provided, one that is consistent with what the concept denotes and will add important constraint to the application of it.

NOTES

This is a revised and updated version of a paper presented at the symposium "Lessons from the Past, Prospects for the Future: Honoring the Fortieth Anniversary for the Voting Rights Act," Yale University, April 21–23, 2005. It has also served as the basis for presentations at the Roscoe C. Siciliano Forum on "The Future of the Voting Rights Act: Democracy in Danger?," University of Utah, October 12, 2006, the Center for Democratic Performance, University of Binghamton, October 28, 2010, and the workshop on "Redistricting California: Cutting Edge Questions," Chief Justice Earl Warren Institute on Law and Social Policy, University of California at Berkeley, March 12, 2011, in Los Angeles. The author wishes to acknowledge the useful comments on the research he received at each of these settings. This version of the paper has benefited from support provided by a Ford Foundation general support grant to the Center for Civil Rights, School of Law, University of North Carolina, Chapel Hill.

1. Other minority groups protected by the VRA are Asian Americans, Native Americans, and Native Alaskans.

2. *Bartlett v. Strickland*, 556 U.S. 1, 13–14 (2009)

3. Canon 2008.

4. As discussed in other chapters of this volume, Section 2 is a nationwide protection against minority vote dilution and Section 5 is a protection against changes in election systems that have a retrogressive impact on minority voting strength in those state and local governments covered by the Section.

5. See, e.g., Canon 1999; Fenno 2003; Tate 2003; Whitby 1997; Whitby and Krause 2001; Grose 2005; Pantoja and Segura 2003: 455; Haynie 2005: 405–6; Gay 2007; and Casellas 2007; and for African American and Latino school board members elected by districts, see Meier et al. 2005: 764–65.

6. The only type of tradeoff the theory deals with concerns substantive representation defined as being on the winning side of legislative votes. It does not address other potential benefits of descriptive representation, such as more attentive constituency service and legislative agenda building, or important symbolic benefits such as minority inclusion in public decision-making processes (see Canon 2008: 8–9, 23; and Casellas 2011: 10, 118–19). For evidence of other benefits, see especially Canon 1999; Fenno 2003; and Tate 2003.

7. See, e.g., Grose 2007: 3 n. 1 (25 to 50 percent in total population) and 2011: 33 (26 to 29 percent African American population); Klarner 2007: 298 (between 35 and 50 percent total population), Casellas 2011: 71 (25 to 49.9 percent Latino in total population); Epstein and O'Halloran 2006: 61 (25 to 40 percent black VAP); Canon 2005: 188 (between 30 and 50 percent black VAP); Barabas and Jerit 2004: 421–22 (35–50 percent in total population); Canon 1999: 11, 132, 146, 253 (30 to 50

percent "black voters," but at 146 Canon identifies districts in which white representatives "should be the most sensitive to racial issues" as beginning at 25 percent African American); Burton 1998: 299–301 (25 to 45 percent total population); Handley, Grofman, and Arden 1998: 34 (between 30 and 50 percent total population are "strong minority influence districts"); and Hagens 1998: 323, 329–32 (between 30 and 50 percent VAP for state legislative districts, but between 20 and 50 percent for congressional districts). One set of authors has explicitly incorporated expected party outcomes into a measure of influence districts. They maintain that influence districts are those at or above "the point of 'partisan equal opportunity.'" This point is, based on a probit analysis, "the level of BVAP at which a candidate of the party supported by minority voters has an equal chance of winning the election" (Epstein and O'Halloran 2008; 644). An application of this procedure based on combining elections in Georgia for the U.S. House and both chambers of the state legislature from 1991 through 2001 states that "the chances of electing a white Democrat *peak* at just over 25% BVAP" (ibid., at 655, emphasis added). (It is not clear however whether this peak is also the point of equal partisan opportunity.)

8. This was also found to be true during Reconstruction (see Cobb and Jenkins 2001: 190–91).

9. In his case studies of southern congressional elections, Glaser reports that in majority-white districts with a substantial African American presence, some Republican candidates introduced the race issue in order to *enhance* their candidacies (1996: 30, 67, and 176).

10. Another recent study of the voting behavior of state legislators, this one examining Georgia state senators (Canon 2008), will be discussed in the following section on *Georgia v. Ashcroft*.

11. Grofman likewise has stated that "to resuscitate a career placed in jeopardy due to close contests with Republicans in the general election, a White Democratic legislator in the South may see himself or herself as better off by reaching out to white voters rather than black voters" (2006: 261).

12. For previous references to the concept in Supreme Court decisions, see *Reno v. Bossier Parish School Board,* 520 U.S. 471, 491 (1997) (Thomas, J., concurring), *Shaw v. Hunt,* 517 U.S. 899, 947 (1996) (Stevens, J., dissenting), *Hall v. Holder,* 512 U.S. 874, 893 (1994) (Thomas, J. concurring), *Johnson v. DeGrandy,* 512 U.S. 997, 1009 (1994) (Souter, J., for the Court), *Shaw v. Reno,* 509 U.S. 630, 675 (1993) (White, J., dissenting), and *Voinovich v. Quilter,* 507 U.S. 146, 149, 154 (1993) (O'Connor, for the Court).

13. The state's figures for African Americans include not only those who reported to the census that they were solely African American, but also anyone who reported being any part African American. This method is known as the "combo" method. The United States Department of Justice identified the African American percentage of the VAP in these districts to be 50.31, 50.66, and 50.80. These figures include people who self-identified as African American or both African American and white, but not another minority group [*Georgia v. Ashcroft,* 539 U.S. 451, 472–474 n. 1 (2003)]. Georgia maintains records of the number of African Americans registered to vote. These figures reveal that African Americans constituted less than a majority of the registered voters in these districts, 48.5 percent, 47.76 percent, and 48.68 percent, respectively. The number of majority–African American districts based on voter registration in the plan overall was eight, which was five fewer than in the previous plan [see *Georgia v. Ashcroft,* 195 F. Supp. 2d 25, 56 (D.D.C., 2002)].

14. The equal opportunity to elect under the Voting Rights Act of course concerns the opportunity provided within a plan overall, not within a particular district. As pointed out in the Supreme Court Amicus Curiae Brief for the Georgia Coalition for the Peoples' Agenda in Support of Appellees, at 5, "A 50-50 chance to win is also a 50-50 chance to lose."

15. Crossover districts were not distinguished from coalition districts in this opinion. That distinction was made later in *Bartlett v. Strickland,* 556 U.S. 1, 13–14 (2009), in which the Court acknowledged that the districts it had referred to in *Georgia* as coalitional were of the crossover variety (8).

16. Fannie Lou Hamer, Rosa Parks, and Coretta Scott King Voting Rights Act Reauthorization and Amendments Act of 2006, sec. 2(b)(6) (hereinafter VRARA). The VRARA ultimately passed the U.S. House by a vote of 390-33 and the U.S. Senate by a vote of 98-0. For an extensive account of the legislative history of the act, see Tucker 2007.

17. Section 5(3)(d).

18. Some have warned, however, that the Supreme Court may interpret the revised act in a way that would "reinstate a standard akin to that articulated in Ashcroft" (Persily 2006: 236; see also Canon 2008: 4–5, 23–24).

19. This chapter does not review literature and court decisions that apply the label "influence district" to districts that are allegedly coalition or crossover districts.

20. *Jurisdictional Statement,* at i and 18–26, *Brief of Appellant State of Georgia,* at i and 30–39.

21. 2003 U.S. Trans Lexis 45, at 12, see also, 10, 11–17.

22. This mistaken view even appears in some of the scholarly literature; see, e.g., Karlan 2004: 35 ("The [Supreme] Court found that the 2001 plan 'offset' the potential retrogression in the three identi-

fied districts with an increase in the black
voting age percentage in other districts");
Chang 2005: 244 ("the Ashcroft Court
affirmed Georgia's disaggregation of safe
districts"); and also Harris and Hardy
2007: 240; Swain 2007: 36; Dawood 2008:
1426 n. 76; and Bullock and Gaddie 2009:
99, all stating that the Supreme Court
upheld Georgia's senate redistricting plan.
One article maintains that the Supreme
Court "reversed" the district court, "approved" the plan, and had itself granted
preclearance to it, although later noted
that the Court had "vacated and remanded" the decision (Faget 2007–2008: 46, 48,
49, 52, and 54).

23. Justice O'Connor utilized three different VAP ranges for influence districts at
various places in her opinion. These were
districts that were less than 50 percent
but above 30 percent in African American
VAP (470, 471, 487), or above 25 percent
(470, 471, 487), or even 20 percent (489).
No basis was identified for any of these
thresholds other than that districts above
20 percent tended to be above 50 percent
"Democratic" in an index the state created
(489). The utility of this index, which was
based on voting in statewide elections, for
inferring partisan voting in senate district
elections, in which white crossover voting
was less frequent (as had been shown to be
the case in Senate Districts 2, 12, 26), was
questioned by Justice David Souter (dissenting, at 507). On remand, following the
2002 elections, the United States argued
that the index was not a reliable predic-
tor of outcomes, as nine of the seventeen
districts in which the index identified the
Democratic Party strength to be between
50 and 55 percent were represented by
Republicans at the time the subsequent
legislative session began (six the result
of the election and three the result of the
winning Democratic candidates switching to the Republican Party). United
States' Response to Order to Show Cause,

at 13–14, 17–18, and United States' Reply
to Georgia's Response to Order to Show
Cause, at 9.

24. The Court also referenced the
testimony of African American senators,
stating that the plan was designed to help
the Democratic Party maintain control of
the state senate, which would be beneficial to the state's African Americans, and
also the fact that ten of the eleven African
Americans in the senate voted for it, as
did thirty-three of the thirty-four African
Americans in the House (469–72). For
commentary on the appropriate weight
to be given to the votes of the African
American legislators, see Becker (2007:
240–46).

25. The District Court found, based
partly on this author's study of voting in
the three districts at issue, that elections in
them had been racially polarized [Georgia
v. Ashcroft, 195 F. Supp. 2d 25, 69–71, 85–88,
91, 94 (D.D.C. 2002) and 204 F. Supp. 2d
5, 12 (D.D.C. 2002)]. This finding was not
disturbed by the Supreme Court.

26. For an excellent discussion of the
overall evidence provided in this case, see
Becker 2007.

27. Plaintiff's Brief in Response to
United States' and Defendant-Intervenors'
Responses to Order to Show Cause.

28. Georgia v. Ashcroft, 204 F. Supp. 2d
4 (D.D.C. 2002). African Americans constituted a majority of the registered voters
in each of these districts as well, 55.8, 51.58,
and 54.7 percent, respectively (ibid., 7).

29. The plan was described similarly
as "not substantially different" from the
2001 plan by the court in Georgia (1324),
which has been labeled "a clear partisan
gerrymander" designed to maintain a
Democratic majority in the face of declining electoral support (Winburn 2008: 90).
The decision has been called a "backdoor"
invalidation of a partisan gerrymander
(Engstrom 2005a: 320–321). Although the
District Court had dismissed a complaint

that the plan was a partisan gerrymander in favor of the Democrats (1322), the state's justifications for the population deviations in the plan were rejected because they were applied in a manner that favored the Democrats (1347–48, 1352).

30. United States Response to Order to Show Cause, at 15–18.

31. Three of these districts, 3, 41, and 44, are identical in the interim plan and the 2001 proposed senate plan. The difference in the African American VAP in six of them, 5, 6, 14, 20, 25, and 40, is less than 1 percentage point between these two plans, and two more, 11 and 13, differ by less than 1.5 percentage points. District 4 in the interim plan is 4.66 percentage points less in African American VAP than the corresponding district in the proposed plan, and District 18 in the interim plan is 2.78 percentage points less in African American VAP than is District 16 in the proposed plan.

32. This analysis was performed for the Department of Justice by the author. This procedure has been employed by King and others, including this author, to estimate the levels of racially polarized voting in elections while serving as expert witnesses in court cases involving retrogression or dilution issues under the VRA. See Engstrom 2005b.

33. In addition, the winning candidate in District 22, in which 51.5 percent of the VAP was African American, was a Republican, despite only 8.0 percent of the African Americans voting for him.

34. Plaintiff's Brief in Response to United States' and Defendant-Intervenors' Responses to Order to Show Cause, at 14.

35. Pamela Karlan states that these party switchers left the African American voters in their districts "completely high and dry" (2004: 35). The districts of the party switchers were 38.15, 36.86, 26.69, and 25.85 percent African American in their voting age populations (Canon 2008: 22).

36. The changes in the percentage of African American VAP in four of these adjacent districts were negative, −3.90, −1.37, −1.22, and −0.22, while one was positive, 0.87. These percentage differences were all smaller than the increases in the VAP percentages in the three majority–African American districts, Districts 2, 12, and 26, and did not occur in nearly as critical a range of VAP. The Epstein and O'Halloran study also finds that there were seventeen influence districts, based on their measure (see n. 2) in the state's 2001 plan as a whole, and also seventeen in the interim plan used for the 2002 election (2008: 658). The need to place the Senate Districts 2, 12, and 13 at risk by shaving the BVAP percentage in them to below 51 percent likewise appears, under their analysis, to have been unnecessary to create influence districts.

37. It must be noted that this conclusion by Canon also depends on the fact that the Democrats lost their majority in the state senate as a result of the 2002 election and the subsequent postelection switch by the four white Democratic senators, all elected in "influence" districts, to the Republican Party (2008: 23).

38. Canon also references data from the 2003 legislative session concerning the four senators in apparent influence districts that switched their party affiliation from the Democratic Party to the Republican Party after the 2002 election. He states that "while the switchers were not especially strong supporters of black interests even as Democrats . . . they became even less so when they switched parties" (2008: 22). He reports that on a ten-point scale of support scores for "poor and minority constituents" on key votes, with higher scores being more supportive, their 1999 scores of 5.15, 5.5, 6.75, and 7.9 dropped respectively to 3.8, 1.6, 4.8, and 4.0 in 2003. These were statistically significant reductions in all but one case, and was close to significant on the fourth (ibid. at 22 n. 56).

39. Epstein and O'Halloran (2008) provide a contrary conclusion about the substantive representation implications of the 2001 plan. They report that the level of substantive representation in the 2001 plan would be expected to increase over that in the previous plan. This is based on an analysis of all 892 "non-unanimous" roll calls in the state senate from 1999 through 2002. No minimum degree of disagreement on a roll call vote is specified to qualify for inclusion, which is a common feature of roll call studies by political scientists. In those studies a minimum of 10 percent is usually required. Unlike Canon, they ignore the substantive content of the legislative measures being voted upon. They calculate a "Black Support Score" based on whether a legislator was on the same side of a vote as was a majority of the African American senators, including a bare majority of them, regardless of the substantive content of the item (ibid. at 656). Only 33.3 percent of these legislative votes, allegedly measuring the substantive representation of African Americans, were divided along party lines, with a majority of black and white Democrats voting contrary to a majority of Republicans (ibid. at 657). This collection of roll calls resulted in the "Black Support Score" for Republican state senators in Georgia of 50.2 percent (ibid.). While well below the corresponding figures of 92.0 percent for white Democrats and 94.6 for African American Democrats (ibid.), the Republican figure of 50.2 certainly raises questions about the validity of this procedure as a measure of *substantive* representation for African Americans, especially when compared to the results of Canon's analysis of roll calls on matters identified as being of specific substantive concern to them. Based on this, Epstein and O'Halloran report that the overall Black Support Scores for the previous plan was 62.3 percent, while that for the 2001 plan was 66.6 (and that for the

interim plan used in 2002 was 65.9) (ibid. at 659).

40. See, e.g., *Cousin v. McWherter*, 904 F. Supp. 686, 713 (E.D. Tenn. 1995) (30 percent African American VAP); *Johnson v. Miller*, 922 F. Supp. 1556, 1568, 1571 (S.D. Ga. 1995) (32.8 percent African American VAP); *Johnson v. Mortham*, 926 F. Supp. 1460, 1491 (N.D. Fla. 1996) (several districts ranging between 25.0 percent and 47.5 percent in African American VAP); *Johnson v. Miller*, 929 F. Supp. 1529, 1554 (S.D. Ga. 1996) (44.76 percent African American VAP); *Harper v. City of Chicago Heights*, 1997 U.S. Dist 2509, slip op. at 5 (N.D. Ill. 1997) (40 percent Latino VAP); *McCoy v. Chicago Heights*, 6 F. Supp. 2d 973, 979 (N.D. Ill. 1998) (44.1 percent Latino VAP); *Frank v. Forest County*, 109 F. Supp. 2d 867, 877 (E.D. Wisc. 2002) (49.35 percent Native American VAP); *Sessions v. Perry*, 298 F. Supp. 2d 451, 489 (E.D. Tx. 2004) (45.8 percent Latino citizen CVAP); *Larios v. Cox*, 314 F. Supp. 2d 1357 (N.D. Ga. 2004) (districts ranging from 30 percent to 49 percent in African American voter registration); *Woullard v. State of Mississippi*, 2006 U.S. Dist. LEXIS 46561, 18–19 (S.D. Miss. 2006) (32.5 percent and 38.21 percent in African American VAP); and *Gonzales v. City of Aurora*, 535 F. 3d 594, 596, 600 (7th Cir. 2008) (districts with Latino CVAP of 43 percent and 28 percent are identified as influence districts, and three more with more than 1,000 Latino CVAP in absolute terms but without any percentage figures provided are considered "likely" to be influence districts). None of these examples appear, based on the opinions, to include any situations in which the district identified as an influence district would more appropriately be called a coalition district. One court has determined that an illustrative district that was barely a majority in African American VAP, 50.23 percent, was "in reality only an influence district" because

participation rates in elections in that district were expected to be lower among African Americans than other voters [*Thompson v. Glades County Board of Commissioners,* 2004 U.S. Dist. LEXUS 30989, at 40, 42 (2004)].

41. The totality of circumstances test allows judges to consider almost anything and provides them with enormous discretion in deciding a case. The things courts typically reference in making such determinations have been described by Justice Clarence Thomas as "a list of possible considerations that might be consulted by a court attempting to develop a *gestalt* view of the political and racial climate in a jurisdiction, but a list that cannot provide a rule for deciding a vote dilution claim" [*Holder v. Hall* 512 U.S. 874 (1994) (Thomas, J. concurring)].

42. For a review of these various aspects of the bill, see Engstrom 1988.

43. Senator Thurmond's votes on these matters can be found readily in Congressional Quarterly 1982: 31S–33S.

44. For another example, see the testimony of U.S. Representative Robert Livingston, a Louisiana Republican, in *Major v. Treen,* 574 F. Supp. 325 (E.D. La. 1983), Livingston testimony, transcript (March 10, 1083), p. 23. As noted elsewhere, "When asked at the trial how he responded in the past to the concerns of his black constituents, Livingston did not mention a single bill introduced, amendment offered, or vote cast by him in Congress, reciting instead a list of services and favors performed for black individuals and groups" (Engstrom 1986: 119).

45. A more common description of Duke would be McKaskle's identification of him as "ultraconservative and racist" (McKaskle 1995: 24). On Duke's political career in Louisiana, see generally Rose 1992 and Kuzenski, Bullock, and Gaddie 1995.

46. In Louisiana's election system at the time, all candidates for an office competed in one election, with their party affiliations listed on the ballot. If no one received a majority of the votes in that election, a runoff election would be held between the top two, regardless of their party affiliation.

47. Grofman and Brunell have stated, to the contrary, that "we see good evidence that black or Hispanic elected officials are at least as likely to be sensitive to the views of their white constituents as white representatives are to be sensitive to the views of minorities within the district" (2006: 318). See also McClain's and Stewart's rejection of "asymmetric representation assumptions" (1995: 25). Justice David Souter, in his dissent in *Georgia v. Ashcroft,* dismissed footnote 17 in *Hays* as "footnote dictum" (495).

48. Canon also states that "on average, the white members of the 103rd Congress who represent districts that were at least 25 percent black did not show much interest in racial issues" (1999: 200).

49. Another illustration of this selectivity was provided by a political scientist testifying as an expert witness for the plaintiffs in *Hays.* He testified, relying on the *McWherter* standard of 25 percent, about the presence of African American influence districts. When asked on cross-examination whether majority–African American districts that were more than 25 percent white were white influence districts, he appeared stunned and answered, "My recollection of the discussion of influence districts has to do with the, what we call minority influence, *not* majority influence" (emphasis added). Asked then if the concept of influence districts did not apply when whites were the quantitative minority in districts, he answered, "That's true, yes." After acknowledging that he used the concept "in the context of the majority minority districts," he did state that "I think, you know, you could *stretch the definition* to say that a district that is 25

percent white to 50 percent white *might* be considered a white influence district" (emphasis added). But this was then qualified by stating that in the context of majority–African American districts, "You'd have to look at the actual analysis to determine that," rather than rely on the 25 percent threshold. Testimony of Ronald Weber, transcript (October 30, 1995, afternoon session, at 163–64), and personal observation. Scholarly studies continue to ignore the possibility of white influence districts (see, e.g., Grose 2011: 33–34).

50. The racially selective application of the concept of "opportunity district" was rejected by a three-judge panel in *Black Political Task Force v. Galvin*, 300 F. Supp. 2d 291, 311–312 (D C. Mass. 2004).

51. For an extensive discussion of this re-redistricting, including the issues of partisan gerrymandering and mid-decade redistricting, see Bickerstaff 2007.

52. In its 122-page brief for the Supreme Court, the only specific thing the state offered to demonstrate that Bonilla had been responsive to his Hispanic constituents was a letter from the American GI Forum, the national organization to which the GI Forum of Texas was affiliated, stating that he had been"'a voice and effective advocate' for Hispanic veterans" (State Appellees' Brief, at 101). In contrast, the GI Forum of Texas, the major protagonist concerning District 23, noted that on a set of roll calls during the congressional session leading up to the 2002 election, Bonilla "voted for Latino interests a mere 18 percent of the time" (Reply Brief for Appellants GI Forum, *Et Al.*, at 4 n. 10, referencing the National Hispanic Leadership Agenda Congressional Scorecard 107th Congress).

Justice Stevens, in a footnote in his separate opinion, described District 24 in the previous plan, located in the Dallas/Fort Worth area, as a "strong influence district" (concurring in part and dissenting in part,

at 2645 n. 15; see also Gringer 2008: 209 and Tolson 2008: 326). This district was 25.7 percent African American in CVAP. African Americans had been strong supporters of Martin Frost, an Anglo Democrat who had represented the district since 1979. The Jackson appellants, the main party opposing the dismantling of this district in the 2003 plan, argued however that it was not an influence district, but rather an opportunity-to-elect district for African Americans, who controlled the outcomes of both the Democratic primary and general election (see oral argument of Paul Smith, transcript at 33, and Reply Brief for Appellants, at 10–15). The majority of the Court, this time consisting of Kennedy and the other four justices generally described as the "conservative block," did not find the dismantling of the district for partisan purposes to be a violation of the VRA or the federal Constitution.

53. General Election Analysis, Congressional Districts – Plan 01440C, Texas Legislative Council, 8/7/06.

54. In special elections in Texas all candidates, regardless of party, compete as a single group, with the top candidates, regardless of party, advancing to a runoff if no candidate receives a majority of the votes. Bonilla came close to winning in the first election, receiving 48.6 percent of the total vote. His closest competitor was Rodriguez with 19.9 percent of the votes.

55. On remand the district court, in *Vecinos de Barrio UNO v. City of Holyoke* [960 F. Supp. 515 (D.C. Mass. 1997)], noted the testimony of the Anglo candidate that won the district in 1993, in which he had "credibly" reported that he was "actively vying for the Hispanic votes and offering to serve the interests of the Hispanic community" (523). He had, the court stated, "garnered 74.4% of the Hispanic vote in Precinct 4 A, which is 45.2% Hispanic, against an Hispanic opponent" (ibid.), although the source for this figure was not

identified. The winner in the following election, in 1995, was also an Anglo who "did well even in the more heavily Hispanic precinct, while his Hispanic opponent was "unable to attract significant Hispanic voter turnout" (527). Once again, specifics about how well the candidate did, or what the turnout was, were not provided. As to whether the district was an influence district, the court concluded, "The picture in this ward is still not crystal clear, but it is hard to imagine any viable candidate of whatever ethnicity ignoring the interests of its large Hispanic population" (ibid.).

56. The expression "substantial, if not decisive" has, however, been interpreted differently by the North Carolina Supreme Court. Citing O'Connor's use of the expression, the court stated "an influence district is one in which a minority group is merely large enough to influence the election of candidates but too small to determine the outcome" [*Pender County v. Bartlett*, 649 s.e.2d 364, 371 (2007)]. It may be that the court was interpreting "too small to determine the outcome" as *independently* determining the outcome, regardless of how the rest of the electorate votes, which would be an ability-to-elect district. But O'Connor did not say "but not decisive," but rather "if not decisive." The expression "if not," as in "the candidate got a plurality, if not a majority," denotes that the candidate certainly received a plurality, and might have received a majority.

57. Grofman expresses skepticism about a "potentially 'pivotal'" African American vote in the Deep South producing representatives sensitive to African American concerns and preferences. A threat of African Americans voting for a Republican candidate, or even declining to vote in an election, he maintains, might not be viewed by the representative as credible. In addition, the representative might choose to become more responsive to his or her white constituents in an effort to expand their electoral support for him or her (Grofman 2006, 261).

This raises a question of whether the simple percentage threshold approach to identifying influence districts will not only result in errors of inclusion, but errors of exclusion as well. In the Texas congressional redistricting case, the G.I. Forum argued that two districts with small Latino percentages in the court-drawn plan were Latino influence districts. The incumbents in these districts, Democrats Chet Edwards and Charles Stenholm, were targeted for defeat in the Republican plan adopted to replace the court's plan. This plaintiff argued that the districts were Latino influence districts because the Latinos in the districts were an important part of the electoral constituency of these representatives. In Edward's district, District 11, Latinos constituted 14.1 percent of the vap according to the 2000 census, and at the time of the 2002 election, 9.5 percent of the registered voters. In Stenholm's district, District 17, these figures were 16.6 percent and 12.1 percent respectively. Edwards was re-elected in 2002, under the court's district plan, with 52.3 percent of the vote cast for the two major-party candidates, and Stenholm was re-elected with 52.0 of the two-party vote. An analysis of the 2002 elections held in these districts indicates that non-Latino voters were sharply divided between the candidates. Edwards received an estimated 51.9 percent of the votes cast by non-Latinos, and Stenholm 50.6 percent. Latino voters, however, strongly supported of the Democratic incumbents. Latinos cast an estimated 96.5 percent and 90.0 percent of their votes for these candidates. Although these estimates do not indicate that Latino voters were decisive, the serious divisions in the non-Latino vote and in the outcome overall would likely result in representatives being highly sensitive to Latino interests and preferences. The estimated divisions in the vote reported above were derived through King's EI procedure by the author; see Richard L. Engstrom, *Report*, G.I. Forum v. Texas, November 17, 2003, and the trial testimony of Richard L. Engstrom, *Sessions v. Perry*, December

16, 2003, at 14–22, 31–40, and 47–48. The court's opinion in *Sessions*, however, did not address this evidence or argument.

58. Grofman warns, however, that such determinations should not rely on "mere assertions by a representative" (2006: 260).

REFERENCE

Aleinikoff, T. Alexander, and Samuel Issacharoff. 1993. "Drawing Constitutional Lines after Shaw v. Reno." *Michigan Law Review* 92 (December): 583–87.

Ardoin, Phillip J., and Ronald J. Vogel. 2006. "African Americans in the Republican Party: Taking the Road Less Traveled." *American Review of Politics* 27 (Summer): 93–113.

Barabas, Jason, and Jennifer Jerit. 2004. "Redistricting Principles and Racial Representation." *State Politics and Policy Quarterly* 4 (Winter): 415–35.

Becker, David. 2007. "Saving Section 5: Reflections on *Georgia v. Ashcroft* and its Impact on the Reauthorization of the Voting Rights Act." In Ana Henderson, ed., *Voting Rights Act Reauthorization of 2006: Perspectives on Democracy, Participation, and Power*. Berkeley, Calif.: Berkeley Public Policy Press.

Bedoya, Alvard. 2006. "The Unforeseen Effects of Georgia v. Ashcroft on the Latino Community." *Yale Law Journal* 115 (June): 2112–46.

Bickerstaff, Steve. 2007. *Lines in the Sand: Congressional Redistricting in Texas and the Downfall of Tom Delay*. Austin: University of Texas Press.

Bullock, Charles S., III, and Ronald Keith Gaddie. 2009. *The Triumph of Voting Rights in the South*. Norman: University of Oklahoma Press.

Burton, Orville Vernon. 1998. "Legislative and Congressional Districting in South Carolina." In Bernard Grofman, ed.,

Race and Redistricting in the 1990s. New York: Agathon Press.

Cameron, Charles, David Epstein, and Sharyn O'Halloran. 1996. "Do Majority-Minority Districts Maximize Substantive Black Representation in Congress?" *American Political Science Review* 90 (December): 794–812.

Canon, David T. 1999. *Race, Redistricting, and Representation: The Unintended Consequences of Black Majority Districts*. Chicago: University of Chicago Press.

———. 2005. "Representing Racial and Ethnic Minorities." In Paul Quirk and Sarah Binder, eds., *The Legislative Branch and American Democracy: Institutions and Performance*. New York: Oxford University Press.

———. 2007. "The Future of the Voting Rights Act." *Election Law Journal* 6, no. 3: 266–369.

———. 2008. "Renewing the Voting Rights Act: Retrogression, Influence, and the *Georgia v. Ashcroft* Fix." *Election Law Journal* 7, no. 1: 3–24.

Casellas, Jason F. 2007. "Latino Representation in Congress: To What Extent Are Latinos Substantively Represented?" In Rodolfo Espino, David Leal, and Kenneth Meier, eds., *Latino Politics: Identity, Mobilization, and Representation*. Charlottesville: University of Virginia Press.

———. 2011. *Latino Representation in State Houses and Congress*. New York: Cambridge University Press.

Chang, Felix B. 2005. "After Georgia v. Ashcroft: The Primacy of Proportionality." *Michigan Journal of Race and Law* 11 (2005): 219–46.

Chervenak, Edward. 1998. "1992 Congressional Redistricting in Louisiana: Drawing the Line(s) on Race." *The Urban Lawyer* 30 (Winter): 209–31.

Clarke, Monet. 2005. "Race, Partisanship, and the Voting Rights Act (VRA): African-Americans in Texas from Reconstruction to the Republican Redistricting of 2004." *Texas Journal on Civil Liberties and Civil Rights* 10 (Spring): 223–44.

Cobb, Michael D., and Jeffery A. Jenkins. 2001. "Race and the Representation of Black Interests During Reconstruction." *Political Research Quarterly* 54 (March): 181–204.

Congressional Quarterly. 1982. *Congressional Roll Call 1982*. Washington, D.C.: Congressional Quarterly Inc.

Dawood, Yasmin. 2008. "The Antidomination Model and the Judicial Oversight of Democracy." *Georgetown Law Journal* 96, no. 5: 1411–85.

Earls, Anita. 2006. "Introduction: Advancing Minority Voting Rights: How Do We Get from Here to There?" In David A. Bositis, ed., *Voting Rights and Minority Representation: Redistricting, 1992–2002*. Lanham, Md.: University Press of America, Inc.

Engstrom, Richard L. 1986. "Repairing the Crack in New Orleans' Black Vote: VRA's Results Test Nullifies 'Gerryduck.'" *Publius* 16 (Fall): 109–21.

———. 1988. "Black Politics and the Voting Right Act: 1965–1982." In James F. Lea, ed., *Contemporary Southern Politics*. Baton Rouge: Louisiana State University Press.

———. 2002. "The Post-2000 Round of Redistricting: An Entangled Thicket within the Federal System." *Publius* 32 (Fall): 51–70.

———. 2005a. "Missing the Target: The Supreme Court, 'One Person, One Vote,' and Partisan Gerrymandering." In Peter F. Galderisi, ed., *Redistricting in the New Millennium*. Lanham, Md.: Lexington Books.

———. 2005b. "Expert Witness Testimony." *Encyclopedia of Social Measurement*, vol. 1. London: Elsevier Inc.

———. 2005c. "Prepared Statement of Richard L. Engstrom." *Voting Rights Act: The Continuing Need for Section 5*, Hearing before the Subcommittee on the Judiciary, House of Representatives, 109th Cong., 1st sess., October 25, 2005, Serial No. 109-75, pp. 51–80.

———. 2006. "Race and Southern Politics: The Special Case of Congressional Redistricting." In Robert P. Steed and Laurence W. Moreland, eds., *Writing Southern Politics: Contemporary Interpretations and Future Directions*. Lexington: University Press of Kentucky.

Engstrom, Richard L., and Jason F. Kirksey. 1998. "Race and Representational Redistricting in Louisiana." In Bernard Grofman, ed., *Race and Redistricting in the 1990s*. New York: Agathon Press.

Epstein, David L., and Sharyn O'Halloran. 1999. "Measuring the Electoral and Policy Impact of Majority-Minority Voting Districts." *American Journal of Political Science* 43 (April): 367–95.

———. 2006. "Trends in Minority Representation, 1974 to 2000." In David Epstein, Richard H. Pildes, Rudolfo O. de la Garza, and Sharyn O'Halloran, eds., *The Future of the Voting Rights Act*. New York: Russell Sage Foundation.

———. 2008. "Does the New VRA Section 5 Overrule Georgia v. Ashcroft?" *N.Y.U. Annual Survey of American Law* 63, no. 4: 631–59.

Faget, Kyle. 2007–2008. "GEORGIA V. ASHCROFT: A New Statistical Model?" *Georgetown Public Policy Review* 13: 45–60.

Fauntroy, Michael K. 2007. *Republicans and the Black Vote*. Boulder, Colo.: Lynne Rienner Publishers.

Fenno, Richard F., Jr. 1978. *Home Style: House Members in Their Districts*. Boston: Little, Brown and Company.

———. 2003. *Going Home: Black Representatives and Their Constituents*. Chicago: University of Chicago Press.

Frymer, Paul. 1999. *Uneasy Alliances: Race and Party Competition in America*. Princeton, N.J.: Princeton University Press.

Gay, Claudine. 2007. "Legislating Without Constraints: The Effect of Minority Districting on Legislators' Responsiveness to Constituency Preferences." *Journal of Politics* 69 (May): 442–56.

Glaser, James M. 1996. *Race, Campaign Politics, and Realignment in the South*. New Haven, Conn.: Yale University Press.

Gringer, David. 2008. "Why the National Popular Vote Plan Is the Wrong Way to Abolish the Electoral College." *Columbia Law Review* 108 (January): 182–230.

Grofman, Bernard. 2006. "Operationalizing the Section 5 Retrogression Standard of the Voting Rights Act in Light of *Georgia v. Ashcroft*: Social Science Perspectives on Minority Influence, Opportunity and Control." *Election Law Journal* 5, no. 3: 250–82.

Grofman, Bernard, and Thomas Brunell. 2006. "Extending Section 5 of the Voting Rights Act: The Complex Interaction between Law and Politics." In David Epstein, Richard H. Pildes, Rudolfo O. de la Garza, and Sharyn O'Halloran, eds., *The Future of the Voting Rights Act*. New York: Russell Sage Foundation.

Grofman, Bernard, Lisa Handley, and Richard G. Niemi. 1992. *Minority Representation and the Quest for Voting Equality*. New York: Cambridge University Press.

Grose, Christian R. 2005. "Disentangling Constituency and Legislator Effects in Legislative Representation: Black Legislators or Black Districts." *Social Science Quarterly* 86 (June): 427–43.

———. 2007. "Black-Majority Districts or Black Influence Districts? Evaluating the Representation of African Americans in the Wake of *Georgia v. Ashcroft*." In Ana Henderson, ed., *Voting Rights Act Reauthorization of 2006: Perspectives on Democracy, Participation, and Power*. Berkeley Calif.: Berkeley Public Policy Press.

———. 2011. *Congress in Black and White: Race and Representation in Washington and at Home*. New York: Cambridge University Press.

Hagens, Winnett W. 1998. "The Politics of Race: The Virginia Redistricting Experience, 1991–1997." In Bernard Grofman, ed., *Race and Redistricting in the 1990s*. New York: Agathon Press.

Handley, Lisa, Bernard Grofman, and Wayne Arden. 1998. "Electing Minority-Preferred Candidates to Legislative Office: The Relationship Between Minority Percentages in Districts and the Election of Minority-Preferred Candidates." In Bernard Grofman, ed. *Race and Redistricting in the 1990s*. New York: Agathon Press.

Harris, David H., Jr., and Trish Hardy. 2007. "A Good Fix But Not the Cure – Fannie Lou Hamer, Rosa Parks, and Coretta Scott King Voting Rights Act Reauthorization and Amendments Act of 2006." *North Carolina Central Law Journal* 29, no. 2: 224–49.

Haynie, Kerry L. 2005. "African Americans and the New Politics of Inclusion: A Representational Dilemma?" In Lawrence C. Dodd and Bruce Oppenheimer, eds., *Congress Reconsidered*, 8th ed. Washington DC: CQ Press.

Hoston, William T. 2007. "African-American Legislators Post-Katrina: Race, Representation, and Voting Rights Issues in the Louisiana House." Ph.D. dissertation, University of New Orleans, 2007.

Huerta, Juan Carlos, and Adolfo Santos. 2006. "Latino Representation in the U.S. Congress: How Much and by Whom?" *American Review of Politics* 27 (Summer): 115–28.

Hutchings, Vincent L. 1998. "Issue Salience and Support for Civil Rights Legislation Among Southern Democrats." *Legislative Studies Quarterly* 23 (November): 521–44.

Hutchings, Vincent L., Harwood K. McClerking, and Guy-Uriel Charles. 2004. "Congressional Representation of Black Interests: Recognizing the Importance of Stability." *Journal of Politics* 66 (May): 450–68.

Karlan, Pamela S. 2004. "*Georgia v. Ashcroft* and the Retrogression of Retrogression." *Election Law Journal* 3, no. 1: 21–36.

Kerr, Brinck, and Will Miller. 1997. "Latino Representation, It's Direct and Indirect." *American Journal of Political Science* 41 (July): 1066–71.

King, Gary. 1997. *A Solution to the Ecological Inference Problem: Reconstructing Individual Behavior from Aggregate Data.* Princeton, N.J.: Princeton University Press.

Klarner, Carl E. 2007. "Redistricting Principles and Racial Representation: A Re-analysis." *State Politics and Policy Quarterly* 7 (Fall): 298–302.

Kousser, Morgan. 1998. "Reapportionment Wars: Party, Race, and Redistricting in California, 1971–1992." In Bernard Grofman, ed., *Race and Redistricting in the 1990s.* New York: Agathon Press.

Kuzenski, John C., Charles S. Bullock III, and Ronald Keith Gaddie, eds. 1995. *David Duke and the Politics of Race in the South.* Nashville, Tenn.: Vanderbilt University Press.

LeVeaux, Christine, and James C. Garand. 2003. "Race-Based Redistricting, Core Constituencies, and Legislative Responsiveness to Constituency Change." *Social Science Quarterly* 84 (March): 32–51.

Liu, Baodong, and James Vanderleeuw. 2007. *Race Rules: Electoral Politics in New Orleans, 1965–2006.* Lanham, Md.: Rowman & Littlefield/Lexington Books.

Lublin, David. 1997. *The Paradox of Representation: Racial Gerrymandering and Minority Interests.* Princeton, N.J.: Princeton University Press.

Lublin, David, and Cheryl Lampkin. 2007. "Racial Redistricting and the Election of African-American County Supervisors in Mississippi." In Ana Henderson, ed., *Voting Rights Act Reauthorization of 2006: Perspectives on Democracy, Participation, and Power.* Berkeley Calif.: Berkeley Public Policy Press.

Lublin, David, and D. Stephen Voss. 2000. "Racial Redistricting and Realignment in Southern State Legislatures." *American Journal of Political Science* 44 (October): 792–810.

———. 2003. "The Missing Middle: Why Median-Voter Theory Can't Save Democrats from Singing the Boll-Weevil Blues." *Journal of Politics* 65 (February): 227–37.

McClain, Paula D., and Joseph Stewart, Jr. 1995. "W(h)ither the Voting Rights Act after *Shaw v. Reno*: Advancing to the Past?" *PS* 28 (March): 24–26.

McCrary, Peyton, Christopher Seaman, and Richard Valelly. 2006. "The End of Preclearance as We Knew It." *Michigan Journal on Race and Law* 11 (Spring): 275–323.

McKaskle, Paul L. 1995. "The Voting Rights Act and the 'Conscientious Redistricter.'" *University of San Francisco Law Review* 30 (Fall): 1–94.

Meier, Kenneth J., Eric Gonzales Juenke, Robert D. Wrinkle, and J. L. Polinard. 2005. "Structural Choices and Representational Biases: The Post-Election Color of Representation." *American Journal of Political Science* 49 (October): 758–68.

Note. 2004. "The Implications of Coalition and Influence Districts for Vote Dilution Litigation." *Harvard Law Review* 117 (June): 2598–2620.

Note. 2008. "Need for Preclearance: Riley v. Kennedy." *Harvard Law Review* 122 (November): 495–504.

Overby, L. Marvin, and Kenneth M. Cosgrove. 1996. "Unintended Consequences? Racial Redistricting and the Representation of Minority Interests." *Journal of Politics* 58 (May): 540–50.

Pantoja, Adrian D., and Gary M. Segura. 2003. "Does Ethnicity Matter? Descriptive Representation in Legislatures and Political Alienation among Latinos." *Social Science Quarterly* 84 (June): 441–60.

Persily, Nathaniel. 2006. "Options and Strategies for Renewal of Section 5 of the Voting Rights Act." In David Epstein, Richard H. Pildes, Rudolfo O. de la Garza, and Sharyn O'Halloran, eds., *The Future of the Voting Rights Act.* New York: Russell Sage Foundation.

Pildes, Richard H. 2002. "Is Voting Rights Law Now at War with Itself? Social Science and Voting Rights in the 2000s." *North Carolina Law Review* 80 (June): 1517–73.

Posner, Mark A. 1998. "Post-1990 Redistrictings and the Preclearance Requirement of Section 5 of the Voting Rights Act." In Bernard Grofman, ed., *Race and Redistricting in the 1990s.* New York: Agathon Press.

Reeves, Keith. 1997. *Voting Hopes or Fears? White Voters, Black Candidates and Racial Politics in America.* New York: Oxford University Press.

Rose, Douglas, ed. 1992. *The Emergence of David Duke and the Politics of Race.* Chapel Hill: University of North Carolina Press.

Segura, Gary M., and Nathan D. Woods. 2007. "Majority-Minority Districts, Co-Ethnic Candidates, and Mobilization Effects." In Ana Henderson, ed., *Voting Rights Act Reaaauthorization of 2006: Perspectives on Democracy, Participation, and Power.* Berkeley, Calif.: Berkeley Public Policy Press.

Shotts, Kenneth W. 2002. "Gerrymandering, Legislative Composition, and National Policy Outcomes." *American Journal of Political Science* 46 (April): 398–414.

———. 2003a. "Does Racial Redistricting Cause Conservative Policy Outcomes? Policy Preferences of Southern Representatives in the 1980s and 1990s." *Journal of Politics* 65 (February): 216–26.

———. 2003b. "Racial Redistricting's Alleged Perverse Effects: Theory, Data, and 'Reality.'" *Journal of Politics* 65 (February): 238–43.

Singh, Robert. 1998. *The Congressional Black Caucus: Racial Politics in the U.S. Congress.* Thousand Oaks, Calif.: Sage Publications.

Swain, Carol M. 1993. *Black Faces, Black Interests: The Representation of African Americans in Congress.* Cambridge, Mass.: Harvard University Press.

———. 2007. "Reauthorization of the Voting Rights Act: How Politics and Symbolism Failed America." *Georgetown Journal of Law and Public Policy* 5 (Winter): 29–39.

Tate, Katherine. 2003. *Black Faces in the Mirror: African Americans and Their Representatives in the U.S. Congress.* Princeton, N.J.: Princeton University Press.

Thernstrom, Abigail M. 1987. *Whose Votes Count? Affirmative Action and Minority Voting Rights.* Cambridge, Mass.: Harvard University Press.

———. 2009. *Voting Rights – and Wrongs: The Elusive Quest for Racially Fair Elections.* Washington, D.C.: The American Enterprise Institute Press.

Tolson, Franita. 2008. "Increasing the Quantity and Quality of the African-

American Vote: Lessons for 2008 and Beyond." *Berkeley Journal of African-American Law and Policy* 10: 313–50.

Tucker, James Thomas. 2007. "The Politics of Persuasion: Passage of the Voting Rights Act Reauthorization Act of 2006." *Journal of Legislation* 33, no. 2: 205–67.

Whitby, Kenny J. 1997. *The Color of Representation: Congressional Behavior and Black Interests*. Ann Arbor: University of Michigan Press.

Whitby, Kenny J., and George A. Krause. 2001. "Race, Issue Heterogeneity, and Public Policy: The Republican Revolution of the 104th U.S. Congress and the Representation of African-American Policy Interests." *British Journal of Political Science* 31 (July): 555–72.

Winburn, Jonathan. 2008. *The Realities of Redistricting: Following the Rules and Limiting Gerrymandering in State Legislative Redistricting*. Lanham, Md.: Lexington Books.

PART TWO

The Debate

The Bull Connor Is Dead Myth: Or Why We Need Strong, Effectively Enforced Voting Rights Laws

LAUGHLIN MCDONALD

THE DEATH OF BULL CONNOR DID NOT SIGNAL THE END OF RACISM

Prior to passage of the Fannie Lou Hamer, Rosa Parks, and Coretta Scott King Voting Rights Act Reauthorization and Amendments Act of 2006,[1] which extended the special preclearance provisions of Section 5 of the act, opponents of the legislation frequently said, "Bull Connor is dead. We don't need Section 5 anymore." Edward Blum, a Visiting Fellow of the American Enterprise Institute, made that argument in his testimony in opposition to the bill before the House of Representatives on October 25, 2005. Quoting a recent law review article that said "Bull Connor is dead," he added, "And so is every Jim Crow–era segregationist intent on keeping blacks from the polls."[2]

Bull Connor was the infamous chief of police of Birmingham, Alabama, who turned attack dogs and fire hoses on peaceful African American civil rights demonstrators during the 1960s. With Bull Connor's death, Blum and others said or implied, all racial prejudice, bias, division, and discrimination also died, and with it the need for federal supervision of voting changes in jurisdictions (most of them in the South) that had traditionally denied racial minorities the right to vote.

Charles Norwood, a congressman from Georgia, introduced an amendment to the House bill that would have rewritten Section 5 and exempted all the covered jurisdictions from preclearance. In doing so, he also invoked Bull Connor. "Georgia and the South now lead the Na-tion in civil rights achievements," he said, "putting to shame the record of those States who continue to point their hypocritical fingers at the grave of Bull Connor."[3] The Norwood amendment was soundly defeated on the floor of the House.

And not every Jim Crow–era segregationist intent on keeping blacks from the polls was in fact dead. One of those who was still alive when Norwood made his comments in the House was Jim Clark, the former sheriff of Dallas County, Alabama. Clark's violent confrontation with civil rights demonstrators on the Edmund Pettus Bridge, which came to be known as Bloody Sunday, led to passage of the Voting Rights Act of 1965. Clark was not only alive, but unrepentant. In an interview with the *Montgomery Advertiser* in 2006, he said, "I'd do the same thing today if I had to do it all over again."[4]

The "Bull Connor is dead" mantra isn't really new. Southerners have something of a tradition of announcing the end of racism. Henry Grady, the managing editor of the *Atlanta Constitution* and a leading spokes-person for the "New South," declared in a speech to the New England Society of New York in 1886 that "There was a South of slavery and seces-sion – that South is dead. There is a South of union and freedom – that South, thank God, is living, breathing, growing every hour." And speak-ing of the Negro he said, "He shares our school fund, has the fullest protection of our laws and the friendship of our people."[5] The reality, however, was that by the turn of the century Georgia and the white South had disfranchised the Negro, reduced him to second-class status, and imposed racial segregation in every area of life.

When Jimmy Carter was inaugurated governor of Georgia in 1971, he also said that "the time for racial discrimination is over. Our people have already made this major and difficult decision."[6] One can appreciate Carter's hope for an end to racism, but when Congress extended the Vot-ing Rights Act in 1975 and 1982, it did not find that racial discrimination and its continuing effects in Georgia and other covered jurisdictions was over.

History and experience show that the "Bull Connor is dead" thesis is deeply flawed. Bull Connor is dead. But so is George Washington. So is Abraham Lincoln. So are Robert E. Lee and William Tecumseh

Sherman. So are the Twelve Apostles and the prophet Muhammad. So is William Shakespeare. And so are a lot of other people whose influence upon us is real and continuing. The notion that the past no longer has any relevance to the present, that it does not speak to us, and that it does not inform the ways we think and act is simplistic. As William Faulkner, who had a profound understanding of his native region, put it, "The past is never dead. It's not even past."[7] And as another perceptive southern writer, W. J. Cash, has said, the mind of the South "is continuous with the past. And . . . in many ways it has actually always marched away, as to this day it continues to do, from the present toward the past."[8]

Humans are capable of much that is generous, selfless, and noble, and they can, and often do, learn from past experiences. But we are also capable of much that is ignoble, and we are often driven by greed, self-interest, prejudice, and fear. Nothing in the past or present suggests we have outgrown our need for strong, effectively enforced civil rights laws.

WE CANNOT IGNORE THE PAST

World War I was described as "the war to end all wars." Many believed that because of the horrors inflicted by that war – up to ten million men were killed on the battlefield and another twenty million were wounded – no nation would ever go to war again. To paraphrase the Bull Connor exemplar: Germany and the central powers were dead and we had learned the lessons of the past; humanity had been fundamentally changed by events, and there would be no more war. But there was more war.

In an effort to ensure that World War I was in fact "the war to end all wars," the League of Nations was established, and a number of treaties limiting military power were enacted, including the Kellogg-Briand Pact outlawing war. While President Woodrow Wilson was a strong supporter of the League of Nations and was the impetus for its founding, the United States never joined it because of congressional opposition and isolationism. Despite some notable successes, the League failed in its mission to achieve disarmament and prevent war. It was unable to halt the military buildup of Germany, Italy, and Japan, and the outbreak of World War II signaled the demise of the League, as well as the conviction that war in the modern age had been buried in the garbage heap of the past.

The United Nations was founded on the ashes of the League by the victorious Allied forces after the end of World War II. The conviction, or at least hope, was that based on the concept of collective security, the UN would prevent conflicts between nations and make future wars impossible. The successes of the UN have been undeniable, but we know wars continue to be fought and sectarian and ethnic violence rage out of control in Iraq and much of the Middle East. It is deeply ironic that the Middle East, regarded as the cradle of humanity and the birthplace of some of the most influential religions of the world – Judaism, Christianity, and Islam – should be the site of some of the most appalling human behavior in modern times – roadside and suicide bombings, assassinations, torture, beheadings, and the indiscriminate killing of women and children.

We are also witnessing some of the worst genocide in the world's history. In 1994, nearly a million people were the victims of genocide in Rwanda. From 1998 to 2002, sectarian war claimed nearly five million lives in the Democratic Republic of the Congo. The Coalition for International Justice has estimated that some four hundred thousand people have been the victims of ethnic cleansing or genocide in Darfur. In Croatia and Bosnia from 1991 to 1995, the Serbian government resorted to ethnic cleansing to kill, terrorize, and expel non-Serbs to create new territories reserved for Serbs only. In Bosnia in the first months of the conflict, more than one hundred thousand people were killed and some three million were forced to leave their homes. In Srebrenica, in eastern Bosnia, several thousand men of military age were ambushed as they tried to escape, and some five to eight thousand others were taken to sites outside the city and shot.

Serbia and Darfur are not, of course, the United States, but the United States has its own regrettable history of betrayal of human rights. The nation's belief in equality was loudly trumpeted in the Declaration of Independence of 1776, which said, "We hold these truths to be self-evident, that all men are created equal." But the nation also tolerated human slavery, which was embodied in the Constitution of 1787 and counted a slave as only three-fifths of a person for purposes of apportionment of the House of Representatives, prohibited Congress from abolishing the slave trade prior to the year 1808, and provided for the return of fugitive slaves to their owners.[9]

Following the Civil War, the nation adopted constitutional amendments to implement the principle of racial equality. The Thirteenth Amendment abolished slavery, the Fourteenth Amendment guaranteed equal rights of citizenship to freedmen, and the Fifteenth Amendment guaranteed the equal right to vote without regard to race, color, or previous condition of servitude. But these amendments were effectively nullified by the southern states in the aftermath of Reconstruction. They passed a variety of laws imposing racial segregation in all its forms and depriving blacks of the ballot through such devices as literacy and understanding tests, poll taxes, voter challenges and purges, cumbersome registration procedures, durational residency requirements, the white primary, the expulsion of blacks from office, the abolition of elected offices, felon disfranchisement laws, and discriminatory redistricting and apportionment schemes. And when these technically legal measures failed to work, the states were more than willing to resort to fraud and violence to smother black political participation and safeguard white supremacy.[10]

The disfranchisement of blacks and their reduction to an inferior status was approved by our highest court. In *Plessy v. Ferguson* the Supreme Court held racial segregation constitutional and reasonable "with reference to the established usages, customs, and traditions of the people."[11] In subsequent decisions, the Court upheld the constitutionality of literacy tests and poll taxes, as well as the outright refusal of state officials to register black voters.[12] As our history shows, a nation founded on the principle that all men are created equal was willing to betray that principle.

CHALLENGES TO SECTION 5 AND ITS EXTENSION IN 1970, 1975, AND 1982

One of the great legacies of the modern civil rights movement, sometimes referred to as the second Reconstruction, was the Voting Rights Act of 1965. But South Carolina and five other southern states immediately challenged it as unconstitutional and an unwarranted intrusion on states' rights. The Supreme Court disagreed, holding in *South Carolina v. Katzenbach* that the act and the Section 5 preclearance requirement were justified by the "insidious and pervasive evil which had been perpetuated in certain parts of our country through unremitting and ingenious defiance of the Constitution," the failure of the case-by-case method to end discrimination, and the repeated attempts by local jurisdictions to evade the law by enacting new and different discriminatory voting procedures.[13]

Congress thought, in retrospect unrealistically, that the five-year "cooling-off" period initially prescribed by Section 5 would be sufficient "to permit dissipation of the long-established political atmosphere and tradition of discrimination in voting because of color" that existed in the covered jurisdictions.[14] The reality, however, proved to be far different.

In 1970, Congress extended Section 5 for another five years. Lester Maddox, who was then the governor of Georgia, probably had as much to do with the extension as anybody. He testified before the Senate in 1969 and railed against the Voting Rights Act, saying it "is illegal, unconstitutional and ungodly and un-American and wrong against the good people in this country . . . And phooey on anything that says otherwise."[15] After listening to Maddox, Congress concluded that extension was "essential . . . in order to safeguard the gains in Negro voter registration thus far achieved, and to prevent future infringements of voting rights based on race or color."[16]

The U.S. attorney general sued the State of Georgia in 1972 for failing to implement a new legislative reapportionment to replace a plan that had been objected to under Section 5. The state argued that Section 5 was not applicable to its plan, but if so, the statute was now unconstitutional. The Supreme Court disagreed and held that "for the reasons stated at length in *South Carolina v. Katzenbach* . . . we reaffirm that the Act is a permissible exercise of congressional power under § 2 of the Fifteenth Amendment."[17]

In 1975, nearly two years after Bull Connor's death, Congress extended Section 5 for seven more years. It again concluded that progress under the act "has been modest and spotty in so far as the continuing and significant deficiencies yet existing in minority registration and political participation." The Senate report noted "[t]his past experience [of evading Section 5] ought not to be ignored in terms of assessing the future need for the Act." It was "imperative," the report said, that Section 5 protection apply to the redistricting that would take place after the 1980 census.[18]

After the 1975 extension, the city of Rome, Georgia, argued that Section 5 violated principles of federalism, or states' rights, and that even if the preclearance requirements were constitutional when enacted in 1965, "they had outlived their usefulness by 1975."[19] The Court rejected the federalism argument, noting that the Fourteenth and Fifteenth Amendments "were specifically designed as an expansion of federal power and an intrusion on state sovereignty." As for the argument that Section 5 had outlived its usefulness, the Court concluded that "Congress' considered determination that at least another 7 years of statutory remedies were necessary to counter the perpetuation of 95 years of pervasive voting discrimination is both unsurprising and unassailable."[20]

In 1982, Congress again extended Section 5, this time for twenty-five additional years. In doing so, it took seriously the testimony of C. Vann Woodward, the dean of southern historians. He said in view of the aggravated history of black disfranchisement in the South:

> it [is] reasonable . . . to warn that a weakening of that act, especially the preclearance clause, will open the door to a rush of measures to abridge, diminish, and dilute if not emasculate the power of the black vote in southern states. Previous testimony before your committee has shown how persistent and effective such efforts have been even with the preclearance law in effect. Remove that law and the permissiveness will likely become irresistible – in spite of promises to the contrary.[21]

Bull Connor had been dead for nearly eight years when Van Woodward testified, but he was under no illusion that every threat or danger to the black vote had died with Connor. Nor was the Congress. As the Senate report concluded:

> There is virtual unanimity among those who have studied the record that Section 5 preclearance should be extended. . . . Continued progress toward equal opportunity in the electoral process will be halted if we abandon the Act's crucial safeguards now. . . . Without the preclearance of new laws, many of the advances of the past decade could be wiped out overnight with new schemes and devices.[22]

After the 1982 extension, Sumter County, South Carolina, filed yet another challenge to the constitutionality of the statute. It contended the 1982 extension was unconstitutional because the coverage formula, known as the "Section 5 trigger," was outdated. The county pointed out that as of May 28, 1982, more than half of the age eligible population in South Carolina and Sumter County was registered, facts it said "distinguish the 1982 extension as applied to them from the circumstances relied upon in *South Carolina v. Katzenbach, supra,* to uphold the 1965 Act."[23] The three-judge court rejected the argument, noting that Section 5 "had a much larger purpose than to increase voter registration in a county like Sumter to more than 50 percent."[24] In support of its conclusion, the court noted that "Congress held hearings, produced extensive reports, and held lengthy debates before deciding to extend the Act in 1982."[25]

Monterey County, one of five counties in California covered by Section 5, also challenged the constitutionality of the statute's "federalism costs." The Supreme Court rejected the challenge and held that Section 5 was constitutional even if it "intrudes into legislative spheres of autonomy previously reserved to the States."[26]

THE 2006 EXTENSION OF SECTION 5:
THE LEGISLATIVE HISTORY

Congress passed the 2006 extension and amendments of the Voting Rights Act by a vote of 390-33 in the House and by a unanimous vote in the Senate. It held a total of twenty-one hearings, heard from more than eighty witnesses, and compiled a comprehensive record of more than sixteen thousand pages of evidence. The legislative history strongly supports Congress's considered finding that "vestiges of discrimination in voting continue to exist as demonstrated by second generation barriers constructed to prevent minority voters from fully participating in the electoral process."[27]

One of the most sobering facts to emerge from the congressional record is the continuing presence of racially polarized voting. As Congress concluded, "[t]he continued evidence of racially polarized voting in each of the jurisdictions covered by the expiring provisions of the Voting Rights Act of 1965 demonstrates that racial and language minorities remain politically vulnerable, warranting the continued protection of the Voting Rights Act."[28]

South Carolina was one of many examples relied upon by Congress of continuing racially polarized voting in the covered jurisdictions. A three-judge federal court concluded in 1992 "that since 1984 there is evidence of racially polarized voting in South Carolina."[29] A subsequent three-judge court held in 1996 that "[i]n South Carolina, voting has been, and still is, polarized by race. This voting pattern is general throughout the state."[30] Still another three-judge court made similar findings in 2002 that racially polarized voting:

> has seen little change in the last decade. Voting in South Carolina continues to be racially polarized to a very high degree, in all regions of the state and in both primary and general elections. Statewide, black citizens generally are a highly politically cohesive group and whites engage in significant white bloc-voting.[31]

The federal judges who wrote that opinion were all South Carolinians. William Traxler was born and raised in Greenville. Matthew Perry practiced law in Columbia for many years before going on the bench, and Joe Anderson was from Edgefield, the home of Benjamin "Pitchfork Ben" Tillman and Strom Thurmond, among others. It may not have been pleasant for them to write about their state as they did, but what they had to say is far more reliable than the claims often made by the casual or uninformed observer that race no longer matters.

Abigail Thernstrom, a Senior Fellow at the Manhattan Institute in New York and who testified before the Senate in opposition to the extension and amendment of the Voting Rights Act in May 2006, wrote several years ago that Charleston "was not a stereotypical southern racist city. To begin with, it had the advantage of being located in South Carolina," which had "an unusual commitment to law and orderly change, stemming perhaps from an aristocratic respect for civility." The state could not be "lumped with . . . the vulgarities and crudities of Mississippi and Alabama." In Charleston, "[a] sense of community and a tolerance of diversity seem to have gone hand-in-hand."[32] But that is not what Judge Patrick Duffy, a Charleston native who attended The Citadel, had to say when he wrote an opinion in 2003 invalidating at-large elections for the Charleston County Council.

According to Duffy, "voting in Charleston County Council elections is severely and characteristically polarized along racial lines." In
addition, "African Americans in Charleston County, on account of their
race, have inherited a depressed socioeconomic posture which hinders
political participation and exacerbates the effect of already severely polarized voting." "The on-going racial separation that exists in Charleston County – socially, economically, religiously, in housing and business
patterns – makes it especially difficult for African-American candidates
seeking county-wide office to reach out to and communicate with the
predominantly white electorate." There was also "significant evidence
of intimidation and harassment" of blacks "at the polls during the 1980s
and 1990s and even as late as the 2000 general election." There were
also "incidents of subtle or overt racial appeals" in campaigns, such as
white candidates distributing darkened photos of their black opponents
to call attention to their race.[33] The court of appeals unanimously affirmed Judge Duffy's opinion.[34] Judicial findings of this sort by the federal courts, as Congress concluded, strongly underscore the continued
need for Section 5.[35] And what the South Carolina legislature did *after*
the decision even further underscores the need for Section 5.

Despite its alleged aristocratic respect for civility and tolerance of
diversity, the legislature, at the urging of the white members of the Charleston County legislation delegation, adopted for the county board of
education the identical method of at-large elections that had just been
invalidated by Judge Duffy for the county council as diluting black voting strength. There is little doubt that is the reason white officials thought
it was such a good method of elections.

Under the existing system, school board elections were nonpartisan,
multiseat contests decided by plurality vote, which allowed minority
voters the opportunity to "single-shot vote," or concentrate their votes
on one or two candidates and elect them to office. That possibility would
have been effectively eliminated under the proposed new partisan system adopted by the state legislature.

In denying Section 5 preclearance to the county's submission, the
Department of Justice concluded that "[t]he proposed change would
significantly impair the present ability of minority voters to elect candi-

dates of choice to the school board and to participate fully in the political process." The department noted further:

> every black member of the Charleston County delegation voted against the proposed change, some specifically citing the retrogressive nature of the change. Our investigation also reveals that the retrogressive nature of this change is not only recognized by black members of the delegation, but is recognized by other citizens in Charleston County, both elected and unelected.[36]

Section 5 thus prevented the state from implementing a new and retrogressive voting practice, one which everyone understood was adopted to dilute black voting strength and ensure white control of the school board.[37]

In extending Section 5, Congress relied on "the hundreds of objections" made to voting changes submitted by covered jurisdictions since the last extension of the statute in 1982.[38] Section 5 objections, requests for more information that resulted in the withdrawal of voting changes from consideration, and Section 5 enforcement actions have blocked implementation of an extraordinary array of devices that would have diluted minority voting strength. Recent voting changes blocked by the statute include state restrictions on registration and voting, discriminatory annexations, voter purges, adoption of at-large elections, bilingual election procedures, high school diploma requirements for holding office, consolidations, anti–single shot provisions, majority vote requirements, re-registration procedures, redistricting, numbered post requirements, abolition of elected offices, residency requirements, staggered terms, de-annexations, elimination or relocation of polling places, and dual registration requirements.[39]

Other voting practices from jurisdictions covered in whole or in part by Section 5 identified in the House and Senate hearings that have had the purpose or effect of discriminating against minority voters include challenges by white voters or elected officials to majority-minority districts;[40] pairing black incumbents in redistricting plans;[41] refusing to draw majority-minority districts;[42] refusing to appoint blacks to public office;[43] maintaining a racially exclusive sole commissioner form of county government;[44] refusing to designate satellite voter registration sites in the minority community;[45] refusing to accept "bundled" mail-in voter registration forms;[46] refusing to allow registration at county offices;[47] refusing to comply with Section 5 or Section 5 objections;[48] transferring duties to an appointed administrator following the election of blacks to office;[49] white opposition to restoring elections in a majority-black town;[50] prohibiting "for sale" and other yard signs in a predominantly white municipality;[51] disqualifying black elected officials from holding office or participating in decision making;[52] refusing to hold elections following a Section 5 objection;[53] maintaining an all-white self-perpetuating board of education;[54] challenges to the constitutionality of the National Voter Registration Act of 1993;[55] failure to provide bilingual ballots and assistance in voting;[56] county governance by state legislative delegations;[57] packing minority voters to dilute their influence;[58] and using discriminatory punch card voting systems.[59] Congress concluded the need for Section 5 was further evident from "the continued filing of section 2 cases that originated in covered jurisdictions," efforts by the Department of Justice to implement the minority language provisions of the act, and "the tens of thousands of Federal observers that have been dispatched to observe elections in covered jurisdictions."[60]

One objection made by the Department of Justice after the extension of Section 5 involved the state of Georgia. Prior to the 2009 election, Georgia adopted a new voter verification program that matched information provided by an applicant for voter registration with information maintained by the state's Department of Driver Services and the Social Security Administration. As of March 2009, nearly 200,000 individuals were flagged as "non-match based on any criteria," while 7,007 individuals were flagged as potential noncitizens who were required to take further, inconvenient steps to be considered registered voters. The racial impact of the new system was also significant. African Americans voters were 60 percent more likely to be flagged than were whites, while Hispanics and Asians were more than twice as likely to appear on the list as were whites. Even though the voter verification program was a change in voting, the state failed to submit it for preclearance under Section 5.

A Hispanic voter who had been flagged as a noncitizen, even though he had been naturalized, filed suit challenging the state's failure to pre-clear its new matching system. On October 27, 2008, a three-judge court ruled that Georgia was required under Section 5 to submit its voter verification program for preclearance before it could be fully implemented.[61] Following the decision, the state submitted its system to the attorney general, who issued an objection, concluding that "[t]his flawed system frequently subjects a disproportionate number of African-American, Asian, and/or Hispanic voters to additional and, more importantly, erroneous burdens on the right to register to vote. These burdens are real, are substantial, and are retrogressive for minority voters. As such, an objection based upon the state's failure to establish the absence of a discriminatory effect is warranted."[62] In light of the objection the state revised its verification process and the new version was precleared by the attorney general.[63]

Another recent Section 5 objection from Georgia involved Randolph County. Shortly before the 2006 election for the school board, local white election officials moved a black incumbent, Henry Cook, out of the majority-black district from which he was elected and put him in a majority (70 percent)-white district. They did so even though neither Cook's residence nor the district lines had been changed and even though Cook's residence had previously been determined by a state superior court judge to be in the majority-black district. Even though moving Cook was a change in voting, the county refused to submit it for preclearance. The ACLU filed suit on behalf of black voters, and a three-judge court enjoined use of the change absent compliance with Section 5.[64] The county made a submission, and on September 12, 2006, the attorney general objected. Citing the "highly unusual" sequence of events surrounding the change and "the history of discrimination in voting in the County," he concluded that the county had not "sustained its burden that the submitted change lacks a discriminatory purpose."[65] As is apparent, and despite the death of Bull Connor, covered jurisdictions remain willing to enact and implement voting changes that suppress minority registration, voting, and political participation.

REASONS FOR THE REDUCTION IN SECTION 5 OBJECTIONS

The reduction in the number of Section 5 objections in recent years does not suggest or mean, as some have argued, that there is no longer a need for preclearance. First, Section 5 has a strong deterrent effect. A recent example of that involves congressional redistricting in Georgia carried out by Republicans in 2005 once they gained control of the house, senate, and governor's office.

The legislature passed resolutions that any redistricting had to be done in conformity with Section 5 and avoid retrogression. And the plan the legislature adopted in 2005 did exactly that.[66] The black percentages in the majority-black districts (represented by John Lewis and Cynthia McKinney), as well as the black percentages in the majority-white coalition districts that had elected blacks (David Scott and Sanford Bishop) were kept at almost exactly the same levels as under the plan passed by the Democrats in 2002. One can only conclude that the legislature was determined it would not have a Section 5 retrogression dispute on its hands after it passed the 2005 plan. Thus, even in the absence of an objection from the Department of Justice, Section 5 played an important role in the redistricting process.

Second, some of the changes that were precleared by the Department of Justice should have been objected to. In 2005, the Georgia legislature, in a vote sharply divided on racial and partisan lines, passed a new voter identification bill that had the dubious distinction of being one of the most restrictive in the United States. To vote in person – but not by absentee ballot – a voter would have to present one of six specified forms of photo ID. Those without such an ID would have to purchase one for $20. Not only are there laws on the books that make voter fraud a crime, but there was no evidence of fraudulent in-person voting in Georgia to justify the stringent photo ID requirement.[67] The new requirement would also have an adverse impact upon minorities, the elderly, the disabled, and the poor, who were disproportionately unlikely to have the required photo ID.

Representative Sue Burmeister, one of the sponsors of the photo ID bill, was quoted in a memo released by the Department of Justice as saying if black people in her district "are not paid to vote, they don't go to the polls."[68] She added that if fewer blacks vote as a result of the photo ID bill it is only because it would end voter fraud.

Georgia submitted its new photo ID bill for preclearance under Section 5, and the Department of Justice approved it, despite the near-unanimous recommendation by the career staff to object. The staff recommendation concluded that "the state has failed to meet its burden of proof to demonstrate that [the photo ID bill] does not have the effect of retrogressing minority voting strength."[69]

Joseph Rich, who served as chief of the Voting Section from 1999 to 2005, testified before a congressional committee that the failure to object to the Georgia photo ID bill was "the brazen insertion of partisan politics into the decision-making under Section 5."[70] Rich's comments were echoed by Bob Kengle, a lawyer who spent twenty years in the Civil Rights Division and served as deputy chief of the Voting Section. He left the section in 2005, he said, after reaching a "personal breaking point" precipitated by "institutional sabotage . . . from political appointees," "partisan favoritism," and the administration's "notorious" Georgia Section 5 decision and its pursuit of "chimerical suspicions of vote fraud."[71]

A challenge to the photo ID law was subsequently filed by a coalition of groups. On October 18, 2005, the federal court preliminarily enjoined its use on the grounds it was in the nature of a poll tax, as well as a likely violation of the equal protection clause.[72] In response to the decision, the state amended its law to provide photo IDs free of charge. Despite its grant of a preliminary injunction, the district court ultimately dismissed the complaint, concluding that none of the plaintiffs had standing, the state was not required to document that "in-person voter fraud exist[s] in Georgia," the burden the law imposed on voters was not "significant," and the photo ID requirement was "rationally related" to a legitimate state interest.[73] The plaintiffs appealed, but the decision of the district court was affirmed.[74]

The absence of an objection to Georgia's photo ID law doesn't show a lack of need for Section 5. What it shows is the need for better Section 5 enforcement by the Department of Justice.

Third, the decision of the Supreme Court known as *Bossier II* (2000) has had the effect of allowing preclearance of changes that would no doubt have been objected to under the previous standard. In *Bossier II* the Court held a voting change was not objectionable under Section 5 if it was enacted with "a discriminatory but nonretrogressive purpose."[75] Thus, a voting change adopted purposefully to discriminate against minorities could not be objected to unless it was intended to make minorities worse off than they were under the existing system.

A principal finding of a recent study of Section 5 objections, one of whose authors is an employee of the Voting Section of the Department of Justice, was that "[i]n the 1990s, fully 151 objections (43 percent) were based on purpose alone."[76] Another 108 (31 percent) were based on purpose and some other ground. The intent prong was involved in 74 percent of all objections in that decade. The recent decline in objections is obviously directly tied to the restrictive *Bossier II* standard. In response to the Supreme Court's decision, the 2006 amendments provide that a voting practice violates Section 5 if it was adopted with "any discriminatory purpose."[77]

Fourth, objections aside, Section 5 has a decided, beneficial impact on court-ordered remedies. In its opinion implementing legislative and congressional redistricting in South Carolina in 2003, for example, the three-judge court held that the state must comply with Sections 2 and 5 of the Voting Rights Act. Accordingly, it rejected plans that had been proposed by the governor and the legislature because they were "primarily driven by policy choices designed to effect their particular partisan goals."[78] Those choices included protecting incumbents and assigning the minority population to maximize the parties' respective political opportunities.[79] The plan implemented by the court increased the number of majority-black house districts from twenty-five to twenty-nine, maintained the existing nine majority black senate districts, and maintained the sixth congressional district as majority-black.

ONGOING ATTEMPTS TO MANIPULATE
THE ELECTORAL PROCESS

The temptation to manipulate the law in ways that will disadvantage minority voters is as great and irresistible today as it was in 1982. Congress concluded that the record it compiled in 2005–2006 "demonstrates that, without the continuation of the Voting Rights Act of 1965 protections, racial and language minority citizens will be deprived of the opportunity to exercise their right to vote, or will have their votes diluted, undermining the significant gains made by minorities in the last 40 years."[80] The brief filed in the Supreme Court by the State of Georgia in a Section 5 preclearance action, *Georgia v. Ashcroft* (2003), and which is discussed in the legislative history, provides a vivid present-day example of the willingness of one of the states covered by Section 5 to manipulate the law to diminish the protections afforded racial minorities.[81]

One of the state's principal arguments was that the retrogression standard of Section 5 should be abolished in favor of a coin toss, or an "equal opportunity" to elect, standard, which it defined as "a 50-50 chance of electing a candidate of choice."[82] The Supreme Court rejected the state's invitation to rewrite Section 5 and held that "Georgia must prove that its plan is nonretrogressive under §5."[83]

The state argued further that "the point of equal opportunity is 44.3% BVAP [black voting age population]."[84] The adoption of Georgia's standard for an equal opportunity election would have permitted the state to abolish *all* of its majority-black districts.

Georgia is not the only covered state to make such arguments. The governor of South Carolina argued in a post-2000 census case involving court-ordered redistricting that a BVAP as low as 45.58 percent was the "point of equal opportunity" and was all the Voting Rights Act required in the way of protecting the rights of minority voters.[85] The three-judge court rejected that argument and concluded "a majority-minority or very near majority-minority voting age population in each district remains a minimum requirement" in order to satisfy the requirements of the Voting Rights Act.[86]

Majority-minority districts have been central to equal political participation by minority voters. Throughout the 1970s and 1980s, only about 1 percent of majority-white districts in the South elected a black to a state legislature. Blacks who were elected were overwhelmingly from majority-black districts.[87] As late as 1988, no black had ever been elected from a majority-white district in Alabama, Arkansas, Louisiana, Mississippi, or South Carolina.[88] The number of blacks elected to state legislatures increased after the 1990 redistricting, but again the gain resulted from an increase in the number of majority-black districts.[89]

In Georgia, of the forty-seven blacks elected to the state legislature in 2002, forty-four (94 percent) were elected from majority-black districts. Of the three elected from majority-white districts, two were incumbents and the third was elected from a multimember three-seat house district.[90]

The pattern of minority officeholding principally in majority-black districts exists at the city and county levels in Georgia as well. A survey conducted in 1989–90 of cities and counties in the state concluded that:

> The increase in black officeholding can in large measure be traced directly to the gradual demise of at-large elections and the implementation of single-member districts containing effective black voting majorities. These changes were neither self-executing nor voluntary, but were coerced through a combination of congressional legislation, favorable judicial decisions, the enforcement of the preclearance requirement, favorable judicial decisions, and litigation efforts of the civil rights and minority communities.[91]

A similar pattern exists in other covered states. Alabama, for example, currently has no officials, including the governor, elected statewide who are black.[92] Almost all black elected officials in the state were elected from majority-black counties, municipalities, or districts. And most of the majority-black districts had to be ordered by federal courts.[93] James Fields, whose election is highlighted by Thernstrom, is in fact the only black legislator in the state elected from a district with a clear white voter majority.[94]

Prior to the 1996 elections, the only black in the twentieth century to win a seat in Congress from a majority-white district in the states of Virginia, North Carolina, South Carolina, Georgia, Florida, Alabama, Mississippi, Louisiana, or Texas was Andrew Young. He was elected in 1972 from the Fifth District in metropolitan Atlanta, in which blacks were 44 percent of the population.[95] In 1990, after serving in Congress, being ambassador to the United Nations, and being elected mayor of Atlanta, Young ran for governor of Georgia. He made it into the runoff in the Democratic primary, but running statewide, where blacks were just 27 percent of the population, he was defeated by a cohesive white majority.[96] Even for a candidate with Young's experience and qualifications, racial bloc voting was still a decisive factor.

The most notable exception to the pattern of blacks losing in majority-white districts in Georgia have been judicial elections. Judicial elections, however, are unusual in that they are subject to considerable control by the bar and the political leadership of the state. Candidates are essentially preselected through appointment by the governor to vacant positions upon the recommendation of a judicial nominating committee dominated by the bar. The chosen candidate then runs in the ensuing election with the advantages of incumbency and typically with no opposition. Judicial elections are low-key, low-interest contests in which voters tend to defer to the choices that have previously been made.[97]

Given the continuing levels of white bloc voting identified by the three-judge court in *Georgia v. Ashcroft*,[98] white candidates are prohibitive favorites to win in most majority-white legislative districts in Georgia, and indeed throughout the South. Abolishing majority-black districts, or providing black voters an opportunity to elect candidates of their choice only in districts with reduced black populations that provide a 50-50 chance of losing, would have caused a significant reduction in the number of black officeholders. The state's advocacy of such positions, and its attempt to implement them, were compelling reasons for extending Section 5.

Georgia further demonstrated its disregard for minority voting rights by arguing in *Georgia v. Ashcroft* that minorities should be excluded from the preclearance process. According to the state, "[n]ot a word in the Voting Rights Act hints that private citizens possess a right to intervene and arrogate to themselves the enormous responsibilities and power of the Attorney General."[99] The state's argument was audacious at the least, for it was directly contrary to decisions of the Court recognizing a private cause of action to enforce Section 5,[100] as well as subsequent acts of Congress making the right of a private cause of action to enforce the Voting Rights Act explicit.[101] The Supreme Court rejected the state's argument, holding that "[p]rivate parties may intervene in §5 actions."[102]

CHALLENGES TO THE 2006 EXTENSION OF SECTION 5

Within days of the president's signing into law the 2006 extension of Section 5, and to no one's surprise, a municipal utility district in Austin, Texas, filed suit claiming that it was entitled to bailout from Section 5, and if not that Section 5 was now unconstitutional. The district was established in the late 1980s and provides infrastructure, waste and wastewater services, and other local services to its approximately 3,500 residents. It is governed by a five-member board elected by residents of the district.

Section 4(a) of the Voting Rights Act allows a jurisdiction that had a clean voting rights record during the preceding ten years, and has engaged in constructive efforts to promote full voter participation, to bail out from Section 5 coverage.[103] The three-judge court held that the district was not entitled to bail out because it did not meet the definition of a "political subdivision" in §14(c)(2) of the act, which includes only counties, parishes, and other subdivisions that conduct registration for voting.[104] The utility district was neither a county nor a parish, while voter registration for district elections was conducted by Travis County. This interpretation of the bailout provision had been consistently applied by the Department of Justice and endorsed by Congress in the legislative history of the 1982 extension of Section 5.[105]

The utility district's arguments that Section 5 was unconstitutional were similar to those raised by plaintiffs in the prior challenges – that the statute imposed "disproportionate burdens and [was] a badge of shame on covered jurisdictions [based] on an ancient formula and conditions that existed thirty or more years ago but have long since been remedied."[106] In rejecting these arguments, the three-judge court applied the Fifteenth Amendment standard used in *South Carolina v. Katzenbach* and concluded that "given the extensive legislative record documenting contemporary racial discrimination in covered jurisdictions, Congress's decision to extend section 5 for another twenty-five years was rational and therefore constitutional." In the alternative, it held that applying the Fourteenth Amendment standard set forth in *City of Boerne v. Flores*,[107] "[g]iven Section 5's tailored remedial scheme, the extension qualifies as a congruent and proportional response to the continuing problem of racial discrimination in voting."[108]

The three-judge court found that the argument that Section 5 was overinclusive was addressed by the bailout provision. It also held that the argument that the statute was underinclusive was addressed by the fact that a court that found a constitutional violation of voting rights could "bail-in" a noncovered jurisdiction under Section 5. The court further concluded that the utility district's burden of complying with Section 5 was "trivial."[109] The cost of compliance to the district was, on average, only $233 a year, while there was no evidence the district had ever decided not to pursue a voting change because of Section 5.

The utility district appealed directly to the Supreme Court, which noted probable jurisdiction. In its brief in opposition to the motions to affirm filed by the solicitor general and the intervenors, the district argued that the intervening election of Barack Obama as the nation's first African American president reflects a "deep-rooted societal change" that undermines the continued need for Section 5.[110] There is no question that Obama's election reflects an enormous advance in race relations in the United States. Few would have thought when the Voting Rights Act was passed in 1965 that a black person could win the nation's highest office in the foreseeable future. But an examination of the election results shows that voting, particularly in the southern states covered by Section 5, remains significantly polarized along racial lines.

Of the nine southern states covered in whole or in part by Section 5, six went for McCain – Alabama, Georgia, Louisiana, Mississippi, South Carolina, and Texas.[111] According to exit poll data, the average white vote for Obama in these states was only 18 percent. And in some of the states, the white vote for the Democratic candidate declined compared to the 2004 presidential election. John Kerry got 19 percent of the white vote in Alabama in 2004, while Obama got just 10 percent in 2008. In Louisiana, Kerry got 24 percent of the white vote in 2004, while Obama got only 14 percent in 2008. In Mississippi, Kerry got 14 percent of the white vote, Obama 11 percent.[112]

Obama's election can be attributed to the increase in the minority vote and increased white support in the noncovered jurisdictions, rather than changes in white voting patterns in the covered jurisdictions. Blacks were 11 percent of voters in the 2004 election, and increased to 13 percent in the 2008 election. In addition, while 88 percent of blacks voted for Kerry in 2004, 95 percent voted for Obama in 2008. Nationwide, the white vote for Obama was 43 percent, compared to 41 percent for Kerry. However, in sixteen non-southern states and the District of Columbia, Obama received an absolute majority of the white votes. It was the increased turnout of blacks and the increase in white support outside of the South that produced victory for Obama in 2008, and not the diminution of racial bloc voting in covered jurisdictions.[113]

Progress has been made in minority political participation, much of it attributable to the Voting Rights Act's ban on discriminatory tests or devices for voting and the federal oversight of voting changes in the covered jurisdictions. But nothing in the 2008 election casts doubt on Congress's considered judgment that racially polarized voting shows that racial minorities remain politically vulnerable, warranting the continued protection of Section 5.

The 2009 election for mayor of Atlanta, a city which regards itself as one of the most racially progressive in the South, is a further example of the continuing presence of racially polarized voting in the covered jurisdictions. A white candidate – Mary Norwood – faced a black candidate – Kasim Reed – in a runoff election. In an analysis of city election districts, the *Atlanta Journal-Constitution* concluded that "there was nothing post-racial about" the runoff. "Tuesday's election shows votes were cast sharply along racial lines."[114] Only about 15.6 percent of Reed's votes came from predominantly white districts, while Norwood got only 14.5 percent of the votes from predominantly black districts. Alton Hornsby, Jr., a history professor at Morehouse College who has written on race and politics in Atlanta, said the Reed-Norwood runoff showed that "Obama's election last year was more of a fluke than any indication we are getting closer to post-racialism." Michael Owens, a political science professor at Emory, concurred that "[t]he lid has been lifted off the truth that was already there."[115]

The Supreme Court heard oral argument in the Austin utility district's case on April 29, 2009, and based upon comments by individual justices, it appeared the Court was evenly divided on the issue of Section 5's constitutionality, with Justice Kennedy being the deciding vote. The Court issued its much-anticipated ruling on June 22, 2009, and in a 8-1 opinion written by Chief Justice Roberts, it declined to decide the issue of the constitutionality of Section 5. Instead, it held that the utility district was in fact eligible to bail out from Section 5 coverage, and as a consequence the Court would "avoid the unnecessary resolution of constitutional questions" involving Section 5.[116]

Despite the prior limitations on bailout, the Supreme Court held that "the structure of the Voting Rights Act, and underlying constitutional concerns compel a broader reading of the bailout provision."[117]

As a consequence, it held that the definition of "political subdivision" in §14(c)(2) of the act applied to political units in noncovered states that could be separately designated for coverage, but did not define jurisdictions entitled to bailout from Section 5. Accordingly, "all political subdivisions – not only those described in §14(c)(2) – are eligible to file a bailout suit."[118]

The majority opinion raised questions about the "current burdens" imposed by the act and whether they were "justified by current needs," and whether the "statute's disparate geographic coverage is sufficiently related to the problem that it targets." But it also underscored the vital role the act has played in American politics: "The historic accomplishments of the Voting Rights Act are undeniable," and the improvements in minority political participation "are no doubt due in significant part to the Voting Rights Act itself, and stand as a monument to its success."[119] It also acknowledged that "Congress amassed a sizable record in support of its decision to extend the preclearance requirement," and that "it may be . . . conditions continue to warrant preclearance under the Act."[120]

The meaning of the Court's decision has been the subject of much discussion, but the most likely explanation is that there were not five votes to strike down one of the most important and effective civil rights acts in our nation's history. In any event, Section 5 remains in full force and effect, while its resistance to further constitutional challenges has been strengthened by the fact that the argument that it unfairly burdens covered jurisdictions has been significantly weakened. If any jurisdiction has a clean voting rights record and no longer needs to be covered by Section 5, it can bail out. If it remains covered, it would be a consequence of its own decision not to seek bailout, or because it does not have a clean voting rights record. Continuing coverage under either scenario does nothing to suggest Section 5 is an unconstitutional burden or that geographic coverage is unrelated to the problem that it targets.

Following remand, the utility district, the United States, and the interveners filed a proposed consent decree allowing the utility district to bail out from Section 5 coverage. The consent decree was approved by the three-judge court on November 3, 2009, and the claim challenging the constitutionality of Section 5 was dismissed without prejudice.

A month later, a federal court in South Dakota dismissed yet another challenge to the constitutionality of Section 5. The state argued
that the statute as applied to Shannon County, one of two covered counties in the state, was now outdated and that Shannon County was experiencing high voter registration rates and above national average voter
turnout rates. In rejecting these arguments, the court relied upon prior
Supreme Court decisions upholding the constitutionality of Section 5
and concluded that "South Dakota's history of discriminating against
Native Americans and the risk that such discrimination will increase
in the absence of the preclearance requirement set forth in Section 5
of the Voting Rights Act compels the court to reject state defendants'
argument that Section 5 of the Voting Rights Act is unconstitutional as
applied to Shannon County."[121]

Challenges to the constitutionality of Section 5, however, are ongoing. Six have been filed so far in the district court for the District of
Columbia following the dismissal of the utility district's case. Two were
dismissed as moot,[122] another was dismissed on the merits and is on appeal,[123] and three others are pending in the District of Columbia court.[124]
One of these cases may make its way to the Supreme Court, and if so the
Court may finally resolve the issue of the constitutionality of Section 5
as extended in 2006.

SECTION 5 PROMOTES RACIAL INTEGRATION

Much of Abigail Thernstrom's criticism of Section 5 in the following
section is based on the way the statute was applied by the Department
of Justice during redistricting in the 1990s. In *Shaw v. Reno*, the Court
held that a congressional redistricting plan adopted by North Carolina
in 1991, even though it was precleared by the attorney general under
Section 5, was "so bizarre on its face that it is 'unexplainable on grounds
other than race,'" and was presumptively unconstitutional.[125] In *Miller v.
Johnson*, the Court subsequently found unconstitutional a congressional
redistricting plan enacted by Georgia in 1992, which had been precleared
by the Department of Justice after two earlier plans had been rejected,
because "race was the predominant factor motivating the drawing of the

do with racial discrimination." The Court held that "[t]hese arguments . . . are largely beside the point," and that the trigger was not a mathematical formula but was designed "to describe these areas . . . relevant to the problem of voting discrimination." 383 U.S. at 329.

26. *Lopez v. Monterey County,* 525 U.S. 266, 282–83 (1999).

27. 120 Stat. 577, sec. 2(b)(2).

28. Id. at sec. 2(b)(3).

29. *Burton v. Sheheen,* 793 F. Supp. 1329, 1357–58 (D. S.C. 1992).

30. *Smith v. Beasley,* 946 F. Supp. 1174, 1202 (D. S.C. 1996).

31. *Colleton County Council v. McConnell,* 201 F. Supp. 2d 618, 641 (D. S.C. 2002).

32. Abigail M. Thernstrom, *Whose Votes Count? Affirmative Action and Minority Voting Rights* (Cambridge, Mass.: Harvard University Press, 1987), pp. 166–67. A special "shared" racial intimacy, according to Thernstrom, could be seen at the grocery store where "there would be a black lady and a white lady picking out okra, and they never let things interfere with good manners on either side." Id. at 282 n. 34 (interview with Marybelle Howe).

33. *Moultrie v. Charleston County Council,* 316 F. Supp. 2d 268, 278, 286 n. 23, 291, 294–95, 304 (D. S.C. 2003).

34. *Moultrie v. Charleston County Council,* 365 F.3d 341, 350 (4th Cir. 2004).

35. The evidence of continued discrimination relied upon by Congress included "the section 2 litigation filed to prevent dilutive techniques from adversely affecting minority voters." 120 Stat. 578, sec. 2(b)(8).

36. R. Alexander Acosta, assistant U.S. attorney general, to C. Havird Jones, Jr., South Carolina assistant attorney general, February 26, 2004.

37. For a discussion of South Carolina cases in the legislative history, see *Voting Rights Act: Evidence of Continued Need, Hearing before the Subcommittee on the Constitution of the Committee on the*

Judiciary, House of Representatives, 109th Congress, 2nd sess., March 8, 2006, Serial No. 109-103, Volume I, Appendix to the Statement of Nadine Strossen, "Vote: The Case for Extending and Amending the Voting Rights Act, Voting Rights Litigation, 1982–2006," a report of the Voting Rights Project of the American Civil Liberties Union, at 964–1065 (hereafter "House Hearing, March 8, 2006, Volume I, Appendix").

38. 120 Stat. 577, sec. 2(b)(4)(A).

39. House Hearing, October 25, 2005, Volume I at 104–224 (list of Section 5 objections through October 17, 2005).

40. Coca, Florida, 1994; Georgia congressional, house, and senate redistricting, 1990; Georgetown County, South Carolina, 1983; Louisiana congressional redistricting, 1994; North Carolina congressional redistricting, 1991–2001; Perry County, Mississippi, 1993; Putnam County, Georgia, 1997; South Carolina house and senate redistricting, 1996; South Carolina congressional redistricting, 1996 and 1998; St. Francisville, Louisiana, 1995; Telfair County, Georgia, 1986; Union County, South Carolina, 2002; Virginia congressional redistricting, 1995; South Dakota redistricting, 1996. House Hearing, March 8, 2006, Volume I, Appendix at 477–81, 783–88, 831–33, 883–84, 891–94, 908–11, 915–19, 974–76, 1020–21, 1061–63, 1093–95, 1153–58.

41. West Palm Beach, Florida, 1990. House Hearing, March 8, 2006, Volume I, Appendix at 500–1.

42. Bossier Parish, Louisiana, 1992; Georgia congressional redistricting, 1982. House Hearing, March 8, 2006, Volume I, Appendix at 504–8, 888–89.

43. Ben Hill County, Georgia, 1988; Johnson County, Georgia, 1983. House Hearing, March 8, 2006, Volume I, Appendix at 535–40, 729–31.

44. Bleckley County, Georgia, 1985; Wheeler County, Georgia, 1993. House

Hearing, March 8, 2006, Volume I, Appendix at 543–44, 549.

45. Columbus/Muscogee County, Georgia, 1984. House Hearing, March 8, 2006, Volume I, Appendix at 767–69.

46. Georgia, 2004. House Hearing, March 8, 2006, Volume I, Appendix at 558–62.

47. Fulton County, Georgia, 1986. House Hearing, March 8, 2006, Volume I, Appendix at 37.

48. Georgia judicial elections, 1989; Charlton County, Georgia, 1985; Georgia soil and water conservation elections, 2004; Douglasville, Georgia, 1996; Greene County, Georgia, 1985; Rochelle, Georgia, 1984; Louisiana, 1995; South Dakota, 1976–2002. House Hearing, March 8, 2006, Volume I, Appendix at 564–72, 573–76, 648–52, 692–94, 708–9, 871–72.

49. Kingston, Georgia, 1987. House Hearing, March 8, 2006, Volume I, Appendix at 600.

50. Keysville, Georgia, 1990. House Hearing, March 8, 2006, Volume I, Appendix at 622–23.

51. Avondale Estates, Georgia, 2000. House Hearing, March 8, 2006, Volume I, Appendix at 679–80.

52. Thomaston, Georgia, 1986; Beaufort County, South Carolina, 1983. House Hearing, March 8, 2006, Volume I, Appendix at 862–63, 989–90.

53. Butler, Georgia, 1995. House Hearing, March 8, 2006, Volume I, Appendix at 830.

54. Thomaston, Georgia, 1981. House Hearing, March 8, 2006, Volume I, Appendix at 856.

55. Louisiana, 1995; Virginia, 1995; South Carolina, 1995. House Hearing, March 8, 2006, Volume I, Appendix at 887, 981, 1101–2.

56. Michigan, Buena Vista and Clyde Townships, 1992; Bennett County, South Dakota, 2002. House Hearing, March

8, 2006, Volume I, Appendix at 902–3, 1169–70.

57. South Carolina, 1999. House Hearing, March 8, 2006, Volume I, Appendix at 964–66.

58. Buffalo County, South Dakota, 2003; South Dakota legislative redistricting, 2002. House Hearing, March 8, 2006, Volume I, Appendix at 1155–56, 1171–72.

59. Georgia, 2001; Florida, 2001; California, 2001; Illinois, 2001; Ohio 2002. House Hearing, March 8, 2006, Volume I, Appendix at 1197–1209.

60. 120 Stat. 577, sec. 2(b)(4) and (5). South Dakota, which has two covered counties, Todd and Shannon, has had a particularly egregious history of refusing to comply with Section 5. That history is contained in the legislative history, House Hearing, March 8, 2006, Volume I, Appendix at 1158–61, and is discussed in detail by Bryan Sells in his chapter of this book.

61. *Morales v. Handel,* 1:08-CV-3172 (N.D. Ga.).

62. Loretta King, acting assistant U.S. attorney general, to Thurbert E. Baker, Georgia attorney general, May 29, 2009.

63. T. Christian Herren, Jr., chief of the Voting Section, to Anne W. Lewis, August 18, 2010.

64. *Jenkins v. Ray,* Case No. 4:06-CV-43 (CDL) (M.D. Ga. June 5, 2006).

65. Wan J. Kim, Assistant U.S. Attorney General, to Tommy Coleman, September 12, 2006.

66. HB 499 (2005).

67. The United States Elections Assistance Commission, an independent bipartisan commission created by the Help America Vote Act, issued a report in December 2006 in which it concluded that many of the allegations of voter fraud made in reports and books it analyzed "were not substantiated," even though they were often cited as evidence of fraud. United States Elections Assistance Com-

mission, *Election Crimes: An Initial Review and Recommendations for Future Study* (Washington, D.C.: December 2006), p. 16. Overall, the report found "impersonation of voters is probably the least frequent type of fraud because it is the most likely type of fraud to be discovered, there are stiff penalties associated with this type of fraud, and it is an inefficient method of influencing an election." Id. at 9.

68. "Georgia Voter ID Memo Stirs Tension," *The Oxford Press,* November 18, 2005.

69. Section 5 Recommendation: August 25, 2005, p. 20.

70. Testimony of Joseph D. Rich, Oversight Hearing of the Civil Rights Division, House Judiciary Subcommittee on the Constitution, Civil Rights and Civil Liberties, March 22, 2007.

71. Bob Kengle, "Why I Left the Civil Rights Division."

72. *Common Cause/Georgia v. Billups,* 406 F. Supp. 2d 1326 (N.D. Ga. 2005).

73. *Common Cause/Georgia v. Billups,* 504 F. Supp. 2d 1333, 1377, 1381 (N.D. Ga. 2007).

74. *Common Cause/Georgia v. Billups,* 554 F.3d 1340 (11th Cir. 2009).

75. *Reno v. Bossier Parish School Board,* 528 U.S. 320, 341 (2000).

76. Peyton McCrary, Christopher Seaman, and Richard Valelly, *The End of Preclearance As We Knew It: How the Supreme Court Transformed Section 5 of the Voting Rights Act,* 11 Mich. J. of Race & L. 275, 298 (Spring 2006).

77. 120 Stat. 581, sec. 5 (3)(c).

78. *Colleton County Council v. McConnell,* 201 F. Supp. 2d at 628.

79. Id. at 659.

80. 120 Stat. 578, sec. 2(b)(9).

81. House Hearing, March 8, 2006, Volume I, Appendix at 522–29.

82. *Georgia v. Ashcroft,* 195 F. Supp. 2d 25, 66 (D.D.C. 2002).

83. *Georgia v. Ashcroft,* 539 U.S. 461, 478–79 (2003).

84. *Georgia v. Ashcroft,* 195 F. Supp. 2d at 66.

85. *Colleton County Council v. McConnell,* 201 F. Supp. 2d at 643.

86. Id.

87. Lisa Handley and Bernard Grofman, "The Impact of the Voting Rights Act on Minority Representation: Black Officeholding in Southern State Legislatures and Congressional Delegations," in *Quiet Revolution in the South: The Impact of the Voting Rights Act 1965–1990,* ed. Chandler Davidson and Bernard Grofman, pp. 336–37 (Princeton, N.J.: Princeton University Press, 1994).

88. Id. at 346.

89. David A. Bositis, *Redistricting and Representation: The Creation of Majority-Minority Districts and the Evolving Party System in the South* (Washington, D.C.: Joint Center for Political and Economic Studies, 1995), p. 46.

90. *Voting Rights Act: The Judicial Evolution of the Retrogression Standard,* Hearing before the Subcommittee on the Constitution of the Committee on the Judiciary, House of Representatives, 109th Congress, 1st sess., November 9, 2005 (Serial No. 109-74), at 53 (statement of Laughlin McDonald).

91. Laughlin McDonald, Michael Binford, and Ken Johnson, "Georgia," in *Quiet Revolution in the South; The Impact of the Voting Rights Act, 1965–1990,* ed. Chandler Davidson and Bernard Grofman, p. 90 (Princeton, N.J.: Princeton University Press, 1994).

92. James Blacksher, Edward Still, Nick Quinton, Cullen Brown, and Royal Dumas, *Voting Rights in Alabama: 1982–226,* 17 So. Cal. Rev. Law & Soc. Just. 278 (2008).

93. Id. at 260 et seq.

94. Id. at 278.

95. Michael Barone and Grant Ujifusa, *The Almanac of American Politics* (Boston: Gambit, 1974), p. 232.

96. Michael Binford, "Andrew Young and the 1990 Governor's Contest in Georgia," presented at the Voter Education Project Workshop, "From Protest to Politics," Clark-Atlanta University, 1990.

97. Laughlin McDonald, Michael Binford, and Ken Johnson, "Georgia," in *Quiet Revolution in the South; The Impact of the Voting Rights Act, 1965–1990*, ed. Chandler Davidson and Bernard Grofman, p. 85 (Princeton, N.J.: Princeton University Press, 1994).

98. 195 F. Supp. 2d at 69.

99. Brief of Appellant State of Georgia, p. 41.

100. See *Allen v. State Board of Elections*, 393 U.S. 544, 557 (1969); *Perkins v. Matthews*, 400 U.S. 379, 383 n. 3 (1971).

101. See 1970 USCCAN 3284 ("private persons have authority to challenge the enforcement of changed voting practices and procedures"); 42 USC § 1973a; S. Rep. No. 94-295, 94th Congress, 1st sess. 40 (1975); S. Rep. No. 97-417, at 30; HR Rep. No. 97-227, 97th Congress, 1st sess. 32 (1981).

102. 539 U.S. at 477.

103. 42 USC §§ 1973a and b.

104. 42 USC § 1973(c)(2).

105. 52 Fed. Reg. 486, 490–500 (Jan. 6, 1987); HR Rep. No. 97-227, at 2 (1981); S. Rep. No. 97-417, at 2 (1982).

106. *Northwest Austin Mun. Utility Dist. No. One v. Mukasey*, 573 F. Supp. 2d 221, 235 (D.D.C. 2008).

107. 521 U.S. 507 (1997).

108. *Northwest Austin Mun. Utility Dist. No. One*, 573 F. Supp. 2d at 223–24.

109. Id. at 282.

110. *Northwest Austin Mun. Utility Dist. No. One v. Mukasey*, Appellant's Brief Opposing Motions to Affirm, at 1.

111. "Election Results 2008," *New York Times*, December 9, 2008.

112. The source for the 2004 exit poll data is National Election Pool, Edison Media Research, & Mitofsky International, National Election Pool General Election Exit Polls, 2004, available at http://dx.doi.org/10.3886/ICPSR04181. The source for the 2008 exit poll data is MSNBC, Politics, 2008 Results, Exit Polls, http://www.msnbc.msn.com/id/26843704.

113. MSNBC, Politics, 2008 Results, Exit Polls, http://www.msnbc.msn.com/id/26843704. For further discussion of racial bloc voting in the 2008 election, see Brief for Nathaniel Persily, Stephen Ansolabehere, and Charles Stewart III as Amicus Curiae on Behalf on Neither Party, filed in *Northwest Austin Mun. Utility Dist. No. One v. Holder*, No. 08-322.

114. "Atlanta Mayoral Election: Race a Key Factor," *Atlanta Journal-Constitution*, December 3, 2009.

115. Id.

116. *Northwest Austin Mun. Utility Dist. No. One v. Holder*, 129 S.Ct. 2504, 2508 (2009).

117. Id. at 2514.

118. Id. at 2516.

119. Id. at 2511.

120. Id. at 2511–13.

121. *Janis v. Nelson*, Case 5:09-cv-05019-KES-LLP-RLW (D. S.D., Dec. 30, 2009), slip op. at 21–22.

122. In *Georgia v. Holder*, Civ. No. 10-1062 (D.D.C.), the state sought preclearance of its revised voter verification process or in the alternative a declaration that Section 5 was unconstitutional. The verification process was subsequently precleared by the Department of Justice, rendering the constitutional challenge moot. In *Georgia v. Holder* II, Civ. No. 1:10-CV-1970 (D.D.C.), the state sought preclearance of a proof of citizenship requirement for voter registration, or in the alternative a declaration that Section

5 was now unconstitutional. The change was subsequently precleared by the Department of Justice, mooting the constitutional claim.

123. *Shelby County, Alabama v. Holder,* Civ. No. 1:10-CV-651 (D.D.C. September 21, 2011). In a lengthy 151-page opinion, the district court discounted the "Bull Connor is dead" argument and affirmed the considered judgment of Congress that Section 5 was still needed to safeguard racial and language minority voters.

124. *LaRoque v. Holder,* Civ. No. 1:10-561 (D.D.C.); *Arizona v. Holder,* Civ. No. 11-1559 (D.D.C.); *Georgia v. Holder,* Civ. No. 10-1062 (ESH).

125. 509 U.S. 630, 644 (1993).

126. 515 U.S. 900, 917, 919 (1995).

127. Id. at 943. See also *Johnson v. Miller,* 864 F. Supp. 1354, 1396–97 n. 5 (S.D. Ga. 1994) ("The Max-Black plan did influence to some degree the shape of the ultimate Eleventh District . . . [B]ut the actual Eleventh is *not* identical to the Max-Black plan. The Eleventh, to my eye, is significantly different in shape in many ways.") (Edmondson, J., dissenting).

128. 515 U.S. 900, 923 (1995) (a Department of Justice interpretation of Section 5 that raises a serious constitutional question "should not receive deference").

129. 42 USC § 1973(b).

130. *Easley v. Cromartie,* 532 U.S. 234, 253 (2001). See also *Bush v. Vera,* 517 U.S. 952, 958 (1996) ("[s]trict scrutiny does not apply merely because redistricting is performed with consciousness of race") (O'Connor, J., principal opinion); *Miller,* 515 U.S. at 916 (legislatures "will . . . almost always be aware of racial demographics"); *Shaw,* 509 U.S. at 646 (same); *LULAC v. Perry,* 548 U.S. 399, 475 (2006) ("strict scrutiny does not apply merely because race was one motivating factor behind the drawing of a majority-minority district") (Stevens, J., concurring in part and dissenting in part).

131. *LULAC,* 548 U.S. at 475 (compliance with Section 2 of the Voting Rights Act is "a compelling state interest") (Stevens, J., concurring in part and dissenting in part); *Vera,* 517 U.S. at 994 (same) (O'Connor, J., concurring); *LULAC,* 548 U.S. at 475 n. 12 ("compliance with Section 5 of the Voting Rights is also a compelling state interest") (Stevens, J., concurring in part and dissenting in part); id. at 485 n. 2 (Souter, J., concurring in part and dissenting in part); id. at 518–19 (Scalia, J., concurring in part and dissenting in part); *Shaw,* 509 U.S. at 656 (there is a "significant state interest in eradicating the effects of past racial discrimination"); *Miller,* 515 U.S. at 920 (same).

132. Thernstrom, *Whose Votes Count?,* p. 243.

133. Richard H. Pildes, *The Politics of Race,* 108 Harv. L. Rev. 1359, 1367 (1995).

134. Bositis, *Redistricting and Representation,* p. 28.

135. *Miller,* 515 U.S. at 932 (Stevens, J., dissenting); id. at 944–45 (Ginsburg, J., dissenting).

136. A. Leon Higginbotham, Jr., Gregory A. Clarick, and Marcella David, Shaw v. Reno: *A Mirage of Good Intentions with Devastating Racial Consequences,* 62 Fordham L. Rev. 1593, 1632 (1994).

137. *Voting Rights Act: Hearings Before the Subcomm. on the Constitution of the Senate Comm. on the Judiciary,* 97th Congress, 2d sess. 662 (1982) (statement of John H. Bunzel).

138. Id. at 745 (statement of Michael Levin).

139. Id. at 1250 (statement of Henry Abraham).

140. Id. at 1449 (statement of William Van Alstyne).

141. S. Rep. No. 97-417, at 31 (1982). See *Gingles v. Edmisten,* 590 F. Supp. 345, 356 (E.D. N.C. 1984) ("Congress necessarily took into account and rejected as unfounded . . . the risk that creating 'safe'

black-majority single member districts would perpetuate racial ghettos and racial polarization in voting behavior"), *aff'd sub nom. Thornburg v. Gingles,* 478 U.S. 30 (1986).

142. Frank R. Parker, *The Constitutionality of Racial Redistricting: A Critique* *of* Shaw v. Reno, 3 D.C. L. Rev. 1, 19–20 (1995).

143. *Hays v. Louisiana,* 862 F. Supp. 119, 128 (W.D. La. 1994) (Shaw, J., concurring).

144. Id.

145. 120 Stat. 577, sec. 2(a).

146. 129 S.Ct. at 2513.

FIVE

Bull Connor Is Long Dead: Let's Move On

ABIGAIL THERNSTROM

Over time, the Voting Rights Act has evolved into one of the most ambitious legislative efforts in the world to define the appropriate balance between the political representation of majorities and minorities in the design of democratic institutions.

RICHARD H. PILDES, PROFESSOR OF LAW,
NEW YORK UNIVERSITY

In January 2009 Barack Obama became the first black leader of the free world, winner of an election in which his race was clearly no barrier, and may well have been an advantage. He won a larger share of the white vote than the previous two nominees of his party, and turnout for African Americans ages eighteen to forty-four was higher than that for whites.[1] President Obama's victory was unmistakably the end of an era and the welcome beginning of a new one. Whatever one thinks of his politics, his stunning success is a historic turning point. Integration was the aim of the civil rights movement in the 1950s and much of the 1960s, and, by the ultimate test, American politics is now integrated. Blacks have been a major force in American politics for decades – and now they have reached its highest peak.

The narrative of continuing white racism and black exclusion is so embedded in the American zeitgeist that prominent political and civil rights spokesmen, as well as voices in the media, doubted that a black man could win the presidency. In the early months of the 2008 campaign – before the first primary ballots were cast – polls showed Obama as having only modest support from black voters. African Americans, it appeared, believed he had no chance of winning.[2] Senator Obama himself said, "I think here is a protectiveness and a skepticism within the African American community that is grounded in their experiences."[3]

Robert Ford, a black state senator in South Carolina, was one of many who voiced that skepticism. "Obama would need 43% of the white vote in some states to win, and that's humanly impossible," he told a *Time* magazine reporter in January 2007. Southern blacks "don't believe this country is ready to vote for a black president," he added.[4] Referring to Obama's opponent, Hillary Rodham Clinton, Jesse Jackson said, "A white female has an advantage over a black male."[5] And after the first three contests, political scientist Philip Klinkner was ready to conclude that there was a "ceiling" on potential white support for Obama of about 35 percent.[6]

Two nations, separate and unequal – that was still the conventional wisdom, particularly in African American circles. On November 4, 2008, it became crystal clear how dated that picture was, as fears of the "Bradley effect" dissolved in the face of returns that closely matched pre-election predictions.[7] Tears flowed, *Washington Post* writer Kevin Merida reported, not only in response to Obama's victory, "but because many were happily discovering that perhaps they had underestimated possibility in America." In Milton, Massachusetts, novelist Kim McLarin told Merida that she had stood at the polling place overwhelmed. "I've been forced to acknowledge . . . there has been a shift – it's not a sea change. But there's been a decided shift in the meaning of race," she said.[8]

Countless other such stories were heard in the days after the election. Blacks and whites alike acknowledged that their fears of racist resistance to a black president had been misplaced.

Obama's election marked a dramatic turning point, but his victory was the culmination of a quiet revolution in racial politics that had begun many decades before with the passage of the 1965 Voting Rights Act. The statute marked the death knell of the Jim Crow South. The exclusive hold of whites on political power made all other forms of racial subjugation possible. For ninety-five years after the passage of the Fifteenth Amendment, southern blacks had been kept in political chains; the 1965 act was an indispensable and beautifully designed response to a profound moral wrong. Its enactment was one of the great moments in the history of American democracy.

Over time, the Voting Rights Act morphed in an unanticipated direction – a change that has had both benefits and costs. The act's original vision was firmly grounded in the Fifteenth Amendment: Racial equality in the American polity. Blacks would be free to form political coalitions and choose candidates in the same manner as other citizens. This constitutional clarity was partly responsible for the relatively weak southern resistance to black voting rights, in sharp contrast to the fierce (often violent) opposition to school desegregation well into the 1960s.[9]

Political equality was the goal of the statute, but it soon became apparent that equality could not be achieved – as originally hoped – simply by giving blacks the vote. Merely providing access to the ballot was insufficient after centuries of slavery, another century of segregation, ongoing white racism, and persistent resistance to black political power. More aggressive measures were needed.

In response, Congress, as well as courts and the Justice Department, in effect amended the law to ensure the political equality that the statute clearly promised. Blacks came to be treated as politically different – entitled to *in*equality in the form of a unique political privilege. Legislative districts carefully drawn to reserve seats for African Americans became a statutory mandate. Such districts would protect black candidates from white competition; whites would seldom even bother to run in them.[10]

The new power of federal authorities to force jurisdictions to adopt racially "fair" maps was deeply at odds with the commitment to federalism embedded in the Constitution, and the entitlement to safe black seats was equally at odds with traditional American assumptions about representation in a democratic nation. In 1965, however, a century of Fifteenth Amendment violations demanded what might be called federal wartime powers, and, as on other occasions when wartime powers were invoked, the consequence was a serious distortion of our constitutional order.

In the literature on minority voting rights, that distortion – fully justified in the early years – is too seldom acknowledged. The long history of pervasive southern racism justified a temporary abrogation of the traditional right of states to govern their own political processes within constitutional boundaries. Yet the Constitution contains no provision for group representation, "no matter how shamefully treated [its members] were nor how tragic their history," a witness argued at the 1982 Senate hearings on the amendment of Section 2.[11] "This is not India," Henry Abraham, professor of government at the University of Virginia, testified. "There is no right to be represented on the basis of group membership." In a community of equal citizens – one in which identity is fluid and the horizons of trust extend beyond the ethnic, racial, or religious community – individuals, not groups, are the unit of representation.[12]

The principle was right, but there was a problem: In 1965, southern states and counties were not communities of equal citizens. The South, with its racial caste system, *was* Abraham's India, and its long history of group exclusion justified concern that methods of election ensure black inclusion.

What was the measure of inclusion, however? The conviction that the franchise alone would not suffice – that further steps had to be taken to destroy an entrenched caste system – put the enforcement of the statute on a proverbial slippery slope. Ensuring that black and Hispanic ballots carried sufficient political weight became the expanded goal of the act; from there, it was but a short slide down that slope to a constitutionally problematic system of reserved seats for minority group members, even in settings with no history of racist exclusion; and from there, another short slide to proportional racial and ethnic representation as the only logical standard by which to measure true electoral opportunity.[13] Congress, the courts, and the Justice Department could have planted their feet firmly at a point well short of proportionality as an entitlement. But civil rights advocates saw results as the proper measure of opportunity – in employment, education, and contracting, too – and those who wrote, interpreted, and enforced the law consistently took their cues from these advocates.[14]

"Distinctions between citizens solely because of their ancestry are by their very nature odious to a free people whose institutions are founded upon the doctrine of equality," Justice Harlan Fiske Stone said in 1943, but the Supreme Court has never prohibited all race-conscious public policy.[15] Such policies have been treated as morally right when they are essential to opening the doors of opportunity – when the alternative is the perpetuation of all-white (or overwhelmingly white) legislatures, for instance.

The emergence of race-driven districting as an entitlement coincided with a dramatic change in white racial attitudes in the South. In 1982, five black candidates won seats in the North Carolina State House of Representatives, although they ran in districts ranging from 79 to 64 percent white. Nevertheless, the Supreme Court dismissed that record of success in a landmark 1987 decision in which black electoral opportunity in the state was described as generally "impaired."[16] It rested that conclusion mainly on the district court's findings that whites and blacks tended to vote for different candidates – with the court making no distinction between racial preferences and political party preferences. The lower court had acknowledged that it had now "become possible for black citizens to be elected to office at all levels of state government in North Carolina," but the High Court dismissed such black success as "perhaps too aberrational" to be taken seriously.[17] At what point, however, should that electoral possibility have suggested racial inclusion?

THE IMPORTANCE OF BLACK LEGISLATORS

What is the measure of sufficient racial progress? When can decisions about election-related matters be entrusted to elected representatives? Congress, the Justice Department, and the courts (intermittently) have coped with the question by playing down racial progress. Blacks live in a world in which the clock has stopped, they have implied. Without race-conscious districts gerrymandered to elect blacks to public office, "you're not going to have minority representation in Congress. It's just that simple," North Carolina representative Mel Watt stated in response to a 1993 Supreme Court decision allowing constitutional challenges to egregiously race-driven districting maps.[18]

But it wasn't "just that simple." In the 1990s, plaintiffs prevailed in a series of constitutional challenges to racial gerrymandering, but the decisions that struck down what the ACLU once called "max-black" districting plans in Georgia, Louisiana, Texas, and elsewhere did not halt the impressive growth in the number of black elected officials.[19] By the end of the decade, the Congressional Black Caucus was stronger than ever. It is important to note, however, that its enhanced strength was in great part due to the creation of fourteen new black-majority districts after the 1990 census – districts deliberately drawn to elect black representatives. All but two were in the South, and the impact was a jump in the number of southern blacks in the House from five to seventeen.[20]

Such descriptive representation – blacks representing blacks – is important. The history of whites-only legislatures in the South made the presence of blacks both symbolically and substantively important. Racially integrated legislative settings work to change racial attitudes. Most southern whites had little or no experience working with blacks as equals and undoubtedly saw skin color as signifying talent and competence. Their stereotypical views changed when blacks became colleagues.

In addition, southern blacks came to politics after 1965 with almost no experience organizing as a conventional political force. Thus, race-based districts in the region of historic disfranchisement were arguably analogous to high tariffs that helped the infant American steel industry get started: They gave the black political "industry" an opportunity to get on its feet before facing the full force of equal competition.

The North was not the South, which is not to say that northern electoral politics were always free of racial tension. The 1983 Chicago mayoral race that Harold Washington won, for instance, was racially ugly.[21] But blacks had a long history of involvement in Chicago politics; white ethnic doubts about Washington – who had a troubled legal history – bore no resemblance to black political exclusion in the South. The extraordinary measures to protect against disfranchisement contained in the original Voting Rights Act were rightly confined to the region that had kept the majority of blacks from the polls.

CONTEXT MATTERS

Most Americans do not like public policies that distribute benefits and burdens on the basis of race and ethnicity.[22] But while it is relatively easy to take an uncompromising stance against racial classifications in higher education, for instance, it is more difficult when the issue is districting lines drawn to increase black officeholding.

Context matters. Take the racial preferences used by the University of Michigan in admitting college and law students – the issue in two important 2003 Supreme Court decisions.[23] Those preferences were not dismantling a dual system. Moreover, the alternative to preferences in education has never been all-white schools, as William G. Bowen and Derek Bok, in their acclaimed 1998 book *The Shape of the River,* acknowledged. They calculated that approximately half the black students in the selective schools they studied needed no distinctive treatment to gain admission.[24] There is also strong evidence that racial preferences in higher education don't even work as advertised. The rich empirical work by UCLA law professor Richard Sander, for instance, has shown that black students preferentially admitted to law schools have disproportionately low rates in passing the bar exam. It is possible, he finds, that racial preferences have reduced, rather than increased, the supply of black attorneys.[25]

The contrast with the realm of politics is marked. There are no objective qualifications for office – the equivalent of a college or professional degree, a minimum score on the LSATs, a certain grade-point average, or relevant work experience. Race-based districts also work precisely as intended. They elect blacks and Hispanics to legislative seats. In the South such descriptive representation has been particularly important, I have already argued.

In suggesting that race-conscious maps were a temporary necessity, I do not defend what are often called bug-splat districts – constitutionally problematic, racially gerrymandered constituencies. They were the product of an aggressive Justice Department that labeled districting maps as intentionally discriminatory if the NAACP or another civil rights groups had come up with what they regarded as a superior plan.[26] Nor do I deny the serious costs that accompanied race-driven districting – costs that have increased in importance as racism has waned.

Such districting continues to reinforce old notions that blacks are fungible members of a subjugated group that stands apart in American life, requiring methods of election that recognize their racial distinctiveness. In 1993 Justice Sandra Day O'Connor described race-driven maps as "an effort to 'segregate . . . voters' on the basis of race."[27] As such, she said, they threaten "to stigmatize individuals by reason of their membership in a racial group."[28]

That is, most black voters do have a strong sense of belonging to a racially defined community; the law should nevertheless treat them as individuals, free to choose the strength of their own sense of group commitment. The alternative is racial stereotyping built into the law.

Racially gerrymandered districts flash the message "RACE, RACE, RACE," T. Alexander Aleinikoff and Samual Issacharoff have written.[29] Racial sorting creates advantaged and disadvantaged categories – groups that are privileged and groups that are subordinate, they argued.[30] The majority-minority districts upon which the Department of Justice (DOJ) insisted have become safe for black or Hispanic candidates, as intended, but they have also turned white voters into what these two scholars called "filler people."[31] Whites have become irrelevant to the outcome of the elections in districts designed to elect minorities, unless they serve as the swing vote in a black-on-black contest.

Today, the costs of race-conscious districts outweigh their benefits. Indeed, they have become a brake on the pursuit of political equality – tending, as they do, to elect representatives who are generally isolated from mainstream politics and thus on the sidelines of American political life. Indeed, black political progress might actually be greater today had race-conscious districting been viewed simply as a temporary remedy for unmistakably racist voting in the region that was only reluctantly accepting blacks as American citizens.

A LAWLESS JUSTICE DEPARTMENT

The South has changed; the balance between costs and benefits in weighing race-based districting has altered as a result. But the costs would not have been as great, and no Supreme Court Justice would have referred to "segregated" constituencies, had the Justice Department, in its enforcement of Section 5, stayed within the confines of the law.

The department was expected to function as a surrogate court, with the legal standards articulated in judicial opinions guiding administrative decisions. The reality has been quite different. That reality was spelled out clearly in a 1995 Supreme Court decision, *Miller v. Johnson*.[32] The issue was Georgia congressional districting, and the case tells a remarkable story of a lawless Republican Department of Justice that forced a state to accept a plan drawn by the American Civil Liberties Union in its capacity as advocate for the black caucus of the state's general assembly.

The enforcement of the Voting Rights Act has long made for strange bedfellows – although only superficially. John Dunne was the assistant attorney general for civil rights from 1990 to 1993 in the George H. W. Bush administration. He was an unambivalent champion of race-based districting to maximize minority officeholding, and his alliance with the ACLU and the state black caucus also served the Republican Party's interests. What the ACLU called a "max-black" plan was also "max-white" – more black voters in some districts meant fewer in others, and, in the South particularly, districts that had been "bleached" were fertile ground for Republican political aspirations.[33]

Of course, redistricting is not the only area in which Republicans have failed to oppose what Chief Justice John Roberts has called the "sordid business . . . [of] divvying us up by race."[34] But seldom is the magnitude of the gap between alleged principle and a quite different reality so fully on display as it has been in some of the redistricting cases.

The Georgia House and Senate redistricting committees, when they began the map-drawing process following the 1990 census, had no idea of the roadblocks that lay ahead.[35] They drew one map and then another, both of them increasing the number of majority-black congressional districts from one to two.

The state, in fact, had no obligation to draw a map that gave minorities more safe districts than they previously had. The point of preclearance had been to prevent racially suspect states from depriving blacks of the political gains that basic enfranchisement promised, not to ensure a "fair" number of legislative seats, the Supreme Court had held in its controlling 1976 decision, *Beer v. United States*.[36] Georgia had clearly met the demands of the law. Nevertheless, the Justice Department found both maps in violation of Section 5. John Dunne informed the state that it had not adequately explained its failure to create a third majority-minority district.

Dunne wanted, among other changes, a reshuffling of black and white voters. But his reconfiguration would have created a district (CD 11) that connected black neighborhoods in metropolitan Atlanta and poor black residents on the coast, 260 miles away and "worlds apart in culture," as the Supreme Court put it in *Miller*. "In short," the Court continued, "the social, political and economic makeup of the Eleventh

District [told] a tale of disparity, not community."[37] Dunne's insistence on heavy-handed racial gerrymandering forced candidates to run in four major media markets, while leaving CD 2 still less than 50 percent black.[38]

Dunne's communications were entirely guided by ACLU attorney Kathleen Wilde, who had drawn up a "max-black" plan. As the district court noted, "Throughout the preclearance process, from this first objection letter to the final submission, [DOJ] relied on versions of the max-black plan to argue that three majority-minority districts could indeed be squeezed out of the Georgia countryside. Ms. Wilde's triumph of demographic manipulation became the guiding light."[39] Georgia legislators and staff members who met with Justice Department attorneys in Washington were "told to subordinate their economic and political concerns to the quest for racial percentages."[40]

These legislators on the redistricting committee, many of whom were veteran mapmakers, were essentially cut out of the districting process by the Justice Department. Excluding them raised grave constitutional questions. As the Court stated in rejecting the "max-black" plan as unconstitutional, "Electoral districting is a most difficult subject for legislatures, and so the States must have discretion to exercise the political judgment necessary to balance competing interests." Plainly, judicial or Justice Department review "represents a serious intrusion on the most vital of local functions."[41]

To make matters worse, DOJ attorneys had cultivated "informants" within the state legislature; "'whistleblowers' became 'secret agents,'" the district court found.[42] One of these informants described a black state senator who had not toed the line as a "quintessential Uncle Tom" and "the worst friend of blacks in Georgia."[43] By contrast, attorneys from the ACLU and the Voting Section of the DOJ's Civil Rights Division were characterized as "peers working together." They discussed the smallest details of the Wilde plan and its revisions, with the result that "there were countless communications, including notes, maps, and charts, by phone, mail and facsimile."

In fact, the lower court found, the "DOJ was more accessible – and amenable – to the opinions of the ACLU than to those of the Attorney General of the State of Georgia."[44] The DOJ's March 1992 objection letter, quoted above, actually arrived at the state attorney general's office *after* members of the Georgia black caucus were already discussing it with the press, since the Justice Department attorneys had told the ACLU lawyers of their decision before informing any state official.[45] The court found this "informal and familiar" relationship between federal attorneys and an advocacy group "disturbing" and an "embarrassment."[46]

The preclearance process was not supposed to work as it did in Georgia in the early 1990s, as well as in countless jurisdictions (large and small) in the 1980s as well. By 1991, when the Justice Department first reviewed the Georgia plan, the initial vision of the department as a more accessible court had completely broken down. The Voting Section of the Civil Rights Division was operating as a law office for minority plaintiffs, working as partners with civil rights advocacy groups.

As UCLA law professor Daniel Lowenstein has written, "Much is at stake for politicians and the interests they represent in a districting plan, and enacting a plan is typically a difficult and contentious process. Once they strike a deal, they want it to stay struck, and therefore they tend to be risk-averse with respect to possible legal vulnerabilities in a plan."[47] A risk-averse plan was one that accepted racial quotas, which the Justice Department believed in as a matter of principle through Republican and Democratic administrations in the 1980s and 1990s. Blacks here, whites there, in just the right numbers to ensure the election of blacks to public office roughly in proportion to their population numbers.

"A serious intrusion on the most vital of local functions," as the Supreme Court called preclearance, had been fully justified when racist exclusion kept blacks out of legislative office, I have argued above. But the depth of that intrusion would have been much less had the DOJ adhered to the standards established in *Beer*, and greater adherence to the law would have prompted fewer questions about the ongoing legitimacy of the provision in the face of a quiet revolution in white racial attitudes in the South.

A PERIOD PIECE

A serious disconnection from reality surrounds the Voting Rights Act today. By every measure, American politics has been transformed since the 1960s. Blacks hold office at all levels of government and have reached the pinnacles of virtually every field of private endeavor. Racial prejudice has fallen to historic lows. And yet in 2006 Section 5 was renewed (and partially amended) for another quarter-century. The emergency of black disfranchisement has come to be treated as near permanent – even in an era when an African American can be elected president.[48]

The 2006 "Fannie Lou Hamer, Rosa Parks, and Coretta Scott King Voting Rights Act Reauthorization and Amendments Act" (VRARA) was passed with almost no dissent.[49] By the new expiration date, electoral arrangements in the South, the Southwest, Alaska, and a collection of arbitrarily selected counties elsewhere will have been under federal receivership, in effect, for a total of sixty-six years. But Congress had been persuaded that at least until 2031 minority voters in the covered jurisdictions (covered by a formula last updated in 1975) would remain unable to participate in American political life without the benefit of electoral set-asides. Such pessimism is not benign; it distorts the formulation of policies involving race.

The passage of the 2006 VRARA was preceded by a sustained, meticulously organized campaign by civil rights groups to persuade Congress that race relations remain frozen in the past and that America is still plagued by persistent disfranchisement. And in passing the VRARA, Congress signed on to a picture that reflected conventional wisdom in the civil rights community and the media. "Discrimination [in voting] today is more subtle than the visible methods used in 1965. However, the effects and results are the same," the House Judiciary Committee reported. "Vestiges of discrimination continue to exist . . . [preventing] minority voters from fully participating in the electoral process," the statute itself read.

Surely, rarely in the rich annals of congressional deceit and self-deception have more false and foolish words been uttered. No meaningful evidence supported such an extraordinary claim.

It cannot be said too strongly or too often: The skepticism of those, like Georgia representative John Lewis, who cannot forget the brutality of the Jim Crow South is understandable. But today most southern states have higher black registration rates than those outside the region. In the presidential election of 2004, a stunning 68.2 percent of the black population in the original Section 5 states was registered to vote, a rate a few points *higher* than that in the rest of the country.[50]

Black turnout rates, as well, have been impressive. In the 2004 election, roughly 60 percent of blacks cast votes in both covered and non-covered jurisdictions. Alabama, for instance, had a turnout rate of almost 70 percent, Georgia 54.4 percent, Louisiana 62.1 percent, Mississippi 66.8 percent, South Carolina 59.5 percent, and Virginia 49.6 percent. In 2008 black turnout overall increased substantially over 2004; the total share of the national vote represented by black voters rose from 11 percent to 13 percent, according to exit polls. In six states, the increase in the black share of the statewide vote over the previous election was very large. Looking again at the South, we see that in Alabama, the black voting-age population was 25 percent of the total electorate; the black share of the vote rose from 25 percent in 2004 to 29 percent in 2008. In Georgia, where blacks are 24.6 percent of the voting-age population, their share of the electorate was 30 percent. In Virginia and North Carolina, as well, blacks overvoted their share of eligible population in 2008.[51]

Whether candidates preferred by the group are able to win elections is another test of electoral progress. Answering the question of office-holding gains is more difficult than it might seem, however. A sizable minority group that leans strongly Democratic will have less success in electing its preferred candidates in a state whose electorate is strongly tilted in favor of Republicans – the picture in much of the South. Furthermore, it is not possible to determine who was the preferred black candidate in thousands of local and state electoral contests.

With these caveats in mind, the record of electoral success of black candidates in recent decades is impressive. In 1964, only five African Americans held seats in the U.S. Congress. None was from any of the covered states, or indeed any other southern state. In that same year, just ninety-four blacks served in any of the fifty state legislatures, with only sixteen coming from the southern states that held half of the nation's African American population.[52]

By 2008, however, there were forty-one members of the Congressional Black Caucus.[53] Almost 600 African Americans held seats in state legislatures, and another 8,800 were mayors, sheriffs, sheriffs, school board members, and the like. It is remarkable that 47 percent of these

black public officials lived in the seven covered states, though those states
contained only 30 percent of the nation's black population. Especially
striking is that Mississippi, which once had a well-deserved reputation
for the depth of its commitment to white supremacy, now leads the nation in the number of blacks it elects to political office.[54]

Over the years between 1970 and 2002, the number of black elected
officials in the country soared from 1,469 to 9,430, a rise of more than
sixfold. Black political power grew by leaps and bounds. The gain in the
seven covered states was even more rapid, a jump from 407 black elected
officials to 4,404, almost double the overall rate of increase! In 1970, the
covered states had just 28 percent of all black elected officials; by 2002
it was 47 percent. In the covered states, in short, African Americans
made political gains at a dramatically higher rate than elsewhere in the
country.[55] This may have been a reflection of how far those states had to
go – but it is surely also an indication of how far they have come, in an
absolute and meaningful sense.

More recent data are available to gauge the rate of black progress in
winning election to state legislatures. In 2007, the proportion of seats
in the Alabama House of Representatives held by blacks (24.8 percent)
almost exactly mirrored their share of the state's voting-age population
(24.7 percent).[56] In Mississippi, blacks had only 12 percent fewer seats
than their share of the voting-age population, and in Georgia, 13 percent
less. It was lower still in other covered states, with an overall average
of 19 percent short of parity. This is a huge advance over the complete
lack of representation in state legislative bodies at the time the Voting
Rights Act was passed, although it is important to remember that levels
of educational attainment among blacks tend to be relatively low, and
education is highly correlated with political participation.

There is certainly room for further gains. But before leaping to the
conclusion that the covered states thus still need extraordinary oversight
by federal officials, we should notice that the pattern in the six southern
states that are not covered by Section 5 is not significantly different. In
these states, blacks had 16 percent fewer seats in the houses than their
share of the voting-age population. In the covered states they were 19
percent below parity, hardly a large enough difference to support the
claim that preclearance is needed for another generation.

In the six northern states with populations at least 10 percent black, African Americans did win almost exactly their proportional share of seats in the lower house, falling short by only two points. The most likely explanation is not that northern white voters are less afflicted by prejudice than their southern counterparts. It happens that this group of northern states (New York, New Jersey, Illinois, Michigan, Ohio, and Pennsylvania) tended to lean strongly Democratic, so minority candidates running as Democrats find it relatively easy to attract white votes.

Elections to the state senates display a similar pattern. The record of minority electoral success in the covered states is slightly better than that of the southern states that are not covered by Section 5. In the covered states, blacks were 26 percent below parity in the share of senate seats they held in 2007; in the southern states not affected by the provisions of Section 5, they were 29 percent below parity. It's important to note, however, that lower houses are the entry rung in state-level politics. It takes time to move up; in a few years senate numbers are likely to improve as house members throw their hats in the more competitive races in the larger senate districts.

Voting rights advocates argue that elections are still racially polarized – that white voters' preferences are still driven by race. But the highly questionable definition of white bloc voting most commonly used – whites and blacks generally preferring different candidates – means it can be found wherever black candidates run campaigns unlikely to attract a majority of whites. By definition, then, all districts in which whites tend to be more politically conservative than blacks are racially polarized.[57] If 52 percent of blacks vote for the Democratic candidate but only 48 percent of whites do so, there is pernicious racially polarized voting.

The term "polarized voting" suggests racial exclusion – blacks and whites with unequal electoral opportunity. The method of election is said to have "diluted" the minority vote; black ballots had been "made to count less than the votes of the majority."[58] And yet as early as 1971 the Supreme Court recognized that the process of party competition and the principle of majority rule – rather than racism – could deny blacks the representation they sought. Since blacks were Democrats in largely Republican Marion County, Ohio, the "dilution" of their voting strength was a "mere euphemism for political defeat," the Court found.[59]

If one assumes that white candidates lose political races for a variety of reasons, but blacks for one only one – racism – then the Court's 1971 decision will seem willfully blind and thus surely wrong. But four decades later it is surely apparent that party affiliation will often be decisive in races in which a black candidate loses. In fact, it is now also clear that except in solidly Democratic contexts, white Democrats are also dependent on minority support in electoral contests. Since 1964, no Democratic president has won with a majority of the white vote.

In 2008 Barack Obama got 43 percent of the white vote. He needed that degree of support, but if his re-election were held today, it is unlikely that he would have it. In the mid-term elections of 2010 exit polls found that only 37 percent of whites voted for Democrats in House races, while 60 percent backed Republicans – a percentage unmatched in the history of modern polling.[60] The president's approval rating among all whites in a survey taken in late March/early April 2011 stood at only 38 percent.[61] The president's black and Hispanic support has also been falling.[62]

Nevertheless, given the significant drop in the white numbers, black and Hispanic voters who are already a powerful constituency for Democrats are likely to become even more decisive in 2012. Their share of the American electorate is growing. A number of witnesses who testified on behalf of the 2006 amendments argued that Section 5 has a "deterrent effect" – suggesting that perhaps without the threat of federal interference, southern state legislatures will feel free to engage in all sorts of disfranchising mischief.[63] It is literally inconceivable. Black (and Hispanic) votes count. Not even Mississippi can pedal backward; it has over 900 black elected officials.

As a Clarksdale, Mississippi, newspaper editorial noted in June 2008, "section 5 of the Voting Rights Act presumes that minorities are powerless to protect their own election interests in places where they actually have the most clout." Black lawmakers in the state, for instance, didn't have to rely on courts to stop the enactment of a voter ID law; they had the power to do so themselves.[64]

Racial progress rapidly outpaced the law, and the voting rights problems that are now regarded as of greatest concern – felon disfranchisement and other registration obstacles, provisional ballots, glitches in electronic voting, voter identification, and fraud – bear no relationship to those that plagued the South in 1965. Nevertheless, the most radical provisions of the statute live on, addressing yesterday's problems.

African Americans and Hispanics have become politically powerful, I have argued. In addition, an army of activists and lawyers monitor American elections closely. Most important, how many Americans would even want to return to the days of old? Is racism dead? Of course not – neither in America nor in any other country. But the level of contemporary race-driven voting problems does not justify keeping states and counties selected by a statistical trigger last updated in 1975 under federal receivership.

Fifteen years ago, one of the most liberal members of the Court came close to describing blacks and Hispanics as members of normal political interest groups. "Minority voters," Justice David Souter said, "are not immune from the obligation to pull, haul, and trade to find common political ground, the virtue of which is not to be slighted in applying a statute meant to hasten the waning of racism in American politics."[65]

America has changed; the South has changed, and it's time to revise the Voting Rights Act as well. The core provisions that guarantee basic Fifteenth Amendment rights will never and should never be changed. But shelf life of the temporary, emergency provisions – included to protect against virulent racism in the Jim Crow South – has long expired.

THE CONSTITUTIONALITY OF
PRECLEARANCE CHALLENGED

At its inception, the Voting Rights Act stood on very firm constitutional ground; it was pure antidiscrimination legislation designed to enforce basic Fifteenth Amendment rights. A clear principle justified its original enactment: Citizens should not be judged by the color of their skin when states determine eligibility to vote.

That clarity could not be sustained over time. As a result, more than four decades later, the law is not only out of date. It has become what Judge Bruce Selya has described as a "Serbonian bog." The legal land looks solid but is in fact a quagmire, into which "plaintiffs and defendants, pundits and policymakers, judges and justices" have sunk.

In the 2008–2009 term, the Supreme Court had a chance to extricate itself in good measure by declaring preclearance – intended to be very temporary – a relic from a previous era. Regrettably, it took a pass.

Northwest Austin Municipal Utility District Number One v. Holder (NAMUDNO) involved a tiny Texas utility district that was formed in 1987 mainly to provide water to unincorporated areas.[66] Because the Voting Rights Act treats all Texas localities as racially suspect, the Justice Department had to "preclear" the district's decision to move a polling place out of a private garage and into a public school – a move "calculated to increase public access to the ballot." Preclearance, the plaintiffs contended, was an irrational and "burdensome imposition" on the district's "sovereign rights" to manage its own electoral affairs. It had no history of electoral discrimination.[67]

Declaring Section 5 unconstitutional was not the Court's only option. With an interpretive stretch, it could read a "bailout" provision to allow relief from preclearance, and it did so. However, Chief Justice John Roberts, writing for the majority, explicitly said, "The Act's preclearance requirements and its coverage formula raise serious constitutional questions."[68] And he spelled those questions out at considerable length.

Another case, another day, perhaps a different decision, he implied. That day may be on the horizon. Already there are five serious challenges to the continuing constitutionality of preclearance so many decades down the road of racial progress and black electoral power. One involves a suit against the Justice Department brought by voters and potential candidates in Kinston, North Carolina, who challenged the DOJ decision to reject the town's decision to switch to nonpartisan town council elections.[69] The other constitutional suits have been brought by Shelby County, Alabama, Arizona, and Florida. All these jurisdictions make basically the same arguments. Shelby County, for instance, notes that neither the county nor the state of Alabama would be covered if Congress, when it renewed the provision in 2006, had updated the formula for establishing coverage to reflect turnout data from "any of the last three presidential elections" instead of using registration and turnout figures from November 1964." Given the nation's radically altered racial climate, Section 5 is unconstitutional, these covered jurisdictions argue. As I write, the parties to the suit – the Justice Department and the county – are awaiting the court's ruling on the plaintiff's motion for summary judgment.[70]

The picture that Congress accepted in 2006 of an America still spinning its wheels in the racist muck of its Jim Crow past bears no relationship to reality, I argued. In 1966, Justice Hugo Black complained that Section 5 compelled states to "beg federal authorities to approve their policies," and thus so distorted our constitutional structure as to almost erase the distinction between federal and state power.[71] It was a constitutionally serious argument, but at the time, all other attempts to secure Fifteenth Amendment rights had failed. Today, more than four decades later, it is a point that should be remembered.

The Voting Rights Act, Nathaniel Persily has noted, "stands alone in American history in its alteration of authority between the federal government and the states. No other statute applies only to a subset of the country and requires covered states and localities to get permission from the federal government before implementing a certain type of law."[72] Persily's description was actually not of the law in its entirety but only of Section 5. The constitutionally daring design of that provision was essential in 1965; the South of that era – with its elaborate legal arrangements to ensure white supremacy – has disappeared.

A BRAKE ON BLACK POLITICAL ASPIRATIONS

In fact, by now, the Voting Rights Act arguably serves as a barrier to greater racial integration.[73] Race-based districts have worked to keep most black legislators clustered together and on the sidelines of American political life – precisely the opposite of what the statute intended and precisely the opposite of what is needed. Majority-minority districts appear to reward political actors who consolidate the minority vote by making the sort of overt racial appeals that are the staple of invidious identity politics. Cass Sunstein describes a larger phenomenon that is pertinent: People across the political spectrum end up with more extreme views than they would hold otherwise when they talk only to those who are similarly minded.[74]

The point can be logically extended: Most voters in a district drawn for the sole purpose of maximizing black representation will generally talk politics only with people who share their left-leaning, race-conscious values. And aspiring politicians who seek office in such settings have every incentive to run on their racial identity – defining themselves as "authentically" black. "Postracial" has no appeal in such contexts, with the result that very few members of the Congressional Black Caucus (CBC) have a voting record that would attract white support, except in reliably liberal jurisdictions. Only four members of the CBC, as I write, have been elected from majority-white constituencies, and one of the four is a Republican.[75]

Members of the CBC who won their seats in majority-black districts by defining themselves as racially authentic have acquired secure seats but no experience building biracial coalitions. As a result, they've been traveling on a road going nowhere. Thus it is unimaginable that South Carolina representative James Clyburn could build a national or even statewide campaign, even though he holds an important leadership position in the House. He is a *black* politician with a majority-*black* constituency. His race was his ticket to Congress.

In 2010, Rep. Artur Davis took the unprecedented move of risking his safe House seat, making a run to become the Democratic nominee for governor of Alabama as a postracial candidate. He lost; the contest was not even close. He tried to build a biracial coalition and was rejected by both whites and blacks.

Alabama whites saw him as too Obama-like, although their support for any Democrat would have been weak. He obviously needed strong black support, but his profile was not that of most Congressional Black Caucus members. Alone in the CBC, he had opposed Obama's health care bill. The state's two predominantly black organizations, the Alabama Democratic Conference and the Alabama New South Coalition, endorsed his white opponent, Ron Sparks. You couldn't call yourself "black" and vote against Obamacare, Jesse Jackson announced in November – and the Alabama civil rights community had agreed. But if "black" has a political definition – nurtured in majority-minority race-based districts – there is obviously a low ceiling on how far most aspiring black candidates can go in most settings in this center-right country.[76]

Barack Obama has obviously made it all the way to the political top, but his history is instructive. In 1997 he was elected to the Illinois

state senate. In 2000, he tried to climb the political ladder by challenging incumbent congressman Bobby Rush, who handily defeated him in
the Democratic primary in Chicago's heavily black first congressional
district. Rush – in conformity to the usual CBC mold – emphasized his
racial bona fides, his commitment to representing black interests, and
his leftist politics. That defeat, as attorney and voting rights specialist
Michael Carvin has said,

> was the best thing that ever happened to Obama. . . . If he had won, he would
> have just become another mouthpiece for a group that is ghettoized in Congress
> and perceived as representing certain interest groups in the legislature.[77]

Instead, Obama won a seat in the U.S. Senate in 2004, and his status
as a senator from a heavily white state enabled him to transcend that
perception of black politicians as first and foremost representing black
interests.[78]

Blacks running in majority-minority districts, not acquiring the
skills to venture into the world of competitive politics in majority-white
settings – that is not the picture of political integration, equality, and the
vibrant political culture that the Voting Rights Act should promote. By
another measure, as well, equality may be compromised by race-conscious districting. The creation of these districts has not overcome the
heritage of political apathy created by the long history of systematic disfranchisement; their residents are generally less politically engaged and
mobilized, a number of scholars have concluded.[79] Carol Swain found
that turnout in black-majority congressional districts across the country
was especially low. She noted, for example, that just 13 percent of eligible
voters showed up at the polls in 1986 in Major Owens's 78 percent black
district in New York City. If voters in Owens's district felt more empowered with a black man representing them in Washington, it certainly did
not inspire many of them to bother to vote.[80]

James E. Campbell has supported Swain's findings. Campbell found
that in 1994, more than 60 percent of congressional districts in which
minorities were the majority ranked in the bottom *quintile* in levels of
voter turnout.[81] The most recently published review of the scholarly literature on this subject is a 2007 article by Claudine Gay.[82] Summing
up what we have learned from previous investigations, Gay observed,

"Limited electoral competition and low voter turnout are widely viewed as defining features of districts with black or Latino majorities." The "lack of competition" serves to "discourage participation" and reduces "the incentive for candidates or parties to mobilize voters." Thus, "the unique opportunity that majority-minority districts offer for minority self-determination only partially offsets . . . the decrease in turnout associated with noncompetitive electoral environments."[83]

Gay added further empirical evidence showing that the creation of majority-minority districts tends to depress minority voter turnout, and thus generates political disengagement and apathy. In the districts from which members of the California Assembly were elected in 1996, voter turnout exceeded 60 percent (of registered voters) in only *a quarter* of the majority-minority districts. Turnout levels were above 60 percent, by contrast, in *90 percent* of the white-majority districts.[84] In sum, majority-minority districts probably lower the level of black political participation – a significant cost overlooked by advocates of race-based constituencies.

In addition, racially gerrymandered lines that wander all over the landscape may bring black families under one majority-black political roof, but they make organized political activity more difficult. A townwide civic organization, for instance, will find it harder to campaign for an issue or candidate if it has to mobilize in separate congressional districts arbitrarily drawn to further black officeholding.[85]

The civil rights community and its allies in the media and in academe seem to see a static racial landscape. And thus they have been distressed by recent census news that, in increasing numbers, blacks are moving to suburbs.[86] The 2010 census has revealed that the black population is shrinking in urban congressional districts and swelling in suburban ones. Indeed, looking at the newest census numbers, the fifteen districts with the greatest black population growth are all in the suburbs. Conversely, the African American population in eight of the top ten majority-black districts dropped by an average of more than 10 percent. But if blacks keep scattering, as they are doing, black representation by black officeholders will inevitably become harder to ensure. The creation of majority-black legislative districts will become harder to achieve.

Are they needed? In 2011, does black political inclusion still depend on protecting black candidates from white competition in race-based districts? Once upon a time, treating all blacks as members of a "community" made sense; white racism obliterated social class and other distinctions. But today? White racial attitudes have undergone an amazing transformation in recent decades. In 2007, for instance, only 5 percent of Americans said they were unwilling to vote for a "qualified African American candidate," according to a Gallup Organization survey.[87] Before the Reverend Jeremiah Wright, Obama's longtime pastor, surfaced with his racist, anti-American rhetoric, the Illinois senator had won the majority of white votes in the Democratic primaries in Virginia, New Mexico, Wisconsin, Illinois, and Utah, and had received impressive vote totals among whites in other states' primaries, as well. And in November, as noted above, he received 43 percent of the white vote nationally.

In February 2008, voters in an Alabama county more than 96 percent white sent a black man, James Fields, as their representative to the state House of Representatives. "Really, I never realize he's black," a white woman, smiling, told a New York Times reporter.[88] How many Americans today look at the president and think "black"? I know of no polling in which that question has been asked, but I suspect the answer is relatively few. They look to him for leadership in the face of extraordinarily urgent economic and foreign policy problems; if previous surveys are any indication, they are unlikely to judge his accomplishments through the lens of race. America has come a very long way in the decades since the Voting Rights Act was passed.

The 1965 Voting Rights Act is the crown jewel of federal civil rights laws. No one should doubt its importance in making America a very different nation than the one in which I grew up not so many years ago. Race-conscious districting was legitimate as a temporary measure to give blacks what UCLA law professor Daniel Lowenstein has called "a jumpstart in electoral politics." But Lowenstein made a further, important point: "A jumpstart is one thing but the guy who comes and charges up your car when the battery's dead, he doesn't stay there trailing behind you with the cable stuck as you drive down the freeway. He lets it go."[89]

It's time to let race-driven districting go the way of those jumper cables. America is better off with the increase in the number of black elected officials who gained office, in large part due to the deliberate drawing of majority-minority districts. But black politics has come of age, and black politicians can protect their turf, fight for their interests, and successfully compete even for the presidency, it turns out. It's a new world.

The Voting Rights Act has been a magnificent success. But Bull Connor is long dead and it's time to move on.

NOTES

The epigraph is from Richard Pildes, introduction to *The Future of the Voting Rights Act*, ed. David Epstein, Rodolfo de la Garza, Sharyn O'Halloran, and Richard Pildes (New York: Russell Sage Foundation, 2006), xiv.

1. "2008 Surge in Black Voters Nearly Erased Racial Gap," *New York Times*, July 21 2009. http://www.nytimes.com/2009/07/21/us/politics/21vote.html. There was still a racial gap in black-white turnout because older blacks voted at a rate lower than whites of the same age.

2. Once the campaign got underway, black voters began to believe victory was actually possible, ABC reported in February 2008. "Among blacks . . . the surge to Obama since December has been remarkable. In the last pre-primary ABC News/Washington Post poll last year, Clinton led Obama among blacks by 52–39 percent. That changed after Obama established his credentials by winning Iowa [in January]; across all primaries to date he's won African-Americans by 79–17 percent." Gary Langer, "The Role of Race," *The Numbers: A Run at the Latest Data from ABC's Poobah of Polling*, http://blogs.abcnews.com/thenumbers/2008/02/the-role-of-rac.html, February 15, 2008 (accessed April 7, 2009).

3. Quoted in Dewey Clayron, "The Audacity of Hope," *Journal of Black Studies* 38, no. 1 (September 2007): 60.

4. Perry Bacon Jr., "Can Obama Count On the Black Vote? *Time*, January 23, 2007.

5. Adam Nagourney, "The Pattern May Change, If," *New York Times*, December 10, 2006, Week in Review, section 4, 1.

6. Philip Klinkner, "The Obama Ceiling, Again," PolySigh: The Political Science Take on Things, March 10, 2008, http://polysigh.blogspot.com/search?q=klinkner (accessed April 8, 2009).

7. The "Bradley effect" refers to the experience of Tom Bradley, a black candidate in the 1982 California gubernatorial race, who seemed headed for election on the basis of polling data, but who lost. The pre-election polling painted a deceptive picture of his electoral strength.

8. Kevin Merida, "America's History Gives Way to Its Future," *Washington Post*, November 5, 2008, A01.

9. On the contrast between the South's resistance to school desegregation and its relative acceptance of black enfranchisement, see Michael J. Klarman, *From Jim Crow to Civil Rights: The Supreme Court and the Struggle for Racial Equality* (New York: Oxford University Press, 2004), 456.

10. Steve Cohen, a Democrat from Tennessee, is currently the only white member of the U.S. House of Representatives elected from a majority-black district. His 60

percent African American district includes Memphis, and he gained his congressional seat in 2006 after a crowded field of black candidates splintered the vote. With a voting record that the Leadership Conference on Civil Rights called the most liberal in the state , he was re-elected in 2008. See Leadership Conference on Civil Rights, LCCR Voting Record, 33, http://www.civil rights.org/resources/voting/2008/lccr_ voting_record_110th_congress.pdf (accessed December 22, 2008). One might think that the winner in a majority-black district would be regarded as speaking for black interests, but Representative Cohen's request to join the Congressional Black Caucus was rejected. See Michael Barone, ed., *The Almanac of American Politics 2008*, web edition, NationalJournal.com, entry for Steve Cohen.

11. On S. 53, S. 1761, S. 1992, and H.R. 3112. *Bills to Amend the Voting Rights Act of 1965: Hearings on the Voting Rights Act Before the Subcomm. on the Constitution of the S. Comm. on the Judiciary*, 97th Cong., 1, 444 (1982) (testimony of Barry Gross, professor, York College, City University of New York) (hereafter 1982 Senate hearings).

12. Ibid., 1247. The "horizons of trust" argument is from Michael Walzer, *Spheres of Justice: A Defense of Pluralism and Equality* (New York: Basic Books, 1983), 149–50.

13. Vanderbilt Law School professor James Blumstein made this point at the 1982 Senate hearings, declaring that the substitution of discriminatory effect for that of intent turned a "fair shake" into a "fair share." 1982 Senate hearings, 1334.

14. See e.g. *Parents Involved in Community Schools v. Seattle School District No. 1*, 551 U.S. 701 (2007). Chief Justice John Roberts, writing for the Court, repeatedly addressed the misconception that proportionality was assumed by the school district to be the measure of racial fairness. On employment and the question

of proportionality, see, for instance, *Ricci v. DeStefano*. The Second Circuit Court of Appeals had affirmed a lower court's summary judgment for the defendants, 530 F.3d 87 (Second Circuit; June 9, 2008; per curiam). Dissenting from that judgment, Judge José Cabranes wrote, "At its core this case presents a straight-forward question: May a municipal employer disregard the results of a qualifying examination [for promotion in the New Haven fire department] . . . on the ground that the results of that examination yielded too many qualified applicants of one race and not enough of another?" In short, the city had discarded the results of the exam in the belief that statistical parity – racial and ethnic proportionality in the fire department – defined racial fairness.

15. *Hirabayashi v. United States,* 320 U.S. 81, 100 (1943).

16. *Thornburg v. Gingles,* 478 U.S. 30, 75 n. 35 (1986).

17. Ibid., 40. It is not possible to create a timeline of racial change showing the clear point at which black political exclusion switches to black participation. Different scholars read the data differently. I am impressed by the level of black electoral success in overwhelmingly white multimember districts in North Carolina in 1982. On the other hand, testifying at the 2006 Senate hearings on the VRARA, voting rights scholar Richard Pildes stated, "Even in 1982, blacks were still virtually invisible in elective offices; the South remained, for state and local elections, the virtual one-party monopoly it had been throughout the 20th century." *On the Continuing Need for Section 5 Pre-Clearance, Hearing on S. 2703 before the S. Comm. on the Judiciary*, 109th Cong. (May 16, 2006) (testimony of Professor Richard H. Pildes, Sudler Family Professor of Constitutional Law, NYU School of Law). The important point is that by now, surely, the line dividing exclusion from inclusion has been clearly crossed.

18. "Is an All White Congress Inevitable?" *Ethnic NewsWatch: New York Beacon* 2, no. 96 (December 13, 1995): 2.

19. The "max-black" description is quoted in *Miller v. Johnson,* 515 U.S. 900, 907 (1995).

20. The two outside the South were in Maryland and Pennsylvania. Alabama, Louisiana, South Carolina, Texas, and Virginia each created one; Georgia and North Carolina, two apiece; Florida, three.

21. Encyclopedia.com, "Harold Washington." http://www.encyclopedia.com/topic/Harold_Washington.aspx

22. See, for example, David W. Moore, "Public: Only Merit Should Count in College Admissions," Gallup News Service, June 24, 2003. Moore reported on a Gallup Poll finding that 69 percent of Americans and 75 percent of whites believed college applicants "should be admitted solely on the basis of merit, even if that results in few minority students being admitted." Blacks were almost evenly divided, with 44 percent favoring merit-only admissions and 49 percent supporting color-conscious admissions. On American views on racial preferences, see Gallup Organization, "Race Relations Poll," June 4–24, 2007 (unpaginated), as well as Pew Research Center, "Blacks See Growing Values Gap Between Poor and Middle Class," November 2007, 35.

23. See *Grutter v. Bollinger,* 539 U.S. 306 (2003), and *Gratz v. Bollinger,* 539 U.S. 244 (2003).

24. William G. Bowen and Derek Bok, *The Shape of the River: Long-Term Consequences of Considering Race in College and University Admissions* (Princeton, N.J.: Princeton University Press, 1998), 41.

25. Much other data tell basically the same story. For summaries, see Abigail Thernstrom and Stephan Thernstrom, *Secrecy and Dishonesty: The Supreme Court, Racial Preferences, and Higher Education,* 21 Const. Comment. 251 (2004);

Stephan Thernstrom and Abigail Thernstrom, *Reflections on* The Shape of the River, 46 UCLA L. Rev. 1583 (1999); Stephan Thernstrom and Abigail Thernstrom, *America in Black and White: One Nation, Indivisible* (New York: Simon & Schuster, 1997), chapter 14. See also Richard H. Sander, *A Systematic Analysis of Affirmative Action in American Law Schools,* 57 Stan. L. Rev. 367 (2004), and Richard H. Sander, *A Reply to Critics,* 57 Stan. L. Rev. 1963 (2005).

26. Thus, an NAACP brief in a South Carolina State Senate districting case implied that any jurisdiction that failed to implement redistricting suggestions made by that organization was guilty of deliberately obstructing black voting rights. *South Carolina v. United States and the National Association for the Advancement of Colored People, Inc.,* Civil Action No. 83-3626, District Court for the District of Columbia, NAACP-Defendant's Supplemental Response to Interrogatories (April 2, 1984), 3–4: "The redistricting plan as drawn avoidably and deliberately denies Blacks the equal opportunity to elect a candidate of their choice. . . . Moreover, the State . . . failed and or refused to implement suggestions for redistricting made by the NAACP Defendants, as well as other minority organizations." Any minority organization (not just the NAACP) with a plan of its own could veto that of the state, the argument implied.

27. *Shaw v. Reno,* 509 U.S 630, 646–47 (1993).

28. Ibid., 643.

29. T. Alexander Aleinikoff and Samuel Issacharoff, *Race and Redistricting,* 92 Mich. L. Rev. 592, 610 (1993).

30. "As a result, the claim of a right of effective participation in an electoral system not only entails the recognition of an affirmative group right, but – given the zero-sum quality of representation – the claim also assumes the right to subor-

dinate electorally some other group or groups." Aleinikoff and Issacharoff, *Race and Redistricting*, 601.

31. Ibid.

32. *Miller v. Johnson*, 515 U.S. 900 (1995).

33. The connection between Republican gains and race-based districting is a point that has been made frequently by scholars and journalists. See, for example, Abigail Thernstrom, *Whose Votes Count? Affirmative Action and Minority Voting Rights* (Cambridge, Mass.: Harvard University Press, 1987), 6. See also Abigail Thernstrom, "A Republican-Civil Rights Conspiracy," *Washington Post,* September 23, 1991, A11; David Lublin, *The Paradox of Representation: Racial Gerrymandering and Minority Interests in Congress* (Princeton, N.J.: Princeton University Press, 1997); David Lublin, *The Republican South: Democratization and Partisan Change* (Princeton, N.J.: Princeton University Press, 2004); Earl Black and Merle Black, *The Rise of Southern Republicans* (Cambridge, Mass.: Harvard University Press, 2002). I was the first to make this point, I believe, in my 1987 book, and at the time reviewers generally dismissed it as ridiculous; it has now become the conventional wisdom.

34. *League of United Latin American Citizens v. Perry,* 548 U. S. 399 (2006).

35. "While many of their members were veterans of past redistricting wars, the legislators could not have known what the DOJ would require by way of compliance with sections 2 and 5 of the VRA." *Johnson v. Miller,* 864 F. Supp. at 1360.

36. *Beer v. United States,* 425 U.S. 130, 141 (1976).

37. *Miller v. Johnson,* 515 U.S. at 912.

38. *Johnson v. Miller,* 864 F. Supp. at 1365.

39. Ibid., 1363–64. "Ms. Wilde was not simply one of various advocates. Her work was of particular importance to DOJ lawyers, whose criteria for and opinions

of Georgia's submissions were greatly influenced by Ms. Wilde and her agenda." Ibid., 1362.

40. Ibid., 1364 n. 8.

41. *Miller v. Johnson,* 515 U.S. at 915–16.

42. *Johnson v. Miller,* 864 F. Supp. at 1367.

43. Ibid.

44. Ibid., 1362.

45. Ibid., 1368.

46. Ibid., 1362, 1368.

47. Daniel H. Lowenstein, "Race and Representation in the Supreme Court," in *Voting Rights and Redistricting in the United States,* ed. Mark E. Rush, 62 (Westport, Conn.: Greenwood Press, 1998).

48. In fact, when Section 5 was renewed for the second time in 1982, many representatives of the civil rights community voiced their frustration with the temporary nature of preclearance. For instance, in 1980, the President's Commission for a National Agenda, chaired by Benjamin Hooks, referred to the temporary status of the special provisions as a "built-in defect" that marred the act. President's Commission for a National Agenda for the Eighties, *Report of the Panel on Government for the Advancement of Social Justice, Health, Welfare, Education, and Civil Rights* (Washington, D.C.: Government Printing Office, 1980), 15. For other examples, see Thernstrom, *Whose Votes Count?* 93.

49. Voting Rights Act Reauthorization and Amendments Act, Pub. L. No. 109-246, § 2(b)(2), 120 Stat. 577 (2006) (codified at 42 USC § 1973c) ("2006 Amendments"). The statute passed in July 2006 with majorities of 98-0 in the Senate and 390-33 in the House.

50. Senate Judiciary Committee, Fannie Lou Hamer, Rosa Parks, Coretta Scott King, and Cesar E. Chavez Voting Rights Act Reauthorization and Amendments Act of 2006, S. Rep. No. 109-295, at 19, 31, 47, and 52 (2006). Cesar E. Chavez's name,

which was not included in the House bill's name, was dropped from the Senate bill before the final congressional vote so that the two bills would be identical, eliminating the need for further debate.

51. David A. Bositis, *Blacks and the 2008 Elections: A Preliminary Analysis* (Washington, D.C.: Joint Center for Political and Economic Studies, 2008), 15, table 2.

52. U.S. Bureau of the Census, Current Population Reports, Special Studies, P-23-80, *The Social and Economic Status of the Black Population in the United States: An Historical View, 1790–1978* (Washington, D.C.: U.S. Government Printing Office, 1979), 156–57.

53. That number does not include the two African Americans elected from the District of Columbia and the U.S. Virgin Islands who are nonvoting members of the House.

54. U.S. Census Bureau, *Statistical Abstract: 2009*, 251, table 398, http://www.census.gov/prod/2008pubs/09statab/election.pdf (accessed April 3, 2009).

55. Joint Center for Political and Economic Studies, *Black Elected Officials: A Statistical Summary, 2000*, Appendix, Black Elected Officials in the U.S., 28.

56. David Lublin, Tom Brunnell, Bernard Grofman, and Lisa Handley, "Has the Voting Rights Act Outlived Its Usefulness? In a Word, No," January 2009, unpublished paper available at http://papers.ssrn.com. Table 1. Data on voting-age population is drawn from the Census Bureau's American FactFinder 2005–2007 American Community Survey 3-Year Estimates.

57. That was the definition of racial bloc voting used by Justice William Brennan, writing for the Court in *Thornburg v. Gingles*, 478 U.S. 30 (1986), a Section 2 case. It was a definition joined by only three other justices, however. It eliminated from racially driven choices the logically essential element of racism:

white resistance to black candidacies. "The reasons black and white voters vote differently have no relevance to the central inquiry of § 2," he concluded. "It is the difference between the choices made by blacks and whites – not the reasons for that difference – that results in blacks having less opportunity than whites to elect their preferred representatives." (478 U.S. at 55.)

58. This was the commonly understood definition of vote dilution. The language quoted here is from *H. Comm. on the Judiciary, Voting Rights Act Extension*, HR Rep. No. 94-196 at 30 (1975), 18.

59. *Whitcomb v. Chavis*, 403 U.S. 124, 153 (1971).

60. Edison Research exit poll, reported in Ronald Brownstein, "Obama Struggling With White Voters," *National Journal*, April 7, 2011. http://hotlineoncall.nationaljournal.com/archives/2011/04/pew-poll-obama.php.

61. Pew Research Center national poll released April 7, 2011. Brownstein, "Obama Struggling With White Voters."

62. Leonard Greene and Jennifer Fermino, "Base in the Hole," *New York Post*, April 8, 2011.

63. See, for instance, the testimony of Theodore M. Shaw, president and director-counsel of the NAACP Legal Defense and Educational Fund, Inc., before the House Judiciary Committee's Subcommittee on the Constitution, Voting Rights Act Renewal Oversight Hearing on the Judicial Evolution of the Retrogression Standard, November 9, 2005; and testimony of Laughlin McDonald, director, Voting Rights Project, American Civil Liberties Union, Fnd., before the House Committee on the Judiciary Subcommittee on the Constitution, The Voting Rights Act: The Continuing Need for Section 5, Tuesday, October 25, 2005.

64. *Clarksdale Press Register*, "Voting Rights Act Is Antiquated," June 13, 2008.

65. *Johnson v. De Grandy,* 512 U.S. 997, 1020 (1994).

66. *Citizens v. Perry,* 548 U.S. 399 (2006).

67. Complaint, *Northwest Austin Mun. Util. Dist. No. One v. Mukasey,* 557 F.Supp. 2d 9 (D.D.C. 2008), 6. In a number of states, only some counties are covered by Section 5. There was thus nothing novel about the notion that a particular jurisdiction could be treated differently than others in the same state.

68. *Citizens v. Perry,* 548 U.S. 399 (2006).

69. *LaRoque v. Holder,* No. 10-0561, 2010 U.S. Dist. LEXIS 134464 (D.D.C. Dec. 20, 2010). The case was dismissed on December 20, 2010, after a federal judge determined that the plaintiffs lacked standing. It is on appeal to the Court of Appeals for the District of Columbia Circuit.

70. *Shelby County v. Holder,* 270 F.R.D. 16, 2010 U.S. Dist. LEXIS 96970 (D.D.C. Sept. 16, 2010).

71. *South Carolina v. Katzenbach,* 383 U.S. 301, 358 (1966).

72. "The Promise and Pitfalls of the New Voting Rights Act," 117 *Yale Law Journal,* 174, 177 (November, 2007). Persily is Charles Keller Beekman Professor of Law and Political Science and the director of the Center for Law and Politics at Columbia Law School.

73. This discussion of the high costs of continuing to insist on race-based electoral arrangements rests heavily on Abigail Thernstrom, *Voting Rights – and Wrongs: The Elusive Quest for Racially Fair Elections* (Washington, D.C.: American Enterprise Institute Press, 2009), 214–20. A forthcoming article by Jason Rathod makes almost the identical argument, noting that the Voting Rights Act "currently encourages formation of majority-minority districts that reward racially polarizing candidates, handicap minorities from winning politically powerful statewide races, and reproduce race as an organizing principle of American society." Race-based districts, he continues, "typically reward race-baiters who resort to fanning the flames of racial extremism." As a consequence, "campaigns degenerate into battles of who is the blacker candidate.... Because majority-minority districts reward race-baiting candidates and punish post-racial candidates," he continues, "they elect candidates who lack the cross-racial appeal to win statewide races." These are precisely the arguments I make below (and in my 2009 book), but Rathod goes on (as I do not in this chapter) to urge a solution: maps that contain many more crossover districts in which minority candidates must appeal to white voters. Such districts would reward postracial campaigns. And he places his argument an interesting larger theoretical context, depicting the country as torn between civic nationalism and racial nationalism, concepts he discusses at length. Jason Rathod, *A Post-Racial Voting Rights Act,* 13 Berkeley J. Afr.-Am. L. & Pol'y 139 (2011).

74. Cass R. Sunstein, *Why Groups Go to Extremes* (Washington, D.C.: American Enterprise Institute Press, 2008). Sunstein is professor law at Harvard University, currently on loan to the Obama administration.

75. The lone Republican is Allen West, representing FL-22; as a Republican, his politics appeal to southern whites. The other three are Keith Ellison (MN-5), Emanuel Cleaver (MO-5), and Andre Carson (IN-7). Ellison's election is probably explained by the heavy concentration of University of Minnesota students and faculty in the district. Cleaver had been a very successful Kansas City mayor and had supported President Bill Clinton's changes in welfare policy. In a race to fill the seat

vacated by the death of his grandmother, Carson won the Democratic nomination with a plurality of votes against two other candidates. In the special election in 2007, he got extensive assistance from the Democratic Congressional Campaign Committee.

76. Massachusetts is an obvious exception; Deval Patrick is in his second term as governor, but the state is the bluest in the nation.

77. Michael Carvin, remarks, book event, American Enterprise Institute, May 5, 2008.

78. No African American had made a serious bid for the presidency before Obama. Jesse Jackson, never elected to any office, ran in 1984 and 1988. He raised his national profile, and perhaps his speaking fees, but he had no chance of winning the Democratic nomination. Likewise, in 1972, Representative Shirley Chisholm, a Democrat from New York, declared her candidacy, but she was not a politically serious contender.

79. Is should be noted, however, that some scholarly work has found a mixed picture. Kimball Brace, Lisa Handley, Richard Niemi, and Harold Stanley, "Minority Turnout and the Creation of Majority-Minority Districts," *American Politics Quarterly* 23, no. 2 (April 1995): 190–203, for example, found no consistent pattern in elections for the Florida State House and Senate and the U.S. House of Representatives. In some newly created black-majority districts, black turnout rose modestly; in many others it declined. "Overall, we cannot yet conclude that the creation of minority-dominated districts has a consistent effect on minority turnout," the authors wrote.

80. Carol Swain, *Black Faces, Black Interests: The Representation of African Americans in Congress* (Cambridge, Mass.: Harvard University Press, 1993), 203. Swain is

professor of law at Vanderbilt University Law School.

81. James E. Campbell, *Cheap Seats: The Democratic Party's Advantage in U.S. House Elections* (Columbus: Ohio State University Press, 1996). Campbell is a political scientist at the University of Buffalo.

82. Claudine Gay, "Legislating Without Constraints: The Effect of Minority Districting on Legislators' Responsiveness to Constituency Preferences," *Journal of Politics* 69, no. 2 (May 2007): 442–56. Gay is professor of government at Harvard University.

83. Ibid., 443.

84. Ibid., 446 n. 6.

85. Judge Edith Jones (U.S. Court of Appeals, Fifth Circuit) made this point in *Vera v. Richards*, 861 F. Supp. 1304, 1335, n. 43 (S.D. Tex. 1994): "Organized political activity takes place most effectively within neighborhoods and communities; on a larger scale, these organizing units may evolve into media markets and geographic regions. When natural geographic and political boundaries are arbitrarily cut, the influence of local organizations is seriously diminished. After the civic and veterans groups, labor unions, chambers of commerce, religious congregations, and school boards are subdivided among districts, they can no longer importune *their* Congressman and expect to wield the same degree of influence that they would if all their members were voters in his district. Similarly, local groups are disadvantaged from effectively organizing in an election campaign because their numbers, money, and neighborhoods are split." Jones was hearing this district court case as a circuit judge.

86. Aaron Blake, "The Decline of the Majority-Black District, and What It Means," Washington Post, April 20, 2011. http://www.washingtonpost.com/

blogs/the-fix/post/the-decline-of-the-majority-black-district-and-what-it-means/2011/04/19/AFTqqACE_blog.html.

87. Frank Newport and Joseph Carroll, "Analysis: Impact of Personal Character-istics on Candidate Support: Americans Most Comfortable Voting for a Black or Female Candidate," Gallup News Service, March 13, 2007.

88. Adam Nossiter, "Race Matters Less in Politics of South," *New York Times,* February 21, 2008, A1.

89. Daniel Lowenstein, remarks, book event for Anthony A. Peacock, American Enterprise Institute, Washington, D.C., May 5, 2008, edited transcript from audio tapes, http://www.aei.org/events/event ID.1710/event_detail.asp (accessed April 1, 2009).

SIX

The Voting Rights Act in South Dakota: One Litigator's Perspective on Reauthorization

BRYAN L. SELLS

South Dakota received relatively little attention in the debates over re-authorization of the Voting Rights Act. The state is hardly mentioned in the legislative history of the 2006 reauthorization. It got not a word in the Supreme Court's opinion upholding that reauthorization.[1] Few people, including many voting-rights advocates, are even aware that the state was affected by the reauthorization. South Dakota is not one of the seven states originally covered by the special provisions of the Voting Rights Act,[2] but it is a prime example of the need for continued – and expanded – coverage.

In the seven years preceding Congress's decision to reauthorize the special provisions for another twenty-five years, Native American[3] voters brought eight voting rights cases challenging virtually every level of government in the state.[4] Together, those cases and the volumes of evidence they generated offer a compelling demonstration of the present-day impact of the Voting Rights Act and the continuing need for close federal oversight of state election processes. The cases also suggest that Congress may not have gone far enough to protect minority voters from the kinds of invidious voting discrimination that they face today.

A LONG HISTORY OF DISCRIMINATION

Throughout the American West, Native Americans have faced voting discrimination ranging in form from outright vote denial to more subtle restrictions on political participation similar to those used to disenfranchise African Americans in the American South.[5] South Dakota is no exception, and its long history of voting discrimination against Native Americans stretches back to the earliest days of the Dakota Territory.

The act of Congress that created the territory in 1861 denied Indians the right to vote by restricting suffrage in the first legislative election to free white men.[6] The act also limited suffrage and officeholding in the territory to citizens of the United States and persons who intended to become citizens.[7] Because virtually no Indians in the territory were citizens of the United States, the act effectively prohibited Native Americans from voting or holding office in the territory.

The first territorial assembly, meeting in 1862, limited the rights of suffrage and officeholding to free white men.[8] The assembly passed the territory's first comprehensive election law in 1864, and that law restricted the rights of suffrage and officeholding to "[e]very free white male person above the age of twenty-one ... who is a citizen of the United States, or who has declared upon oath his intention to become such."[9]

When the territory enacted its first civil code in 1866, the code contained a special provision expressly denying Indians the most basic civil rights, including the right to "vote or hold office."[10] This rights-stripping provision was redundant, however, because the franchise was still restricted to free white men.

After Congress enacted the Civil Rights Act of 1866, which granted citizenship and civil rights to "all persons born in the United States ... excluding Indians not taxed,"[11] the territorial assembly struck the word "white" from the qualifications of electors but added the proviso that "no person shall have the right to vote by reason of the passage of this act, except such persons as are declared to be citizens of the United States by act of Congress of April 9, 1866." This made it clear that it did not intend to extend the franchise to Native Americans, who were not considered citizens of the United States.[12] Although voting was no longer limited to white male citizens, it was still limited to male *citizens,* and virtually no Indians in the territory had yet obtained citizenship.[13] Striking the word "white" also had no effect on the civil code's affirmative prohibition on Indian voting and officeholding, which remained in full effect.

When South Dakota became a state in 1890, its new constitution continued to limit suffrage and officeholding to male citizens and men who declared an intention to become citizens.[14] The new state also carried forward the Dakota Territory's anti-Indian civil rights statute that categorically denied Indians the right to "vote or hold office."[15]

In 1903, the state legislature softened the anti-Indian civil rights statute by limiting it to Indians who "maintain[ed] tribal relations."[16] Indian men were thus eligible to vote in South Dakota for the first time in 1903, but only if they had severed all ties with their tribes and only if the individual had either become a citizen of the United States or expressed an intention to become a citizen.

This new formula for Indian suffrage became a recipe for confusion. Most Indians were ineligible to vote, and it was not easy to identify those that were. Numerous judicial decisions and opinions issued by South Dakota's attorneys general between 1908 and 1924 grappled with the problem.[17] The test for eligibility that emerged was whether the Indian seeking the franchise "has severed his tribal relations and adopted the habits of civilized life."[18] That test, moreover, was "a question of fact that must be determined as to each Indian offering to vote."[19]

In 1924, Congress passed the Indian Citizenship Act, which granted citizenship to "all non-citizen Indians born within the territorial limits of the United States."[20] Even that apparently did not resolve the question of Indian suffrage in South Dakota, however, because the state's anti-Indian civil rights statute continued to require Native Americans to sever their tribal ties before they could be eligible to vote or hold office.

In 1940, the state's attorney in Winner, South Dakota, requested an opinion from the South Dakota attorney general on the question of whether an Indian who maintained tribal relations was eligible to vote and to hold office.[21] The attorney general indicated his view that the Indian Citizenship Act had "nullified" the state law insofar as it conditioned Indian voting rights on the severance of tribal relations.[22] The anti-Indian civil rights statute nonetheless remained on the books, unamended, until 1951 – making South Dakota one of the last states in the nation officially to grant voting rights to all Native Americans.[23]

Even after Native Americans gained the right to vote, moreover, South Dakota officially continued to deny them the right to vote for and hold certain offices until the early 1980s. Under state law, residents of an "unorganized" county (that is, a county with no organized government) were ineligible to vote for or hold county offices in the neighboring "organized" county that had administrative control over the unorganized county's affairs.[24] While these restrictions technically applied to Indians and non-Indians alike, the only unorganized counties in South Dakota after the 1910s were Shannon, Todd, and Washabaugh (now part of Jackson County), all three of which were wholly within the boundaries of the Pine Ridge and Rosebud Sioux Indian Reservations and were overwhelmingly Indian in population.[25]

In 1975, a federal court struck down the voting restriction as a violation of the Fourteenth Amendment, rejecting the state's argument that reservation Indians "do not share the same interest in county government as residents of organized counties."[26] The same court struck down the restriction on officeholding five years later,[27] and the state legislature finally repealed the laws in 1982.[28]

With that repeal, South Dakota became the last state in the nation to end its official disfranchisement of Native Americans. But the voting discrimination did not end there.

THE VOTING RIGHTS ACT COMES TO SOUTH DAKOTA

Like all other states, South Dakota is covered by the nationwide and permanent provisions of the Voting Rights Act of 1965. Among other things, those provisions prohibit voting discrimination on the basis of "race or color" and the use of any "test or device," such as a literacy test, as a prerequisite for registering or voting in any federal, state, or local election.[29] The permanent provisions of the act were aimed primarily at voting discrimination against African Americans in the South, but Native Americans were also covered as a cognizable racial group.[30]

South Dakota did not become covered by the special provisions of the Voting Rights Act, however, until 1975, when Congress amended the act to expand the geographic reach of the act's special provisions, to cover discrimination against language minorities, and to require certain jurisdictions to provide language assistance to voters with limited English proficiency.[31] As a result of those amendments, Shannon and

Todd Counties in South Dakota, which are home to the Pine Ridge and
Rosebud Indian Reservations respectively, became subject to Section
5's preclearance requirement.[32] Eight counties in the state – Todd, Shannon, Bennett, Charles Mix, Corson, Lyman, Mellette, and Washabaugh
(which is now part of Jackson County) – were required to provide language assistance in the local Indian dialect because of their significant
Indian populations with limited English proficiency and high illiteracy
rates.[33]

Reaction to the new coverage in South Dakota was eerily reminiscent of the southern strategies of interposition and nullification in the
1950s and 1960s. William Janklow, who was then the state's attorney general, issued a formal opinion deriding Section 5 as a "facial absurdity" that
imposed an "unworkable solution to a nonexistent problem."[34] He con-
demned the Voting Rights Act as an unconstitutional federal encroachment that rendered state power "almost meaningless"[35] and quoted with
approval Justice Black's famous dissent in *South Carolina v. Katzenbach*[36]
complaining that Section 5 treated covered jurisdictions as "little more
than conquered provinces."[37] Janklow expressed the hope that Congress
would soon repeal "the Voting Rights Act currently plaguing South Dakota."[38] And he advised the secretary of state not to comply with the
preclearance requirement. "I see no need," he concluded, "to proceed
with undue speed to subject our State's laws to a 'one-man veto' by the
United States Attorney General."[39]

Although the 1975 amendments never were in fact repealed, state
officials followed Janklow's advice and essentially ignored the preclearance requirement. From the date coverage began in 1976 until 2002,
South Dakota enacted more than six hundred statutes and regulations
having an effect on elections or voting in Shannon and Todd Counties,
but submitted fewer than a dozen for preclearance. Those submissions,
moreover, were not the result of voluntary compliance with the law but
rather came at the request of the Department of Justice. As a result,
South Dakota's record of compliance with the special provisions of the
Voting Rights Act is almost certainly the worst in the nation.

Enforcement of the act's permanent provisions was also lacking
in the early years. The extensive voting rights litigation campaign that
swept through the South in the 1970s, '80s, and '90s largely bypassed

South Dakota. At least one scholar has attributed this lack of enforcement to a combination of factors, including a lack of resources and access to legal assistance among Native Americans, lax enforcement of the Voting Rights Act by the Department of Justice, the geographic isolation of Indian reservations, and the debilitating legacy of discrimination by the state and federal government.[40] Whatever the causes, the effect was clear: between 1965 and 1998, the state saw only four cases brought under the permanent provisions of the Voting Rights Act.

In the first such challenge, brought in 1984, four members of the Sisseton-Wahpeton Sioux Tribe sued the Sisseton Independent School District, alleging that the at-large method of electing the district's nine-member school board diluted Native American voting strength. The district court ruled against the Indian plaintiffs, but the court of appeals reversed.[41] It observed that the district court had failed to consider "substantial evidence . . . that voting in the District was polarized along racial lines."[42] Pointing out that the district court had failed to discuss virtually any of the substantial evidence of discrimination offered by the plaintiffs, the court of appeals remanded the case to the district court for further findings.[43] On remand, the parties agreed to settle the case by implementing a system of cumulative voting that enabled Indian voters to elect representatives of their choice to the school board.

The other three South Dakota cases brought under the Voting Rights Act before 1999 involved episodic voting practices (as opposed to permanent structural barriers) that had a disparate impact on Indian voters. In 1984, a member of the Oglala Sioux Tribe successfully obtained a temporary restraining order against county election officials who had rejected voter registrations submitted by Indian voters just before the deadline.[44] In 1986, Alberta Black Bull and other Indian residents of the Cheyenne River Reservation brought a successful Section 2 suit against Ziebach County because of its failure to provide sufficient polling places for school district elections.[45] The same year, Indian plaintiffs on the reservation secured an order requiring the auditor of Dewey County to provide Indians additional voter registration cards and extend the deadline for voter registration.[46]

Following those victories, however, there was no further Indian voting rights litigation in South Dakota for the next thirteen years. The

second wave of voting rights litigation began in 1999 and brought with
it eight cases over the next five years.

United States v. Day County

Day County is a sparsely populated county in the glacial lakes region
of northeast South Dakota. The county lies within the disestablished
reservation of the Sisseton-Wahpeton Sioux Tribe, in what is known as
a "checkerboard" area of non-Indian-owned parcels and adjacent Native American–owned parcels of land. The county is also home to the
Enemy Swim Lake, a glacial lake popular for its fishing and recreational
opportunities.

In the early 1990s, white landowners around the lake organized the
Enemy Swim Sanitary District. (A sanitary district is a special, limited-
purpose government charged with constructing and maintaining sewers
and storm drains.) The sanitary district was made up of several noncontiguous pieces of land owned by whites, which represented only 13
percent of the land area around Enemy Swim Lake, and was drawn to exclude the remaining 87 percent, owned by the Sisseton-Wahpeton Sioux
Tribe and about two hundred of its members. The district was governed
by a board of trustees who were elected at-large and served three-year
staggered terms. All the registered voters in the sanitary district were
white.

In May 1999, the Department of Justice sued the county and the
sanitary district for intentionally excluding Native Americans from their
electoral process.[47] The Department alleged, among other things, that
Indian lands had been excluded from the district out of fear that Native
Americans would become a majority of the district's voters. The result,
according to the complaint, was a *Gomillion*-style[48] denial of the right to
vote in violation of Section 2 of the Voting Rights Act.

Day County promptly agreed to settle the case, but the sanitary district resisted, settling only after the court denied their motion for summary judgment. As part of the settlement agreement, both the county

and the district admitted that the district's boundaries unlawfully denied Indian citizens' right to vote, and they agreed to redraw the boundaries to include the Indian land.[49]

Emery v. Hunt

In 1991, the South Dakota legislature adopted a new legislative redistricting plan using data from the 1990 census.[50] The plan divided the state into thirty-five districts and provided, with one exception, that each district would be entitled to one senate member and two house members elected at large from within the district.

The exception was the new District 28. The 1991 legislation provided that "in order to protect minority voting rights, District No. 28 shall consist of two single-member house districts."[51] House District 28A consisted of Dewey and Ziebach Counties and portions of Corson County, and included the Cheyenne River Sioux Reservation and portions of the Standing Rock Sioux Reservation. House District 28B consisted of Harding and Perkins Counties and portions of Corson and Butte Counties. According to 1990 census data, Indians were 60 percent of the voting-age population of House District 28A, and less than 4 percent of the voting age population of House District 28B.

Five years later, despite its pledge to protect minority voting rights, the legislature abolished House Districts 28A and 28B and required candidates for the house to run at large in District 28.[52] The repeal took place after an Indian candidate, Mark Van Norman, won the Democratic primary in District 28A in 1994. A chief sponsor of the repealing legislation was Eric Bogue, the Republican candidate who defeated Van Norman in the general election.[53] The reconstituted House District 28 had an Indian voting-age population of only 29 percent. Given the prevailing patterns of racially polarized voting, of which members of the legislature were surely aware, Indian voters could not realistically expect to elect a candidate of their choice in the new district.

Steven Emery, Rocky Le Compte, and James Picotte – all residents of the Cheyenne River Sioux Reservation – challenged the repeal in early 2000. They claimed that the changes in District 28 violated Section 2 of the Voting Rights Act, as well as Article III, Section 5 of the South Dakota constitution, which mandated reapportionment once every tenth year, but prohibited all reapportionment at other times. The South Dakota Supreme Court had expressly held "when a Legislature once makes an apportionment following an enumeration no Legislature can make another until after the next enumeration."[54]

The plaintiffs' experts analyzed the six legislative contests between 1992 and 1994 involving Indian and non-Indian candidates in District 28 held under the 1991 plan to determine the existence, and the extent, of any racial bloc voting. Indian voters favored the Indian candidates at an average rate of 81 percent, while whites voted for the white candidates at an average rate of 93 percent. In all six of the contests the candidate preferred by Indians was defeated.[55]

White cohesion also fluctuated widely depending on whether an Indian was a candidate. In the four head-to-head white-white legislative contests, where there was no possibility of electing an Indian candidate, the average level of white cohesion was 68 percent. In the Indian-white legislative contests, the average level of white cohesion jumped to 94 percent.[56] This phenomenon of increased white cohesion to defeat minority candidates has been called "targeting."[57]

Before deciding the plaintiffs' Section 2 claim, the district court certified the state law question to the South Dakota Supreme Court. That court accepted certification and held that, in enacting the 1996 redistricting plan, "the Legislature acted beyond its constitutional limits."[58] It declared the 1996 plan null and void and reinstated the pre-existing 1991 plan. At the ensuing special election ordered by the district court, Tom Van Norman was elected from District 28A, the first Indian in history to be elected to the state house from the Cheyenne River Sioux Indian Reservation.

Bone Shirt v. Hazeltine

The State of South Dakota enacted a new redistricting plan for its 105-member state legislature in November 2001.[59] The plan divided the state into thirty-five districts, each of which elected one member of the state senate and two members of the state house of representatives. Voters elected their two house members at large in each district except District

28, which the plan subdivided into two single-member house districts, Districts 28A and 28B. The plan contained two majority-Indian districts: District 27 and District 28A. District 27 encompassed part of the Pine Ridge Indian Reservation and all of the Rosebud Indian Reservation in the southern part of the state. Native Americans made up approximately 90 percent of District 27's total population and 86 percent of its voting-age population. In majority-white District 26, which bordered District 27 to the north and east and encompassed the remainder of the Pine Ridge Indian Reservation, Native Americans made up approximately 30 percent of the total population and 23 percent of its voting-age population. In the state as a whole, Native Americans are approximately 9 percent of the total population and 7 percent of the voting-age population.

Shortly after the 2001 plan became law, Alfred Bone Shirt and three other Native American voters sued in federal court, alleging that the plan violated Sections 2 and 5 of the Voting Rights Act.[60] The plaintiffs contended that the plan diluted Native American voting strength in violation of Section 2 by "packing" Native Americans into District 27, with the result that Indian voters in the neighboring District 26 were unable to elect representatives of their choice. The plaintiffs also claimed that the defendants, who included the secretary of state and other state officials as well as both houses of the state legislature, had violated Section 5 by implementing the plan without first obtaining federal preclearance.

A three-judge district court heard the plaintiffs' Section 5 claim first. The state argued that preclearance was not required because the boundaries of District 27, the district that encompassed all of Shannon and Todd counties, had not changed significantly from the state's 1991 plan. In fact, the only changes to District 27 occurred in Bennett County, which is not a covered jurisdiction. The plaintiffs argued that Section 5 required the state to preclear the 2001 plan because (a) the plan, as a whole, was very different from the 1991 plan, (b) District 27 had seen significant demographic changes[61] over the 1990s that effectively made it a "new" district despite having similar boundaries to the district in the 1991 plan, and (c) the small changes to the district's boundaries required preclearance even though they occurred in Bennett County. The Department of Justice also weighed in on the case as amicus curiae in support of the plaintiffs' position.

After a hearing, the court ruled in the plaintiffs' favor by a 2-1 margin.[62] In an opinion written by Judge Karen Schreier of Rapid City and joined by Judge Charles Kornmann of Aberdeen, the court agreed with the plaintiffs' second argument, holding that "demographic shifts render the new District 27 a change 'in voting' for the voters of Shannon and Todd counties that must be precleared under § 5."[63] As remedy, the court enjoined the enforcement of the plan in District 27 and ordered the state to submit the plan for preclearance within thirty days.

Circuit Judge James Loken of Minnesota dissented. He adopted the state's position that preclearance was not required because none of the boundary lines within Shannon or Todd Counties had changed. He also disagreed with the court's chosen remedy, arguing that the only proper remedy was to enjoin the implementation of the 2001 plan in Shannon and Todd Counties. In other words, the state would have to implement the 1991 plan in two counties and the 2001 plan in every other county. He also took the position that the court lacked the authority to order the state to submit its 2001 plan for preclearance because the state itself is not a covered jurisdiction.

The state did, however, submit the 2001 plan for preclearance, and the Bush administration precleared it without delay. The state did not appeal, and the parties turned their attention to the plaintiffs' Section 2 claim.

After extensive discovery and a bench trial held over nine days in April 2004, Judge Schreier ruled in a 144-page opinion that the state's plan violated Section 2.[64] The court first considered whether the evidence established the three factors that the Supreme Court identified in *Thornburg v. Gingles*[65] as generally necessary to prove a violation of Section 2. The court then analyzed whether the totality of the evidence had also shown that Indian voters had less opportunity than white voters to participate in the political process and to elect candidates of their choice. In conducting this analysis, the district court examined twelve additional factors: (1) the history of discrimination against Native Americans in South Dakota; (2) the extent of racially polarized voting; (3) the use of voting procedures that could enhance the dilutive effect of "packing"; (4) Native American access to formal and informal candidate slating processes; (5) the extent to which Native Americans in South Dakota bear the effects of discrimination in education, employment, and health, which hinder their ability to participate effectively in the political process; (6) whether political campaigns in South Dakota have been characterized by overt or subtle racial appeals; (7) the extent to which Native Americans have been elected to public office; (8) whether the state legislature is responsive to the particular concerns of Native American voters; (9) whether the state's policy justification for the 2001 plan was tenuous; (10) the extent to which the plan gave white voters control over a disproportionate share of the legislative seats; (11) the lack of Indian legislative candidates; and (12) the role of voter apathy and low turnout as an explanation for the lack of Indian electoral success. The district court made extensive findings of fact on each factor.

With respect to the first *Gingles* factor, the district court found that Native Americans in South Dakota are sufficiently numerous and geographically compact that they could constitute a majority in at least one more legislative district than existed in the state's plan.[66] The court based its finding on the report and testimony of William S. Cooper, the plaintiffs' expert demographer, as well as several redistricting plans drafted by state legislative staffers during the 2001 redistricting process. Cooper had produced five illustrative districting plans, "each one of which creates at least one additional majority-minority legislative district in South Dakota while adhering to traditional redistricting principles."[67] Each of the plans produced by legislative staffers also created at least one additional majority-Indian district.

The district court rejected the defendants' argument that the required threshold for the first *Gingles* factor in this case should be well above 65 percent of the voting-age population. The court noted that the defendants had failed to identify any cases in which a court had ever required such an elevated threshold. The district court also rejected the defendants' contention that the plaintiffs' illustrative plans were based on racial considerations above all else. To the contrary, the court found that the plans did not subordinate traditional race-neutral districting principles to racial considerations and did not consider race any more than reasonably necessary to determine whether an additional majority-Indian district was possible.

After considering all the evidence, the district court concluded that the plaintiffs had satisfied the first *Gingles* factor "as a matter of law."[68]

With respect to the second *Gingles* factor, the district court found that Native Americans in Districts 26 and 27 were politically cohesive. Turning first to the parties' statistical evidence, the court found that despite a difference in methodology, experts for both parties produced reliable results that "demonstrate[d] significant cohesion among Indian voters."[69]

The plaintiffs' expert, Dr. Steven P. Cole, used bivariate ecological regression and homogeneous precinct analysis – the two statistical methods endorsed by the Supreme Court in *Gingles* – to estimate Indian cohesion and white crossover voting. He analyzed a total of forty-five elections in Districts 26 and 27 from 1986 to 2002 and found high levels of political cohesion. The defendants' expert, Dr. Jeffrey S. Zax, used a statistical technique called ecological inference, or EI, which produced estimates of Indian cohesion and white crossover voting as well as estimates of Indian and white voter turnout. Dr. Zax analyzed fifty-three elections for public office in Districts 26 and 27 between 1996 and 2002 and, like Dr. Cole, found high levels of cohesion.

The district court also surveyed the parties' nonstatistical evidence of cohesion at some length. Relying on the testimony of numerous witnesses, both expert and lay, and literally dozens of documentary exhibits, the court concluded that the nonstatistical evidence, like the statistical evidence, established Indian cohesion.[70]

The district court rejected the defendants' contention that Democratic partisanship, not race, was the reason that Native Americans tended to vote the same way at the polls.[71] Relying on statistical and nonstatistical evidence, including two of the defendants' own lay witnesses, the court found that the balance of the evidence did not support the defendants' claim. The district court also rejected the defendants' partisanship claim as a matter of law, reasoning that Section 2 protects a minority voter's right to elect candidates of choice even if the voter chooses candidates solely because they belong to a particular political party.

After considering all the evidence, the district court found that the plaintiffs had satisfied the second *Gingles* factor.[72]

With respect to the third *Gingles* factor, the court found that both Dr. Cole and Dr. Zax had produced results that "show[ed] that non-

Indian voters in District 26 vote sufficiently as a bloc to enable them, particularly in the most probative elections and in the absence of special circumstances, usually to defeat the Indian-preferred candidate."[73] The district court divided the relevant statistical results into four categories according to the probative value it assigned to them: (1) endogenous interracial elections – elections for state legislative offices in District 26 with Indian and non-Indian candidates; (2) endogenous elections with only white candidates; (3) exogenous interracial elections – interracial elections for offices other than the state legislature; and (4) exogenous elections with only white candidates. In all four categories, white voters in District 26 voted sufficiently as a bloc to defeat the vast majority of the candidates preferred by Indian voters.

Across all of the many elections on which the district court relied, regardless of category, Dr. Cole's results showed that white voters in District 26 voted sufficiently as a bloc to defeat twenty-one out of twenty-one (100 percent) Indian-preferred candidates. Dr. Zax's results showed that white voters defeated seventeen out of twenty-five (68 percent) Indian-preferred candidates.

Considering all of this evidence in the aggregate, the district court concluded that the plaintiffs had satisfied the third *Gingles* factor.[74]

Turning to the "totality of the circumstances," the court found that eleven of the twelve totality factors weighed in the plaintiffs' favor, and it rejected the defendants' claim on the twelfth factor that Indian voter apathy alone accounted for the difficulty Indian voters had experienced in electing candidates of their choice in District 26.[75]

According to the Supreme Court, the two "most important" totality factors are (1) the extent to which minorities have been elected under the challenged plan; and (2) the extent to which voting is racially polarized.[76] The district court found that both factors weighed in the plaintiffs' favor. The defendants admitted, and the district court found, that not a single Native American candidate was elected to the state legislature from the area in District 26 between 1982 and 2002.[77] The district court also found that "substantial evidence, both statistical and lay, demonstrates that voting in South Dakota is racially polarized among whites and Indians in Districts 26 and 27."[78] It described that polarization as "extensive" and at a "high level."[79] It also found that white crossover voting dropped precipitously when the Indian-preferred candidate was an Indian.[80]

The district court's analysis of the totality of factors is also noteworthy because of its extensive findings on South Dakota's history of discrimination against Native Americans. The court's review of that history of discrimination covers more than forty pages in its slip opinion.[81] The review synthesizes innumerable documents, many of which were pulled directly from the state's own session laws.

The review also highlights the testimony of Native American witnesses who offered at trial their own experiences of discrimination. For example, Elsie Meeks, a tribal member at Pine Ridge and the first Indian to serve on the U.S. Commission on Civil Rights, told about her first exposure to the non-Indian world and the fact "that there might be some people who didn't think well of people from the reservation."[82] When she and her sister enrolled in a predominantly white school in Fall River County and were riding the bus, "somebody behind us said . . . the Indians should go back to the reservation. And I mean I was fairly hurt by it . . . it was just sort of a shock to me."[83] Meeks said that there is a "disconnect between Indians and non-Indians" in the state.[84] "[W]hat most people don't realize is that many Indians, they experience this racism in some form from non-Indians nearly every time they go into a border town community . . . [T]hen their . . . reciprocal feelings are based on that, that they know, or at least feel that the non-Indians don't like them and don't trust them."[85]

Lyla Young, a Rosebud tribal member, said that the first contact she had with whites was when she went to high school in Todd County.[86] The Indian students lived in a segregated dorm at the Rosebud boarding school and were bussed to the high school, then bussed back to the dorm for lunch, then bused again to the high school for the afternoon session.[87] The white students referred to the Indians as "GI's," which stood for "government issue."[88] Young said that "I just withdrew. I had no friends at school. Most of the girls that I dormed with didn't finish high school . . . I didn't associate with anybody."[89] Even as an adult, Young has had little contact with the white community. "I don't want to. I have no desire to open up my life or my children's life to any kind of discrimination or harsh treatment. Things are tough enough without inviting more."[90]

Testifying in court was particularly difficult for her. "This was a big job for me to come here today. . . . I'm the only Indian woman in here, and I'm nervous. I'm very uncomfortable."[91]

Arlene Brandis, a Rosebud tribal member, recalled walking to and from school in Tripp County: "[C]ars would drive by and they would holler at us and call us names . . . like dirty Indian, drunken Indian, and say why don't you go back to the reservation."[92] Although that was years ago, Brandis did not see much difference between then and now. White families in Winner, where she lives now, do not sit near her family at high school football and basketball games. She believes that this is because she and her husband are Native American.

Almost without exception, the tribal members who testified at trial could recount incidents of being mistreated, embarrassed, or humiliated by whites. Based on "the wealth of evidence and testimony" before it, the court concluded that "there is a long and extensive history of discrimination against Indians in South Dakota that touches upon the right to register and to vote, and affects their ability to participate in the political process on an equal basis with other citizens."[93]

Lastly, the district court returned to the defendants' attempt to attribute the lack of Indian electoral success to voter apathy and low voter turnout. In particular, the defendants claimed that the lack of success was due to a lack of Indian interest in state politics, internal divisions among the tribes, and a fear among Indian voters that voting in state and county elections would erode tribal sovereignty.

The district court found, however, that the record refuted those claims.[94] "Throughout South Dakota's history, Native Americans have made repeated and persistent efforts to participate in the political process at all levels of government despite facing outright discrimination and informal barriers in exercising their right to vote."[95] The court based its conclusion in part on more than two dozen documentary exhibits and the testimony of several Native American lay witnesses who underscored the value of participating in state and federal elections. Even the defendants own expert historian, Dr. Michael Lawson, conceded that Native Americans in South Dakota are not uninterested in state politics. He added, "I think there's a growing number of tribal members who see the importance of political participation at every level."[96]

After reviewing each of the factors in its analysis, the district court found, based on the totality of circumstances, that South Dakota's 2001 legislative redistricting plan "results in unequal electoral opportunity for Indian voters."[97] Accordingly, the court concluded that the plan "impermissibly dilutes the Indian vote and violates § 2 of the Voting Rights Act."[98]

After finding a violation of Section 2, the district court gave the defendants two separate opportunities to propose a remedy. Each time they declined to do so. The court then issued an order adopting one of the plaintiffs' proposed remedial plans and enjoining the defendants from using the unlawful plan in future elections.[99] In the reconfigured District 27, Native Americans make up 73 percent of the total population and 65.66 percent of the voting-age population. In District 26A, Native Americans are 80.88 percent of the total population and 74.36 percent of the voting-age population.

The state appealed, but the Eight Circuit affirmed the decision of the district court.[100] The state did not ask the Supreme Court to hear the case, and the redrawn districts have been used ever since, resulting in Indian voter control over one additional seat in the South Dakota House of Representatives.

Weddell v. Wagner Community School District

The city of Wagner is a border town in Charles Mix County, South Dakota. The county, in the southeastern part of the state along the Missouri River, is home to the disestablished Yankton Sioux Reservation. The county made headlines not long ago when the local police chief was accused of racial profiling in an effort to enforce old bench warrants.[101] A local school later got into trouble for using a German shepherd police dog to search Indian kindergartners for drugs.[102]

The local school district in Wagner was run by a seven-member school board elected at large to staggered three-year terms. Although Indians were 42 percent of the district's total population and 36 percent of the district's voting-age population, Indian voters had not been able to elect a candidate of their choice to the school board for many years.

In March 2002, three members of the Yankton Sioux Tribe filed suit against the school district, alleging that its at-large elections diluted Indian voting strength in violation of Section 2 of the Voting Rights Act.[103] The plaintiffs demonstrated that Native American voters could control at least two seats if the seven board members were elected from single-member districts.

The parties eventually agreed to settle the case by replacing the at-large elections with cumulative voting. The district court approved a consent decree containing the settlement agreement on March 18, 2003.[104]

The very first election under the new system resulted in a tie between an Indian candidate and a non-Indian candidate. Under South Dakota law, the tie was to be settled with a deck of cards, and the Indian candidate prevailed by drawing a queen.

Cottier v. City of Martin

The city of Martin, located in southwestern South Dakota, is a small town of just over 1,100 people. Nearly 45 percent of the city's population is Native American. Martin lies near the border of two Indian reservations, Pine Ridge and Rosebud, and, like many border towns in the American West, the city has seen more than its share of racial conflict.

In the mid-1990s, for example, there were deep racial divisions over the homecoming ceremony at the local high school, in which male students designated as the "Big Chief" and "Little Chief" selected a "Princess" in a mock Indian ceremony while wearing traditional Indian regalia.[105] Also in the mid-1990s, the federal government successfully sued the local bank for systematic lending discrimination against Native Americans.[106] And in early 2002, Native Americans organized two peaceful marches in Martin to protest what they viewed as racial discrimination and police brutality by the non-Indian sheriff and his deputies.

Just weeks after the 2002 march, the American Civil Liberties Union (ACLU) sued the city on behalf of two Native American voters, alleging that the city's recently adopted redistricting plan violated the constitutional principle of one person, one vote.[107] The city responded by changing its plan to correct the malapportionment, but it did so in a way that fragmented the Indian community and gave white voters an overwhelming supermajority in all three council wards. The city also refused to reopen the candidate qualification period so that prospective candidates could decide whether to run under the new plan.

After a hearing in May 2002, the district court held on technical grounds that the plaintiffs could not challenge the city's decision not to reopen the candidate qualification period because none of the plaintiffs had expressed an intention to run for office under the new plan.[108] The court did, however, allow the plaintiffs to amend their complaint to allege that the new plan violated Section 2 of the Voting Rights Act and the Fourteenth Amendment to the United States Constitution.

After more than two years of pretrial discovery, the case went to trial in June 2004. The plaintiffs demonstrated, among other things, that no Indian-preferred candidate had ever been elected to the city council under the challenged plan. The court nonetheless ruled against the plaintiffs in March 2005, finding on the basis of *county* elections that the plaintiffs had not satisfied the third *Gingles* factor.[109]

The plaintiffs appealed, and on May 5, 2006, the Eighth Circuit reversed the decision of the district court.[110] It held that "the plaintiffs proved by a preponderance of the evidence that the white majority usually defeated the Indian-preferred candidate in Martin aldermanic elections."[111] The court described this evidence as "striking proof of vote dilution in Martin."[112] The court also noted the history of ongoing discrimination against Indians in Martin:

> For more than a decade Martin has been the focus of racial tension between Native-Americans and whites. In the mid-1990s, protests were held to end a racially offensive homecoming tradition that depicted Native-Americans in a demeaning, stereotypical fashion. Concurrently, the United States Justice Department sued and later entered into a consent decree with the local bank requiring an end to "redlining" loan practices and policies that adversely affected Native-Americans, and censuring the bank because it did not employ any Native-Americans. Most recently, resolution specialists from the Justice Department attempted to mediate an end to claims of racial discrimination by the local sheriff against Native-Americans.[113]

Finding that the plaintiffs had established all three factors for violation, the Eighth Circuit remanded the case to the district court to determine whether the plaintiffs were entitled to relief.[114]

On remand, the district court found that the city's redistricting plan "fragments Indian voters among all three wards, thereby giving Indians 'less opportunity than other members of the electorate to participate in the political process and to elect representatives of their choice.'"[115] The court concluded the plan diluted Indian voting strength and violated the law.

The district court gave the defendants the first opportunity to propose a remedy. The city refused, arguing instead that no remedy was possible. The district court disagreed and in February 2007 issued a remedial order requiring the city to hold future elections using a cumulative voting system.[116]

The city appealed. Notwithstanding the appeal, the city held its first round of elections under the remedial plan in June 2007. Three pro-Indian candidates ran unopposed and were elected to the city council without a vote.

On December 16, 2008, a three-judge panel of the Eighth Circuit affirmed the district court's judgment in the plaintiffs' favor.[117] The court held that the district court's finding of vote dilution was supported by substantial evidence in the record and that the district court did not abuse its discretion when it imposed cumulative voting as the remedy. The Eighth Circuit subsequently vacated the panel's ruling, however, when it granted the city's petition for rehearing en banc.

In a divided 7-4 opinion, the full Eighth Circuit affirmed the district court's original finding that the plaintiffs had failed to satisfy the third *Gingles* factor.[118] Even though Indian voters had never been able to elect a candidate of choice to the city council under the challenged plan, the en banc court relied on the results of elections for a wide variety of other offices ranging from President of the United States to county coroner. The court recognized that *Indian* candidates generally lost, but it found that those defeats were outweighed by the greater success of Indian-preferred candidates in contests featuring only white candidates. Adding those white-on-white contests to the ledger, the court found that white voters defeated the Indian-preferred candidates in 52 percent of the elections it had considered. It described this evidence as "mixed" and concluded that it did not compel a finding "that a white majority in Martin votes sufficiently as a bloc usually to defeat the Indian-preferred candidate."[119]

After more than eight years in court, Indian voters had lost. Their lack of opportunity to elect candidates of choice to the city council was somehow offset by an opportunity to elect white candidates to offices that nobody cared about. Notwithstanding the ultimate outcome, though, the record in the case still supports the need for federal oversight. Indeed, it suggests that Indians need *more* protection than current law gives them.

Quiver v. Nelson

In August 2002, four Native Americans brought what may be the largest Section 5 enforcement action in the Act's history. During the *Bone Shirt* litigation earlier that year, attorneys from the Department of Justice had produced a list of every Section 5 preclearance request ever submitted by the state of South Dakota in the twenty-five years since two counties in the state became covered jurisdictions in 1976. The list contained fewer than a dozen submissions.

After further investigation, attorneys for the *Bone Shirt* plaintiffs identified hundreds of unprecleared voting changes dating back to 1975. Indeed, the state had made sweeping changes to its election laws without seeking preclearance. Many statutes and regulations had been changed several times over the course of two and a half decades. All of this noncompliance, it turned out, was the result of Attorney General William Janklow's official opinion in 1977 advising state officials to ignore the federal law.[120] And ignore it they did.

The plaintiffs filed suit on August 5, alleging more than six hundred separate violations of Section 5.[121] Chris Nelson, who was then the head of the Elections Division within the South Dakota secretary of state's office, stated in an interview about the suit with South Dakota Public Radio that South Dakota had complied with its obligations under the Voting Rights Act.[122] A few days later, however, the secretary of state sent the Department of Justice a copy of the state's election code along with a two-paragraph letter asking the department to preclear the entire code. The department demurred, responding that the form of the submission was incomplete and demanding that the state comply fully with its preclearance obligations under the act. That brought the state to the negotiating table.

Following several months of settlement discussions, the state agreed to submit all unprecleared voting changes by the end of 2006, and the plaintiffs agreed not to seek any further injunctive relief prohibiting the enforcement of unprecleared voting changes while the submissions were underway.[123] The parties were unable, however, to agree on a schedule for the submissions. The plaintiffs wanted to have the state submit the changes year by year, beginning with the oldest changes, so that the Department of Justice would receive the changes in roughly the order that it would have received them if the state had been complying with the preclearance mandate all along. The state, however, wanted to submit changes by code section, so that all changes to a given code section were submitted at one time. Under the state's proposed method, the baseline for preclearance purposes would normally be whatever was in effect on the date of coverage, and the comparison for measuring retrogression would be the last change that the state sought to enforce. Because the parties were unable to agree, they left the choice of a schedule to the district court.

The court chose the state's method.[124] The effect of the court's choice, however, was significant. It meant that the state could preclear voting changes that were patently retrogressive as long as the final change was not retrogressive compared to whatever was in effect on the date of coverage. In other words, a code section that, for Indian voters, represented two steps forward and one step back looked like one step forward for purposes of preclearance. Had the court chosen the plaintiffs' proposed schedule, or had the state actually been complying with Section 5 all along, the Department of Justice would likely have objected to preclearance for any steps backward.

After the court adopted the defendants' proposed submission schedule, the defendants submitted more than eight hundred voting changes over the next three years. All of them were ultimately precleared, although the Bush administration did ask for additional information on several of the submissions. The court finally dissolved the consent decree in September 2006,[125] and the state has continued to make submissions for new voting changes as they are adopted.

Kirkie v. Buffalo County

In March 2003, the ACLU filed suit on behalf of three members of the Crow Creek Sioux Tribe in a challenge to the county commission districts in Buffalo County, South Dakota.[126] The plaintiffs alleged that the districts were malapportioned in violation of the one-person, one-vote principle and were adopted or maintained for the purpose of discriminating against Native American voters.

Buffalo County, which according to the 2000 census was the poorest county in the United States, had a population of approximately two thousand people, approximately 85 percent of whom were Native American.

The county was governed by a three-member county commission elected from three single-member districts. Those districts, which had been in use for decades, contained populations of approximately 1,550, 350, and 100 people, respectively. Virtually all of the 1,550 people in District 1 were Native American, while not a single Indian lived in the under-populated District 3. The system not only violated the "one person, one vote" standard of the Equal Protection Clause but had also been clearly implemented and maintained to dilute the Indian vote and ensure white control of county government.

The malapportionment persisted, moreover, despite a state law made for decennial redistricting. South Dakota law required a board of county commissioners to redistrict "at its regular meeting in February of each year ending in the numeral 2 . . . if such change is necessary in order that each district shall be as regular and compact in form as practicable and it shall so divide and redistrict its county that each district may contain as near as possible an equal number of residents, as determined by the last preceding federal decennial census."[127] Minutes of the county commission meeting held in February 2002 revealed that the commissioners considered the issue and decided – despite the overwhelming inequality among the districts – that the existing districts "required no change."[128] The commissioners were, in effect, thumbing their noses at state and federal redistricting requirements in order to prevent Native Americans from having a full voice on the commission.

The parties settled the case in early 2004. In a consent decree approved by the court, the county was required to redraw its commissioner districts and to hold a special election for two of the three seats.[129] The county also admitted that its plan was discriminatory and agreed to relief under Section 3 of the Voting Rights Act. That relief included the authorization of federal observers to monitor elections and the activation of the "pocket trigger" in Section 3(c), which effectively made Buffalo County subject to the preclearance requirements of Section 5 of the Voting Rights Act through 2013.

Blackmoon v. Charles Mix County

The litigation against Charles Mix County may be the best example of the continuing need for Section 5. Charles Mix has been, and still is, a county divided. Members of the Yankton Sioux Tribe, who make up approximately 30 percent of the county's population, live mainly in the southern part of the county, along the banks of the Missouri River, and in the small towns of Lake Andes, Marty, and Wagner. Farmers make up the bulk of the county's non-Indian population, and they are concentrated in the northern and eastern parts of the county. Social life remains largely, though informally, segregated. There is a plaque in the main hall of the county courthouse recognizing county residents who served in the Vietnam War, and it lists not a single Indian name even though many served.

The county is governed by a three-member county commission, with each commissioner elected from a single-member district. Before the litigation, no Native American had ever been elected to the commission.

The county's commissioner districts were decades old and badly malapportioned. The total deviation of the districts from equality was greater than 19 percent, and white voters were a majority in all three districts.

In anticipation of redistricting following the 2000 census, the Yankton Sioux Tribe sent a letter to the commission in November 2001 pointing out the malapportionment and proposing a new plan with one majority-Indian district. State law required the commission to redraw its districts at its regular meeting in February 2002 and then prohibited further redistricting for the rest of the decade.[130] The February meeting came and went, however, and the commission decided to leave its existing districts intact.

Four tribal members then sued the county, alleging that the three commissioner districts were malapportioned in violation of the one-person, one-vote standard of the Fourteenth Amendment and had been drawn or maintained to dilute Indian voting strength in violation of Section 2 of the Voting Rights Act.[131] In response to the suit, the county commission took the position that its districts were not unlawful, but it also asked the state legislature to pass legislation establishing a process for emergency redistricting. The purpose of the bill, according to its proponents, was to allow the defendants in the *Blackmoon* case to render the plaintiffs' claims moot by modifying the challenged redistricting plan and thereby avoid liability in the suit. Because of the urgency of that goal, the bill's sponsors brought the bill directly to the House floor, where the House suspended its rules, dispensed with a hearing, and passed the bill on the same day without the usual public notice. In the South Dakota Senate, the defendants' attorneys lobbied aggressively in favor of the bill and testified in support of it. Although many Native Americans, including several from Charles Mix County, testified in opposition to the bill, the Senate passed it shortly thereafter. Because it contained an emergency clause, the law went into effect immediately upon the governor's signature. The new law allowed a county to redistrict any time it became aware of facts that called into question whether its districts complied with state or federal law, and the county commission immediately began the process of redrawing its districts to avoid court-ordered redistricting.[132]

Before the county could complete the redistricting process, however, the plaintiffs in the *Quiver* litigation obtained a temporary restraining order and preliminary injunction prohibiting the state from enforcing the new law unless and until it obtained preclearance under Section 5 of the Voting Rights Act.[133] In a strongly worded opinion granting the injunction, the three-judge district court noted that state officials in South Dakota "for over 25 years . . . have intended to violate and have violated the preclearance requirements" and that the emergency clause in the new law "gives the appearance of a rushed attempt to circumvent the VRA."[134] The injunction effectively put the new law on hold while the litigation against Charles Mix County proceeded.

While the new law was on hold, the district court in *Blackmoon* granted the plaintiffs' motion for partial summary judgment on their malapportionment claim and ordered the defendants to submit a remedial proposal for court approval.[135] The county commission then tried to push through a redistricting plan that would have continued to dilute Native American voting strength. Using noncontiguous districts, the plan included recently developed land along the Missouri River in the district that, according to the 2000 census, contained the most Native Americans. Because the developments didn't exist at the time of the 2000 census, the impact of those voters was not apparent on the county's proposed plan. Residents of the county knew full well, however, that most of the voters in the newly developed area were non-Indian. The county commission held a hearing on its dilutive plan, and Native Americans strongly opposed it. In light of that opposition, the county adopted the plan that had been proposed by the Yankton Sioux Tribe in 2001, and that remedied both the malapportionment and the dilution of Indian voting strength.

Reaction to new districts was swift. Less than a month after the county adopted a redistricting plan with a majority-Indian district, a white resident of the northeast part of the county began circulating a petition to split Charles Mix into two counties, one part of which would be almost all white. The petition received significant news coverage, and it was widely seen as directly related to the Indian victory in the *Blackmoon* case.[136]

The secession movement fizzled after the media coverage, and the petitions to divide the county were never turned in. Instead, a new petitioning effort sprung up – this time seeking to increase the number of county commissioners from three to five. In a thinly veiled reference to an Indian candidate who was running for commissioner in the new majority-Indian district, the circulator of the petition told the media that the purpose of increasing the size of the county commission was to "take . . . power away from one strong commissioner."[137]

Native Americans opposed the increase, but it passed in November 2006 with strong white support. In an effort to stop the increase from being implemented, tribal members successfully circulated a petition to refer the county's five-member plan to the voters. In a special election on the referendum, however, the matter failed and the increase was scheduled to take effect in 2008.

In early 2007, the district court ruled that the plaintiffs' remaining claims could go forward and set them for trial in March 2008.[138] The primary issue was the plaintiffs' request for relief under the "pocket trigger" provisions of Section 3 of the Voting Rights Act, which would require the county to comply with Section 5.

Rather than go to trial, the county requested mediation. In December 2007, the parties negotiated a consent decree that, among other things, activated the "pocket trigger" in Section 3(c) of the Voting Rights Act and required the county to preclear its voting changes until 2024. The county subsequently submitted for preclearance its plan to increase the size of the county commission from three to five. The Department of Justice objected to the change on the ground that the county had not met its burden of proving that the increase was not motivated by a discriminatory purpose. As a result of the objection, the three-member plan with one majority-Indian district remained in place.

The first election under the new districts was held in November 2006, and Sharon Drapeau was elected to be the first woman and the first Native American to serve on the commission.

THE VOTING RIGHTS ACT OUTSIDE THE COURTROOM

Any analysis of the Voting Rights Act in South Dakota would be incomplete without an examination of the act's effect on nonlitigation decisions by legislative and executive policymakers. It is not always easy to measure this effect. Legislators and other officials rarely announce why they are choosing a particular course of action or choosing not to take a particular course of action. Often their actions reflect multiple influences and subtle pressures. In South Dakota, however, there are several excellent examples of the Act's having a significant impact on decisions made outside the courtroom.

Legislative Redistricting

In the 1970s, the state of South Dakota created a special task force consisting of the nine tribal chairs, four members of the legislature, and five lay people to examine the current state of Indian/state government relations. Among other things, the task force examined the state's legislative redistricting plan adopted in 1971. That plan created twenty-eight legislative districts, all of which were majority-white and none of which had ever elected an Indian.[139] The plan also split the Pine Ridge and Rosebud reservations into three multimember legislative districts, none of which contained an Indian majority. The task force concluded in a 1975 report that the plan diluted Indian voting strength by "cracking" or fragmenting the Indian population on the Pine Ridge and Rosebud reservations.[140] The report demonstrated that Native Americans on the reservations were sufficiently numerous and geographically compact to form a majority in at least one majority-Indian multimember legislative district.[141] The report also alleged that the use of multimember districts diluted Native American voting strength by "stacking" or submerging large concentrations of Native Americans within even larger concentrations of non-Indians and demonstrated that Native Americans in several reservation counties, including the Standing Rock and Cheyenne River Reservations, were sufficiently numerous and geographically compact to form a majority in a number of single-member legislative districts.[142] The report concluded, presciently, that:

> if the state wishes to avoid possible litigation . . . it may want to re-apportion its legislative districts to allow for more Indian representation. It is possible that the lack of Indian representation in state government may create problems in Indian-state relations in South Dakota.[143]

The report recommended the creation of a majority-Indian district in the area of Shannon, Washabaugh, Todd, and Bennett Counties.

The legislature initially ignored the task force's recommendation. According to the report's author, the state representatives and senators felt "it was a political hot potato . . . [T]his was just too pro-Indian to take as an item of action."[144]

Five years later, just before the 1980s round of redistricting, the South Dakota Advisory Committee to the U.S. Commission on Civil Rights made a similar recommendation that the legislature create a majority-Indian district in the area of the Pine Ridge and Rosebud Reservations. The committee issued a report in which it said that the existing districts inherently discriminate against Native Americans in South Dakota who might be able to elect one legislator in a single-member district.[145]

Still the legislature did nothing until the Department of Justice, pursuant to its oversight under Section 5, advised the state that it would not preclear any legislative redistricting plan that did not contain a majority-Indian district in the Rosebud/Pine Ridge area. The state legislature finally capitulated and in 1981 drew a redistricting plan creating for the first time in the state's history a majority-Indian district, District 28, which included Shannon and Todd Counties and half of Bennett County.[146] Thomas Shortbull, an early proponent of equal voting rights for Indians, ran for the senate the following year from District 28 and was elected, becoming the first Indian ever to serve in the state's upper chamber.

The Voting Rights Act also figured prominently in the 1990s round of redistricting. In 1989, legislative staffers prepared an issue memorandum for the redistricting committee analyzing the then-current state of redistricting law and demographic trends in the state. Noting the concentration of Native Americans on the Cheyenne River Reservation, the memo advised that the creation of a single-member district in that area "may be the only effective insurance" against a vote-dilution suit under the recently decided *Thornburg v. Gingles.*

A year later, an attorney from the Department of Justice gave similar advice during a presentation to the redistricting committee, noting that the Voting Rights Act would require a single-member district if a dual-member district would dilute minority voting strength. The attorney also advised that the department would review the state's final plan to determine whether it was retrogressive, intentionally discriminatory, or discriminatory in its result. While not specifically mentioning the Cheyenne River Reservation, the implication of the attorney's remarks suggested that the department would not preclear a redistricting plan that failed to create a single-member district in that area.

The redistricting committee and the legislature ultimately followed the advice of its staff and the Department of Justice. At the committee's recommendation, the legislature for the first time incorporated minority voting rights into the state's redistricting policies. And it created, also for the first time, a majority-Indian single-member district on the Cheyenne River Reservation.

Polling Places in Mellette County

In September 2008, officials in sparsely populated Mellette County, South Dakota, voted to close all but one of the county's four polling places. The move was touted as a cost-saving measure designed to save the cash-strapped county about $1,000. But it meant that some voters would have to drive as far as forty miles each way to the county seat in order to cast a vote. And to make matters worse, South Dakota has one of the most restrictive absentee ballot laws in the country, requiring voters to have their absentee ballot applications notarized or witnessed by county officials.

Soon after the county's decision to close the polls, the Rosebud Sioux Tribe contacted the ACLU's Voting Rights Project for help. Mellette County is within the historical boundaries of the Rosebud Indian Reservation, and Native Americans still make up about half of the county's population.

The ACLU analyzed the impact of the county's decision and concluded that the poll closure would have a severe and disparate impact on Native American voters. Not only would a higher percentage of Indians than non-Indians have to travel significant distances to vote or cast an absentee ballot, but Native Americans were also much less likely than whites to have access to a vehicle or the money to pay for gas. And, to add insult to injury, the all-white county commission moved the county's only remaining polling place next door to the sheriff's office, a place that would further deter Indians from voting because of a history of friction between Native Americans and law enforcement in the county. The ACLU prepared a lawsuit alleging violations of Section 2 of the Voting Rights Act as well as the Fourteenth and Fifteenth Amendments to the United States Constitution.

One of the largest television stations in the state ran a story on the poll closure, and word of the ACLU's investigation got out. Less than

twenty-four hours before the ACLU was prepared to file suit against the
county on behalf of Native American voters, county officials hastily ar-
ranged a meeting and rescinded the poll closing ordinance to avoid the
possibility of litigation.

Drivers' Licensing Offices in Todd and Charles Mix Counties

In September 2009, South Dakota announced plans to close seventeen
of its drivers' licensing offices around the state. Among the offices to be
closed were those in Todd and Charles Mix Counties, both of which are
covered jurisdictions subject to the act's preclearance mandates (Todd
by Section 5 and Charles Mix by Section 3(c)). Residents of those counties would in many instances have to drive long distances to get a drivers'
license or photo ID. Several residents of those counties complained, and
the ACLU began an investigation.

The closure would affect both voter registration and voting. Under
the National Voter Registration Act, drivers' license offices in South
Dakota conduct voter registration, and the closure of drivers' licensing
offices would mean that residents of Todd and Charles Mix Counties
would have less access to motor-voter registration. Access to drivers'
licenses would also affect voting because South Dakota is one of several
states that require each voter to show identification before voting in
person or by absentee ballot.[147] The closure would likely mean that some
voters would not be able to meet the identification requirements because
they would not have an up-to-date driver's license or state-issued photo
identification card. Census data showed that Native Americans in Todd
and Charles Mix Counties had a lower socioeconomic status and less access to cars than their white counterparts, which would mean less access
to gas money and the ability to travel long distances to obtain or renew
the necessary identification.

The ACLU asked the Department of Justice to send the state a "please
submit" letter asking the state to submit its closure plan to the attorney
general for preclearance. It is unclear whether the department did, in
fact, send such a letter or make an oral request for a submission, but the
state announced three weeks later that it was reversing the decision to
close the offices in Todd and Charles Mix Counties. The state's Depart-

ment of Public Safety, which oversees the licensing program, issued a statement specifically citing the preclearance provisions of the Voting Rights Act and the state's desire to avoid potential litigation as a reason for its decision.

CONCLUSION: THE IMPACT OF THE VOTING RIGHTS ACT AND THE NEED FOR EXPANDED COVERAGE

The Voting Rights Act has had an obvious impact in South Dakota. Section 2 has contributed, directly or indirectly, to the enfranchisement of thousands of Indian voters. In the last decade alone, it has contributed to the enfranchisement of thousands of Native American voters in Buffalo County, Charles Mix County, Day County, Mellette County, Wagner Community School District, and the City of Martin. It led to the creation of a new majority-Indian legislative district in the area of the Pine Ridge and Rosebud reservations and before that to the creation of a majority-Indian legislative district in the area of the Cheyenne River and Standing Rock Reservations.

The preclearance provisions of the act, Section 3(c) and Section 5, have had their successes as well. Section 5 had everything to do with the creation of the first majority-Indian legislative district in 1981. It played a significant role in the creation of the second majority-Indian district in 1991. And it seems to have been responsible for state officials' recent decision not to close a drivers' licensing office in Todd County. Section 5 also contributed to the success of the *Blackmoon* litigation in Charles Mix County. Had the *Quiver* plaintiffs been unable to obtain a temporary restraining order against the emergency redistricting bill under Section 5, the county would almost certainly have drawn new districts that would have remedied the one-person, one-vote defect in their existing plan but that would have also made a Section 2 challenge more difficult, time-consuming, and expensive. Section 3(c)'s preclearance requirement has already had a significant success even though it has been in place in only two jurisdictions and only for a short time. It almost single-handedly stopped Charles Mix County's plan to increase the size of its county commission after losing the *Blackmoon* litigation. The remedial plan in the *Blackmoon* case created one majority-Indian commissioner district out of three. Because of the demographics and geographic concentration of the county's Indian population, it was impossible to draw two majority-Indian districts out of five. Were it not for the activation of the act's pocket trigger in the *Blackmoon* consent decree and the attorney general's objection, Native American voters would have a smaller voice on the county commission and native American plaintiffs would be embroiled in another difficult and expensive lawsuit – one probably relying on a claim of intentional discrimination.

Notwithstanding these successes, the Voting Rights Act has had some failures in South Dakota as well. The biggest among them is the state's lousy record of compliance with the preclearance mandate. How did the Department of Justice, which is expressly charged with enforcing the Act, and the civil rights community overlook twenty-five years of defiant noncompliance? It is a record of which we should all be deeply ashamed. I view the *Quiver* litigation to bring the state back into compliance as a partial failure, too. There was not a single objection to any of the more than eight hundred preclearance submissions that the state made between 2003 and 2006, but not because there was nothing objectionable in them. Rather, the district court's decision to allow the state to submit by code section rather than by session law let the state off the hook for a number of retrogressive changes that would not likely have survived preclearance review if the state had been in compliance all along. Another set of objectionable changes likely fell by the wayside because of the Supreme Court's two decisions in *Reno v. Bossier Parish School Board,*[148] which significantly limited the department's ability to object. Those decisions were overturned when Congress reauthorized the act in 2006, but by then it was too late to help South Dakota. And a third set of objectionable changes likely fell on deaf ears because of the politicization of the Voting Section during the Bush Administration. South Dakota is a reliably red state, and it was a congressional battleground in 2002, 2004, and, to a lesser extent, in 2006. The Bush administration made few objections overall, and fewer still to the kinds of anti–voter fraud measures that were popular among Republicans in the South Dakota legislature.

The successes and failures of the Voting Rights Act in South Dakota over the past decade point to the continuing need for its protections, and particularly for Section 5. They also point to a need for expanded Section 5 coverage in parts of the state as non-Indian decision makers, following the lead of places like Charles Mix County, start using more and more sophisticated techniques to discriminate against Indian voters. Hard-fought gains in places like Charles Mix and Wagner are vulnerable to backsliding. Other border communities not currently covered by Section 5, like Mellette County, are likely to be the next battlegrounds.

In its decision upholding the 2006 reauthorization of the Voting Rights Act, the Supreme Court seemed to invite Congress to rework Section 5's coverage formula, which it viewed as both overinclusive and underinclusive.[149] This litigator hopes that Congress accepts the invitation. Indian voters in South Dakota need more protection, not less.

NOTES

1. See *Northwest Austin Municipal Utility District Number One v. Holder*, 129 S.Ct. 2504 (2009).

2. The special provisions are those that were set to expire in 2007 unless reauthorized by Congress. See Laughlin McDonald, *Voting Rights Act in Indian Country: A Case Study*, 29 Am. Indian L. Rev. 43, 71–74 (2004–2005) (discussing the expiring and nonexpiring provisions of the Voting Rights Act). The special provisions are contained primarily in Sections 4 though 9 of the act, and coverage was determined by a formula set forth in Section 4(b), 42 USC § 1973b. The seven states originally covered by the special provisions were Alabama, Georgia, Louisiana, Mississippi, South Carolina, Virginia, and forty counties in North Carolina. See Jurisdictions Covered Under Section 4(b) of the Voting Rights Act, as Amended, 28 CFR § 51 (Appendix).

3. I use the terms "Native American," "Indian," and "American Indian" interchangeably throughout this chapter because there is no consensus in the law or culture on a single term to describe the indigenous peoples of the United States. I recognize, however, that there are often very significant differences between tribal groups.

4. I have been lead counsel or co-counsel in seven of those eight cases, including *Emery v. Hunt*, No. 01-3008 (D.S.D. Aug. 10, 2000); *Weddell v. Wagner Community School District*, No. 02-4056 (D.S.D. Mar. 18, 2003) (consent decree); *Bone Shirt v. Hazeltine*, 336 F. Supp. 2d 976 (D.S.D. 2004), aff'd 461 F.3d 1011 (8th Cir. 2006); *Quick Bear Quiver v. Nelson*, 387 F. Supp. 2d 1027 (D.S.D. 2005) (three-judge district court), *appeal dismissed*, 546 U.S. 1085 (2006) (mem.); *Cottier v. City of Martin*, 445 F.3d 1113 (8th Cir. 2006), *remanded to* 466 F. Supp. 2d 1175 (D.S.D. 2006), rev'd 604 F.3d 553 (8th Cir. 2010) (en banc); *Kirkie v. Buffalo County*, No. 03-5024 (D.S.D. Feb. 10, 2004) (consent decree); and *Blackmoon v. Charles Mix County*, No. 05-4017, 2005 WL 2738954 (D.S.D. Oct. 24, 2005).

5. See generally Jeanette Wolfley, *Jim Crow, Indian Style: The Disenfranchisement of Native Americans*, 16 Am. Indian L. Rev. 167 (1990); Orlan Svingen, *Jim Crow, Indian*

Style, 11 Am. Indian Quarterly 275 (1987); Daniel McCool, "Indian Voting," in *American Indian Policy in the Twentieth Century,* ed. Vine Deloria Jr., 105–34 (Norman: University of Oklahoma Press, 1985).

6. Act to Provide a Temporary Government for the Territory of Dakota, 1862 Dakota Terr. Laws 21.

7. Id.

8. An Act Prescribing the Manner of Conducting Elections; Of Canvass and Return of the Same, ch. 32, 1862 Dakota Terr. Laws 274.

9. Act of January 14, 1864, ch. 19, § 51, 1864 Dakota Terr. Laws 26, 40.

10. An Act to Establish a Civil Code, § 26, 1866 Dakota Terr. Laws 1, 4 ("Indians resident within this territory have the same rights and duties as other persons, except that: 1. They cannot vote or hold office; and that, 2. They cannot grant, lease, or incumber [*sic*] Indian lands, except in the cases provided by special laws.")

11. The Civil Rights Act of 1866, § 1, ch. 31, 14 Stat. 27.

12. An Act to Strike the Word "White," ch. 33, 1868 Dakota Terr. Laws 255.

13. The first practical opportunity for Native Americans in the territory to obtain citizenship came in the 1868 Fort Laramie Treaty, 15 Stat. 635, reprinted in II Charles J. Kappler, *Indian Affairs: Laws and Treaties* 998 (1904). The treaty offered citizenship to any member of a signatory tribe who could occupy a plot of land for three years and make at least two hundred dollars' worth of improvements. It is unclear how many Native Americans, if any, obtained citizenship under the treaty.

14. S.D. Const. Art. VII (1890).

15. S.D. Stat. § 3424 (Parsons 2d rev. ed. 1901).

16. S.D. Rev. Civ. Code § 26 (1903).

17. See Right of Indians to Vote, Op. S.D. Att'y Gen., 1923–1924 Rep. S.D. Att'y Gen. 171 (March 13, 1924); Right of Indi-

ans to Vote, Op. S.D. Att'y Gen., 1917–1918 Rep. S.D. Att'y Gen. 262 (March 11, 1918); Indians Entitled to Hold Office-When, Op. S.D. Att'y Gen., 1909–1910 Rep. S.D. Att'y Gen. 340 (May 10, 1910) (finding that the fact that an Indian has an allotment is one indication that he has severed his tribal relations, thereby entitling him to vote and to hold office); Right to Vote, Op. S.D. Att'y Gen., 1909–1910 Rep. S.D. Att'y Gen. 257 (June 22, 1909); Right of Indians to Vote, Op. S.D. Att'y Gen., 1909–1910 Rep. S.D. Att'y Gen. 166 (June 10, 1909) (stating that an Indian who "has severed his tribal relation, and has adopted the habits of civilized life . . . is a voter regardless of whether he has a patent in fee simple, or a patent in trust, or no patent at all"); Right of Suffrage of Indians, Op. S.D. Att'y Gen., 1907–1908 Rep. S.D. Att'y Gen. 123 (August 28, 1908); see also *State v. Nimrod,* 30 S.D. 239, 138 N.W. 377 (1912) (holding that an Indian who had abandoned tribal relations and taken land in severalty separate and apart from tribe and had adopted the habits of civilized live thereby became a citizen of the United States and of South Dakota).

18. Right of Indians to Vote, Op. S.D. Att'y Gen., 1909–1910 Rep. S.D. Att'y Gen. 166 (June 10, 1909).

19. Right to Vote, Op. S.D. Att'y Gen., 1909–1910 Rep. S.D. Att'y Gen. 257 (June 22, 1909).

20. Indian Citizenship Act, ch. 233, 43 Stat. 253, reprinted in IV Charles J. Kappler, *Indian Affairs: Laws and Treaties* 420 (1929).

21. Member of Highway Board of Unorganized County May Be a Member of Legislature – Indians are Citizens and Entitled to Vote and Hold Office, Op. S.D. Att'y Gen., 1939–1940 Rep. S.D. Att'y Gen. 579 (April 4, 1940).

22. Id.

23. Act of February 27, 1951, ch. 471, 1951 S.D. Laws 432 (repealing § 65.0801 of

1939 S.D. Code relating to certain disabilities of Indians).

24. S.D.C.L. § 12-3-2 (1968) (authorizing elections in unorganized counties for state and national officers and members of the legislature, highway board and school board, but not for county officers).

25. See Virginia Driving Hawk Sneve, ed., *South Dakota Geographic Names* (Sioux Falls, S.D.: Brevet Press, 1973), 18–36.

26. *Little Thunder v. South Dakota*, 518 F.2d 1253, 1255 (8th Cir. 1975).

27. See *United States v. South Dakota*, 636 F.3d 241 (8th Cir. 1980).

28. Act of March 2, 1982, ch. 28, 1982 S.D. Laws 91 (repealing provisions relating to elections in unorganized counties).

29. 42 USC §§ 1973, 1973b.

30. See *Rice v. Sioux City Mem'l Park Cemetery*, 349 U.S. 70, 76 (1955) (acknowledging that Native Americans are protected by laws that prohibit discrimination on the basis of race or color).

31. See An Act to Amend the Voting Rights Act of 1965, Public Law 94-73, 89 Stat. 400 (1975).

32. See 41 Fed. Reg. 784 (Jan. 5, 1976).

33. See 41 Fed. Reg. 30002 (July 20, 1976).

34. Voting Rights Act of 1965, As Amended by Public Law 94-73: Bilingual Elections, Op. S.D. Att'y Gen. No. 77-73, 1977–1978 Rep. S.D. Att'y Gen. 175 (August 23, 1977). In an opinion issued two years earlier, Janklow had used similar rhetoric in advising that state officials should ignore federal regulations on Indian education. See Conflict of Proposed Federal Regulations Part 403 to Implement P.L. 93-638 and South Dakota Statutes, Op. S.D. Att'y Gen. No. 75-174, 1975–1976 Rep. S.D. Att'y Gen. 399 (October 16, 1975) (declaring federal regulations regarding Indian education to be in conflict with state statutes and advising that state officials "are bound to give

precedence to carrying out the legal mandates of our state law") (Janklow, A.G.)).

35. Id.

36. 383 U.S. 301 (1966).

37. Id. at 328 (Black, J., dissenting).

38. 1977–1978 Rep. S.D. Att'y Gen. 175 (August 23, 1977).

39. Id.

40. McDonald, *Voting Rights Act in Indian Country*, 53.

41. *Buckanaga v. Sisseton Indep. Sch. Dist.*, 804 F.2d 469, 478 (8th Cir. 1986).

42. Id. at 473.

43. Id. at 478.

44. *American Horse v. Kundert*, Civ. No. 84-5159 (D.S.D. 1984).

45. *Black Bull v. Dupree Sch. Dist.*, No. 86-3012 (D.S.D. May 14, 1986).

46. *Fiddler v. Sieker*, No. 85-3050 (D.S.D. Oct. 24, 1986).

47. Am. Consent J., *United States v. Day County*, S.D., Civ. No. 99-1024 (D.S.D. June 16, 2000).

48. See *Gomillion v. Lightfoot*, 364 U.S. 339 (1960) (holding that African American could challenge the discriminatory manipulation of city boundary lines as a denial of the right to vote under the Fifteenth Amendment).

49. Am. Consent J., *United States v. Day County*, S.D., Civ. No. 99-1024 (D.S.D. June 16, 2000), at 4–8.

50. 1991 S.D. Laws ch 1, codified at S.D.C.L. § 2-2-23 –31.

51. An Act to Redistrict the Legislature, ch. 1, 1991 S.D. Laws 1st Spec. Sess. 1, 5 (codified as amended at S.D.C.L. § 2-2-24 through 2-2-31).

52. An Act to Eliminate the Single-member House Districts in District 28, ch. 21, 1996 S.D. Laws 45 (amending S.D.C.L. § 2-2-28).

53. Minutes of House State Affairs Committee, January 29, 1996, p. 5.

54. *In re Legislative Reapportionment*, 246 N.W. 295, 297 (S.D. 1933).

55. *Emery v. Hunt,* Civ. No. 00-3008
(D.S.D.), Report of Steven P. Cole, Tables
1 & 2.

56. Id., Tables 1 & 3.

57. See *Clarke v. City of Cincinnati,*
40 F.3d 807, 457 (6th Cir. 1994) ("[w]hen
white bloc voting is 'targeted' against
black candidates, black voters are denied
an opportunity enjoyed by white voters,
namely, the opportunity to elect a candidate of their own race").

58. *In re Certification of a Question of
Law,* 615 N.W.2d 590, 597 (S.D. 2000).

59. 2001 S.D. Laws ch. 2, codified at
S.D.C.L. §§ 2-2-33 –40.

60. *Bone Shirt v. Hazeltine,* Civ. No. 01-
3032 (D.S.D. Dec. 26, 2001).

61. The plaintiffs identified two changes, in particular. First, Native Americans
made up 87 percent of the total population
and 82 percent of the voting-age population of District 27 in 1991. In 2001, Native
Americans made up 90 percent of the total
population and 86 percent of the district's
voting-age population. Second, District 27
was underpopulated by 4.1 percent in 1991
and was the sixth most underpopulated
district in the entire 1991 plan. In 2001, the
district was overpopulated by 4 percent
and was the third most overpopulated district in the 2001 plan.

62. *Bone Shirt v. Hazeltine,* 200 F. Supp.
2d 1150 (D.S.D. 2002).

63. Id. at 1154.

64. See *Bone Shirt v. Hazeltine,* 336 F.
Supp. 2d 976, 1053 (D.S.D. 2004).

65. 478 U.S. 30, 50–51 (1986).

66. *Bone Shirt v. Hazeltine,* 336 F. Supp.
2d at 995.

67. Id. at 989.

68. Id. at 995.

69. Id. at 1004.

70. Id. at 1004–08.

71. Id. at 1008–10.

72. Id. at 1010.

73. Id. at 1016.

74. Id. at 1017.

75. Id. at 1017–52.

76. *Gingles,* 478 U.S. at 48–49 n. 15;
accord *Harvell v. Blytheville Sch. Dist. No.
5,* 71 F.3d 1382, 1390 (8th Cir. 1995) (en
banc).

77. *Bone Shirt,* 336 F. Supp. 2d at 1043.

78. Id. at 1036.

79. Id. at 1035.

80. Id. at 1035.

81. Id. at 1018–34.

82. Id. at 1032.

83. Id. at 1032.

84. Id. at 1032.

85. Id. at 1032.

86. Id. at 1032.

87. Id. at 1032.

88. Id. at 1033.

89. Id. at 1033.

90. Id. at 1033.

91. Id. at 1033.

92. Id. at 1033.

93. Id. at 1034.

94. Id. at 1050–52.

95. Id. at 1052.

96. Id. at 1052.

97. Id. at 1052.

98. Id. at 1052.

99. *Bone Shirt v. Hazeltine,* 387 F. Supp.
2d 1035, 1044 (D.S.D. 2005).

100. *Bone Shirt v. Hazeltine,* 461 F.3d 1011
(8th Cir. 2006).

101. "American Indians Say They Are
Targeted by Wagner Police for Arrests,"
Yankton Press & Dakotan, April 24, 2000;
"Officials Deny Racial Profiling," *Yankton
Press & Dakotan,* May 30, 2000; David
Ledford, "Barnett Shoots the Messenger,"
Yankton Press & Dakotan, May 31,
2000.

102. "School Agrees to Payments in Dog
Lawsuit," *Yankton Press & Dakotan,* October 10, 2003.

103. *Weddell v. Wagner Community
School District,* Civ. No. 02-4056 (D.S.D.
March 22, 2002).

104. *Weddell v. Wagner Community School District*, Civ. No. 02-4056 (D.S.D. March 18, 2003).

105. See generally Paula L. Wagoner, *They Treated Us Just Like Indians: The Worlds of Bennett County, South Dakota* (Lincoln: University of Nebraska Press, 2002).

106. *United States v. Blackpipe State Bank*, No. 93-5115 (D.S.D.).

107. *Wilcox v. City of Martin*, No. 02-5021 (D.S.D.).

108. *Wilcox v. City of Martin*, No. 02-5021 (D.S.D. May 29, 2002).

109. *Cottier v. City of Martin*, No. 02-5021 (D.S.D. Mar. 22, 2005).

110. *Cottier v. City of Martin*, 445 F.3d 1115 (8th Cir. 2006).

111. Id. at 1117.

112. Id. at 1121.

113. Id. at 1115–16.

114. Id. at 1115–67, 1121–22.

115. *Cottier v. City of Martin*, 466 F. Supp. 2d 1175, 1199 (D.S.D. 2006).

116. *Cottier v. City of Martin*, 475 F. Supp. 2d 932, 936, 942–43 (D.S.D. 2007).

117. *Cottier v. City of Martin*, 551 F.3d 733 (8th Cir. 2008).

118. *Cottier v. City of Martin*, 604 F.3d 553 (8th Cir. 2010) (en banc).

119. Id. at 560.

120. Voting Rights Act of 1965, As Amended by Public Law 94-73: Bilingual Elections, Op. S.D. Att'y Gen. No. 77-73, 1977–1978 Rep. S.D. Att'y Gen. 175 (August 23, 1977).

121. *Quiver v. Nelson*, Civ. No. 02-5069 (D.S.D. Aug. 5, 2002).

122. See "Voting Rights Suit," Morning Edition, National Public Radio, August 5, 2002, available at http://www.npr.org/templates/story/story.php?storyId=1147824.

123. Consent Order, *Quiver v. Nelson*, Civ. No. 02-5069 (D.S.D. Dec. 27, 2002).

124. See Order, *Quiver v. Nelson*, Civ. No. 02-5069 (D.S.D. Mar. 24, 2003).

125. Order Dissolving Consent Decree, *Quiver v. Nelson*, Civ. No. 02-5069 (D.S.D. Sept. 18, 2006).

126. Complaint, *Kirkie v. Buffalo County*, Civ. No. 03-5024 (D.S.D. Mar. 20, 2003).

127. S.D.C.L. § 7-8-10.

128. See Answer, *Kirkie v. Buffalo County*, Civ. No. 03-5025 (D.S.D. Apr. 28, 2003), at 10.

129. Consent Decree, *Kirkie v. Buffalo County*, Civ. No. 03-5024 (D.S.D. Feb. 12, 2004).

130. S.D.C.L. § 7-8-10.

131. Complaint, *Blackmoon v. Charles Mix County*, Civ. No. 05-4017 (D.S.D. Jan. 27, 2005).

132. 2005 S.D. Laws, ch. 43.

133. *Quiver v. Nelson*, 387 F. Supp. 2d 1027 (D.S.D. 2005) (three-judge district court).

134. Id. at 1034.

135. *Blackmoon v. Charles Mix County*, 2005 WL 2738954 (D.S.D. 2005).

136. See Kimberly Kolden, "Residents in Charles Mix Consider Plan to Split County," *Mitchell Daily Republic*, Feb. 14, 2006.

137. Monica Wepking, "Petition to Change County Commission Numbers," *Lake Andes Wave*, June 14, 2006.

138. *Blackmoon v. Charles Mix County*, 505 F. Supp. 2d 585 (D.S.D. 2007).

139. *Bone Shirt*, 336 F. Supp. 2d at 980–81.

140. Thomas H. Shortbull, *Tribal-State Relations in South Dakota* (1975), at 167.

141. See id. at 171.

142. See id. at 167–69, 171–74.

143. Id. at 186.

144. *Bone Shirt*, 336 F. Supp. 2d at 981.

145. Report of the South Dakota Advisory Committee to the U.S. Commission on Civil Rights 35, 52 (1981).

146. *Bone Shirt*, 336 F. Supp. 2d at 981.

147. See S.D.C.L. § 12-18-6.1, 12-19-2.

148. *See Reno v. Bossier Parish Sch. Bd.,*
528 U.S. 320 (2000) (holding that Section
5 does not prohibit preclearance of a voting change enacted with a discriminatory
but nonretrogressive purpose); *Reno v.
Bossier Parish Sch. Bd.,* 520 U.S. 471 (1997)
(holding that preclearance under Section
5 of the Voting Rights Act may not be
denied solely because a voting change
violates Section 2 of the Voting Rights
Act).

149. See *Northwest Austin Municipal
Utility District Number One v. Holder,* 129
S.Ct. 2504, 2512 (2009).

SEVEN

Realistic Expectations: South Dakota's Experience with the Voting Rights Act

CHRIS NELSON

BACKGROUND ON ELECTION ADMINISTRATION IN SOUTH DAKOTA'S INDIAN COUNTRY

For thirteen years, from 1989 through 2002, I served as the election supervisor for the state of South Dakota. In 2002 I was elected secretary of state in a three-way race with 56 percent of the vote. In 2006 I was unopposed for re-election, which was the first time in the history of South Dakota that a candidate for secretary of state was unopposed. My involvement in election administration ended in 2011 when term limits prevented me from running for re-election. I mention these facts only to establish with the reader my long-term and respected involvement in administering elections in South Dakota.

Native Americans are the largest minority population in South Dakota. The 2010 census reported that 8.8 percent of our population was American Indian. Of South Dakota's 814,180 residents, 71,817 reported being full American Indian. An additional 10,229 residents report some American Indian racial background.[1]

Approximately one-third of the time I spent on election-related responsibilities as secretary of state was devoted to Native American voter needs. Some of that time involved compliance with the temporary provisions of the Voting Rights Act such as Section 5 (preclearance) and Section 203 (minority-language provisions). Significant amounts of time were involved defending the state in ACLU-inspired lawsuits involving Native American voting issues.

Additional time was invested in working with local election administrators on the conduct of elections in Native American Indian reservation counties. Election administration in those counties is significantly
more difficult than in other parts of the state due to limitations on state
legal jurisdiction, the low property tax base, and lack of citizen interest
in serving as trained poll workers.

Criminal jurisdiction on Indian reservations is divided between the
federal government and tribal government. State and county law enforcement has no jurisdiction over Native Americans on reservation land.
The normal avenue for enforcement of state election criminal statutes
involves action by the county sheriff and state's attorney. If warranted, the
attorney general and state division of criminal investigation agents may
assist. None of these resources are available to investigate or prosecute
election crimes by Native Americans on reservation land. That fact adds
an additional element to the complexity of election administration in
those areas.

County government functions, including election administration
for primary and general elections, are predominantly funded with taxes
paid on real property. Reservation counties contain large percentages of
land that is tribal or held in trust for Native Americans. That land does
not generate any property tax dollars, leaving those county governments
struggling to fund basic county services such as road maintenance, law
enforcement, and election administration.

The county auditor is in charge of election administration for his or
her county. Finding poll workers who will attend election training, staff
a polling place, and properly enforce election laws and regulations is a
difficult task for a county auditor in Indian country. A typical example
of this difficulty occurred at Shannon County's Pine Ridge #3 precinct
on the day of the 2010 general election. Two of the three poll workers, including the precinct superintendent who had all the ballots and election
supplies for that precinct, didn't show up at the polling place until after
poll opening time. Fortunately no voters were prevented from voting
during this unfortunate circumstance. Polls were left open an additional
half-hour to compensate for the tardy election workers. County auditors
in reservation areas work diligently to ensure that elections are properly
conducted despite these hurdles.

Given this background on election administration challenges in South Dakota, this chapter will focus on three areas. The first will review practical impacts of ACLU-inspired voting rights litigation in South Dakota. The second and third portions will outline South Dakota's experience with Section 5 and Section 203, focusing on realistic expectations for what reauthorization of those sections of the Voting Rights Act will accomplish.

ACLU-INSPIRED LITIGATION

During the twenty-three years that I worked in South Dakota election administration, there were nine voting rights cases in the state, eight of which were ACLU-inspired. I do not intend to relitigate those cases in this chapter. The courts have spoken. It will, however, be profitable for the reader to examine with the benefit of hindsight what those cases and decisions have accomplished or, more realistically, not accomplished.

There are two threads that tie each of these cases together. The first is that each time a case was filed and litigated and a decision rendered, it served to remove a scab from old racial wounds. Litigation rehashed wrongs that were committed in some cases more than a hundred years ago. The cases always pitted Native Americans against their elected leaders. Lawsuits were seen by plaintiffs as the first course of action instead of the last resort. In some cases litigation could have been avoided entirely by the plaintiff's simply sitting down with election officials and working out the issue.

In none of these nine cases did any plaintiff attempt to talk to me about their grievance prior to filing a lawsuit. In my position as election supervisor or secretary of state I would have eagerly listened to a voter's complaint and worked with them to find a solution. In many cases that solution would have necessitated my working with a local unit of government to resolve their differences with a Native American constituent. Playing that mediating role would not have been unique or unusual. In fact, I played that role hundreds, maybe thousands, of times throughout my years in election administration. Nine more times would not have been too much to ask.

The second thread is that while most cases focused on increasing the number of Native Americans elected in various jurisdictions, the prevailing court decisions have almost universally failed to accomplish that objective. The following review shows the lack of impact these cases have had on Native American representation.

United States v. Day County

To settle this 1999 lawsuit brought by the Department of Justice, Day County and the Enemy Swim Sanitary District agreed to expand the boundaries of the district to include tribally owned land that contained about two hundred tribal members, thereby allowing those voters to participate in and run for sanitary district office.

What has been the long-term result of this litigation? In 2011 there are no Native Americans on the board of the sanitary district.

Emery v. Hunt

South Dakota has thirty-five single-member state senate districts. Each district contains two statehouse members elected at large within the senate district. Following the 1990 census District 28 was broken into two single-member house districts, 28A and 28B, with the intention of giving Native American candidates in District 28A a better chance of getting elected. In the middle of the decade the legislature reversed course and recombined the house districts to once again give the voters in District 28 two representatives in the state house instead of one representative. The *Emery* decision found that mid-decade redistricting was unconstitutional per South Dakota's constitution. The district was once again split into 28A and 28B.

What has been the long-term result of this litigation? In 2011 there are no Native American legislators from Districts 28, 28A, or 28B.

Bone Shirt v. Hazeltine

Following the 2000 census the South Dakota legislature conducted legislative redistricting. After conducting a number of hearings focusing on redistricting the most heavily Native American area of the state, the legislature adopted a plan for District 27 (Bennett, Shannon, and Todd

Counties), which the ACLU testified was their "favorite" plan during the hearings.[2] The plan essentially left this district the same as it had been for the past twenty years, a configuration encouraged during the 1981 redistricting by the Department of Justice, the state Civil Rights Commission, and a tribal/state government task force examining tribal/state relations in the late 1970s. Little did the redistricting committee realize that when the ACLU said this was their "favorite" plan they meant it was their favorite plan on which to base a lawsuit against the state.

The suit resulted in the federal district court ordering District 27 to be reconfigured with districts 21 and 26. This essentially split District 27 in half, placing Shannon and Bennett Counties in the new District 27 and Todd County in the new District 26, while creating two single-member statehouse districts within District 26.

What has been the long-term result of this litigation and court-ordered reconfiguration? At the time the litigation was commenced, there were three Native American legislators from that area. In 2011 there are still three Native American legislators from that same area. Despite the magnitude of this case there has been no change in the number of Native Americans in the South Dakota legislature from this area.

Weddell v. Wagner Community School District

This 2002 lawsuit complained that the at-large election process used in the Wagner School District prevented the election of Native Americans to the school board. The at-large election process is provided by state law and is used in nearly all school districts in the state. The consent decree settling the case replaced the at-large elections with a cumulative voting process not provided in state law.

What has been the long-term result of this litigation? In 2011 there are no Native Americans on the school board in the Wagner Community School District.

Cottier v. City of Martin

The plaintiffs in this case alleged that the city council, when redistricting their city wards, had purposely fragmented Native American voters among the three wards, thereby diluting the voting strength of those voters. The suit was originally dismissed for failure to find a violation of Section 2 of the Voting Rights Act. Eight years after the 2002 filing of this litigation the Eighth Circuit Court of Appeals sitting en banc ruled that the district court had properly dismissed this case in 2005 and that subsequent remedies be vacated.

Quiver v. Nelson

This 2002 case involved a failure by Todd and Shannon Counties to file Section 5 preclearance submissions. The net effect resulted in no denials of preclearance for any of the 3,048 statute or rule changes in question. The details of this case will be covered later in this chapter.

Kirkie v. Buffalo County

This case involved the failure of Buffalo County to redistrict its county commissioner districts following the 2000 census. There was no excuse for this nonperformance on the part of the county commission.

What has been the long-term result of this litigation? At the time of the redistricting failure, one of the three county commissioners was Native American. In 2011 two of the three are Native American. Of the nine cases cited here, this is the only case where Native American representation has increased.

Blackmoon v. Charles Mix County

The Blackmoon case began, as did the Buffalo County case, with a failure to redistrict county commissioner districts in 2002. The county quickly realized the error of its ways, asked the state legislature for emergency authority to redistrict, which was granted, and proceeded with reapportionment, ultimately adopting a plan proposed by the Yankton Sioux Tribe. In settling the case, the county agreed to submit for preclearance any election changes until the year 2024.

What happened after this redistricting was a theft of direct democracy from Native American and white voters alike in Charles Mix County.

Of the sixty-six counties in South Dakota, Charles Mix County was one of only six that had three county commissioners in 2006. The other sixty counties had five county commissioners. That year three of those six counties, including Charles Mix, saw citizen-circulated petitions filed to place a question on the county ballot to increase the number of commissioners from three to five.

In the 2006 general election voters in all three counties approved increasing their representation to five commissioners. Charles Mix County approved the increase with a 70 percent "yes" vote. Some have argued that this increase would hurt Native Americans. Apparently Native American voters didn't think so. The most predominantly Native American precinct, with 70 percent Native American population, had a 63 percent "yes" vote. Every precinct in the county supported increasing the number of county commissioners to five.

Per the county's agreement to subject itself to preclearance, the voter-approved increase in county commissioners was submitted to the Department of Justice, which denied approval of the change. The "yes" votes of 2,532 voters in Charles Mix County were essentially thrown away by this decision of the Department of Justice.

Because the department failed to preclear this voter-approved increase, Charles Mix County remains one of only four counties in the state with three commissioners. The Department of Justice unfairly denied the citizens of the county the ability to have five commissioners even though the size of the county warrants representation by five commissioners. The county's population is five and a half times larger than the other three counties that have only three commissioners.[3]

What has been the long-term result of this litigation? In 2011 Charles Mix County has only three county commissioners, none of whom are Native American.

Janis v. Nelson

If there is a quintessential example of how one phone call on the part of the plaintiff could have avoided the circumstances that led to a lawsuit, this case is it.

Prior to the 2008 general election, plaintiffs Eileen Janis and Kim Colhoff were convicted and sentenced to probation for a federal felony. Under South Dakota law felons receiving prison time as part of their sentence lose their voting rights until the sentence is complete.[4] Felons receiving only probation don't lose those rights. An unfortunate error on the part of county election officials led to the removal of the plaintiffs' names from the voter registration file.

The facts of exactly what occurred when the plaintiffs, one of whom was a poll worker, attempted to vote at her polling place in the 2008 general election remain unclear. What is known is that neither plaintiff cast a ballot in that election and neither plaintiff called the secretary of state's office for assistance in resolving the conflict at the polling place. Large posters at the polling place as required by the Help America Vote Act encourage any voter whose rights are being violated to call the secretary of state using a toll-free telephone number, which is listed on the poster. A call to the secretary of state would have triggered an immediate investigation into why the plaintiffs' names were not on the voter registration list, the authorizing of an emergency voting card by the county auditor, and ballots being given to the plaintiffs.

After failing to take any initiative to solve their election-day problem, the plaintiffs teamed up with the ACLU to file a lawsuit three months after the election contending that their voting rights had been violated by the secretary of state, State Board of Elections, county election officials, and precinct workers.

What was the result of this litigation? In 2010 the case was settled through mediation with the state admitting no liability and agreeing to expand notices regarding felon disenfranchisement.

It is clear that the Voting Rights Act gives voters a legal avenue to redress grievances. It is unfortunate and counterproductive when that right encourages litigation instead of conversation to solve problems. The act is used by ACLU lawyers as an opportunity to earn hundreds of thousands of dollars in reimbursed legal fees at the expense of taxpayers.

As has been illustrated, several of these lawsuits could have been avoided by potential plaintiffs bringing their concerns to the secretary of state and working together for a resolution. A willingness to constructively resolve issues instead of running to litigate would save taxpayer dollars and foster an atmosphere of cooperation in election administration instead of confrontation.

An excellent example of working to resolve instead of litigate occurred just prior to the 2010 general election. The ACLU made the secretary of state aware of some inconsistencies in a felon's records that may have cast doubt on whether that person could vote on election day. That notification, instead of *Janis v. Nelson*–type litigation, allowed the secretary of state to work with the office maintaining criminal records to correct the data error and ensure that the person would have no problem receiving a ballot on election day. Perhaps this successful resolution can serve as a model for future circumstances affecting voting rights in South Dakota.

TEMPORARY PROVISIONS – SECTIONS 5 AND 203

In any evaluation, anomalies to the accepted rule can be invaluably instructive. South Dakota's experience with the temporary provisions (Section 5 and Section 203) of the Voting Rights Act is that anomaly. South Dakota's experience, which is shared with no other jurisdiction, provides unique insight into why the virtuous claims of VRA temporary provision supporters are based on quicksand logic.

South Dakota may have the only Section 5–covered jurisdictions in the nation that did not comply with the preclearance requirements for nearly thirty years. This unique distinction provides crucial evidence for the discussion on the need for a federal preclearance requirement.

The "temporary" provisions of the Voting Rights Act – which now look more permanent than temporary – have been extended to 2032. Supporters of the 2006 extension can lay claim to a political victory. But what are the realistic expectations for what this extension or this "permanency" of the statute will accomplish? The most important question is, "Will this extension find more persons who are racial minorities participating in the election process?"

Based on South Dakota's experience the answer to that question is "no."

On June 30, 2006, the *Argus Leader,* South Dakota's largest newspaper, proclaimed in a headline that "Indian Vote Affected if Crucial Act

Expires."[5] The underlying article postulated that the failure to extend the
temporary provisions would mean "taking away powerful deterrents to
discrimination against Indian voters" that would "halt an upward trend
in voter turnout on reservations." The story went on to claim that these
provisions "are the underpinning of a renaissance in Indian voting."

None of these claims are realistic nor will they be fulfilled in South
Dakota by the extension of the temporary provisions. This chapter will
detail why these claims fail and what will occur in South Dakota from
the extension of the provisions.

BACKGROUND OF SECTION 5 PRECLEARANCE COVERAGE IN SOUTH DAKOTA

Section 5 of the Voting Rights Act requires changes in election law or
procedure in covered jurisdictions to be precleared – approved – by the
Department of Justice prior to the change becoming effective in the
covered jurisdictions.

Which jurisdictions throughout the country are considered covered
jurisdictions? Section 5 coverage for a jurisdiction is determinate upon
having less than 50 percent of the voting age population registered to vote
or less than 50 percent voter turnout in the 1972 general election coupled
with a "test or device" as a "prerequisite for voting or registration."[6]

Two counties in South Dakota have been covered by Section 5's pre-
clearance requirements since 1975.[7] Todd County, which is part of the
Rosebud Indian Reservation, is 86 percent Native American. Shannon
County, which is part of the Pine Ridge Indian Reservation, is 94 percent
Native American.[8]

In 1977 Democratic secretary of state Lorna Herseth asked Republican attorney general William Janklow if South Dakota needed to comply with the recently imposed preclearance requirement. In a strongly
worded opinion, Attorney General Janklow said he could not recom-
mend "obtaining immediate preclearance."[9] Instead he stated that "South
Dakota is currently preparing for such 'bail out' litigation," referring to
a Section 5 provision which allows covered jurisdictions to be judicially
excused from preclearance requirements in certain circumstances. Janklow also noted that an amendment being then considered in Congress

would repeal the preclearance requirement. The attorney general prag-matically recommended waiting on the outcome of the bailout litigation and congressional action before submitting preclearance requests that might eventually become moot.

The year 1978 saw the election of a new secretary of state and a new attorney general, and for unknown reasons no bailout proceeding was ever commenced. The congressional amendment was never adopted.

From 1975 through 2002, the South Dakota legislature made thou-sands of statutory changes regarding the state's election process. The State Board of Elections similarly made hundreds of administrative rule changes. These changes were not submitted for preclearance, though several times during this period the Department of Justice requested preclearance submissions for major election law changes, such as the implementation of the National Voter Registration Act. Such submis-sions were made and preclearance was granted.

How could this failure to preclear have gone unquestioned for so many years? There is no record of any request from any person in either Todd or Shannon Counties for preclearance submissions to be made between 1975 and 2002. Failure to preclear election changes simply was not an issue of importance or concern for the citizens in these counties.

In 2002, at the height of an open-seat statewide congressional cam-paign that featured Stephanie Herseth, granddaughter of the former secretary of state, running against former attorney general William Jank-low, the ACLU filed suit against the state of South Dakota and Todd and Shannon Counties over the preclearance requirement. "Quiver v. Hazeltine" was pronounced by the ACLU as the "largest voting rights suit ever filed."[10] Their news release goes on to criticize the former attorney general's recommendation and states that he is a current candidate for the United States House of Representatives. This author's opinion is that the timing of this lawsuit was essentially a political maneuver to embar-rass Janklow in his congressional race, and the filing of the lawsuit was an effort to raise reimbursed legal fees for the ACLU.

To settle the suit, Secretary of State Joyce Hazeltine agreed to sub-mit for preclearance on behalf of Todd and Shannon Counties all elec-tion law and rule changes dating back to November 1, 1972.[11] The submis-sions commenced in May of 2003 and were concluded in June of 2006.

These submissions contained 3,048 changes to election statutes, administrative rules, and the state constitution. The Department of Justice examined each of these changes individually. They asked follow-up questions regarding any issues that were unclear. In many cases the ACLU provided written arguments to the Department of Justice opposing individual changes. Following a Department of Justice examination of each change, their written determination was rendered.

Every one of these changes were precleared by the Department of Justice.[12] None were denied preclearance. Not a single change was found to retrogress the voting rights of Native Americans. This fact destroyed the ACLU's claims in the *Quiver* suit that South Dakota election statutes discriminated against Native American voters.

LESSONS LEARNED FROM SOUTH DAKOTA'S UNIQUE EXPERIENCE WITH SECTION 5

There are three logical conclusions that can be learned from South Dakota's unique experience with Section 5.

First, South Dakota's experience negates claims of preclearance supporters that Section 5 provides some kind of deterrent effect to protect minority voters from lawmakers and election officials. For thirty years, South Dakota legislators made changes to election statutes, the State Board of Elections made and changed administrative rules, and voters approved constitutional amendments without any regard for whether those changes would pass Section 5 examination. Changes were made 3,048 times without any regard for Section 5. There was no deterrence effect during those years. When those changes were finally submitted to the Department of Justice, none were found to be retrogressive to the voting rights of Native Americans.

South Dakota lawmakers and election board members have made fair election-related decisions for the past thirty years without an active Section 5 hammer over their heads. South Dakotans should be allowed to continue to make just laws and rules to protect and improve all voters' rights – including Native Americans – without unnecessary federal intervention. For Section 5 advocates to claim that all of a sudden in year thirty-one these lawmakers and election board members will hatch evil plans to hinder minority voting without a Section 5 inhibitor is illogical. To imagine that local county commissions, city councils, or school boards that are 60 to 100 percent Native American would begin working to undermine the ability of their people to vote is not rational.

On the contrary, over the thirty years in which South Dakota operated without any regard for Section 5, progressive changes have been made to election law. Poll hours have been expanded, notarization requirements have been removed from voter registrations and absentee ballot envelopes, voter registration forms have been made readily available on the Internet, and absentee voting is now allowed without any required excuse.

Second, the basis for two South Dakota counties to remain covered by Section 5 escapes logic. The basis for coverage of these counties from now until 2032 is voter registration and turnout from 1972. What possible reason could there be for the law to require data that is thirty-five to sixty years old? The unfortunate answer is that this is the only data that could perpetuate Section 5 coverage.

This raises the question: Why not use contemporary data?

In 2004, voter registration in Shannon County was 104 percent and in Todd County was 101 percent.[13] Turnout was 59 percent and 66 percent respectively.[14] These numbers are a far cry from the "less than 50 percent" threshold of 1972. Turnout in these two counties also outpaced the national average 2004 turnout of 55 percent.[15]

In three federal elections (2002, 2004, and 2006) the average registration was 99 percent in Shannon County and 96 percent in Todd County.[16] Voter turnout was 44.4 percent and 48.5 percent respectively.[17] While these turnout numbers do not exceed the 50 percent threshold, they easily exceed the national average turnout of 42.9 percent in these three election years.[18] Using this expanded and averaged data set or a comparison to contemporary national averages would provide a more accurate picture of the electorate in those counties than an archaic number from 1972.

Section 5 coverage is also determinate upon the jurisdictions employing in 1972 some "test or device" as a "prerequisite for voting or registration." What was the onerous "test or device" employed by Shannon and Todd Counties that triggered Section 5 coverage? Answer: Those counties conducted their elections in English![19] Not only is that "test or device" standard absurd on its face, but it is ridiculous because tribal government elections in South Dakota are conducted in English.

Todd and Shannon Counties have voter registration at or exceeding 100 percent of the voting age population. They have general election turnout that routinely exceeds the national average. Despite this reality, these two counties are bound under Section 5 to comply with the preclearance requirement until 2032. This does not make for rational law.

Third, Section 5 can be used by litigants to create consequences never intended by Congress. Although only two South Dakota counties are covered in federal law by Section 5, the ACLU has been successful in using the federal court system to apply Section 5 statewide.

In 2005 at the request of Charles Mix County (a noncovered county), the South Dakota legislature passed a bill allowing county commissioner districts to be redrawn under a narrow set of circumstances if the existing districts are not correctly drawn.[20] There was no need or attempt to use this provision in Todd or Shannon County nor would this provision be used in those counties prior to preclearance.

The ACLU asked the federal court to prevent implementation in the *noncovered* county prior to preclearance in Todd and Shannon Counties.[21] They were successful in convincing a three-judge panel to buy this argument, thus effectively spreading the preclearance requirement statewide. The state appealed this ruling to the United States Supreme Court, where the case was dismissed as moot upon preclearance of this statute for Todd and Shannon Counties.

Any implication by Section 5 proponents that Section 5 is a narrowly drawn preventive medicine applying only to uniquely defined jurisdictions was eradicated by this three-judge ruling. The effect of the court's ruling makes Section 5 an invasive statute the true boundaries of which are yet to be defined.

MINORITY-LANGUAGE COVERAGE (SECTION 203)

Eighteen of South Dakota's sixty-six counties are covered by the minority-language provisions of the Voting Rights Act for the Lakota or

Dakota languages.[22] Coverage is based on census determinations of the illiteracy rate and English proficiency.

The first coverage determination of English proficiency is whether more than 5 percent of the language minority speaks English less than "very well" as reported to the census.[23] This doesn't mean that these persons can speak or understand Lakota or Dakota, it just means that they feel they don't speak English "very well." There is an obvious disconnect between the census statistic of self-proclaimed English-speaking ability and any ability or inability to only speak Lakota or Dakota.

The second coverage determination is the illiteracy rate.[24] An illiterate person is defined as someone of voting age who has not finished the fifth grade. It doesn't matter if the person can read and write English or not. If a person hasn't finished the fifth grade, the person is illiterate in the eyes of the federal law. If a county's illiteracy rate is above the national average of 1.35 percent, minority-language coverage is triggered. If that county is part of an Indian reservation, every county in the reservation is covered by default.

What does this mean in South Dakota according to the 2000 census? There are twenty-seven people of limited English proficiency located in four South Dakota counties who haven't finished the fifth grade. The 1.35 percent threshold for coverage would be eleven people. The mathematical progression is simple from there. Sixteen people ($27 - 11 = 16$) located in four Indian reservation counties who didn't finish the fifth grade trigger minority-language provision requirements for eighteen counties.[25]

Is there any rationality in this coverage formula? Should the census response by sixteen people be able to drive Section 203 coverage requirements for eighteen counties? This author would argue that this formula lacks the precision required for a law whose consequences are large and far-reaching.

Typically Section 203 would require election materials translated in the covered language. Because Lakota and Dakota are unwritten languages, ballots cannot be printed in Lakota or Dakota to meet the minority-language requirement in these counties.[26] Election announcements, notices, and materials are translated into Lakota and broadcast on local radio stations. Interpreters are stationed at polling places to translate the ballot should any voter need such assistance. Local election officials report that the interpreters are rarely, if ever, used.

The Section 203 mandate with its associated cost does not have any positive impact on voter turnout or ability to participate in the process. It is simply not needed.

As required by the Help America Vote Act, each polling place in these counties is also equipped with an AutoMark voter assist terminal, which contains an audio version of the ballot in Lakota. The total cost involved in translation, recording, programming, and management to place Lakota on the AutoMark was about $28,000 for the 2006 primary and general elections. In the 2006 general election this feature was used by approximately ten voters, despite numerous local Lakota radio advertisements about the availability of Lakota on the AutoMark.[27] The cost per voter for placement of Lakota on the HAVA-mandated AutoMarks is beyond outrageous. Once again, Section 203 requirements exceed commonsense application.

Readers will wonder why there are few if any voters who need Lakota or Dakota assistance. The Lakota Language Consortium, an organization whose "primary mission is the complete revitalization of the Lakota language,"[28] explains the current Lakota language situation:

> Unfortunately, Lakota is dangerously close to extinction. Recent linguistic surveys, anecdotal evidence, and the 2000 US Census reveal that the situation for the language is very serious.
>
> According to these figures, Lakota speakers of all abilities, on and around the reservations of North Dakota and South Dakota amounted to between 8300 and 9000 persons, representing just 14% of the total Indian population. [Census numbers show a] . . . differing linguistic situation on the reservations, ranging from a high of 25% on the Pine Ridge Reservation to a low of 4% on the Lower Brule Reservation. National statistics for the Sioux also mirror this analysis. Among the 102,619 Sioux, age 5 and over, in 2000, only 15% spoke their language (2000 US Census).
>
> Not only are Lakota speakers becoming fewer in number, they are also becoming older. According to earlier linguistic surveys, in 1993 the median age was for a Lakota speaker was over 50 years old. Today, the average Lakota speaker is near 65 years old. These existing speakers are dying and are not being replaced by new Lakota-speaking generations. According to our recent analysis, the language stopped being transmitted inter-generationally during the mid-1950s. Our effort to reverse this language shift relies on creating new generation of Lakota speakers while there are still native speakers available to be teachers.[29]

The broad-brush Section 203 approach lumps the vanishing Lakota language into the same category as rapidly expanding minority languages such as Spanish and Chinese.

While the actual need for Lakota minority-language assistance is very small, Native Americans have repeatedly told the secretary of state's office they appreciate the effort to make this assistance available because it "honors our culture." This appreciation of Lakota culture is the only real benefit in South Dakota created by the minority-language requirements of the Voting Rights Act.

REALISTIC EXPECTATIONS

On the eve of the signing of the renewal of the temporary provisions of the Voting Rights Act by President George W. Bush, the Lawyers' Committee for Civil Rights Under Law, a leading advocate for renewal, issued a press release heralding the event. The press release stated that "[t]he renewed and restored V R A will open the doors for millions of Americans to participate in the political process."[30]

While this statement's validity elsewhere in America is debatable, it holds no truth in South Dakota. As has been demonstrated in this chapter, the sweeping, one-size-fits-all mandates of the temporary provisions of the Voting Rights Act simply do not have any helpful applicability in jurisdictions like South Dakota. The costs associated with compliance by state and local governments provide no return. Conversely, the time and money spent in compliance robs energy and resources that could be spent further improving the administration of elections, which would have a positive impact on all voters in the state.

Given this assessment, what are the realistic expectations in South Dakota for the Voting Rights Act's temporary provisions now having been made nearly permanent?

1. The State Legislature and Board of Elections will continue to exercise their responsibility to the people by giving primary consideration to passing legislation and promulgating rules to ensure the integrity and availability of our election process just as they have before and since South Dakota was first covered by Section 5 provisions in 1975.

2. The county auditors will continue the paper chase of documenting election process and procedure changes for the Department of Justice to preclear.

3. South Dakotans will continue to marvel at how Section 5 expands our traditional concept of federalism. The legislature can pass a law and the governor can sign the law or the voters can pass a constitutional amendment or statutory initiative, and an unelected federal employee can veto that law or amendment.

4. The ACLU will continue to appropriate the federal courts to attempt to expand Section 5 requirements from two counties to statewide coverage. The state will resist any expansion of Section 5 coverage beyond that enumerated in the federal law.

5. South Dakota counties will continue to provide Lakota interpreters and AutoMark ballot-marking devices containing Lakota audio in the polling place even though those services will be seldom used.

6. South Dakota will continue to see statewide voter turnout that ranks from number 1 to number 7 in the nation for each general election.

7. Just as it has since 1972, Native American voter turnout in South Dakota will not be determined or encouraged by the temporary provisions of the Voting Rights Act, but will be determined by:

   a. Interest or lack thereof in the particular candidates on the ballot;

   b. Political activity and encouragement by candidate campaigns and activist groups; and

   c. Increasing realization that tribal government is not the only government entity that affects Native Americans' lives.

Supporters of extending the temporary provisions of the Voting Rights Act are to be congratulated for their political victory in the nation's capital. Supporters worked diligently and played their political cards well. Let no one, however, be misled by claims of what will actually be accomplished. South Dakota's documented reality highlights the practical problems and failures that are the outcome of the temporary provisions of the Voting Rights Act, and it casts a proper light on realistic expectations.

NOTES

1. U.S. Census Bureau website: factfinder2.census.gov/faces/tableservices/jsf/pages/productview.xhtml?fpt=table.

2. South Dakota Legislative Redistricting Committee Minutes, October 9, 2001.

3. U.S. Census Bureau website: factfinder2.census.gov/faces/tableservices/jsf/pages/productview.xhtml?pid=DEC_10_PL_P1&prodType=table.

4. SDCL 12-4-18.

5. Peter Harriman, *Sioux Falls Argus Leader,* June 30, 2006.

6. 42 USC §1973b(b).

7. Appendix to Part 51 of 28 CFR.

8. U.S. Census Bureau website: http://factfinder.census.gov/home/saff/main.html.

9. South Dakota Attorney General Official Opinion 77-73, August 23, 1977.

10. ACLU News Release, August 5, 2002: www.aclu.org/votingrights/minority/13037prs20020805.html.

11. Consent Order in *Quick Bear Quiver v. Hazeltine,* filed December 27, 2002; Civ. 02-5069.

12. Department of Justice preclearance letters to South Dakota secretary of state dated July 1, 2003; August 29, 2003; October 21, 2003; November 3, 2003; November 7, 2003; December 15, 2003; December 31, 2003; January 2, 2004; January 9, 2004; January 20, 2004; March 8, 2004; March 12, 2004; May 3, 2004; May 24, 2004; July 6, 2004; July 13, 2004; August 2, 2004; August 30, 2004; September 7, 2004; October 5, 2004; November 1, 2004; December 6, 2004; December 20, 2004; January 3, 2005; January 31, 2005; February 25, 2005; March 7, 2005; April 4, 2005; May 2, 2005; June 6, 2005; June 30, 2005; August 4, 2005; August 31, 2005; September 29, 2005; October 13, 2005; November 14, 2005; November 23, 2005; December 5, 2005; January 3, 2006; January 13, 2006; February 6, 2006; March 9, 2006; April 12, 2006; April 13, 2006; June 5, 2006; August 7, 2006; and September 18, 2006.

13. U.S. Census Bureau website: www.census.gov/popest/counties/asrh/files/CC-EST2005-agesex-46.csv, for 2004 voting age population estimates; South Dakota secretary of state website: www.sdsos.gov/electionsvoteregistration/pastelections_electioninfo04_generalvoterregistrationtotals.shtm, for 2004 general election voter registration numbers by county. National Voter Registration Act restrictions on voter registration list maintenance combined with aggressive voter registration outreach efforts occasionally push voter registration lists past 100 percent of the voting age population.

14. U.S. Census Bureau website: www.census.gov/popest/counties/asrh/files/CC-EST2005-agesex-46.csv, for 2004 voting age population estimates; South Dakota secretary of state website: www.sdsos.gov/electionsvoteregistration/pastelections_electioninfo04_voterturnoutbycounty.shtm, for 2004 general election turnout by county.

15. George Mason University, United States Election Project website maintained by Dr. Michael P. McDonald: http://elections.gmu.edu/Voter_Turnout_2004.htm.

16. U.S. Census Bureau website: www.census.gov/popest/counties/asrh/files/

CC-EST2005-agesex-46.csv, for 2002,
2004 and 2006 voting age population estimates; South Dakota secretary of state
website: www.sdsos.gov/electionsvote
registration/pastelections.shtm, for 2002,
2004 and 2006 general election voter registration numbers by county.

17. U.S. Census Bureau website: www
.census.gov/popest/counties/asrh/files/
CC-EST2005-agesex-46.csv, for 2002, 2004
and 2006 voting age population estimates;
South Dakota secretary of state website:
www.sdsos.gov/electionsvoteregistration/
pastelections.shtm, for 2002, 2004, and
2006 general election voter turnout by
county.

18. George Mason University, United
States Election Project website maintained
by Dr. Michael P. McDonald: http://elec
tions.gmu.edu/Voter_Turnout_2002.htm,
http://elections.gmu.edu/Voter_Turnout
_2004.htm, http://elections.gmu.edu/
Voter_Turnout_2006.htm.

19. 42 USC §1973b(f)(3).

20. South Dakota House Bill 1265 from
2005 session: http://legis.state.sd.us/ses-
sions/2005/1265.htm.

21. Plaintiffs' Motion for a Preliminary
and Permanent Injunction filed March 25,
2005, Civ. 02-5069.

22. Department of Commerce, Bureau
of the Census publication, Federal Register, Volume 67, No. 144, pages 48871–77.

23. U.S. Census Bureau website: www
.census.gov/rdo/www/voting%20rights.
htm, for Voting Rights Determination File
from the 2000 census.

24. U.S. Census Bureau website: www
.census.gov/rdo/www/voting%20rights.
htm, for Voting Rights Determination File
from the 2000 census.

25. U.S. Census Bureau website: www
.census.gov/rdo/www/voting%20rights.
htm, for Voting Rights Determination File
from the 2000 census.

26. SDCL 12-3-9.

27. South Dakota secretary of state.
Cost includes direct and indirect expen-
ditures. Usage levels were determined
through interviews with county auditors
and polling place workers.

28. Lakota Language Consortium website: www.lakhota.org/html/about.html.

29. Lakota Language Consortium website: www.lakhota.org/html/status2.html.

30. Lawyers' Committee for Civil
Rights Under Law press release, July 26,
2006, www.lawyerscomm.org/2005
website/publications/press/press072606
.html.

EIGHT

The Continuing Need for the Language-Assistance Provisions of the Voting Rights Act

JAMES THOMAS TUCKER

The bilingual election requirements in the Voting Rights Act ("VRA" or "Act") are straightforward.[1] A permanent provision in the 1965 Act, Section 4(e), requires that Spanish-speaking Puerto Rican voters be provided with voting materials and assistance in their native language.[2] The Act's temporary language-assistance provisions, including Section 203, help millions of non-English-speaking voting-age U.S. citizens overcome language barriers to political participation.[3] The requirements apply to four language groups: Alaska Natives; American Indians; Asian Americans; and persons of Spanish heritage and the distinct languages and dialects within those groups.[4] Covered jurisdictions must provide written voting materials in the covered language unless it is oral or unwritten, or if it is an Alaska Native or American Indian language that is "historically unwritten."[5] "Voting materials" are defined as "registration or voting notices, forms, instructions, assistance, or other materials or information relating to the electoral process, including ballots."[6]

In addition, oral language assistance must be provided to the extent necessary to allow language minority citizens to participate effectively.[7] Language assistance is required for all stages of the electoral process, such as voter registration, "the issuance, at any time during the year, of notifications, announcements, or other informational materials concerning the opportunity to register, the deadline for voter registration, the time, places and subject matters of elections, and the absentee voting process."[8] That means that covered jurisdictions must recruit and train bilingual election workers to provide oral language assistance that effectively communicates all voting materials, information, and publicity to language-minority voters.

Congress adopted Section 203 in 1975, extending it for ten years in 1982 and for fifteen years in 1992.[9] During the 1992 reauthorization, the section's coverage formula was expanded to include urban areas with ten thousand or more language-minority voting-age citizens with limited English skills. Coverage also was extended to Indian reservations on which 5 percent or more of voting-age citizens had limited English skills in an American Indian language.[10] In 2006, Congress reauthorized Section 203 by substituting "2032" for "2007" in the sunset date specified in the section. The only substantive amendment was a change to make future coverage determinations using the 2010 American Community Survey ("ACS") census data with subsequent determinations made every five years.[11]

This chapter summarizes the case for Section 203's reauthorization and constitutionality. It begins by briefly responding to some of the arguments against bilingual ballots made by Roger Clegg in the following chapter. Next, the constitutional discussion provides an overview of the controlling legal framework, including a quartet of United States Supreme Court decisions upholding similar requirements under the Act. That is followed by a summary of the discrimination in education, voting, and other areas against the four covered language groups necessitating the enactment of the bilingual assistance remedy in 1975. Section 203's coverage formula is then examined to show how language assistance is carefully targeted to cover voters in jurisdictions where there is a current need because of ongoing discrimination and the present effect of past discrimination. Finally, the chapter concludes with the impact of the VRA's language-assistance requirements on the political participation of covered minorities. Against this extensive factual record and controlling case law, a constitutional challenge to Section 203 is unlikely to succeed.

A RESPONSE TO "POLICY" MYTHS PROMOTED BY SECTION 203'S CRITICS

Section 203's critics make several arguments against language assistance in voting that are unsupported by the facts. For instance, Mr. Clegg raises what he describes as three "policy" problems with Section 203: the statute allegedly "encourages balkanization," "facilitates voter fraud," and "wastes government resources." Representative Steve King of Iowa and other opponents of Section 203 made similar arguments during the recent reauthorization debate. Factual evidence categorically refutes each of their criticisms.[12]

Before turning to Mr. Clegg's arguments, it is necessary to correct his mischaracterizations of the congressional record. Contrary to Mr. Clegg's contention, Congress did not merely go through the motions and avoid developing strong documentary evidence to justify the most recent reauthorization of Section 203. Instead, the 109th Congress carefully deliberated the continued need for language assistance in voting based upon over fourteen thousand pages of reports and testimony submitted both in support of and in opposition to the Voting Rights Act Reauthorization Act ("VRARA"). The debate on the bill in the House and the Senate and at hearings held by the House and Senate Judiciary Committees was lively and often contentious. About a hundred witnesses testified at nearly two dozen hearings held from October 2005 through July 2006. They included opponents of language assistance, such as Mr. Clegg and Linda Chavez, as well as its supporters. Few pieces of federal legislation have been subjected to such intense scrutiny as the VRARA. Members of Congress did not march in lockstep with the civil rights community to pass the bill; they rejected several proposals to expand coverage under Section 203.[13]

"Balkanization" Argument

A bipartisan majority in the House and the Senate found no validity to Mr. Clegg's assertion that Section 203 "balkanizes" our country by discouraging English language acquisition by immigrants. Today's new arrivals lose their native language quickly, with 88 percent of second-generation Latino immigrants reporting that they speak English fluently.[14] Native-born and naturalized language-minority U.S. citizens want to learn English. As discussed later in this chapter, the greatest barriers they face are lack of English-as-a-second-language (ESL) courses and unequal educational opportunities in the public schools. Therefore, the House Judiciary Committee determined, "Citizens should not be penalized for trying to learn English and exercising their right to vote. Section 4(f) and 203 level the playing field for language minority citizens, ensuring that the most fundamental right of all citizens is preserved regardless of one's ability to speak English well."[15]

Mr. Clegg's balkanization argument likewise is premised upon his erroneous contention that few native-born U.S. citizens need language assistance, leading him to conclude that Section 203 promotes noncitizen voting. According to the Census Bureau's 2002 coverage determinations under Section 203, the V R A mandated that language assistance be provided to *over four million voting age U.S. citizens with limited English skills* in covered jurisdictions.[16] Most of those who need language materials and assistance in one of the four covered language groups are native-born U.S. citizens and not naturalized. The 1986 G A O study discussed by Mr. Clegg found that 77 percent of U.S. citizens using Spanish-language materials and assistance in Texas were born in the United States. All Alaska Natives and American Indians and 98.6 percent of Puerto Ricans are native-born, as are a majority of U.S. citizens of Japanese, Cambodian, Hmong, and other Asian ethnicities.[17]

Like many other Section 203 opponents, Mr. Clegg also plays upon the fear among some people that English-language hegemony in this country (itself a myth) is threatened by a widespread growth of bilingual ballots. The number of jurisdictions covered by Section 203, however, is not growing rapidly, as Mr. Clegg maintains. When Section 203 was originally enacted in 1975, there were 385 covered counties. In 2002, there were 296 covered jurisdictions in thirty states. Today, just 248 counties, parishes, and townships in twenty-five states are covered under the 2011 census determinations. In 1975, three states (Alaska, Arizona, and Texas) were covered in their entirety under the separate language trigger in Section 4(f)(4) of the Act. In 2002, two additional states were added to statewide coverage for Spanish under Section 203, California and New Mexico; nearly all the counties in those states were covered when Section 203 was added in 1975. In 2011, New Mexico lost its statewide coverage, while Florida became covered statewide for Spanish; five counties in Florida have been covered under Section 4(f)(4) of the Act since 1975.

Mr. Clegg's contention of an impending language crisis caused by "bi-lingual ballots" is unsupported by the reality that the number of covered jurisdictions has actually decreased dramatically since Section 203 was added to the V R A.[18]

"Vote Fraud" Argument

Evidence of fraud convictions linked to bilingual ballots is conspicu-ously absent in Mr. Clegg's discussion of his "vote fraud" argument. The reason is clear: vote fraud convictions of any kind are extremely rare, much less those of ineligible aliens. For example, Texas, which has more counties covered under Section 203 than any other state, reported only twenty-two convictions statewide for vote fraud in a six-year period from 2002 to 2007; almost all of those involved mailed ballot fraud by eligible voters and not registration or voting by noncitizens.[19] Between 2000 and March 2008, the Office of the State Court Administrator reported just two convictions in Florida of unqualified electors willfully voting, without any indication of their citizenship status. Nearly one hundred counties in Arizona, Indiana, Missouri, New York, and Ohio reported a combined total of just twelve successful vote fraud prosecutions between 2000 and 2006, with none linked to noncitizens. Eighty-six percent of responding prosecutors in those states disagreed with the assertion that vote fraud was a problem in their counties, with only one percent saying it was. None identified noncitizen voting as a concern.[20]

Much of what Mr. Clegg offers as evidence of vote fraud are discred-ited allegations by partisan officials that were never proven in a court of law. He also draws on the specter of noncitizens illegally casting ballots, without identifying any causal link between bilingual voting materials and illegal voting other than his own speculative assumptions. Repub-lican House Judiciary Committee chairman James Sensenbrenner re-jected a similar argument during the committee markup of the VRARA. He explained, "We are not dealing with illegal immigrants, we are deal-ing with United States citizens, and they are people who have either attained citizenship by reason of birth in the United States . . . or have been naturalized."[21]

Section 203 deters vote fraud by ensuring that covered jurisdictions offer eligible voters with limited English skills uniform and official translations of ballots and voting information. Federal regulations provide, "It is essential that material provided in the language of a language minority group be clear, complete and accurate."[22] Absent bilingual voting materials, language-minority voters are more susceptible to being victimized by inaccurate information. Official translations make it more likely that the votes of language minorities will accurately reflect their own political judgment, not that of others.

"Wasted Resources" Argument

Mr. Clegg's remaining "policy" argument, that "bilingual ballots" are wasteful, is also unsupported by the facts. It is curious that Mr. Clegg and other Section 203 opponents largely omit any discussion of bilingual election workers. That may be for a couple of reasons. Section 2 of the Act prohibits discriminatory practices, requiring that election workers reflect the racial, ethnic, and language diversity of voters, even those in jurisdictions not covered by Section 203.[23] Few people would object to election officials and poll workers who are representative of language minorities in the community, including those able to assist voters who do not speak English proficiently. But more critically, bilingual election workers undercut the critics' argument that language assistance is costly. It is not. The 1986 and 1997 GAO studies and the 2005 study I conducted with Professor Rodolfo Espino found that most jurisdictions incurred no additional costs for oral language assistance, primarily because bilingual poll workers are paid the same as other poll workers and poll workers must be hired regardless of Section 203.[24]

Additionally, critics of Section 203 often pull cost data out of context. For example, Mr. Clegg refers to $1.1 million spent by Los Angeles County in 1996 on its language-assistance program. He fails to mention that the county reported to the GAO that those costs only amounted to 3.6 percent of its total election expenses. Deborah Wright, a Los Angeles County election official, testified in the Senate during the VRARA hearings that "the percentage of election expenses for language assistance is reasonable and is virtually the same as the percentage of voters who need assistance."[25] Similarly, the 1997 GAO report, cited by Mr. Clegg, refutes his contention that "frequently the cost of multilingual voter assistance is more than half of a jurisdiction's total election costs." That study only included data from 28 jurisdictions, in which bilingual costs averaged just 4.9 percent of total election costs.[26]

In my 2005 nationwide study with Professor Espino, a majority of jurisdictions covered by Section 203 reported no additional costs for providing language assistance, whether oral or written. Of those that did have costs, a majority incurred average expenses of less than 1.5 percent for oral language assistance and less than 3 percent for written language assistance. About 10 percent of all covered jurisdictions that responded to our survey were outliers, reporting bilingual costs that were disproportionately high. Many outliers attributed all election expenses, including costs for hiring election workers and poll workers required regardless of Section 203, to language assistance. Sixty percent of 154 responding jurisdictions reported no additional costs for oral language assistance, and more than 54 percent of 144 responding jurisdictions reported no additional costs for bilingual materials.[27]

South Dakota secretary of state Chris Nelson contends that few, if any, language-minority voters have requested language assistance in his state, forcing it to waste money. His argument rests on the erroneous assumption that the burden is on language-minority voters to request language assistance before compliance becomes necessary. Section 203 says otherwise: covered jurisdictions have the responsibility to reach out to voters to determine their language needs, not the other way around.[28] Courts have rejected similar "good faith" arguments premised upon a lack of voter complaints.[29] Geographic or linguistic isolation, combined with the lack of bilingual election officials or a toll-free way of contacting them, can be insurmountable barriers for many language-minority voters. Where election officials adopt a passive approach that shifts the burden to limited-English-speaking voters, they are more likely to violate Section 203. The cost of noncompliance by election officials in covered jurisdictions is far greater than the very low cost of working with language groups to provide effective language assistance.[30]

Finally, the examples offered by Mr. Clegg and Secretary Nelson of jurisdictions that spent money on bilingual voting materials that went unused also says nothing about the need for or reasonableness of the cost of Section 203's requirements. Low use or nonuse of language assistance often is attributable to the failure of election officials to conduct adequate outreach to inform language minorities that it is available. Assistance cannot be used if voters do not know about it. Proper use of targeting, which is discussed later in this chapter, also ensures that language assistance is only offered where it is needed.[31]

CONSTITUTIONALITY OF BANS ON LITERACY TESTS AND ENGLISH-ONLY ELECTIONS

More than thirty-five years after Congress enacted Section 203 and five years after its most recent reauthorization, no constitutional challenge to it has been brought. According to Ms. Chavez, "It may be that there simply has not been someone who has been aggressively interested in challenging it."[32] That explanation seems unlikely in light of intense opposition by anti-immigrant organizations, English-only groups, and witnesses such as Ms. Chavez, Mr. Clegg, and Secretary Nelson to Section 203's reauthorization.[33] English-only organizations have challenged other federal bilingual language requirements. English Language Advocates, English First Foundation, and U.S. English filed amicus briefs opposing use of Title VI of the Civil Rights Act to compel language assistance for Alabama's English-only driver's license examination.[34] In 2003, a federal court rejected ProEnglish's attempt to strike down Executive Order 13166, a Clinton policy reaffirmed by President Bush requiring bilingual materials and assistance for certain federal agencies and programs.[35] Nevertheless, Ms. Chavez insists Section 203 "will, in fact, probably be challenged if it is reauthorized."[36]

Debating the constitutionality of Section 203 with critics of the provision sometimes can seem like ships passing in the night. The reason for the disconnect lies in the legal sources of arguments made by the respective sides in this debate. Ms. Chavez and Mr. Clegg have not acknowledged the Court's decisions evaluating the constitutional basis for language-assistance requirements and suspension of English literacy requirements. Rather, they focus on inapplicable cases such as *Washington v. Davis* and *Village of Arlington Heights v. Metropolitan Housing Development Corp.* that have nothing to do with either Section 203 or the constitutional authority Congress exercised in passing it. In both of these cases, the Court's decisions construed congressional power under the first section of the Fourteenth and Fifteenth Amendments, the so-called self-executing provisions. But Congress enacted the bilingual voting requirements pursuant to its broad authority under the enforcement sections of the Fourteenth and Fifteenth Amendments (sections 5 and 2, respectively) to the U.S. Constitution. Consequently, the United States Supreme Court has not wavered in its deference to congressional choices to enact and amend federal requirements for bilingual voting materials and assistance.[37]

Constitutionality of the VRA's Literacy Test Ban

In *Lassiter v. Northampton County Board of Elections,* the Supreme Court acknowledged that states have great discretion in setting voter qualifications, including establishing literacy requirements.[38] The Constitution makes that explicit, providing that "the Electors in each State shall have the Qualifications requisite for Electors of the most numerous branch of the State Legislature."[39] That discretion, however, is not boundless. Voter qualifications must be nondiscriminatory and consistent with "any restriction that Congress, acting pursuant to its constitutional powers, has imposed." A literacy test could be suspended if it was shown to have a racially discriminatory impact on a particular group. Since there was no evidence presented of "discrimination in the actual operation of the ballot laws in North Carolina," the Court in *Lassiter* could not address the discriminatory effect of the literacy test for the first time on appeal.[40] Where such evidence was presented shortly before the VRA was enacted, the Court enjoined the literacy tests.[41]

The Supreme Court examined the constitutionality of the VRA's ban on literacy tests and English-only elections in four cases decided between 1966 and 1970.[42] Each of those decisions focused on congressional powers to pass remedial legislation under the Reconstruction Amendments. In *Ex Parte Virginia,* the Court described the breadth of those powers:

> [The Reconstruction Amendments were] intended to be ... limitations of the
> power of the States and enlargements of the power of Congress.... Congress is
> authorized to enforce the prohibitions by appropriate legislation. Some legisla-
> tion is contemplated to make the amendments fully effective. Whatever legisla-
> tion is appropriate, that is, adapted to carry out the objects the amendments have
> in view, whatever tends to enforce submission to the prohibitions they contain,
> and to secure to all persons the enjoyment of perfect equality of civil rights ... if
> not prohibited, is brought within the domain of congressional power.[43]

That standard provided a strong basis for enacting Section 203 to remedy
the effects of voting and educational discrimination against language
minorities.

SOUTH CAROLINA V. KATZENBACH   In the first case, *South Carolina
v. Katzenbach,* the Supreme Court upheld the constitutionality of the
Act's protections, including the temporary suspension of literacy tests.[44]
The Court found that Section 2 of the Fifteenth Amendment allowed
Congress to "use any rational means to effectuate the constitutional
prohibition of racial discrimination in voting."[45] As a result, Congress
could exercise its powers in an "inventive manner," as it did in suspend-
ing literacy tests "without any need for prior adjudication" because the
states easily circumvented court decisions by adopting new discriminatory procedures. Use of a triggering formula was permissible because it
identified jurisdictions where there was a "significant danger" of voting
discrimination, as documented by "a low voting rate" caused by the application of literacy tests and other devices.[46] It did not matter that the
formula excluded localities that engaged in voting discrimination but
did not use literacy tests or other devices. Instead, "widespread and persistent discrimination in voting during recent years ... typically entailed
the misuse of tests and devices, and this was the evil for which the new
remedies were specifically designed." Therefore, the Court found that
"the Fifteenth Amendment has clearly been violated" and unanimously
concluded that the V R A's ban on literacy tests was constitutional.[47]

GASTON COUNTY V. UNITED STATES   The second case involved the
same North Carolina literacy test upheld in *Lassiter.* In *Gaston County
v. United States,* the Court denied a county's petition to reinstate the lit-

eracy test, which was suspended after the county became covered under Section 4 of the VRA.[48] The Court found that even though educational discrimination itself could not be remedied under the Fifteenth Amendment, its effects on voters could be.[49] Congress was "fully cognizant of the potential effect of unequal educational opportunities upon exercise of the franchise" when it temporarily suspended literacy tests in covered jurisdictions.[50] There was "substantial evidence" that Gaston County "deprived its black residents of equal educational opportunities, which in turn deprived them of an equal chance to pass a literacy test." Congress could use a coverage formula derived from voting or registration data because a formula "based on educational disparities, or one based on literacy rates would be administratively cumbersome: the designation of racially disparate school systems is not susceptible of speedy, objective, and incontrovertible determination."[51] According to the Court, even if covered jurisdictions eliminated educational discrimination against current students, it did "nothing for their parents" who were voters and who continued to suffer from the effects of past discrimination. As a result, with only Justice Black dissenting, *Gaston County* recognized congressional authority to impose a localized and temporary ban on literacy tests.[52]

OREGON V. MITCHELL The third case was the last to be decided. In *Oregon v. Mitchell,* the Court unanimously upheld the nationwide ban on literacy tests adopted in the 1970 amendments to the VRA.[53] Although the justices disagreed on which enforcement section sustained the ban, they all agreed that Congress had broad discretion to impose it.[54] Justice Black found the ban constitutional because of the discriminatory use of literacy tests, their impact on voter participation, and the "denial of equal protection to condition the political participation of children educated in a dual school system upon their educational achievement."[55] Justice Douglas reasoned that the ban was an appropriate response that did not require "findings as to the incidence of literacy."[56] Justice Stewart explained that the need for the ban "need not turn on whether literacy tests unfairly discriminate against Negroes in every State" and did not require "state-by-state findings" concerning educational equality and the impact of literacy tests on voting. Congress could choose to "paint with a much broader brush" and had great discretion in using the "[e]xperience gained under the 1965 Act" with a localized ban "to conclude it should go the whole distance."[57]

KATZENBACH V. MORGAN The fourth case addressed the constitutionality of the permanent suspension of English-only elections for Puerto Rican voters covered under Section 4(e) of the Act. Under that provision, no person who demonstrates he has successfully completed a sixth grade education in a school in the United States "in which the predominant classroom language was other than English, shall be denied the right to vote in any Federal, State, or local election because of his inability to read, write, understand, or interpret any matter in the English language."[58] Congress considered the "clear racial purposes" behind application of New York's literacy requirement to deny political participation to immigrants and non-English-speaking Puerto Ricans:

> Estimates were offered that of 730,000 Puerto Ricans in the city of all ages, 150,000 registered to vote but close to 330,000 were prevented from registering. Accounts were given about how literacy test certificates would "suddenly disappear" causing delays of hours, if not the entire day, to replace them, or how basic supplies like pencils would be missing whenever Puerto Ricans sought to take the test. Finally the witnesses sought to defuse the "myth in our State of New York that a citizen can be an intelligent, well-informed voter only if he is literate in English."[59]

Therefore, Section 4(e) required that bilingual voting materials[60] and Spanish-language assistance be provided for Puerto Rican voters illiterate in English.[61]

In *Katzenbach v. Morgan*, the Court described congressional enforcement powers as "a positive grant of legislative power authorizing Congress to exercise its discretion in determining whether and what legislation is needed to secure the guarantees of the Fourteenth Amendment."[62] As long as Congress did not exceed its discretion, the Court had no authority to second-guess it:

> It was well within congressional authority to say that this need of the Puerto Rican minority for the vote warranted federal intrusion upon any state interests served by the English literacy requirement. It was for Congress, as the branch

that made this judgment, to assess and weigh the various conflicting considerations – the risk or pervasiveness of the discrimination in governmental services,
the effectiveness of eliminating the state restriction on the right to vote as a
means of dealing with the evil, the adequacy or availability of alternative remedies, and the nature and significance of the state interests that would be affected
by the nullification of the English literacy requirement as applied to residents
who have successfully completed the sixth grade in a Puerto Rican school.[63]

Turning to the constitutionality of Section 4(e), the Court reasoned
that Congress had made valid legislative choices to limit the scope of the
provision to Puerto Ricans.[64] The Court explained:

> In the context of the case before us, the congressional choice to limit the relief
> effected in § 4(e) may, for example, reflect . . . a recognition of the unique historic
> relationship between the Congress and the Commonwealth of Puerto Rico,
> an awareness of the Federal Government's acceptance of the desirability of the
> use of Spanish as the language of instruction in Commonwealth schools, and
> the fact that Congress has fostered policies encouraging migration from the
> Commonwealth to the States.[65]

The Court rejected the assertion that New York's English-language requirement was created to give language minorities an incentive to learn
English. Instead, the Court found that Congress may have "questioned
whether denial of a right deemed so precious and fundamental in our
society was a necessary or appropriate means of encouraging persons
to learn English, or of furthering the goal of an intelligent exercise of
the franchise." Consequently, the requirement that New York provide
language assistance to Spanish-speaking Puerto Rican voters, like the
ban on literacy tests, was constitutional.[66] Only two justices, Harlan and
Stewart, dissented.

Impact of NAMUDNO on Section 203

The Court's recent decision in *Northwest Austin Municipal Utility District
Number One (NAMUDNO) vs. Holder*,[67] which challenged the preclearance requirements in Section 5 of the VRA, leaves intact the framework
from this quartet of cases.[68] Chief Justice Roberts's majority opinion,
joined by seven other justices, explicitly reaffirmed that the "Fifteenth
Amendment empowers 'Congress,' not the Court, to determine in the
first instance where legislation is needed to enforce it." Justice Roberts

acknowledged that assessing the constitutionality of any of the VRA's provisions enacted by "a coequal branch of government" required being "mindful of our institutional role." In deference to its limited role in reviewing congressional remedies enforcing the right to vote, the Court applied the principle of constitutional avoidance. As Justice Roberts explained, "it is a well-established principle governing the prudent exercise of this Court's jurisdiction that normally the Court will not decide a constitutional question if there is some other ground upon which to dispose of the case."[69]

Any challenge to the VRA's language-assistance provisions therefore would entail two herculean tasks. It would require convincing the Court to decide the constitutional question in the first instance. Next, it would mean overturning the judgment of Congress in enacting the provisions pursuant to its broad remedial powers under the Fifteenth Amendment. In the process, it would lay waste to the principle of *stare decisis* by reversing more than four decades of precedent affirming the constitutionality of language assistance in public elections. For a Court expressing a desire to exercise judicial restraint, such a constitutional Armageddon is unlikely.

HISTORICAL DISCRIMINATION AGAINST LANGUAGE-MINORITY VOTERS

In *NAMUDNO*, the Court reaffirmed the analytical approach in *South Carolina v. Katzenbach* requiring "the constitutional propriety" of the VRA to "be judged with reference to the historical experience which it reflects."[70] As one congressman explained, the historical experience of language minorities "is tragically reminiscent of the . . . problems experienced by blacks" in the South.[71] In 1975, Congress considered evidence documenting the disenfranchisement of Spanish-speaking voters in Texas, particularly those of Mexican descent.[72] Other groups likewise experienced discrimination through denial of equal educational opportunities that left them illiterate, English literacy tests that deterred registration and voting, gerrymandering and annexations that excluded them from local elections, and physical and economic intimidation.[73]

Denial of Equal Citizenship Rights

American Indians were the victims of wars of extermination and forced relocation to reservations until the late nineteenth century. Alaska Natives fared somewhat better, but like the native peoples of the lower forty-eight, they were victimized by the destruction of their culture, loss of lands and natural resources, and Jim Crow practices perpetuated by whites in Alaska for whom the word "*Indian* was synonymous with *nigger*."[74] Alaska Natives and American Indians were not fully admitted to citizenship until 1924, when Congress conferred citizenship on "all noncitizen Indians born within the territorial limits of the United States."[75] Nevertheless, American Indians would not gain the right to vote in Arizona and New Mexico until 1948[76] and in Utah until 1956, just nine years before the passage of the VRA.[77] Use of literacy tests, English-only elections, and other discriminatory practices also disenfranchised native voters even after they formally obtained the right to vote.[78] Illustrative of that discrimination, Apache County, Arizona, unlawfully refused to certify a Navajo elected to one of the three seats on the county commission.[79] To prevent Indian voters from controlling the commission, the three white commissioners then packed nearly 24,000 Indians and 83 percent of Apache County's population into a single district, with just 370 Indians included in the remaining two districts.[80]

Native-born Asian Americans were denied citizenship until 1898. The Chinese Exclusion Act of 1882 and other laws limiting Asian immigration and citizenship were repealed beginning in 1943. Asian Americans, particularly the Chinese, were vilified, with opponents raising the specter of hordes of "Mongol voters" or "coolie voters" if they were granted citizenship.[81] The last of the restrictions on Asian American citizenship were not removed until 1965, the same year the VRA was enacted.[82] Economic, educational, political, and social discrimination lasted just as long. California and Washington enacted anti-alien land laws in the 1920s that barred Chinese and Japanese from owning land well into the 1940s and 1950s. Antimiscegenation laws in states like Arizona and California banned whites from marrying those of "Mongolian" and "Malay" blood, including all Chinese, Filipinos, and Japanese. California's law was in force until 1948,[83] Arizona's law until 1962,[84] and other state antimiscegenation laws that included Asians, such as Virginia's, were not struck down until 1967.[85] Racism against Asians culminated in the forcible removal and internment of more than one hundred thousand Japanese Americans during World War II, despite the absence of any individual determinations of their disloyalty.[86]

While citizenship was more accessible to native-born Latinos, the fruits of civic and political participation were not. Congress documented discrimination against Puerto Ricans in New York when it included Section 4(e) in the original 1965 Act.[87] Communities in Arizona segregated non-Hispanics from Mexican Americans in public facilities such as swimming pools and schools until at least the mid-1950s.[88] In 1975, Congress cited extensive judicial findings and testimony to support its enactment of temporary language requirements protecting all Spanish-speaking citizens in covered jurisdictions. It found discrimination in Texas against Mexican Americans "in ways similar to the myriad forms of discrimination practiced against blacks in the South." Other evidence showed that the exclusion of Latinos was "further aggravated by acts of physical, economic, and political intimidation" when they attempted to vote. Similar findings were presented from other states.[89]

Educational Discrimination

The U.S. Supreme Court has long held that language-minority students have a right under the Fourteenth Amendment to an equal education that addresses their unique language needs. In 1923, the Court struck down a prohibition on teaching languages other than English in the public schools. In doing so, the Court concluded that "the protection of the Constitution extends to all, to those who speak other languages as well as those born with English on the tongue."[90] In 1927, the Court struck down a Hawaii law that restricted private Japanese foreign-language schools.[91] Despite these decisions and the landmark ruling of *Brown v. Board of Education*,[92] millions of language-minority citizens continued to be denied equal learning opportunities.

AMERICAN INDIANS Congress described the education of American Indians as a "national tragedy," with "the school and the classroom . . . a primary tool of assimilation." Education was provided as a means to "emancipate . . . the Indian child from his home, his parents, his extended family, and his cultural heritage." The purpose was "to wash the 'savage habits' and 'tribal ethic' out of a child's mind and substitute a white middle-class value system in its place."[93] To achieve those goals, a federal "civilization fund" was in effect between 1819 and 1873 to introduce Indian tribes to "the habits and cultures of civilization" by converting them from hunters into farmers.[94]

The congressionally appointed Peace Commission of 1868 used compulsory school attendance laws to ensure that "Indian children's 'barbarous dialects should be blotted out and the English language substituted.'" Echoing the tone of some of today's commentators, the commission sought to remove "the boundary lines" that divided Indians "into distinct nations, and fuse them into one homogenous mass" through "uniformity of language." Eradication of languages was enforced through strict English-only policies in the schools that included physical punishment such as beating an offending child or washing their mouth out with distasteful tonics "to take away the taint of the Indian language."[95]

Boarding schools played a key role in efforts "to dissolve the Indian social structure." The schools were paid for by the sale of Indian lands taken from tribes under the Dawes Severalty Act, or General Allotment Act of 1887. "They were designed to separate a child from his reservation and family, strip him of his tribal lore and mores, force the complete abandonment of his native language, and prepare him for never again returning to his people." When Indian families refused to send their children away, the secretary of the interior withheld their subsistence. Nevertheless, thousands of Indian families resisted. By 1919, the government documented that just 2,089 out of 9,613 Navajo children were attending school.[96] At the same time, Indian children were kept out of the public schools. In 1900, just 1 percent of Indian children were enrolled in public schools.[97]

Segregated schooling and forced assimilation continued, off and on, until the 1960s, when Indian students began to enter public schools in large numbers following passage of the Civil Rights Act of 1964 and the Bilingual Education Act of 1968.[98] But much of the damage had been done. In 1948, it was reported that as many as 90 percent of American Indians in Arizona were illiterate.[99] In 1962, the average education of American Indians in Arizona climbed to 3½ years among some tribes, with others as low as one year.[100]

Indian children entering public schools for the first time encountered a hostile environment in which the American Indian was portrayed as "dirty, lazy, and drunk."[101] "After almost 200 years of a federal 'civilization' policy, one-half to two-thirds of Indian children enter school with little or no skill in the English language, and only a handful of teachers and administrators speak Indian languages."[102] In *Natonabah v. Board of Education,* cited in the 1975 Senate Report, the court held that the Gallup-McKinley School District in New Mexico systematically deprived Navajo students of equal opportunities by denying Indians, most of whom did not speak English, equal funding for educational services.[103] In San Juan County, New Mexico, non-Indians unsuccessfully tried to block use of school bond funds to provide public education on the Navajo reservation, which would have required Indian children to travel 150 miles to school every day.[104] Pervasive educational discrimination against American Indians led the U.S. Commission on Civil Rights to find in 1971 that "American Indians . . . do not obtain the benefits of a public education . . . equal to that of their Anglo classmates."[105]

ALASKA NATIVES Segregated schooling was the norm in Alaska for more than a hundred years. The only schooling available to Natives after Russia's cession of Alaska to the United States in 1867 was provided by missionaries and private companies.[106] Later, "a dual school system emerged unofficially in Alaska" because of "resentment among the relatively few whites over emphasis on education for Natives and a belief that integrated schools would give only inferior education."[107] The policy of separation was born under federal laws governing the territory, which Alaska subsequently used as an excuse to repudiate much of its obligation to provide public schooling for Alaska Natives. It remained in place until the early 1980s.

In 1905, Congress enacted the Nelson Act, which authorized the creation and maintenance of schools in Alaska. The law was written in stark racial terms, limiting attendance to "the education of white children and children of mixed blood who lead a civilized life."[108] The act allowed local school boards to admit Native children, but few did. Often, school boards exercised their discretion to exclude Native children whose "presence is detrimental to the best interests of the school."[109] By 1929, segregated schools existed in at least nineteen communities.

The effects of racist education policies are graphically illustrated in a 1908 court decision. In *Davis v. Sitka School Board,* a federal judge denied a request by Alaska Native children for admission into an all-white school, using reasoning that paralleled the "one-drop" rule applied to sustain southern Jim Crow laws.[110] In 1929, a federal court ordered that an Alaska Native child living in the corporate limits of Ketchikan be admitted to the city's all-white schools.[111] In 1939, an Alaska Indian Service official testified about a case in Valdez in which "an eighth-grade Native girl 'wanted to attend high school, but the school board didn't see fit to take her.'"[112] Despite a 1956 opinion by the secretary of the interior advising the territorial attorney general that Alaska had to provide schools to Alaska Native children, those instructions would be ignored until the mid-1980s.[113]

In 1959, out of thirty-four public secondary schools operated by the new state government, just six were in communities in which at least half of the population was Alaska Native. By the mid-1970s, there were about 2,783 secondary-school-age children who lived in villages with a public or Bureau of Indian Affairs (BIA) elementary school but without a secondary school or daily access to such a school. More than 95 percent of those children were Native; statewide, only 120 white children of secondary school age had no ready access to a secondary school.[114]

Alaska's dual school system was especially pronounced for secondary education. Few Natives were selected for a program that removed them from their villages and sent them to boarding schools in the lower forty-eight, thousands of miles away. By 1960, just 1,832 out of 5,365 Native children between the ages of fourteen and nineteen were enrolled in high school.[115] In *Hootch v. State Operated School System,* a case cited by the 1975 Senate Report, a class of Eskimo, Aleut, and Indian parents and children sued the state to remedy the separate and unequal schooling.[116] The case was settled in 1976, twenty-two years after *Brown v. Board of Education,* when Alaska agreed for the first time to establish a public secondary school in all 126 native villages that wanted one. The settlement ultimately cost Alaska $137 million to open public secondary schools in 105 villages beginning in the early 1980s.[117]

Educational discrimination resulted in illiteracy rates among Natives rivaling rates of African Americans in southern states. According to 1960 census data considered by Congress in 1975, 38.6 percent of Alaska's nonwhite population age twenty-five years and older failed to complete the fifth primary grade, rendering them illiterate.[118] Alaska's 1960 illiteracy rate was higher than the rates for African Americans in Alabama, Florida, North Carolina, and Virginia. By 1970, the illiteracy rate of Natives had improved little. It stood at "approximately 36 percent," exceeding the illiteracy rate for African Americans in every state covered by Section 5 of the Act.[119]

ASIAN AMERICANS Asian Americans have been the victims of educational discrimination since their arrival in this country. Nowhere is that more evident than in California, which has the largest Asian American population in the United States.[120] The state legislature repeatedly enacted school segregation laws, which were upheld by the courts.[121] In 1860, the legislature barred Asian Americans, African Americans, and Native Americans from public schools. After the law was declared unconstitutional, local officials established segregated schools in many parts of the state.[122] The California Supreme Court supported the segregation, describing the Chinese as "a race of people whom nature has marked as inferior, and who are incapable of progress or intellectual development beyond a certain point."[123] Schooling was denied altogether for Chinese students in San Francisco until 1885.[124] The city's school board responded by establishing a separate school for "Mongolians."[125]

When Japanese and Koreans immigrants began arriving in California in larger numbers around 1900, they were placed in the Chinese schools.[126] In 1921, the state legislature formalized the policy by amending its education law to specifically identify Japanese students as a group that could be segregated.[127] During World War II, nearly three-quarters of all interned Japanese minors were from California and received inferior educations that reflected their underfunded schools. California maintained separate schools for Asian American students until they were struck down as a result of a case brought by Thurgood Marshall on behalf of Latinos in 1947.[128] In many other states, segregation laws that included Asian Americans would remain on the books until the practice was prohibited by *Brown v. Board of Education*.

In 1971, the U.S. Supreme Court determined that the San Francisco school board had never changed any school attendance lines to reduce or eliminate racial imbalance toward Chinese students as required by *Brown*.[129] Following that decision, a class of Chinese students sued the school district for failing to give supplemental English instruction to about 1,800 of the district's 2,856 Chinese English language learner (ELL) students.

In *Lau v. Nichols*, the U.S. Supreme Court found that equal treatment was not met with "the same facilities, textbooks, teachers, and curriculum" because "students who do not understand English are effectively foreclosed from any meaningful education." Otherwise, "those who do not understand English are certain to find their classroom experiences wholly incomprehensible."[130] Federal regulations under Title VI of the Civil Rights Act required that "affirmative steps" be taken to rectify language deficiencies in schools "where inability to speak and understand the English language excludes national origin-minority children from effective participation in the educational program offered by a school district.[131] Since the district failed to take affirmative steps to address the language barrier for Chinese ELL students, the Court concluded that it violated Title VI.[132] *Lau* was a watershed for language minorities. Equal educational opportunities were required for language minorities, even if materials and instruction had to be provided in a language other than English. Section 203 was greatly informed by *Lau*, providing a comparable remedy in voting for limited-English-proficient (LEP) voting-age citizens denied equal schooling.[133]

PERSONS OF SPANISH HERITAGE Latinos suffered from severe educational discrimination. Many were the children of migrant workers and jumped from school to school, limiting their progress. Language barriers also prevented many children from obtaining any meaningful education in public schools in which the curriculum was in English-only. Officials relied on stereotypes of Latinos as only fit for manual labor to justify establishing separate and unequal schooling, condemning them to an inferior socioeconomic status.[134] In California, segregation was practiced widely until integration began following the 1947 decision by the state's highest court in *Westminster School District v. Mendez* and *Brown,* which came seven years later.[135]

In Arizona, separate schooling was sanctioned by the state Supreme Court[136] and state legislature, which passed a statute permitting school districts "to make such segregation of pupils as they may deem advisable."[137] Spanish-speaking Latino students were targeted for segregation because of their language.[138] It was not until the 1950s that Latino students began to integrate into Arizona's public schools.[139] Latinos suffered from the discriminatory effects of "1C classes" mandated by Arizona from 1919 until 1965, which required that all school courses be taught in English. Under that policy, Spanish-speaking students only received English lessons at a low-level, simplified curriculum that placed Latinos years behind English-speaking students.[140]

Texas discriminated against Latinos in education from its earliest days as a republic, and later as a state.[141] Discrimination took two insidious forms. First, the educational system "was to reproduce the caste society of the Southwest, with Anglos at the top and Mexicans, Indians, and Blacks at the bottom." A Texas school superintendent remarked, "Most of our Mexicans are of the lower class. They transplant onions, harvest them, etc. The less they know about everything else the better contented they are. . . . If a man has very much sense or education either, he is not going to stick to this kind of work."[142] Consistent with that policy, the state exempted Latino children from its mandatory school attendance law.[143] Second, state officials intentionally segregated Latinos from Anglos in the schools, just as they did in virtually every other facet of public life.[144] By 1930, their efforts proved so successful that 90 percent of all Texas schools were segregated.[145] State courts initially sanctioned that discrimination, citing the language needs of Latinos to receive a separate education in their own language.[146] Although Texas took an incremental step to integrate Latinos into Anglo schools in 1948, full integration did not begin in earnest until after 1970, when Latinos were recognized as "an identifiable ethnic minority" for purposes of the desegregation mandate in *Brown*.[147] By 1975, many schools in Dallas and Midland were desegregated for Latinos for the first time.[148]

Nevertheless, linguistic segregation and failure to provide adequate resources for Spanish-speaking students in Texas schools remained. The 1975 Senate Report cited extreme dropout rates among Latinos that resulted in an illiteracy rate of 18.9 percent among those twenty-five years of age and older, including more than 33 percent of all Mexican Americans in Texas. More than half of all Mexican American children in Texas entering the first grade never finished high school.[149] That evidence led the U.S. Commission on Civil Rights to find "a systemic failure of the educational process, which not only ignores the educational needs of Chicano students but also suppresses their hopes and ambitions," making "the Chicano . . . the excluded student."[150]

Disenfranchising English Literacy Tests

Literacy tests are commonly associated with disenfranchisement of African Americans beginning in the late nineteenth and early twentieth centuries. Some opponents of language assistance, such as Ms. Chavez, perpetuate a myth that other groups were not victimized by literacy tests, arguing that they "were used in the South primarily to keep Blacks from voting."[151] But the addition of literacy tests to the southern arsenal of methods of disenfranchisement began decades after their use against another group of Americans: the foreign born and other non-English-speaking citizens. Language minorities were the first to suffer the pernicious effects of what would become one of America's most successful disenfranchisement schemes.[152]

A majority of the states that adopted literacy tests did so for the express purpose of disenfranchising immigrants and language minorities. Connecticut and Massachusetts each adopted their literacy tests by 1857 to target newer arrivals to their shores more than three decades before the first southern state, Mississippi, adopted a literacy test targeted at African Americans. Sixteen additional states enacted literacy tests between 1889 and 1924.[153] Of those, half were states in the Northeast and the West that required literacy to vote, principally to exclude immigrants from the franchise: Wyoming in 1889, Maine in 1892, California in 1894, Washington in 1896, New Hampshire in 1902, Arizona in 1913, New York in 1921, and Oregon in 1924.[154] The inequity of literacy tests was heightened when combined with the secret ballot and unequal schooling. Absent assistance, the secret ballot could disenfranchise illiterate voters just as effectively as a literacy test did. Illiterate language minorities and African Americans were especially vulnerable to the discriminatory effects of English-only ballots they could not understand without assistance.[155] This section describes the discriminatory purpose and effect of some of those state literacy tests.

ALASKA'S ENGLISH LITERACY TESTS   In 1922, illiterate Native voters from southeastern Alaska were registered to vote for the first time, electing William Paul, the first Native to serve in the territorial House of Representatives. For the next three years, the legislature considered a literacy test to disenfranchise Native voters and remove Paul. Debates focused on race. One representative said that the "question of whether illiterates should vote 'resolves itself into whether or not the Senate and House and the Territory shall remain white.'" A senator echoed the reports of many newspapers by saying, "We do not want to be ruled by an inferior race, nor dominated by an illiterate one," arguing that Alaska was "white man's country" and that "the man who curries favor with the Indian vote by opposing this bill" would not be re-elected. Local newspapers such as the *Alaska Daily Empire* charged that if Indians voting as a bloc had their way, "they will create a chasm between the races in Alaska that will . . . make this either a white man's country or an Indian's country for many years to come." Ads asked voters to "Keep Alaska and Its Schools Free from Indian Control."[156]

In 1925, the territorial legislature enacted a compromise bill that exempted from the literacy requirement anyone who previously voted. It ensured that Paul's Native supporters in southeastern Alaska could continue to vote, but it satisfied many proponents of a literacy test by excluding Natives in the rest of the territory. Unless a person had previously voted, they had to demonstrate that they were "able to read and write the English language." In 1927, proponents of a literacy test without exceptions took their campaign to Congress, only managing to secure a law duplicating the 1925 territorial act.[157] The territorial legislature later enacted a law providing that the literacy test was satisfied by "reading ten lines of the federal constitution chosen at random by the election judge and legibly writing ten lines dictated by the judge."[158] High illiteracy rates in a majority of Alaska Native villages without schools prevented thousands of Natives from qualifying as voters under the literacy test, even when it was relaxed.[159]

Alaska perpetuated the literacy test in its 1959 state constitution, providing that qualifications for voting required a citizen "who is able to read or speak the English language as prescribed by the Legislature." The constitution included a grandfather clause tracking the 1925 state act and the 1927 federal act, providing that the "section shall not apply to any citizen who legally voted at the general election of November 4, 1924."[160] Even with that standard, the literacy test had a discriminatory impact on Natives, including thousands of limited-English-speaking Natives outside of southeastern Alaska. White citizens had full access to Alaska's public schools and low illiteracy rates; among those who were illiterate, nearly all spoke English fluently. On the other hand, Native adults not only suffered from high illiteracy rates because of Alaska's segregated schooling, but many in geographically isolated villages spoke little, if any, English. Alaska did not repeal its constitutional literacy test until August 25, 1970, which was two months after Congress amended the VRA to impose a nationwide ban on literacy tests.[161]

ARIZONA'S ENGLISH LITERACY TEST   Arizona enacted its first English literacy test in 1912, the same year it became a state. The statute only permitted an eligible resident to register to vote "if he . . . [i]s able to read the Constitution of the United States in the English language in such manner as to show he is neither prompted nor reciting from memory, unless prevented from doing so by physical disability" and is "able to write his name, unless prevented from doing so by physical disability."[162] According to historian David Berman, the literacy test was enacted "to limit 'the ignorant Mexican vote'. . . . As recently as the 1960s, registrars applied the test to reduce the ability of blacks, Indians and Hispanics to register to vote." Berman explained, "Anglos some-times challenged minorities at the polls and asked them to read and explain 'literacy' cards. Intimidators hoped to discourage minorities from standing in line to vote."[163] William Rehnquist, later a Supreme Court justice, was said to have used the literacy test to challenge African American and Latino voters during his participation in the Republican Party's ballot security program from 1958 to 1968.[164]

In *Oregon v. Mitchell,* the Supreme Court unanimously upheld Sec-tion 201's nationwide ban on literacy tests.[165] In doing so, the Court re-jected Arizona's argument that the ban could not be enforced to the extent that it was inconsistent with its state literacy test requirement. The Court observed that Congress enacted the ban because literacy tests were used to discriminate against voters on account of their race. Over-whelming evidence also showed that the VRA's ban on tests or devices substantially increased minority registration in the states where it had been applied. In contrast, other states like Arizona continued to suffer from depressed registration: "only two counties out of eight with Spanish surname populations in excess of 15% showed a voter registration equal to the state-wide average. Arizona also has a serious problem of deficient voter registration among Indians."[166] As Justice Douglas explained, lit-eracy tests such as Arizona's "have been used at times as a discriminatory weapon against some minorities, not only Negroes but Americans of Mexican ancestry, and American Indians."[167]

The Court concluded that American citizens could be informed in their own native language and responsibly and knowledgably cast a ballot. Arizona did not repeal its English literacy test until two years later, in 1972.[168] In the report submitted by the U.S. Commission on Civil Rights into the *Congressional Record* in 1975, the commission ob-served that the "requirement of English-language literacy disenfran-chised many otherwise qualified voters in jurisdictions such as New York, California, and Arizona."[169]

CALIFORNIA'S ENGLISH LITERACY TEST   California was home to the American Protective Association, "a powerful anti-immigrant politi-cal party which advocated an English literacy requirement as a method of disenfranchising voters of foreign ancestry." In 1891, an English literacy requirement was introduced before the State Assembly. Its lead sponsor was Assemblyman A. J. Bledsoe, a past member of the "vigilante Committee of Fifteen which expelled every person of Chinese ancestry from Humboldt County." Bledsoe explained that the provision was intended to "protect the purity of the ballot-box from the corrupting influences of the disturbing elements ... from abroad."[170] A separate constitutional provision adopted in 1879 excluded "natives of China" from voting.

Bledsoe and other Nativists also wanted to ensure that the children of Chinese immigrants were excluded. A literacy test would have that effect because most Chinese Americans retained their Chinese language and customs. Newspaper accounts from 1892 confirmed the discriminatory purpose of the literacy test. A Redlands paper urged adoption to "Wipe out the ignorant foreign vote." The *Anaheim Gazette* stated that the provision would prevent voting by "the increasing flood of debased and ignorant Europeans." The *San Bernardino Weekly Courier* cited the "ignorant and vicious foreigners who are a constant menace to our free institutions."[171] Chinese and Mexican Americans remained the primary targets of the literacy test.[172] The California Assembly adopted the test in 1893, and it was approved in a statewide vote in 1894.[173] The constitutional provision provided that "no person who shall not be able to read the Constitution in the English language and write his or her name, shall ever exercise the privileges of an elector in this State."[174]

U.S. citizens from Los Angeles County who were literate in Spanish but not in English sued the state in 1967 to bar its use of the English literacy test. In *Castro v. State,* the Supreme Court of California held that the English literacy test violated the Fourteenth Amendment. *Castro* concluded that it would be "ironic" if the Spanish-speaking applicants, "who are heirs of a great and gracious culture, identified with the birth of California and contributing in no small measure to its growth, should be disenfranchised in their ancestral land, despite their capacity to cast an informed vote."[175] Congress cited the landmark ruling in *Castro* when it extended the VRA's limited language-assistance requirements to language minorities including Spanish-speaking and Chinese-speaking voters.[176]

TARGETED LANGUAGE ASSISTANCE

Language assistance has been part of the VRA since its enactment in 1965. Prior to 1975, three provisions of the original Act offered limited relief from English-only elections for language minorities denied equal educational opportunities. First, Section 4's temporary suspension of literacy tests in certain parts of the country included some areas with large language-minority populations. Second, Section 4(e) includes permanent bilingual election procedures protecting Puerto Rican voters educated in Spanish. Third, the permanent antidiscrimination provision in Section 2 protects all voters nationwide from qualifications or practices denying or limiting the right to vote.[177]

Those protections proved inadequate. Millions of language minorities denied equal educational opportunities by their state and local governments were victimized again when they encountered English-language voting materials they could not read. Court decisions requiring that voters be allowed to receive assistance at the polls did little to alleviate the situation. Instead, they shifted the burden to the victims of educational discrimination to obtain the help they needed to cast an informed ballot. Moreover, election officials often denied the right to receive assistance because it conflicted with local procedures, they claimed it promoted vote fraud, or it simply was unavailable under state law. Of seventeen states without voter assistance laws, eleven had substantial language-minority populations and were among the first to be covered by the VRA's bilingual election provisions in 1975.[178] Only a handful of jurisdictions offered bilingual materials and assistance, and many of those did so after threat of federal action.[179]

Congress responded by broadening the VRA's protection for language minorities because "the denial of the right to vote of such minority group citizens is ordinarily directly related to the unequal educational opportunities afforded them, resulting in high illiteracy and low voting participation."[180] The Senate Judiciary Committee concluded that "these high illiteracy rates are not the result of choice or happenstance. They are the product of the failure of state and local officials to afford equal educational opportunities."[181] Relief was needed from "the current effect that past educational discrimination has on today's [language-minority] adult population" and to overcome "present barriers to equal educational opportunities."[182] Rather than attempting to "correct the deficiencies of prior educational inequality," a remedy was needed allowing "persons disabled by such disparities to vote now."[183] Therefore, Congress declared in Section 203 that "in order to enforce the guarantees of the fourteenth and fifteenth amendments to the United States Constitution, it is necessary to eliminate such discrimination" by prohibiting English-only elections in covered jurisdictions.[184]

Regular Coverage Determinations

A jurisdiction is covered under Section 203 if the director of the census determines that two criteria are met. First, a population threshold must be met. Within a jurisdiction, limited-English-proficient (LEP) voting-age U.S. citizens in a single language group must either: (a) number more than ten thousand; (b) make up more than 5 percent of all voting-age citizens; or (c) make up more than 5 percent of all American Indians or Alaskan Native voting-age citizens of a single language group residing on an Indian reservation.[185] A person is LEP if he or she is "unable to speak or understand English adequately enough to participate in the electoral process."[186] Second, the illiteracy rate of the language-minority voting-age citizens meeting the population threshold must exceed the national illiteracy rate.[187] "Illiteracy" means "the failure to complete the 5th primary grade"[188] and was adopted to conform to the census definition of that term.[189] In 2002, the national illiteracy rate for voting-age citizens was 1.35 percent.[190]

In *NAMUDNO*, the Court acknowledged that use of a geographically based formula was permitted to trigger coverage under the VRA's temporary provisions. *South Carolina v. Katzenbach* made it clear that "equality of the States . . . does not bar . . . remedies for *local* evils which have subsequently appeared." Justice Roberts explained that to justify "a departure from the fundamental principle of equal sovereignty" between the states, there must be "a showing that a statute's disparate geographic coverage is sufficiently related to the problem that it targets."[191] Such a showing was made for Section 5 in 1965 and after each of its previous reauthorizations.[192] The Court also described factors that may be considered in assessing the reasonableness of a coverage formula, including whether (1) the evil the statute is "meant to address" is "concentrated in the jurisdictions singled out" under the formula; (2) the coverage formula uses more recent data; and (3) the formula accounts "for current political conditions."[193]

Section 203 satisfies those factors because coverage determinations are made regularly using a trigger tied to the most current demographic data. Mr. Clegg's contrary contentions bear no semblance to either the statutory language or the evidentiary record supporting its reauthorization in 2006. Since the VRA defines the need for language assistance based on the number or percent of voting-age citizens who are LEP and illiterate, jurisdictions enter and exit from coverage more frequently than they do under the Section 5 trigger.[194] Coverage under Section 203 has been fluid, adapting to the dynamics of changing demographics and areas with rising illiteracy rates. In 2011, thirteen states had a decrease in the number of covered jurisdictions, compared to thirteen states in which the number of covered jurisdictions increased. Seven states lost their coverage entirely (Idaho, Louisiana, Montana, North Dakota, Oklahoma, Oregon, and South Dakota). Only two new jurisdictions were added, Fairfax County in Virginia and Milwaukee, Wisconsin, with both now required to provide language assistance in Spanish.

The director of the census may update census data and publish Section 203 coverage determinations as new data becomes available.[195] Previously, more current data was available only every ten years. Following each decennial census, the director made new Section 203 determinations. In future censuses, the existing method of collecting data used for the determinations, the decennial long-form data, will be replaced by American Community Survey (ACS) data, which will "provide long-form type information every year instead of once in ten years."[196] Coverage determinations will be made using "the 2010 American Community Survey census data and subsequent American Community Survey data in 5-year increments, or comparable census data."[197] The director of the census has been using and will continue to use the most current census data available to identify areas where language assistance is needed. Because the director made the most recent coverage determinations in 2011, the next coverage determinations will be made in 2016.

The trigger in Section 203 also relies upon more precise census data – county-level LEP and illiteracy data – than what was available for other formulas upheld by the Court. In *Gaston County,* the Court affirmed the suspension of literacy tests based solely on political participation data. At that time, the Census Bureau did not collect illiteracy data. While opponents of Section 203 such as Mr. Clegg and Ms. Chavez have suggested that a direct linkage to education discrimination is required, the Court has rejected that argument. Determinations based upon such data would be "administratively cumbersome" because even today, "the designation of racially disparate school systems is not susceptible of speedy, objective, and incontrovertible determination."[198] In *Oregon v. Mitchell,* all nine justices concluded that such a particularized inquiry was unnecessary because Congress could establish a more general linkage between unequal educational opportunities and depressed voting opportunities on a nationwide basis. *Katzenbach v. Morgan* likewise permitted a permanent ban on English-language ballots in jurisdictions with large numbers of Puerto Rican voters based upon a generalized assessment of the legislative choices that Congress *may have made* in passing it. Therefore, opponents of Section 203 would be hard-pressed to attack the Section 203 coverage formula.

Determining Who Needs Language Assistance

Secretary Nelson has criticized the manner in which the director of the census defines "LEP" under the Section 203 trigger. The director determines which jurisdictions meet the population threshold through responses to a census question "inquiring how well they speak English by checking one of the four answers provided – 'very well,' 'well,' 'not well,' or 'not at all.' The Census Bureau has found that most respondents over-estimate their English proficiency and therefore, those who answer other than 'very well' are deemed LEP."[199] According to Ms. Chavez, making the determination based upon "people who do not speak English at least 'very well' . . . is not a good way of . . . determining how many people it is that need such assistance."[200] Disagreement with the census determinations fails to provide a legal basis upon which to challenge Section 203 and does not render the Section 203 trigger unconstitutionally overbroad.

Section 203 does not define which responses to the census language question qualify as LEP, leaving it to the discretion of the census director to make that determination.[201] The Census Bureau found "[t]hose who indicated they spoke English 'Well,' 'Not well,' or 'Not at all' were considered to have difficulty with English – identified also as people who spoke English less than 'Very well.'"[202] The bureau conducted a follow-up study through a series of tests given to a sample of those responding to the language question. It determined that "persons reporting ability levels as 'well' or worse had significantly higher levels of failure" than the English-speaking control group. Moreover, the data confirmed that persons reporting they spoke English "well" felt more comfortable speaking in their native tongue: 77.9 percent with family at home and 77.1 percent with friends. Forty-nine percent spoke their native tongue more frequently than English, with another 26 percent reporting that they spoke it "about the same" as English.[203] Therefore, the director reasonably concluded that LEP should be defined as anyone speaking English less than "very well."

The English proficiency required to understand voting materials and to cast a meaningful ballot supports the director's findings. Contrary to what Secretary Nelson claims, voters who speak English "well" often struggle with the complicated terms they encounter. That is due, in part, to the low threshold in the Section 203 trigger for English literacy, "the failure to complete the 5th primary grade,"[204] which applies to many language-minority voters who speak English "well." A fifth grade education falls far short of what is needed to understand a voter registration application or ballot proposition, typically drafted at the high school level or greater.[205] To illustrate, a linguist determined in 2008 that the readability of many of Alaska's voting materials required a college graduate reading level or higher. The listening, reading, and comprehension skills required to cast an effective ballot require the highest level of English abilities that LEP voting-age citizens routinely lack.[206] That is why it is commonplace for those who speak English "well" to prefer receiving voting materials and assistance in their native language because they are more likely to understand them.

Section 203 provides that those determinations are not reviewable in any court and are effective upon publication in the Federal Register.[207] When the Court was confronted with similar language pertaining to Section 5 determinations in *Briscoe v. Bell*, it unanimously held that federal courts had no jurisdiction to consider the challenge.[208] The Court noted that "the finality of determinations ... like the preclearance requirements of section 5, may well be 'an uncommon exercise of congressional power.'" Nevertheless, all justices agreed that "there can be no question that in attacking the pervasive evils and tenacious defenders of voting discrimination, Congress acted within its 'power to enforce' the Fourteenth and Fifteenth Amendments 'by appropriate legislation'" by permitting such determinations.[209] *NAMUDNO* left intact the census director's broad authority to make coverage determinations. The Court did not question the process by which coverage determinations were made. Instead, a majority acknowledged *Briscoe's* rule that coverage could be broader than necessary as long as there was a reasonable opportunity for jurisdictions free of discrimination to exit coverage.[210]

Ongoing Educational Discrimination

The Supreme Court observed in *NAMUDNO* that its precedent sustaining the VRA required not only a showing of historical discrimination, but also that the Act's "current burdens" are "justified by current needs."[211] Mr. Clegg ignores the *Congressional Record* in arguing that that standard was not met for Section 203. In 2006, Congress satisfied constitutionality through evidence documenting the need for language assistance and the prevalence of educational discrimination against covered language-minority citizens. Evidence of voting discrimination and other unequal treatment in many of those jurisdictions is described elsewhere in this book.

Despite substantial progress, educational barriers impede equal political participation for LEP voters and contribute to the high rates of limited English proficiency and illiteracy. The top six states with LEP students are California with 1,511,646, Texas with 570,022, Florida with

254,517, New York with 239,097, Illinois with 140,528, and Arizona with 135,248. Four of those states, Arizona, California, Texas, and Florida are covered statewide, and the remaining two states are partially covered by Section 203. Twenty-seven of the twenty-eight school districts that had 10,000 or more ELL students in 2004–2005 are in Section 203–covered jurisdictions, including all of the top twenty-five and seven with more than 50,000 ELL students.[212]

Millions of ELL students have become the unwilling beneficiaries of language assistance in elections because of this discrimination.[213] State and local jurisdictions have been found liable for denying equal educational opportunities to ELL students in public schools. Since 1975, at least twenty-four successful educational discrimination cases have been brought on behalf of ELL students in fifteen states, fourteen of which are presently covered in whole or in part by the language-assistance provisions. Since 1992, when the language-assistance provisions were last reauthorized, at least ten successful ELL cases have been brought or plaintiffs have had additional relief granted under existing court decrees.[214] During the 2006 reauthorization of the VRA, other cases brought on behalf of ELL students also were pending, including one in Alaska[215] and one in Illinois.[216] Consent decrees or court orders were in effect for ELL students statewide in Arizona and Florida, and in the cities of Boston, Denver, and Seattle, each of which is covered by the language-assistance provisions. Successful school funding cases have been brought in at least fifteen of the twenty-five states covered in whole or in part by Section 203, with school funding cases pending in 2006 against four additional states covered by Section 203.[217] Those cases likely represent only a small number of the successful education cases brought because so many of the decisions are unpublished. The House Judiciary Committee specifically described the evidence of ongoing educational discrimination in its report.[218]

UNEQUAL SCHOOLING FOR COVERED LANGUAGE MINORITIES
Educational disparities persist for each of the four covered language-minority groups. Alaska, which has the single largest indigenous population in the United States, reported that only 75 percent of Alaska

Natives currently enrolled in school complete high school, compared to 90 percent of non-Natives.[219] More than 80 percent of Alaska Native graduating seniors are not proficient in reading comprehension and have failure rates on standardized tests more than 20 percent higher than non-Native students.[220] In 1999, an Alaska superior court concluded that Alaska has a dual, arbitrary, unconstitutional, and racially discriminatory system for funding school facilities.[221] In 2007, another court found that Alaska had violated its "constitutional responsibility to maintain a public school system" by failing to sufficiently oversee the quality of secondary education in many Alaska Native villages and to provide a "meaningful opportunity to learn the material" on a graduation exam.[222] Today, many Native adults require language assistance when they vote because of their illiteracy and limited-English-proficiency rates caused by the state's educational discrimination. In the Bethel area of Alaska, where LEP plaintiffs obtained a preliminary injunction against the state in 2008 for violating Sections 203 and 208 of the VRA, 34.7 percent of Yup'ik voters have not graduated from high school, nearly three and a half times the rate for non-Natives. Among Yup'iks aged sixty and older, 91.7 percent lack a high school diploma and 86.3 percent have less than a ninth grade education.[223]

American Indians have not fared any better. In Arizona, more than three-quarters of all Indian students failed Arizona's mandatory graduation test in 2004.[224] Similarly, in South Dakota, Indian students lagged behind non-Indians in every statistical category. Among Indians twenty-five years old and older, 29 percent have not completed high school, more than twice the rate of non-Indians. The dropout rate for Indians aged sixteen to nineteen is 24 percent, four times the rate for non-Indians.[225] Indian pupils in Montana's public schools trail non-Indian students in every category of educational attainment as a direct result of educational discrimination.[226] Although American Indians made up only 11.4 percent of Montana's public school K-12 students in 2005, they constituted 72 percent of the total junior high dropout rate and 24 percent of high school dropouts. On average, only 39 percent of American Indian students in grades 4, 8, and 11 scored proficient or advanced in reading, compared to 79 percent for non-Indians. Twenty-nine out of sixty-nine districts in Montana failing to make adequate yearly progress (the state's measure for performance) in 2005 have 50 to 100 percent American Indian student populations.[227] Montana and South Dakota were both covered for Section 203 in several counties for American Indian languages following the 2002 determinations, but both states are no longer covered as a result of the 2011 coverage determinations.

Asian American students also have been subjected to educational discrimination. For example, in *Y.S. v. School District of Philadelphia*,[228] a successful class action brought on behalf of 6,800 Asian ELL students, one of three named plaintiffs was a Cambodian refugee enrolled in English-only ESL courses who was placed in a class for mentally handicapped students after failing to make progress for three years. As a result, the court entered a consent decree requiring judicial oversight of the treatment of Asian-language students, which was extended by stipulation in 2001. Students in jurisdictions covered under Section 203 for Asian languages have been the beneficiaries of successful education cases in those localities.[229]

Spanish-speaking students likewise continue to be affected by educational discrimination. In Texas, a federal court determined that the state did not monitor and enforce compliance with requirements for non-English-speaking students, was understaffed, and needed to "commit substantial additional resources" to remedy the discrimination,[230] the effects of which remain today.[231] In 2005, a federal court cited Arizona for contempt for failing over the course of the preceding thirteen years to provide opportunities for Spanish-language students to learn English in the public schools, which affected more than 175,000 current ELL students and hundreds of thousands of former students.[232] As recently as 2002, California was under a consent decree for *Lau* violations against ELL Mexican American students, which the court reluctantly terminated after noting the state's "disappointing, and even offensive" showing of lackluster compliance.[233] Other jurisdictions covered by Section 203 for Spanish have been held liable for educational discrimination against Latino students including school districts in the states of Florida, Illinois, and New York and in the cities of Boston, Denver, and Seattle, to name just a few.[234]

INSUFFICIENT ESL RESOURCES Educational discrimination and underfunding in public schools is aggravated by insufficient adult ESL programs in most of the covered jurisdictions. A majority of surveyed ESL providers in sixteen states covered by Section 203 reported that they have lengthy waiting lists. For example, in Phoenix, the state's largest ESL provider has a waiting list of more than a thousand people, who wait for up to eighteen months for the highest-demand evening classes. In Albuquerque, the largest provider reported waiting times of twelve to fourteen months. In Boston, where Massachusetts has mandated class sizes of no more than twenty students, there are at least 16,725 adults on ESL waiting lists, with waiting times as long as three years. In New York City, where an estimated one million adults need ESL instruction, only 41,347 adults were able to enroll in 2005 because of limited availability; most adult ESL programs no longer keep waiting lists because of the extreme demand, but use lotteries in which at least three out of every four applicants are turned away and the waiting time can be several years. ESL providers that do not have waiting lists often have overcrowded classrooms, insufficiently trained instructors, place ESL students in the wrong level of English class, and even turn adults away because of insufficient resources.[235]

EFFECTS OF UNEQUAL LEARNING OPPORTUNITIES The congressional findings of the presence of unequal educational opportunities and the resulting high rates of limited-English proficiency, illiteracy, and low political participation, continue to be valid.[236] According to the 2000 census (the 2010 census data is not yet available), an average of 13.1 percent of voting-age citizens are LEP in the languages triggering coverage in the covered jurisdictions. In jurisdictions covered for Alaska Native languages, an average of 22.6 percent of all voting-age citizens are Alaska Native LEP citizens; 40 percent of covered reservations have LEP rates greater than 50 percent. In jurisdictions covered for American Indian languages, an average of 16.3 percent of all voting-age citizens are American Indian LEP citizens; more than a quarter of covered reservations have LEP rates greater than 50 percent. In jurisdictions covered for Spanish, an average of 10.4 percent of all voting-age citizens are Spanish-speaking LEP citizens. Twenty-five of the twenty-seven jurisdictions covered for Asian languages have more than ten thousand Asian American LEP citizens.[237]

Among LEP voting-age citizens, the average illiteracy rate is nearly fourteen times the national illiteracy rate of 1.35 percent. An average of 28.3 percent of Alaska Native LEP voting-age citizens are illiterate, nearly twenty-one times the national rate; 40 percent of covered Alaska Native reservations have illiteracy rates greater than 50 percent. An average of 11.7 percent of all LEP American Indian voting-age citizens are illiterate, nearly nine times the national rate; more than one-quarter of covered American Indian reservations have illiteracy rates greater than 50 percent. An average of 20.8 percent of all LEP Spanish-speaking voting-age citizens are illiterate, more than fifteen times the national rate. On average, 8.5 percent of all LEP Asian American voting age citizens are illiterate, which is more than six times the national rate.[238]

High LEP and illiteracy rates among covered language minorities have contributed to depressed voter participation. In the 2008 presidential election, unequal educational opportunities and lack of language assistance resulted in Alaska Native voter turnout of just 47 percent,[239] nearly 20 percent lower than the statewide turnout rate of 66 percent.[240] In Arizona, American Indian turnout remains low, with just over 54 percent of all registered American Indian voters voting in the 2004 presidential election, compared to statewide turnout of 76 percent.[241] Nationwide in 2004, Hispanic voting-age U.S. citizens had a registration rate of 57.9 percent and Asian voting-age U.S. citizens of only 52.5 percent, compared to 75.1 percent of all non-Hispanic white voting-age U.S. citizens.[242] Despite the progress that has been made as a result of the language-assistance provisions, this data shows that there is still a long way to go.

Reasonableness of Fit between Section 203's Coverage and the Need for Assistance

NAMUDNO recognized that the Court's prior examinations of Section 5 required a demonstration that the VRA's "disparate geographic coverage is sufficiently related to the problem that it targets."[243] The majority declined to examine the constitutionality of the coverage formula in *NAMUDNO*. However, in dicta, the Court indicated that a formula may be at risk if overbreadth of coverage is insufficiently addressed by the statute.[244] *NAMUDNO* adopted a liberal construction of jurisdictions eligible to be removed or to "bail out" from Section 5 coverage. According to the Court, doing so facilitated an exodus of covered jurisdictions where a need for federal oversight no longer existed, thereby avoiding "the underlying constitutional concerns."[245] Section 203 does not raise those concerns. Instead, it ensures coverage is reasonably related to the present need for language assistance for protected language-minority voters.

COVERAGE OF JURISDICTIONS NOT IDENTIFIED BY THE SECTION 203 TRIGGER   Mr. Clegg points out that notwithstanding the precision of the Section 203 trigger, many language minorities are excluded from coverage in places where there is a great need for language assistance. During the 2006 reauthorization, some civil rights organizations proposed lowering the formula's population threshold to expand coverage, particularly for LEP Asian American voters in predominantly urban areas who could not meet the ten thousand persons or 5 percent requirements. Those efforts failed after intense opposition by English-only lobbyists trying to scuttle reauthorization of bilingual voting requirements.[246] The VRA separately accounts for the underinclusiveness of Section 203's coverage formula. Spanish-speaking Puerto Rican voters may seek relief from English-only elections under Section 4(e) of the Act. LEP voters from the four covered language groups residing in jurisdictions not covered under Section 203 may rely upon Section 2, the Act's nationwide permanent nondiscrimination provision.[247] A common legal basis for obtaining relief under Section 2 is where a jurisdiction has failed to hire bilingual poll workers proportionate to the number of LEP voters in a voting precinct.[248] As early as 1974, a federal court relied upon Section 2 to require a New York school district to provide language assistance where English-only voting materials and procedures denied Chinese- and Spanish-speaking voters an effective opportunity to register and vote.[249] Since then, Section 2 has helped secure language assistance in other jurisdictions not covered by Section 203, such as Spanish-speaking voters in Osceola County, Florida (shortly before that county became covered)[250] and Chinese and Vietnamese voters in Boston.[251] It also has provided recourse for language-minority groups not covered by Section 203 at all, such as Arabic- and Bengali-speaking voters in Hamtramck, Michigan (which just became covered for Bengali under the 2011 coverage determinations).[252] The V R A provides other mechanisms for language minority voters who suffer from educational and voting discrimination to become covered even if they are left out of Section 203 coverage. The Act's additional remedies help cure any concerns about Section 203 coverage being too narrow.[253]

Furthermore, it is unlikely that the Supreme Court will second-guess the legislative judgment of Congress in crafting the Section 203 coverage formula the way it did. While educational discrimination and its resulting high LEP and illiteracy rates for language-minority voters is not unique among jurisdictions covered by Section 203, it is most prevalent there. Coverage is targeted not at every area, but at the areas with the greatest need, namely, jurisdictions that have a well-documented history of discrimination against language minorities and large numbers or percentages of LEP voters in the four covered language groups.

Congress has adjusted that trigger when necessary to add excluded jurisdictions where there was an established need for language assistance, most recently in the 1992 amendments.[254] It also carefully weighed the federalism costs and minimal economic expenses some jurisdictions incur under the temporary bilingual elections mandate – two of the arguments Mr. Clegg makes against it. Against that backdrop, the Section 203 trigger is a "rational means to effectuate the constitutional prohibition" through relief from English-only elections on LEP voters denied equal schooling opportunities.[255] Consequently, the Court will be reluctant to overturn the judgment of Congress "to determine in the first instance what legislation" was necessary to secure the fundamental right to vote of language minority citizens.[256]

TARGETING TO REDUCE THE POSSIBILITY OF OVERBREADTH

NAMUDNO restated the Court's long-standing recognition that a geographically based triggering formula "might bring within its sweep governmental units not guilty of any unlawful discriminatory voting practices."[257] Overbroad coverage does not raise constitutional concerns if jurisdictions inadvertently covered are provided with a mechanism to be relieved from the federal requirements. There are two circumstances in which the Section 203 trigger results in coverage of jurisdictions with few, if any, LEP voters. In each instance, jurisdictions in which there is no need for language assistance are relieved from their responsibility to provide it.U.S. Department of Justice guidelines provide that when a county is covered under Section 203, "all political units that hold elections within that political subdivision (e.g., cities, school districts) are subject to the same requirements" under the Act as the county.[258] Opponents of language assistance argue that the guidelines require language assistance to be provided everywhere in a covered jurisdiction, even in political subdivisions where there are no LEP voters. They cite the small town of Briny Breezes in Palm Beach County, Florida, which is covered for Spanish under Section 203. According to these critics, Briny Breezes is required to provide "bilingual ballots" even though 99 percent of the community's residents speak English "very well."[259] The letters that the department sends to jurisdictions such as Palm Beach County following each census determination, however, repudiate that argument, providing that Section 203 "does not require that information in minority languages be provided to people who have no need for it."[260]

Similarly, the 1992 amendments to the Section 203 trigger occasionally lead to some anomalies. Sometimes the reservation trigger results in coverage of a handful of jurisdictions where there are no members of the covered language minority group. In the 2002 coverage determinations, a few counties were covered for Alaskan Native or American Indian languages because they contained a portion of a reservation that satisfied the 5 percent population trigger, even though there were no voters in those counties who spoke the covered languages. However, that anomalous coverage does not render the trigger unconstitutional. Like Briny Breezes, the handful of counties covered for languages where there is no need for assistance are not required to provide it.

Targeting allows a covered jurisdiction to comply with the bilingual election requirements by providing bilingual materials and assistance "only to the language minority citizens and not to every voter in the jurisdiction."[261] Although the VRA does not expressly provide for targeting, the legislative history of the Act demonstrates that Congress intended to allow covered jurisdictions flexibility in devising appropriate methods to provide bilingual language assistance.[262] Targeting is permissible as long as it ensures that language-minority voters face no unequal burden in obtaining access to bilingual materials.[263] The Justice Department's regulations make that explicit by providing that "a targeting system will normally fulfill the Act's minority language requirements if it is designed and implemented in such a way that language minority group members who need minority language materials and assistance receive them."[264] Therefore, the Section 203 formula is not unconstitutionally overbroad because language assistance must be provided only in areas where it is needed.

BAILOUT WHERE THERE IS LITTLE OR NO NEED FOR LANGUAGE ASSISTANCE   Bailout is another way in which a geographically based coverage formula can cure overbreadth. In *NAMUDNO*, the Court recognized that bailout allowed the "release" of jurisdictions covered by the geographically targeted Section 5 formula if they satisfied certain conditions.[265] In 1982, Congress amended Section 5 to facilitate bailout through a "piecemeal" approach that allowed political subdivisions to exit from coverage if they demonstrated that they had been free of voting discrimination for at least ten years. Few eligible localities availed themselves of bailout, however, because it had been restricted to only those jurisdictions that registered their own voters. *NAMUDNO* determined that limiting bailout in that manner misconstrued the more liberal application that Congress intended. The majority reasoned that the "underlying constitutional concerns compel a broader reading of the bailout provision."[266]

Section 203 has its own bailout provision, providing that a covered jurisdiction may be removed from coverage if it can demonstrate "that the illiteracy rate of the applicable language minority group" that triggered coverage "is equal to or less than the national illiteracy rate."[267] Congress used this bailout mechanism so that language assistance was no longer required after the effects of educational discrimination were eliminated. As the House floor manager of the 1975 amendments to the VRA explained, "Having found that the voting barriers experienced by these citizens is in large part due to disparate and inadequate educational opportunities," this bailout procedure "rewards" jurisdictions able to remove these barriers.[268] Consequently, this provision ensures "that the reach" of Section 203 is "limited to those cases in which constitutional violations were most likely (in order to reduce the possibility of overbreadth)."[269] In most cases Section 203 coverage has not been terminated by successful bailout lawsuits. Instead, jurisdictions generally leave through an automatic "bailout" mechanism in place under the Section 203 trigger. The census director makes regular coverage determinations under Section 203. In the past, those determinations were made every ten years following the new decennial census, causing a multitude of jurisdictions to enter and exit coverage.[270] Determinations will be made even more frequently starting with the release of those derived from the 2010 ACS data (used for the 2011 determinations). Subsequent coverage determinations will be made every five years. When the need for language assistance drops below the population threshold or the illiteracy rate of a language group no longer exceeds the national average, coverage ends. The language-assistance requirements are thereby only applied to places where they are actually needed. In that manner, Section 203 does not implicate any of the concerns that led the Court in *NAMUDNO* to liberally interpret Section 5's bailout provision.

IMPACT OF LANGUAGE ASSISTANCE IN VOTING

Just over thirty-five years after Section 203 of the VRA was enacted, it has had a profound impact on voting participation by language-minority voters. Among American Indians, registration and turnout have increased between 50 percent and 150 percent in many places as a direct result of language assistance.[271] Similarly, between 1996 and 2004, Asian American voter registration and turnout increased 58 percent and 71 percent respectively following increased coverage resulting from the 1992 amendments to Section 203.[272] By the end of 2005, at least 346 Asian Americans had been elected to office, including six to federal offices, an increase from 120 elected officials in 1978.[273]

Although Hispanic registration still lags far behind non-Hispanic registration, increased enforcement of Section 203 partially contributed to the increase of registered Hispanic voters from 7.6 million to 9.3 million between 2000 and 2004.[274] The Hispanic voter registration rate, which was 34.9 percent in 1974, has nearly doubled since Section 203 has been in effect.[275] Increased voter registration and turnout have improved Hispanic representation at all levels of the government. Between 1973 and 2006, the number of Hispanic elected officials in six covered states (Arizona, California, Florida, New Mexico, New York, and Texas) increased more than 347 percent, from 1,280 to 4,532.[276] As of January 2006, there were more than 5,100 Hispanic elected officials in the United States. Following the November 2006 election, Hispanic elected officials nationwide included three U.S. Senators, 23 U.S. Representatives, five statewide officials (including three from New Mexico alone), approximately 60 state senators, and 180 state representatives.[277]

Recent election data shows that language minorities continue to experience low political participation because of the impact of past and ongoing discrimination. Language assistance continues to be necessary "to bar discrimination against Spanish-speaking Americans, American Indians, Alaska [N]atives, and Asian Americans."[278] As Congress recognized in its findings supporting the language-assistance provisions, which it reaffirmed in 2006, the barriers posed by educational discrimination, the absence of sufficient ESL classes, and high illiteracy result in extremely depressed voter participation. That evidence provided Congress with a compelling basis for extending the language-assistance provisions for an additional twenty-five years.

NOTES

1. For a thorough accounting of the language-assistance provisions, including the legislative history, policy, and factual evidence supporting the provisions and a more detailed discussion of the evidence described in this chapter, see James Thomas Tucker, *The Battle Over Bilingual Ballots: Language Minorities and Political*

Access under the Voting Rights Act (Burlington, Vt.: Ashgate Publishing 2009).

2. See 42 USC § 1973b(e). For more information about Section 4(e), see Tucker, *The Battle Over Bilingual Ballots*, 27–51.

3. Jurisdictions covered under Section 4(f)(4) of the Act also must comply with Section 203, as well as administrative preclearance requirements under Section 5. See 28 CFR § 55.8(b) (1976). This chapter does not address the constitutionality of the coverage formula for Section 4(f)(4), which is included elsewhere in this book.

4. See 42 USC §§ 1973l(c)(3), 1973aa–1a(e) (2006); 121 *Cong. Rec.* 16246 (1975) (statement of Rep. Edwards); S. Rep. No. 94-295 at 24 n. 14 (1975) (quoting letter from Meyer Zitter, chief, Population Division, Bureau of the Census, to House Judiciary Committee, April 29, 1975).

5. 42 USC § 1973aa–1a(c) (2006).

6. 42 USC § 1973aa–1a(b)(3)(A) (2006); see 28 CFR § 55.18 (1976).

7. See 42 USC § 1973aa–1a(b)(3)(A) (2006); 28 CFR § 55.20 (1976).

8. 28 CFR § 55.15 (1976).

9. See Voting Rights Act Amendments of 1975, Pub. L. No. 94-73, 89 Stat. 400 (1975); Voting Rights Act Amendments of 1982, Pub. L. No. 97-205, 96 Stat. 131 (1982); Voting Rights Language Assistance Act of 1992, Pub. L. No. 102-344, 106 Stat. 921 (1992).

10. Tucker, *The Battle Over Bilingual Ballots*, 78–88.

11. See The Fannie Lou Hamer, Rosa Parks, and Coretta Scott King Voting Rights Act Reauthorization and Amendments Act of 2006, Pub. L. No. 109-246 §§ 7–8, 120 Stat. 581 (2006) (codified as amended at 42 USC § 1973aa–1a(b)(1) (2006)).

12. Tucker, *The Battle Over Bilingual Ballots*, 205–31.

13. Tucker, *The Battle Over Bilingual Ballots*, 165–203.

14. Tucker, *The Battle Over Bilingual Ballots*, 211–12.

15. H.R. Rep. No. 109-478, at 61 (2006).

16. On October 13, 2011, the director of the census issued new determinations for coverage under Section 203. See Voting Rights Act Amendments of 1992, Determinations Under Section 203, 76 Fed. Reg. 63602 (October 13, 2011) (to be codified at 28 C.F.R. pt. 55) ("2011 Census Determinations"). The Census Bureau has not yet released the data files identifying the number of limited-English-proficient voting-age citizens who speak the languages triggering coverage.

17. Tucker, *The Battle Over Bilingual Ballots*, 207–10.

18. Tucker, *The Battle Over Bilingual Ballots*, 76, 80. For maps depicting the changes in Section 203 coverage following the 2011 census determinations, see the Client News Alert I, available at http://www.lbbslaw.com.

19. Karen Brooks, "Backers Pressed on Whether Requiring Proof at Polls Deters Violators," *Dallas Morning News*, January 26, 2008.

20. Michelle Rupp and Julianne Yee, "Vote Fraud and the Role of Picture Identification Requirements: An Analysis of Ten American States" (senior honors thesis, Arizona State University, 2008). Thirteen percent of responding prosecutors were neutral on the question of whether vote fraud was a problem in their county. Id.

21. Tucker, *The Battle Over Bilingual Ballots*, 179.

22. 28 CFR § 55.19(b).

23. See *Harris v. Graddick*, 593 F. Supp. 128, 132–33 (M.D. Ala. 1984).

24. Tucker, *The Battle Over Bilingual Ballots*, 155–60, 224–27.

25. Tucker, *The Battle Over Bilingual Ballots*, 225–26.

26. Tucker, *The Battle Over Bilingual Ballots*, 225.

27. Tucker, *The Battle Over Bilingual Ballots*, 155–60.

28. See 42 USC § 1973aa–1a(b)(1); see also 28 CFR § 55.19(b) (compliance with requirements for bilingual written materials is measured by whether a jurisdiction has consulted with the covered language minority group); 28 CFR § 55.20(c) (providing that "the jurisdiction will need to determine" the location and amount of oral language assistance to be provided).

29. See *Chinese for Affirmative Action v. Leguennec*, 580 F.2d 1006, 1008 (9th Cir. 1978), *cert. denied*, 439 U.S. 1129 (1979); Tucker, *The Battle Over Bilingual Ballots*, 261–89 (discussing the *Nick* litigation in Alaska).

30. Tucker, *The Battle Over Bilingual Ballots*, 261–89.

31. Tucker, *The Battle Over Bilingual Ballots*, 213–21.

32. Linda Chavez, president of One Nation Indivisible, prepared statement (November 8, 2005), reprinted in *Voting Rights Act: Section 203 – Bilingual Election Requirements (Part I): Hearing Before the Subcomm. on the Const. of the H. Comm. on the Judiciary*, 109th Cong., 1st Sess. 22, 44 (2005).

33. Tucker, *The Battle Over Bilingual Ballots*, 165–203.

34. See *Alexander v. Sandoval*, 532 U.S. 275 (2001).

35. See *ProEnglish v. Bush*, 2003 WL 21101726 (4th Cir. 2003).

36. Linda Chavez, president of One Nation Indivisible, prepared statement (November 8, 2005), reprinted in *Voting Rights Act: Section 203 – Bilingual Election Requirements (Part I): Hearing Before the Subcomm. on the Const. of the H. Comm. on the Judiciary*, 109th Cong., 1st Sess. 22, 45 (2005).

37. See James Thomas Tucker, *The Battle Over "Bilingual Ballots" Shifts to the Courts: A Post-Boerne Assessment of Sec-*

tion 203 of the Voting Rights Act, 45 Harv. J. on Legis. 507, 515–17 (2008).

38. 360 U.S. 45 (1959).

39. See U.S. Const. art. I, § 2; U.S. Const. amend. XVII.

40. *Lassiter*, 360 U.S. at 51–54.

41. See *United States v. Mississippi*, 380 U.S. 128 (1965); *Louisiana v. United States*, 380 U.S. 145 (1965).

42. See Tucker, *The Battle Over "Bilingual Ballots" Shifts to the Courts*; Daniel P. Tokaji, *Intent and Its Alternatives: Defending the New Voting Rights Act*, 58 Ala. L. Rev. 349 (2006).

43. 100 U.S. 339, 345–46 (1879).

44. 383 U.S. 301, 324 (1966).

45. Id. at 324.

46. Id. at 314, 327–30.

47. Id. at 329–37. Even Justice Black, who dissented with the Court's holding that the administrative preclearance requirements of Section 5 were constitutional, agreed that Congress had the authority to impose the ban on literacy tests. Id. at 355–56 (Black, J., concurring and dissenting in part).

48. 395 U.S. 285 (1969).

49. In so holding, eight justices in *Gaston County* explicitly rejected Mr. Clegg's suggestion that Section 203 can only be constitutional if it eliminates education discrimination.

50. 395 U.S. at 289.

51. 395 U.S. at 291–92.

52. 395 U.S. at 293, 296–97.

53. 400 U.S. 112, 118 (1970).

54. Justices Black, Marshall, and White concluded that the ban was a proper exercise under Section 5 of the Fourteenth Amendment, while the remaining justices concluded it was proper under Section 2 of the Fifteenth Amendment.

55. 400 U.S. at 132–33.

56. 400 U.S. at 147.

57. 400 U.S. at 283–84.

58. 42 USC § 1973b(e)(2) (2006).

59. Juan Cartagena, *Latinos and Section 5 of the Voting Rights Act: Beyond Black and White*, 18 Nat'l Black L.J. 201, 205 (2005). The evidence Congress considered in 1965 refutes the contention that New York's literacy test was used "to determine voter eligibility" but not "in a discriminatory manner." Linda Chavez, *Out of the Barrio* (New York: Basic Books, 1992), 41. For further treatment of the discriminatory purpose and effect of New York's test, see Tucker, *The Battle Over Bilingual Ballots*, 28–37.

60. See *Torres v. Sachs*, 381 F. Supp. 309 (S.D. N.Y. 1974).

61. See *Torres v. Sachs* 1974: 309; *Coal. for Educ. in Dist. One v. New York City Bd. of Elections*, 370 F. Supp. 42 (S.D. N.Y. 1974), aff'd, 495 F.2d 1090 (2d Cir. 1974); *Lopez v. Dinkins*, No. 73 Civ. 695 (S.D. N.Y. Feb. 14, 1973).

62. 384 U.S. 641, 648–51 (1966).

63. Id. at 654.

64. Id. at 657–58.

65. Id. at 654.

66. Id. at 657–58.

67. 2009 WL 1738645 (U.S. June 22, 2009).

68. The constitutionality of Section 5 is discussed elsewhere in this book.

69. 2009 WL 1738645, at *9.

70. 2009 WL 1738645, at *5.

71. 121 *Cong. Rec.* H4711 (daily ed., June 2, 1975) (statement of Rep. Rodino).

72. See David H. Hunter, *The 1975 Voting Rights Act and Language Minorities*, 25 Cath. U. L. Rev. 250, 254–57 (1976); S. Rep. No. 94-295, 1975: 25–30.

73. See S. Rep. No. 94-295, 1975: 24–31, 37–39; 121 *Cong. Rec.* H4709-13, H4716-18 (daily ed., June 2, 1975) (statement of Rep. Edwards).

74. Terrence M. Cole, "Jim Crow in Alaska: The Passage of the Alaska Equal Rights Act of 1945," in *An Alaska Anthology: Interpreting the Past*, ed. Stephen W. Haycox and Mary Childers Mangusso,

314, 316 (Seattle: University of Washington Press, 1996).

75. Indian Citizenship Act of June 2, 1924, 43 Stat. 253 (codified at 8 USC § 1401(b)).

76. See *Harrison v. Laveen*, 196 P.2d 456 (Ariz. 1948); *Trujillo v. Garley*, No. 1353 (D. N.M. Aug. 11, 1948) (three-judge court).

77. See Dan McCool et al., *Native Vote: American Indians, the Voting Rights Act, and the Right to Vote* (Cambridge: Cambridge University Press, 2007), 95–97.

78. See Tucker 2009: 4, 7, 13, 20–21, 24–25, 63, 248–57; McCool, *Native Vote*; Jeanette Wolfley, *Jim Crow, Indian Style: The Disenfranchisement of Native Americans*, 16 Am. Indian L. Rev. 368 (1990); Orlan J. Svingen, *Jim Crow, Indian Style*, 11 Am. Indian Q. 275 (1987).

79. *Shirley v. Superior Court*, 513 P.2d 939, 941 (Ariz. 1973).

80. *Goodluck v. Apache County*, 417 F. Supp. 13, 14 (D. Ariz. 1975), aff'd, 429 U.S. 876 (1976).

81. For illustrative examples of efforts to limit citizenship under the guise of suppressing the Chinese vote, see Tucker, *The Battle Over Bilingual Ballots*, 22; Lithograph by J. A. Wales from *Puck* magazine, March 12, 1879, p. 16, Library of Congress, Prints & Photographs Division, Washington, D.C., Reproduction no. LC-USZC2-1235 (color film copy slide).

82. See Terry M. Ao, "Impact of Section 203 on Asian American Voters," in Tucker, *The Battle Over Bilingual Ballots*, 295.

83. See *Perez v. Sharp*, 1098 P.2d 17 (Cal. 1948).

84. See James Thomas Tucker and Rodolfo Espino et al., *Voting Rights in Arizona: 1982–2006*, 17 S. Cal. Rev. L. & Soc. Just. 283, 283–84 (2008).

85. See *Loving v. Virginia*, 388 U.S. 1 (1967). For a more detailed discussion of the impact of antimiscegenation laws on

Asian Americans, see Hrishi Karthikeyan and Gabriel J. Chin, *Preserving Racial Identity: Population Patterns and the Application of Anti-Miscegenation Statutes to Asian Americans, 1910–1950*, 9 Asian L.J. 1 (2002).

86. See, e.g., Report of the Comm'n on Wartime Relocation and Internment of Civilians, Personal Justice Denied 27–46 (1997); Angelo N. Ancheta, Race, Rights, and the Asian American Experience 19–40 (1998); Thomas Sowell, Ethnic America: A History 133–79 (1981). Published by the U.S. Commission on Civil Rights.

87. Tucker, *The Battle Over Bilingual Ballots*, 25, 28, 31–39.

88. Tucker and Espino, *Voting Rights in Arizona*, 283–84.

89. S. Rep. 94-295, 1975: 25–26; see U.S. Commission on Civil Rights, The Voting Rights Act: Ten Years After (Jan. 1975). Published by the U.S. Commission on Civil Rights.

90. 262 U.S. 390, 401 (1923).

91. *Farrington v. Tokushige*, 273 U.S. 284 (1927).

92. 347 U.S. 483 (1954).

93. Special Subcomm. on Indian Education, Comm. on Labor and Public Welfare, *Indian Education: A National Tragedy – A National Challenge*, S. Rep. No. 501, 91st Cong., 1st Sess. 106 (1969).

94. Thomas Alton, *Politics, Economics, and the Schools: Roots of Alaska Native Language Loss Since 1867*, 20 Alaska Hist. 18, 21 (Fall 2005).

95. Id. at 22–27.

96. Special Subcomm. on Indian Education, Comm. on Labor and Public Welfare, *Indian Education: A National Tragedy – A National Challenge*, S. Rep. No. 501, 91st Cong., 1st Sess. 106 (1969), 11–12.

97. Margaret Connell Szasz, "Listening to the Native Voice: American Indian Schooling in the Twentieth Century," in *The American Indian, Past and Present*, 5th ed., ed. Roger L. Nichols (New York: McGraw-Hill, 1999), 267, 270.

98. Special Subcomm. on Indian Education, Comm. on Labor and Public Welfare, *Indian Education: A National Tragedy – A National Challenge*, S. Rep. No. 501, 91st Cong., 1st Sess. 106 (1969), 12–17; Szasz, "Listening to the Native Voice," 270–75.

99. Tucker and Espino, *Voting Rights in Arizona*, 103.

100. Testimony of Joe Sanders Before the U.S. Commission on Civil Rights, Phoenix, Arizona, February 3, 1962, 96.

101. Special Subcomm. on Indian Education, Comm. on Labor and Public Welfare, *Indian Education: A National Tragedy – A National Challenge*, S. Rep. No. 501, 91st Cong., 1st Sess. 106 (1969), 22.

102. Daniel M. Rosenfelt, *Indian Schools and Community Control*, 25 Stan. L. Rev. 489, 506–7 (1973). For a similar perspective, see Alison McKinney Brown, *Native American Education: A System in Need of Reform*, 2 Kan. J. L. & Pub. Pol'y 105 (1993).

103. 355 F. Supp. 716 (D.N.M. 1973).

104. See *Prince v. Board of Educ. of Cent. Consol. Indep. Sch. Dist. No. 22*, 543 P.2d 1176 (N.M. 1975).

105. S. Rep. 94-295, 1975: 29.

106. Tucker, *The Battle Over Bilingual Ballots*, 218–19.

107. Settlement Agreement, *Hootch v. State Operated Sch. Sys. ex rel. Tobeluk v. Lind*, Case No. 72-2450-CIV (Alaska Super. Ct. Sept. 3, 1976), at ¶ 9 ("Hootch Settlement").

108. Act of January 27, 1905 § 7, 33 Stat. 616, 619 (1905).

109. Jim Lethcoe and Nancy Lethcoe, "Changes Affecting Native Communities: 1917–1941," in *A History of Prince William Sound, Alaska* (Valdez, Alaska: Prince William Sound Books, 1987); see Tucker, *The Battle Over Bilingual Ballots*, 238–48.

110. 3 Alaska 481 (D. Alaska Terr. 1908). The "one-drop" rule provides that anyone with any trace of African ancestry is con-

sidered "black" unless they can establish another basis for their non-white ancestry. See Pauli Murray, ed., *States' Laws on Race and Color* (Athens: University of Georgia Press, 1997).

111. *Jones v. Ellis,* 8 Alaska 146, 147 (D. Alaska Terr. 1929).

112. Cole, "Jim Crow in Alaska," 319.

113. U.S. Department of Interior (DOI), *Organization of School Districts on Indian Reservations in Alaska,* 63 Interior Dec. 333, 335 (September 17, 1956).

114. Tucker, *The Battle Over Bilingual Ballots,* 245–48.

115. State of Alaska, Governor's Comm. on Educ., *An Overall Education Plan for Rural Alaska* 2 (rev. Feb. 26, 1966).

116. First Amended Complaint, *Hootch v. State Operated Sch. Sys.,* Case No. 72-2450-CIV (Alaska Super. Ct. Oct. 5, 1972).

117. Tucker, *The Battle Over Bilingual Ballots,* 248.

118. See *Extension of the Voting Rights Act of 1965: Hearings on S. 407, S, 903, S. 1297, S. 1409, and S. 1443 Before the Subcomm. on Const'l Rts. of the Senate Comm. on the Judiciary* (1975 Senate Hearings), 94th Cong., 1st sess., at 664 (1975) (Ex. 23 to the testimony of J. Stanley Pottinger).

119. 1975 Senate Hearings at 529 (statement of Sen. Gravel) ("Gravel Testimony").

120. According to the 2000 census, more than 4.1 million Asian Americans (more than one-third of all Asian Americans in the United States), reside in California. New York has the second highest total with more than 1.1 million Asian Americans. See U.S. Census Bureau, Census 2000 Brief, *The Asian Population: 2000,* at 5 (Feb. 2002), available at http://www.census.gov/prod/2002pubs/c2kbr01-16.pdf. Combined, the two states account for ten of the sixteen counties covered for Asian languages under Section 203 of the VRA.

121. See statement of Karen K. Narasaki, president and executive director of

the Asian American Justice Center (June 13, 2006), reprinted in Hearing Before the Committee on the Judiciary of the United States Senate, *The Continuing Need for Section 203's Provisions for Limited English Proficient Voters,* S. Hrg. 109-669, at 108–10 (June 13, 2006).

122. Ancheta, Race, Rights, and the Asian-American Experience, 29.

123. *People v. Hall,* 4 Cal. 399, 404, 1854 WL 765, at *5 (Cal. 1854).

124. See *Tape v. Hurley,* 6 P. 129 (Cal. 1885).

125. Charles Wollenberg, *All Deliberate Speed: Segregation and Exclusion in California Schools, 1855–1975* (Berkeley: University of California Press, 1978), 40–42.

126. Wollenberg, *All Deliberate Speed,* 54.

127. See Cal. Educ. Code §§ 8003–8004 (West 1921).

128. See *Westminster Sch. Dist. of Orange County v. Mendez,* 161 F.2d 774 (9th Cir. 1947).

129. *Lee v. Johnson,* 404 U.S. 1215, 1215–1216 (1971).

130. *Lau v. Nichols,* 414 U.S. 563, 564–67 (1974).

131. 35 Fed. Reg. 11595.

132. *Lau v. Nichols,* 414 U.S. at 568–69.

133. See, e.g., S. Rep. No. 94-295, 1975: 28–29; S. Rep. No. 102-315 at 6 (1992).

134. See Tucker, *The Battle Over "Bilingual Ballots" Shifts to the Courts,* 562–68.

135. See Juan F. Perea, *Buscando América: Why Integration and Equal Protection Fail to Protect Latinos,* 117 Harv. L. Rev. 1420, 1420–24, 1428–29, 1437–46 (2004); Daniel Aaron Rochmes, Note, *Blinded by the White: Latino School Desegregation and the Insidious Allure of Whiteness,* 13 Tex. Hisp. J. L. & Pol'y 7, 9–10, 12–14 (2007).

136. See *Dameron v. Bayless,* 14 Ariz. 180, 126 P. 273 (Ariz. 1912).

137. Ariz. Rev. Code 1913 § 2750 (1913).

138. Laura K. Muñoz, *Separate But Equal? A Case Study of* Romo v. Laird *and*

Mexican American Education, at 1 (Organization of American Historians), *available at* http:/www.oah.org/pubs/magazine/deseg/munoz.html.

139. See *Ortiz v. Jack,* No. Civ-1723 (D. Ariz. 1955); *Gonzalez v. Sheeley,* 96 F. Supp. 1004, 1008–9 (D. Ariz. 1951).

140. Kellie Rolstad, Kate S. Mahoney, and Gene V. Glass, *Weighing the Evidence: A Meta-Analysis of Bilingual Education in Arizona,* 29 Bilingual Res. J. 1, 47–48 (2005).

141. See Nina Perales, Luis Figueroa, and Criselda G. Rivas, *Voting Rights in Texas: 1982–2006,* 17 S. Cal. Rev. L. & Soc. Just. 713, 722–727 (2008).

142. Perea, *Buscando América,* 1439 (quoting from Herschel T. Manuel, *The Education of Mexican and Spanish-Speaking Children in Texas* (Austin: University of Texas Press, 1930), 70).

143. See Lupe S. Salinas and Dr. Robert H. Kimball, *The Equal Treatment of Unequals: Barriers Facing Latinos and the Poor in Texas Public Schools,* 14 Geo. J. on Poverty L. & Pol'y 215, 222 (2007).

144. See *United States v. Texas,* 506 F. Supp. 405, 412 (E.D. Tex. 1981), *rev'd and remanded on different grounds,* 680 F.2d (5th Cir. 1982); Jorge C. Rangel and Carlos M. Alcala, *Project Report: De Jure Segregation of Chicanos in Texas Schools,* 7 Harv. C.R.-C.L. L. Rev. 307 (1972).

145. Rubén Donato, Martha Menchaca, and Richard R. Valencia, "Segregation, Desegregation, and Integration of Chicano Students: Problems and Prospects," in *Chicano School Failure and Success,* ed. Richard R. Valencia, 35 (London, Falmer Press, 1991).

146. See *Independent Sch. Dist. v. Salvatierra,* 33 S.W.2d 790 (Tex. Civ. App. 1930), *cert. denied,* 284 U.S. 580 (1931).

147. *Cisneros v. Corpus Christi Indep. Sch. Dist.,* 324 F. Supp. 599, 606 (S.D. Tex. 1970).

148. See *United States v. Midland Indep. Sch. Dist.,* 519 F.2d 60 (5th Cir. 1972) (Midland schools); *Tasby v. Estes,* 517 F.2d 92 (5th Cir. 1975) (Dallas schools).

149. S. Rep. 94-295, 1975, 28.

150. U.S. Commission on Civil Rights, "The Excluded Student, Mexican American Education Study," report III, 23 (May 1972) (cited in S. Rep. No. 94-295, 1975, 28).

151. Chavez, *Out of the Barrio,* 41.

152. Tucker, *The Battle Over Bilingual Ballots,* chapters 1–2, 9.

153. Alexander Keyssar, *The Right to Vote: The Contested History of Democracy in the United States* (New York: Basic Books, 2000), 362–67.

154. Keyssar, *The Right to Vote,* 145; Arthur W. Bromage, *Literacy and the Electorate,* 24 Am. Pol. Sci. Rev. 946, 950–51, 955–56 n. 27 (November 1930).

155. Keyssar, *The Right to Vote,* 142–43.

156. Stephen W. Haycox, *William Paul, Sr., and the Alaska Voters' Literacy Act of 1925,* 2 Alaska Hist. 16, 17 (Winter 1986–1987); Tucker, *The Battle Over Bilingual Ballots,* 250–54.

157. Haycox, *William Paul, Sr.,* 28–30.

158. Gordon S. Harrison, *Alaska's Constitutional "Literacy Test" and the Question of Voting Discrimination,* 22 Alaska Hist. 23, 36 n. 14 (Spring/Fall 2007).

159. Tucker, *The Battle Over Bilingual Ballots,* 254.

160. State of Alaska, Report of the Committee on Suffrage, Elections, and Apportionment to the Hon. William A. Egan, President of the Alaska Constitutional Convention (December 5, 1955).

161. See Natalie Landreth and Moira Smith, *Voting Rights in Alaska 1982–2006,* 17 S. Cal. Rev. L. & Soc. Just. 79, 91 n. 67 (2007); Haycox, *William Paul, Sr.,* 32–35.

162. Ariz. Rev. Stat. Ann. § 16-101(A) (4)–(5) (1956).

163. David R. Berman, *Arizona Politics and Government: The Quest for Autonomy, Democracy, and Development* (Lincoln: University of Nebraska Press, 1998), 75–76.

164. See Chandler Davidson et al., *Vote Caging as a Republican Ballot Security Technique*, 34 Wm. Mitchell L. Rev. 533, 543–59 (2008); Paul Butler, *Rehnquist, Racism, and Race Jurisprudence*, 74 Geo. Wash. L. Rev. 1019, 1021–22 (2006).

165. 400 U.S. at 118.

166. Id. at 132–33.

167. Id. at 147 (Douglas, J., dissenting).

168. Tucker and Espino, *Voting Rights in Arizona*, 283–88, 320–24.

169. U.S. Commission on Civil Rights, The Voting Rights Act, 16–17.

170. *Castro v. State*, 466 P.2d 244, 247–48 (Cal. 1970).

171. Id. at 248–49.

172. Keyssar, *The Right to Vote*, 145.

173. *Castro v. State*, 466 P.2d at 245–46.

174. Cal. Const. art. II, § 1 (1894).

175. *Castro v. State*, 466 P.2d at 258–59.

176. S. Rep. 94-295, 1975, 33.

177. Tucker, *The Battle Over Bilingual Ballots*, 43–56.

178. S. Rep. 94-295, 1975, 39.

179. Tucker, *The Battle Over Bilingual Ballots*, 43–56.

180. 42 USC § 1973aa–1a(a) (2006).

181. S. Rep. 94-295, 1975, 28.

182. S. Rep. 102-315, 1992, 5.

183. 121 *Cong. Rec.* H4719 (daily ed., June 2, 1975) (statement of Rep. Edwards).

184. 42 USC § 1973aa–1a(a) (2006).

185. See 42 USC § 1973aa–1a(b)(2)(A)(i) (2006).

186. 42 USC § 1973aa–1a(b)(3)(B) (2006).

187. See 42 USC § 1973aa–1a(b)(2)(A)(ii) (2006).

188. 42 USC § 1973aa–1a(b)(3)(E) (2006).

189. See 121 *Cong. Rec.* H4719 (daily ed., June 2, 1975) (statement of Rep. Edwards).

190. See Dr. James Thomas Tucker and Dr. Rodolfo Espino et al., Minority Language Assistance Practices in Public Elections (2006), 29, reprinted in *Voting Rights Act: Evidence of Continued Need, Hearing Before the Subcomm. on the Constitution of the H. Comm. on the Judiciary*, 109th Cong. 2124, 2163 (2006).

191. NAMUDNO 2009: *8.

192. NAMUDNO 2009: *6. In NAMUDNO, the Court did not reach the question of whether Section 5, as reauthorized in 2006, was constitutional. Rather, it decided the case through a statutory construction of the bailout provision in Section 4(a) of the Act. NAMUDNO 2009: **10–13.

193. NAMUDNO 2009: *8. Despite what Mr. Clegg argues, separation of powers requires the Supreme Court to defer to legislation enacted within the scope of the enforcement sections of the Fourteenth and Fifteenth Amendments, even if the Court thinks that law "is not fashioned to do the best job to guarantee the right to vote."

194. Tucker, *The Battle Over Bilingual Ballots*, 106–7.

195. See *Doi v. Bell*, 449 F. Supp. 267, 272 (D. Haw. 1978).

196. U.S. Census Bureau, American Community Survey: A Handbook for State and Local Officials (Dec. 2004), 1.

197. VRARA § 8, enacted as Pub L. No. 109-246 § 8, 120 Stat. 581.

198. *Gaston County*, 395 U.S. at 291–92.

199. H.R. Rep. No. 102-655, at 8 (1992), reprinted in 1992 USCCAN 766, 772.

200. Testimony of Linda Chavez, president of One Nation Indivisible, Hearing Before the Committee on the Judiciary of the United States Senate, *The Continuing Need for Section 203's Provisions for Limited English Proficient Voters*, S. Hrg. 109-669, at 16 (June 13, 2006).

201. See 42 USC § 1973aa–1a(b)(3)(B) (2006).

202. U.S. Census Bureau, Census 2000 Brief, Language Use and English-Speaking Ability: 2000 (October 2003), 2, http://www.census.gov/prod/2003pubs/c2kbr-29.pdf.

203. Robert Kominski, U.S. Census Bureau, Population Division, *How Good Is*

"How Well"? An Examination of the Census English-Speaking Ability Question (1989).

204. 42 USC § 1973aa–1a(b)(3)(E) (2006).

205. See Ana Henderson, "English Language Naturalization Requirements and the Bilingual Assistance Provisions of the Voting Rights Act" (2006) (unpublished manuscript on file with author).

206. See James Thomas Tucker, "The ESL Logjam: Waiting Times for Adult ESL Classes and the Impact on English Learners appendices C-F (October 2006) (tables identifying reading comprehension skills at different levels of English proficiency), available at http://www.naleo.org/downloads/ESLReportLoRes.pdf.

207. 42 USC § 1973aa–1a(b)(4) (2006).

208. 432 U.S. 404, 410 (1977).

209. *Briscoe v. Bell,* 432 U.S. at 414. A federal district court reached the same conclusion in a challenge to the census director's Section 203 determinations. *Doi v. Bell,* 449 F. Supp. at 267.

210. *NAMUDNO* 2009: *5.

211. *NAMUDNO* 2009: *8.

212. Tucker, *The Battle Over Bilingual Ballots,* 127–28. School districts with more than 50,000 ELL students include Los Angeles with 328,684; New York with 122,840; Chicago with 82,540; Miami-Dade with 62,767; Houston with 61,319; Clark County (Las Vegas), Nevada, with 53,517; and Dallas with 51,328. Id.

213. Anneka L. Kindler, "U.S. Department of Education, Survey of the States' Limited English Proficient Students and Available Educational Programs and Services 2000–2001 Summary Report" (2002), 3, 10, 13, available at http://www.ncela.gwu.edu/policy/states/reports/seareports/0001/sea0001.pdf.

214. Tucker, *The Battle Over Bilingual Ballots,* 128–29.

215. See *Moore v. State of Alaska,* Case No. 3AN-04-9756-CIV (Alaska Superior Ct.) (alleging that "every Alaska child receives an inadequate education because

the funding of that education is grossly inadequate").

216. See *Leslie v. Board of Educ. for Ill. Sch. Dist. U-46,* 379 F. Supp. 2d 952 (N.D. Ill. 2005) (denying motion to dismiss case brought under the EEOA on behalf of LEP Hispanic students and African American students).

217. Tucker, *The Battle Over Bilingual Ballots,* 127–28. Successful cases were brought in Alaska, Arizona, California, Connecticut, Idaho, Kansas, Maryland, Massachusetts, Montana, New Jersey, New Mexico, New York, North Dakota, Texas, and Washington. Id. Cases were pending in Colorado, Nebraska, Oklahoma, and Oregon. Id.

218. H.R. Rep. No. 109-478, 2006: 50–52.

219. *Modern Enforcement of the Voting Rights Act: Hearing Before the S. Comm. on the Judiciary,* 109th Cong. 125 (2006) (statement of Natalie Landreth, staff attorney, Native American Rights Fund).

220. Natalie Landreth and Moira Smith, "RenewtheVRA.org, Voting Rights in Alaska 1982–2006" (2006), 27, reprinted in *Voting Rights Act: Evidence of Continued Need, Hearing Before the Subcomm. on the Constitution of the H. Comm. on the Judiciary,* 109th Cong. 2124, 2163 (2006), 1308, 1335.

221. *Kasayulie v. State,* No. 3AN-97-3782 CIV (Alaska Super. Ct. September 1, 1999).

222. Decision and Order, *Moore v. State of Alaska,* Case No. 3AN-04-9756-CIV (Alaska Super. Ct. June 21, 2007) (unpublished opinion), at 194–95. Information about this case was provided to Congress in 2006.

223. Tucker, *The Battle Over Bilingual Ballots,* 260–61.

224. Pat Kossan, "Minorities Score Low on AIMS: Requirement for Graduation Looms Large, Study Indicates," *Arizona Republic,* April 22, 2005, 1B.

225. Laughlin McDonald, Janine Pease, and Richard Guest, "Voting Rights in South Dakota 1982–2006" (2006), 12, reprinted in *Voting Rights Act: Evidence of*

Continued Need, Hearing Before the Sub-comm. on the Constitution of the H. Comm. on the Judiciary, 109th Cong. 2124, 2163 (2006), 1986, 1997.

226. See *Columbia Falls Elementary Sch. Dist. No. 6 v. State,* No. BDV-2002-528, 2004 WL 844055, at *31 (Mont. Dist. Ct. April 15, 2004) (holding that Montana's public schools remained underfunded and that the state had shown "no commitment in its educational goals to the preservation of [American Indian] cultural identity"), *aff'd,* 109 P.3d 257 (Mont. 2005); *Helena Elementary Sch. Dist. No. 1 v. State,* 769 P.2d 684, 690 (Mont. 1989) (holding that the state's education finance system unconstitutionally denied Indian students an equal education); *Heavy Runner v. Bremner,* 522 F. Supp. 162 (D. Mont. 1981) (charging the state school districts with failure to provide its Blackfeet Indian students an equal education).

227. See Mont. Office of Pub. Instruction, American Indian Education Data Fact Sheet (2007), available at http://www.opi.mt.gov/pdf/indianed/IEFA-DataFactSheet.pdf.

228. No. 85-6924 (E.D. Pa. May 4, 1988) (consent decree continued by stipulation in 2001).

229. Tucker, *The Battle Over Bilingual Ballots Shifts to the Courts,* 559–68.

230. See *United States v. Texas,* 506 F. Supp. 405, 427–428 (E.D. Tex. 1981), *rev'd and remanded on different grounds,* 680 F.2d (5th Cir. 1982).

231. In 2007, a federal court found "that over eighty percent of LEP students in the seventh through ninth grade failed to perform satisfactorily" on the state achievement exam. In addition, the progress "towards closing the achievement gaps between LEP students and students overall is less rapid at the secondary level than the elementary level." See *United States v. Texas,* 2007 WL 2177369, at *17 (E.D. Tex. July 27, 2007).

232. *Flores v. Arizona,* 405 F. Supp. 2d 1112, 1113, 1120 (D. Ariz. 2005).

233. *Comite De Padres De Familia v. O'Connell,* 2004 WL 179212, at *4 (Cal. 3d Cir. 2004).

234. Tucker, *The Battle Over Bilingual Ballots,* 127–28.

235. See James Thomas Tucker, *The ESL Logjam: Waiting Times for ESL Classes and the Impact on English Language Learners,* 96 Nat'l Civic Rev. 30 (March 2007).

236. See 42 USC § 1973aa–1a(a).

237. Tucker, *The Battle Over Bilingual Ballots,* 120–26.

238. Tucker, *The Battle Over Bilingual Ballots,* 130–31.

239. See National Congress of America Indians, *Election 2008: Impact in Indian Country* (November 6, 2008), http://www.ncai.org/fileadmin/pdfElection2008AnalysisFINALCompatibilityMode.pdf.

240. See State of Alaska, Division of Elections, Official Results of the Nov. 4, 2008 General Election, http://www.elections.alaska.gov/08general/data/results.pdf.

241. Dr. James Thomas Tucker and Dr. Rodolfo Espino, "Voting Rights in Arizona 1982–2006" (2006), 19, *reprinted in Voting Rights Act: Evidence of Continued Need, Hearing Before the Subcomm. on the Constitution of the H. Comm. on the Judiciary,* 109th Cong. 2124, 2163 (2006), 1363, 1381.

242. Bureau of the Census, U.S. Dep't of Commerce, Current Population Reports, Series P20-556, Voting and Registration in the Election of November 2004, tbl.4a. The census data did not track registration and turnout for Alaska Natives and American Indians. See id.

243. *NAMUDNO* 2009: *8.

244. *NAMUDNO* 2009: *5, *8.

245. *NAMUDNO* 2009: *10, *13.

246. Tucker, *The Battle Over Bilingual Ballots,* 165–203.

247. See 42 USC § 1973 (2006).

248. See *United States v. Osceola County,* 475 F. Supp. 2d 1220, 1235 (M.D. Fla. 2006); *Cottier v. City of Martin,* 466 F. Supp. 2d 1175, 1185, 1193 (D. S.D. 2006); see also *Harris v. Graddick,* 593 F. Supp. at 132–33 (reaching a similar conclusion where the state hired a disproportionately small number of black poll workers).

249. See *Coal. for Educ. in Dist. One v. New York City Bd. of Elections,* 370 F. Supp. 42 (S.D. N.Y.), *aff'd,* 495 F.2d 1090 (2d Cir. 1974).

250. See Complaint, *United States v. Osceola County, FL,* Civil Action No. 6:02-CV-738-ORL-22JGG (M.D. Fla. 2002), available at http://www.usdoj.gov/crt/voting/sec_2/osceola_comp.htm. The Osceola complaint was resolved by consent decree on July 22, 2002, just four days before the county became covered for Spanish under Section 203. See Consent Decree, *Osceola County,* supra (M.D. Fla. July 22, 2002), available at http://www.usdoj.gov/crt/voting/sec_2/osceola_comp.htm.

251. See generally Consent Decree, *United States v. City of Boston,* Civil Action No. 05-11598-WGY (D. Mass. Oct. 18, 2005), available at http://www.usdoj.gov/crt/voting/sec_203/documents/boston_cd2.pdf.

252. See Complaint, *United States v. City of Hamtramck, MI,* Case No. 00-73541 (E.D. Mich. filed Aug. 1, 2000).

253. *South Carolina v. Katzenbach,* 383 U.S. at 331–32.

254. Tucker, *The Battle Over Bilingual Ballots,* 78–88.

255. *South Carolina v. Katzenbach,* 383 U.S. at 324.

256. NAMUDNO 2009: *9.

257. NAMUDNO 2009: *5.

258. 28 CFR § 55.9 (2006).

259. Tucker, *The Battle Over Bilingual Ballots,* 216–21.

260. Ralph F. Boyd, Jr., assistant attorney general, Civil Rights Division, to Ms. Nadine Parkhurst, clerk of the Board,

Cochise County, Arizona (July 26, 2002), available at http://www.usdoj.gov/crt/voting/sec_203/july_ltr02.htm.

261. S. Rep. 94-295, 1975: 39.

262. See 121 *Cong. Rec.* S13,650 (daily ed., July 24, 1975) (statement of Sen. Tunney).

263. S. Rep. 94-295, 1975: 69.

264. See 28 CFR § 55.17 (1976).

265. NAMUDNO 2009: *5.

266. NAMUDNO 2009: *10–*13.

267. 42 USC § 1973aa–1a(d) (2006).

268. 121 *Cong. Rec.* H4719 (daily ed., June 2, 1975) (statement of Rep. Edwards).

269. *City of Boerne v. Flores,* 521 U.S. 507, 533 (1997); see also *South Carolina v. Katzenbach* 1966: 331–32 (reaching a similar conclusion).

270. Elsewhere, I have summarized the complete history of Section 203 determinations, by year, jurisdiction, and covered language (Tucker, *The Battle Over Bilingual Ballots,* appendix B).

271. First Americans Education Project, "Native Vote 2004" (2005), 7, reprinted in *Voting Rights Act: Section 203 – Bilingual Election Requirements (Part II): Hearing Before the Subcomm. on the Constitution of the H. Comm. on the Judiciary,* 109th Cong. 11, 17 (2005).

272. See *Continuing Need for Section 203's Provisions for Limited English Proficient Voters: Hearing Before the S. Comm. on the Judiciary,* 109th Cong. 230–231 (2006) (statement of Margaret Fung, executive director, Asian American Legal Defense and Education Fund).

273. See *Fannie Lou Hamer, Rosa Parks, and Coretta Scott King Voting Rights Act Reauthorization and Amendments Act of 2006 (Part II): Hearing on H.R. 9 Before the Subcomm. on the Constitution of the H. Comm. on the Judiciary,* 109th Cong. 43 (2006) (statement of Karen K. Narasaki, president and executive director, Asian American Justice Center).

274. Bureau of the Census, U.S. Dep't of Commerce, Current Population Reports,

Series P20-542, Voting and Registration
in the Election of November 2000, tbl.4a;
Bureau of the Census, U.S. Dep't of Com-
merce, Current Population Reports, Series
P20-556, Voting and Registration in the
Election of November 2004, tbl.4a.

275. *Continuing Need for Section 203's
Provision for Limited English Proficient Voters: Hearing Before the Senate Committee
on the Judiciary,* 109th Cong. 347 (2006)
(statement of John Trasviña, interim president and general counsel, Mexican American Legal Defense and Education Fund).

276. National Association of Latino
Elected and Appointed Officials (NALEO)

Education Fund, 1985 National Roster of
Hispanic Elected Officials xiii (1985);
NALEO Education Fund, 2006 Latino
Election Handbook (2006), 11, 15, 25, 37,
41, 45. Published by the National Asso-
ciation of Latino Elected and Appointed
Officials.

277. See "Latinos Achieve New Political
Milestones in Congress and State Houses." NALEO press release, November 11,
2006, available at http://www.naleo.org/
pr110906.html.

278. President Gerald R. Ford, remarks
upon signing HR 6219 into Law, 11 Weekly
Comp. Pres. Doc. 837 (August 11, 1975).

NINE

Policy and Constitutional Objections to Section 203 of the Voting Rights Act

ROGER CLEGG

This chapter discusses Section 203 of the Voting Rights Act.[1] Section 203 requires some jurisdictions to print ballots and offer election-related materials in foreign languages. As a constitutional matter, this provision raises serious federalism concerns and equally serious concerns about Congress exceeding its authority to enforce the right to vote regardless of race. Its constitutionality aside, this provision is also objectionable on a variety of policy grounds.

THE LEGISLATIVE CONTEXT: CONGRESS ABDICATES ITS RESPONSIBILITY

In August 2006, President George W. Bush signed into law Congress's amended reauthorization of the Voting Rights Act, which, among other things, extended Section 203[2] of the Voting Rights Act for another twenty-five years. Though it and other provisions did not expire for another year, their reauthorization was a priority for the 109th Congress. Congress appeared to recognize the need for a strong documentary record justifying the reauthorization of these provisions. But the hearings in the House stand out for their one-sidedness, with few witnesses suggesting any policy or legal doubt for reauthorization. The hearings in the Senate included more witnesses expressing these policy and legal doubts. Ultimately, however, Congress chose to adopt without revision the bill as reported by the House Judiciary Committee.[3] The refusal to adopt even modest changes to the structure of the reauthorization and the desire to secure a reauthorization one year prior to expiration suggest that while Congress went through the motions of fulfilling the doctrinal requirement of demonstrating an ongoing pattern of discrimination to justify reauthorization, substantively its deliberative process and constitutional obligations gave way to political expediency.

Just as Congress mistakenly ignored the data demonstrating clear achievements in ballot access with regard to race – as discussed in other chapters of this book – it exercised poor judgment in its treatment of non-English-speaking voters. At a time when the nation is struggling to assimilate a substantial and concentrated number of Spanish-speaking immigrants,[4] Congress set back their full participation in the American political community by discouraging English acquisition and requiring, in instances where there are substantial concentrations of foreign-language speakers, the provision of foreign-language ballots.[5] On policy grounds, these judgments are lamentable. Rather than encouraging ethnic integration, they promote balkanization through foreign-language ballots, as well as by perpetuating the racial gerrymandering and racial segregation that is now an inextricable by-product of the Section 5 preclearance process.[6]

These shortcomings are disappointing but hardly surprising. Rather than answer the serious policy and constitutional concerns brought forward in committee, Congress determined to pass a bill crafted by the House of Representatives in consultation with civil rights groups.[7] The bipartisan participation in this did not result from open political debate but from a bargain between elected federal representatives and these interest groups. Even though a reduction in racial gerrymandering might redound to the benefit of the Democratic Party, its members refused to offend minority incumbents and some of their minority constituents. Meanwhile, Republicans participated in order to avoid accusations of racial and ethnic insensitivity and to maintain segregated congressional districts and the resulting incumbent protection. The result is a law that is inconsistent with America's constitutional principles.

POLICY OBJECTIONS TO SECTION 203

While most of the commentary and testimony during the reauthorization process focused on the impact of the reauthorization of Section
5 of the Voting Rights Act, as noted above Congress also decided to
reauthorize for twenty-five years the foreign-language ballot provisions
of the Voting Rights Act, commonly referred to as Section 203, which is
accomplished by Section 7 of the new bill.[8]

Section 203 requires certain jurisdictions to provide all election-
related materials, as well as the ballots themselves, in foreign languages.[9]
The jurisdictions are those where more than 5 percent of the voting-age
citizens (or simply ten thousand of them) are members of a particular
language minority, and where the illiteracy rate of such persons is higher
than the national illiteracy rate.[10] The language minority groups are limited to American Indians, Asian Americans, Alaskan Natives, and those
"of Spanish heritage."[11] Where the language of the minority group is oral
or unwritten, then oral voting assistance is required in that language.[12]

There are three policy problems with Section 203. First, it encourages balkanization. Second, it facilitates voter fraud. And third, it wastes
government resources. In addition, Section 203 is unconstitutional because although Congress asserts it has enacted this law pursuant to its
enforcement authority under the Fourteenth and Fifteenth Amendments,[13] this statute actually exceeds that authority.

Section 203 Balkanizes Our Country

America is a multiethnic, multiracial nation. This is increasingly so, as
dramatized by the fact that we now have a multiethnic, multiracial president. Our country always has been multiethnic and multiracial, of course,
and this is a source of national pride and strength. But our motto has been
E pluribus unum – out of many, one – and this means that, while we come
from all over the globe, we are also united as Americans.

This unity means that we hold certain things in common. We celebrate the same democratic values, for instance, share the American
dream of success through hard work, cherish our many freedoms, and

champion political equality. Our common bonds must also include an ability to communicate with one another. Our political order and our economic health demand it.

Accordingly, the government should be encouraging our citizens to be fluent in English, which, as a practical matter, is our national language. And in any event, the government certainly should not discourage people from mastering English and should not send any signals that mastering English is unimportant. Indeed, doing so does recent immigrants no favor, since true participation in American democracy requires knowing English.[14]

Inevitably, however, the federal government engages in just that kind of discouragement when it demands that ballots be printed in foreign languages. It also devalues citizenship for those who have mastered English as part of the naturalization process. As Boston University president John Silber noted in his 1996 congressional testimony, bilingual ballots "impose an unacceptable cost by degrading the very concept of the citizen to that of someone lost in a country whose public discourse is incomprehensible to him."[15]

In a nation of immigrants, the importance of assimilation needs to be better recognized. Encouraging English fluency is a critical element of assimilation, and it and others are discussed in testimony I presented to Congress in 2007 (see appendix).

Section 203 Facilitates Voter Fraud

Most Americans are baffled by the foreign-language ballot law. They know that with few exceptions, only citizens can vote. And they know that, again with only few exceptions, only those who speak English can become citizens. So why is it necessary to have ballots printed in foreign languages?

It is a good question, and there really is no persuasive answer to it. As a practical matter, there are very few citizens who need non-English ballots.

There are, however, a great many noncitizens who can use non-English ballots. And the problem of noncitizens voting is a real one. The

Justice Department has brought, for instance, numerous criminal prosecutions regarding noncitizen voting just in Florida, as documented in a
recent official report.[16] This nationwide problem was noted years ago by
Linda Chavez[17] and has been extensively reported on in the press.[18] Hans
von Spakovsky, a former Justice Department voting-rights specialist now
at the Heritage Foundation, more recently (July 10, 2008) published a
paper on "The Threat of Non-Citizen Voting" that further documents
this problem.[19] And there is an obvious interest – by federal, state, and
local governments, and by legitimate voters themselves – in preventing
fraudulent voting.[20]

Section 203 Wastes Government Resources

As just noted, there are few citizens who need ballots and other election materials printed for them in languages other than English. The
requirement that, nonetheless, such materials must be printed is therefore wasteful.

On the one hand, the cost of printing the additional materials is
high. It is a classic, and substantial, unfunded federal mandate. For example, Los Angeles County had to spend over $1.1 million in 1996 to
provide Spanish, Chinese, Vietnamese, Japanese, and Filipino language
assistance.[21] Six years later, in 2002, it had to spend $3.3 million.[22] There
are 296 counties in thirty states that, after the 2000 census, were required
to have such materials.[23] Frequently the cost of multilingual voter assistance is more than half of a jurisdiction's total election costs.[24] If corners
are cut, the likelihood of translation errors increases. Indeed, the inevita-
bility of some translation errors, no matter how much money is spent, is
another argument for why all voters need to master English rather than
rely on translated ballots and election materials.[25]

Conversely, the use made of the additional materials is low. According to a 1986 General Accounting Office study, nearly half of the jurisdictions that provided estimates said *no one* – not a single person – used oral
minority-language assistance, and more than half likewise said *no one*
used their written minority-language assistance. Covered jurisdictions
said that generally language assistance "was not needed" by a ten to one

margin, and an even larger majority said that providing assistance was either "very costly or a waste of money."[26] According to the registrar of voters in Yuba County, California, "In my 16 years on this job, I have received only one request for Spanish literature from any of my constituents." Yet in 1996 the county had to spend $30,000 on such materials for primary and general elections.[27] The problem may be aggravated by the dubious way in which non-English-proficient voters are identified by the census.[28]

What's more, to quote John J. Miller's *The Unmaking of Americans,* getting rid of foreign-language ballots "does not mean that immigrant voters who still have difficulty communicating in English would not be without recourse. There is a long tradition in the United States of ethnic newspapers – often printed in languages other than English – providing political guidance to readers in the form of sample ballots and visual aids that explain how to vote. It would surely continue."[29] Mr. Miller concluded that "Congress should amend the Voting Rights Act to stop the Department of Justice from coercing local communities to print election materials in foreign languages."[30]

In sum, as a simple matter of dollars and cents, foreign-language ballots are just not worth it. The money would be much better spent on improving election equipment and combating voter fraud.

CONSTITUTIONAL OBJECTIONS TO SECTION 203

Section 203 raises constitutional issues for two reasons, which indeed may create judicial concerns greater than their sum alone. First, there are federalism concerns insofar as it substitutes federal for state authority in areas traditionally – and often textually, by the language of the Constitution itself – committed to state discretion.[31] These federalism concerns are heightened by the fact that some jurisdictions are covered and others are not, especially if there is no compelling factual justification for the distinction or for the requirement at all.[32] Second, it is unlikely that Section 203 is a "congruent and proportional" – the relevant legal standard – means to enforcing the Fourteenth or Fifteenth Amendments.

A Changing Factual Landscape

Congress may have been confident that it was acting within its authority when it first passed Section 203 in 1975, but both the facts and the law have changed over the past thirty or forty years.

Congress ignored the changed factual landscape when it reauthorized Section 5 of the Voting Rights Act,[33] and it did so when it reauthorized Section 203 too. Few would dispute that a great deal of progress has been made over the past several decades in eliminating the scourge of state-sponsored racial and ethnic discrimination. No one would deny that there is still additional progress to be made against such discrimination generally, and against voting discrimination specifically, but the facts simply do not exist to justify singling out the jurisdictions delineated under Section 5 and Section 203 for the intrusive requirements of those sections.

Indeed, not only has the factual landscape changed, but part of the current landscape that the Supreme Court will have before it is the unwillingness of Congress to consider that change. Nine U.S. Representatives[34] and two U.S. Senators[35] were willing to state for the record that the reauthorization bill was hurried through without acknowledging the lack of an evidentiary predicate for the reauthorization. Any concerns with the constitutionality of the bill as well as public policy concerns were given short shrift.[36] In sum, the record reads like an after-the-fact justification rather than a serious effort to provide constitutional justification for the reauthorization.

Given the shortcomings in the legislative process, it seems likely that the courts will look hard at a law that substitutes federal for state authority in areas that are traditionally, even textually, committed to state discretion under the Constitution, and that sets a much more difficult standard for legality than is found in the Constitution itself. This is especially so since, as discussed next, the Supreme Court's more recent decisions make clear that Section 203 is inconsistent with principles of federalism and limitations on Congress's authority, particularly because it is not needed to stop disparate racial treatment – and, indeed, is contrary to the idea of *E pluribus unum*. Section 203 of the Voting Rights Act is not fashioned to do the best job it can to guarantee the right to vote regardless of ethnicity, and does so in a way that is inconsistent with principles of federalism – which, after all, is also a bulwark against government abridgment of our rights as citizens.

A Changing Legal Landscape

Not only has the factual landscape changed since Section 203 was first enacted, the legal landscape has changed too. When the two are considered together, Section 203 raises serious constitutional problems. It lacks all congruence and proportionality to the end of stopping purposeful racial and ethnic discrimination by the states and should be struck down as unconstitutional.

During the time since the Voting Rights Act was first enacted in 1965, the Supreme Court has made clear that the Fourteenth Amendment bans only disparate treatment, not state actions that have only a disparate impact and were undertaken without regard to race.[37] A plurality of the Court has drawn the same distinction for the Fifteenth Amendment.[38]

The Supreme Court has also ruled even more recently that Congress can use its enforcement authority under the Fourteenth Amendment to ban actions with merely a disparate impact only if those bans have a "congruence and proportionality" to the end of ensuring no disparate treatment.[39] This limitation ought also to apply to the Fifteenth Amendment: There is no reason to think that Congress's enforcement authority would be different under the Fourteenth Amendment than under the Fifteenth, when the two were ratified within nineteen months of each other, have nearly identical enforcement clauses, were both prompted by a desire to protect the rights of just-freed slaves, and indeed have both been used to ensure our citizens' voting rights.

Finally, the Supreme Court has, in a number of recent decisions, stressed its commitment to principles of federalism and to ensuring the division of powers between the federal government and state governments.[40] It has also stressed what is obvious from the text of the Constitution: "The Constitution creates a Federal Government of enumerated powers."[41]

The Supreme Court's federalism concerns in this area were the focus of much of Chief Justice Roberts's 2009 opinion in *Northwest Austin*

Municipal Utility District Number One v. Holder, which was joined by seven other justices (the ninth, Justice Thomas, went even further in his partial dissent).[42] While the Court did not actually decide the presented issue in that opinion of the constitutionality vel non of Section 5 of the Voting Rights Act – an issue, incidentally, that has been reraised since then in at least two new lawsuits that are likely headed back to the Supreme Court – it clearly signaled that it took that challenge extremely seriously, and in particular the act's tension with division of power principles.

In sum: The Supreme Court has now made it clear that only purposeful discrimination – actually treating people differently on the basis of race or ethnicity – violates the Fourteenth and Fifteenth Amendments.[43] The Court has ruled even more recently that Congress can use its enforcement authority to ban actions that have merely a disparate impact only if those bans have a "congruence and proportionality" to the end of ensuring no disparate treatment.[44] This limitation is likely to be even stricter when the federal statute in question involves areas usually considered a matter of state authority.[45]

Considering Section 203's Constitutionality Today

Now, it is very unlikely that the practice of printing ballots in English and not in foreign languages would be a violation of the Fourteenth or Fifteenth Amendments – that is, it is very unlikely that this practice is rooted in a desire to deny people the right to vote because of race or ethnicity.[46] Rather, it is overwhelmingly likely to have perfectly legitimate roots: to avoid facilitating fraud, to discourage balkanization, and to conserve scarce state and local resources.[47] Accordingly, Congress cannot plausibly assert that in order to prevent discrimination in voting, it has authority to tell state and local officials that they must print ballots in foreign languages.

The rather garbled text of Section 203, however, apparently says that Congress was concerned not with discrimination in voting per se, but with educational disparities.[48] That is, the "unequal educational opportunities" that, say, Latinos receive is what makes foreign-language ballots necessary.

Today, however, it is unlikely that most educational disparities are rooted in discrimination. And if these disparities are not rooted in discrimination, then there is a problem with Congress asserting its power under Section 5 of the Fourteenth Amendment or Section 2 of the Fifteenth Amendment to require foreign-language ballots. In this regard, it is worth noting that the language of Section 203 uses words like "effectively" and "resulting" – words used when disparate treatment is lacking.

But let us assume that Congress did have in mind unequal educational opportunities rooted in educational discrimination, presumably by the states. Even then there are insurmountable problems. There is, in short, a lack of congruence and proportionality between the asserted discrimination in education and the foreign-language ballot mandate in Section 203. Consider just these questions:

Are all the language minorities covered by Section 203 subjected to government discrimination in education – and, if not, why are all of them covered?

Are there language minorities that are subject to government discrimination that are not covered by Section 203 – and, if so, why are they not covered?

How often does education discrimination result in an individual not becoming fluent enough in English to cast a ballot?

Is it not much more likely that this lack of fluency has some other cause (like recent immigration, most obviously, or growing up in an environment where English is not spoken enough)?

Finally, is it a congruent and proportional response to education discrimination to force states to make ballots available in foreign languages?

For example, how likely is Section 203 to result in the elimination of education discrimination? And how likely is it, really, to enable someone to vote who would not otherwise be able to vote because of state discrimination he or she suffered?

In sum, does this "remedy" justify Congress's overruling of the legitimate reasons that states have for printing ballots in English and not in foreign languages – particularly when added to the federalism concerns that are already raised by Congress's entering into an arena (voting) that is typically a state province and by the fact that Congress is singling out some jurisdictions for this intrusive treatment?

And finally, can it really be plausibly argued that the real reason for Section 203 has anything to do with remedying state discrimination in education? With all respect, the answer must be no. As discussed in Linda Chavez's *Out of the Barrio,* the Voting Rights Act of 1965 was motivated by a desire to stop racial discrimination; but the later expansion of the Voting Rights Act at the behest of Latino special interest groups was simply about identity politics.[49] There was little factual record established even to show that Hispanics were being systematically denied the right to vote.[50] This disenfranchisement would have been particularly difficult to demonstrate in light of the number of Hispanics who had previously been elected to office, which included governors, U.S. Senators, and members of the House of Representatives, as well as numerous state legislators and local officials, with many of these officials serving in jurisdictions that would be subject to the special provisions of the Voting Rights Act.[51] There is really no credible way to equate the discrimination that African Americans in the South suffered to the situation of Latinos, who had voted – and been elected to office – in great numbers for decades. That was true when Section 203 was first enacted, and it is even truer now. The reason for the bilingual ballot provision is not and never has been about discrimination – it is about identity politics.

*   *   *

In the previous chapter, Professor Tucker struggles at length to justify Section 203 constitutionally and as a matter of policy, but with all respect he can succeed only if one loses sight of the forest for the trees.

With regard to the policy problems my chapter identifies, he is largely silent, and probably wisely so. After all, we can quibble over the amounts, but it cannot really be denied that it is costly to have to print ballots in foreign languages. We can argue over how many fraudulent ballots are cast by facilitating the voting of non–English speakers – when, after all, the ability to speak English is required of nearly all legal voters – but surely there must be some. And we can readily admit that it may be difficult to measure how much balkanization is caused by removing an important incentive for learning English, but that does not make the balkanization disappear.

And with regard to the constitutional problems, the four principal opinions (often dicta and none written after 1970) cited by Professor Tucker are either readily distinguishable or of questionable authority because of intervening precedent or both. Administering a literacy test, for example, is just not the same thing as expecting voters to be able to understand English. Bear in mind always the fundamental questions. First, how plausible is it that the reason many of some group are not fluent in English is because they were deliberately discriminated against by a state in violation of the Fourteenth and Fifteenth Amendments? (And how much of what Professor Tucker cites, especially that which was not stale – that is, involved evidence that substantial numbers of citizens voting today are unable to speak English because of government discrimination against them on the basis of race or national origin – was before Congress?) For example, if there are a lot of non-English-speaking immigrants, and the state has not taught them English, that may be lamentable but it is not unconstitutional (and the federal government cannot turn this into a constitutional violation by passing a statute that requires such teaching as a condition of federal funding). The same is true if there are a lot of non-English-speaking Indians in a state. And, second, even if you find the existence of such a remedial predicate plausible, is a good remedy for this wrong to force the state to print ballots in a foreign language? It's a terrible fit – completely lacking any tailoring, narrow or otherwise – and thus unconstitutional.

Finally, even if it is a good enough fit to be constitutional, as a policy matter again we have to ask whether the benefit (of helping some of these people vote) is worth the costs (the balkanization, the expense, the fraud). The costs (which cannot be ignored) overwhelm any conceivable benefits (which remain vague).

CONCLUSION: VOTING RIGHTS IN A BROADER CONTEXT

In conclusion, there is a wide divergence between what the Voting Rights Act was supposed to be and what it has become.[52] The purpose of the Voting Rights Act was to stop racial discrimination in voting. In some jurisdictions prior to 1965, specifically in the Deep South, there was no question that African Americans, in particular, were disenfranchised. It is disturbing to see this civil rights statute twisted into a partisan political device, and both parties bear blame for this abuse.

The same kind of abuse can also happen in ways that do not involve racial gerrymandering – the principal evil advanced now by Sections 2 and 5 of the Voting Rights Act – but do involve other voting practices or procedures that are objected to, ostensibly because they are racially discriminatory, but really for partisan purposes. For instance, the lack of concern that one party has with voter fraud – including the noncitizen voting facilitated by Section 203 – can be traced in part to its belief that it is more helped than hurt by such fraud.

Other examples include absentee ballot procedures, limitations on felons voting, and voter identification laws, which are all challenged sometimes, not because anyone really believes that they are intended to be racially discriminatory, but because one side thinks these rules will hurt their voter turnout, and their disparate racial impact allows the Voting Rights Act to be invoked for, again, a partisan political end.[53]

Now let me put this in a broader context. The other day (June 23, 2007, to be precise) I read a couple of letters to the editor of *The New York Times,* from people who were sincerely offended that, as had been discussed in a recent *Times* article, mentally deranged people are often not allowed to vote.

Here's part of one letter: "I am very troubled by [your article], which reports political efforts to prevent people with mental disorders and elderly people with dementia from voting. Our constitutional right to vote does not require that any one of us make a rational choice. . . ."

Here's part of the other: "I was appalled to learn that the mentally ill can be kept from voting, and that some are trying to make it even harder for them to participate in the democratic process. . . . Our government's just powers must be derived from the consent of all the governed, not merely an elite comprised of mentally sound elders."

The former letter, by the way, is from a doctor; the latter letter also cites with approval the lowering of the voting age in Austria to sixteen. I should add that the American Bar Association voted favorably at its annual convention recently on a resolution that will urge jurisdictions to make it easier for mentally incompetent people to vote. And there is a much-publicized, multifront effort to curtail the practice in many states of disenfranchising felons, and there are even activists who think that noncitizens should be allowed to vote.

It is a pretty basic question for our system of government, isn't it? Who should be allowed to vote?

There are, as just indicated, only four groups of people who are generally not allowed to vote in the United States now, and the left wants to enfranchise more of all of them: children, criminals, noncitizens, and the mentally ill.

Now, no doubt much of this is driven simply by politics: The left thinks that all these groups (with the possible exception of the latter) are more likely to vote with them than against them, and it may well be right. But I also think that part of it is more deep-seated than that. This is one fundamental, instinctive difference between right and left: The former believes in standards (or, to be less charitable, is elitist), and the latter does not (or, to be more charitable, embraces egalitarianism more passionately). In addition, the left benefits more from illegal voting, and so resists measures aimed at deterring it (such as voter ID) or that even have the effect of deterring it (like providing ballots only in English); the right's constituencies tend to be more conscientious and orderly, and so they are more likely to jump successfully through any hoops that are put in place.

To be sure, most liberals and most conservatives agree with the basic approach of letting nearly everyone vote these days. I think there is a moral reason for this and also a utilitarian reason. They are not mutually exclusive. The moral reason is that if the government is going to boss you around, then you ought to have some say in how it is run and what rules it makes. No taxation without representation and all that. The utilitarian reason is that the government will make wiser choices if we let most people vote. If we had some way of knowing which particular people would most skillfully foresee who the best candidates and referenda are, then it would obviously lead to better government if we let only those people vote. But knowing these electors is impossible, and it is not even easy to choose their credentials. Many of us suspect that, as William F. Buckley, Jr., once famously observed, the first two thousand names in the Boston phonebook really are wiser in these matters than the Harvard faculty. Moreover, the few are foolish but the many are wise, so it makes no sense to limit yourself to the first two thousand names if you can get input from the whole directory.

But if these are the two reasons that we have (nearly) universal suffrage, then this also suggests why there ought to be some limits on it.

The moral justification, for instance, is less compelling if the person who wants to vote is unwilling to obey the government or follow its laws. Thus, criminals are generally limited in their voting. Likewise, since noncitizens are typically bossed around less, and more temporarily, than citizens, it's less offensive that we not let them vote, even if they do have to pay taxes and so forth. And illegal aliens, by the way, are both – that is, illegal and aliens.

With regard to the utilitarian rationale, while we may not be sure who the wisest people are, we may be pretty confident that some people really do have poor judgment. Children and the mentally incompetent are good examples. And we may also be reasonably confident in our skepticism that some people have the nation's interests at heart, and so we are less interested in their input; here again, those who are criminals or noncitizens come to mind (although, in both cases, that skepticism may change: once a felon has shown he has turned over a new leaf, and of course once a noncitizen becomes a citizen).

Here's an additional note: Rejecting people for either rationale is troubling if the rejection is subjective and, thus, more liable to being abused, but less troubling if based on the failure to meet an objective criterion that has its origins outside the voting context. Thus we might be nervous about giving exams or even simple literacy tests to determine who votes, especially in light of past abuses; on the other hand, basing the decision on age or criminal record or citizenship or prior medical determinations of mental incompetence is – or at least ought to be – less troubling (although it should be noted that the fact that some racial and ethnic groups are overrepresented among felons has fueled challenges to their disenfranchisement).

And one last note: Voting is, of course, not the only way that power is exercised in our republic. Other ways – lobbying, running for office, litigating, and so forth – have grown and adapted over time. There are sound, Burkean reasons why none of this should be radically altered, and that includes dramatically expanding or contracting the franchise.

APPENDIX

TESTIMONY OF
ROGER CLEGG,
PRESIDENT AND GENERAL COUNSEL,
CENTER FOR EQUAL OPPORTUNITY
ON
"COMPREHENSIVE IMMIGRATION REFORM:
BECOMING AMERICANS – U.S. IMMIGRANT INTEGRATION"
BEFORE
THE SUBCOMMITTEE ON
IMMIGRATION, CITIZENSHIP, REFUGEES, BORDER SECURITY,
AND INTERNATIONAL LAW
OF THE
HOUSE JUDICIARY COMMITTEE

MAY 23, 2007
RAYBURN HOUSE OFFICE BUILDING, ROOM 2226

Thank you very much, Mr. Chairman, for the opportunity to testify today. My name is Roger Clegg, and I am president and general counsel of the Center for Equal Opportunity, a nonprofit research and educational organization that is based in Falls Church, Virginia. Our chairman is Linda Chavez, and our focus is on public policy issues that involve race and ethnicity, such as civil rights, bilingual education, and immigration and assimilation.

I am especially glad that you are holding hearings at this time on the issue of assimilation. The current debate over immigration has not given assimilation the attention that it deserves. This is unfortunate not only because assimilation is an extremely important component of the immigration question, but also because it ought to be an issue on which some who are divided on other immigration problems can find common ground.

Left versus Right versus Right

Frequently political differences are about means rather than ends. For instance, no one likes war and we all prefer peace, but folks have very different ideas about the best foreign and defense policies to achieve that end. Likewise, no one desires an impoverished nation and everyone wants prosperity, but there is much disagreement about which policies are best for the economy.

But it's not so clear that this is the case with respect to racial and ethnic relations. There may have been a brief moment when there existed something of a national consensus – a shared vision eloquently articulated in Martin Luther King, Jr.'s "I Have a Dream" speech, with deep roots in the American Creed, distilled in our national motto, *E pluribus unum*. Most Americans still share it, but by no means all.

There is now a lot more disagreement about the kind of society that people envision – a disagreement not just about means, but also about ends.

It is fair to say that we have a tri-polar model with respect to these visions. The hard left sees an American society that is not only multiracial and multiethnic, but multicultural as well. People will speak different languages and have very different traditions, behaviors, and lifestyles. Governments, universities, companies, and other institutions – even statues – must ensure that these different groups are all represented. "Underrepresentation" of a group is unacceptable, and it is groups that are the focus, not individuals.

This multicultural vision is rejected by the right, but in two different ways. The first vision on the right tries to avoid multiculturalism by avoiding multiethnicity. The best way to ensure that Americans continue to share a common culture is by being extremely careful about admitting very many people from non-Western, non-Anglo countries.

The third vision is conservative and also rejects multiculturalism, but without rejecting multiethnicity. It envisions an America of many racial and ethnic groups, but with a common language, common values, and a common culture. It favors relatively liberal immigration policies, but insists on the assimilation of immigrants. In this vision, no group is entitled to a particular degree of representation in any institution; the standards are based on merit and are applied evenhandedly to individuals, and the chips are allowed to fall where they may.

The Center for Equal Opportunity embraces the third vision.

Assimilation: The Unaddressed Issue

Assimilation is the unaddressed issue that needs to be addressed, at whatever level of immigration we have. If the American economy needs relatively high levels of immigration (and we believe it does), and if social conservatives are right to be concerned if there are large numbers of unassimilated immigrants (and we believe that can be a legitimate concern), then we must do a better of job of figuring out how to improve our assimilation policies.

It should be acknowledged at the outset that a successful immigration policy will require some use of generalizations. At some level we must look at immigrants group by group, rather than assuming that an immigrant is an immigrant is an immigrant. That said, however, it does not follow that the U.S. can go back to a quota system where immigration from some countries is welcomed more than immigration from other countries.

On the one hand, of course there are some cultures that are more easily assimilable than others, and there are some individual immigrants who are more welcome than others. On the other hand, it cannot be the case that immigrants from any country are completely unassimilable, nor is it realistic to think we will begin barring all immigrants from any country for no reason other than their national origin. It is too late in the day, and too inconsistent with the American Creed, to have a racially exclusive immigration policy. We cannot announce, "People from Freedonia are, by and large, not welcome, because they come from a hopelessly backward culture." No: The task is to have a realistic, market-driven ceiling on immigration, standards that are nonracial and apply to all countries, and a better policy for assimilation.

We should welcome people who want to come here, work hard, and build better lives for themselves and families. Instead of turning such people into temporary sojourners with no stake in our society, we ought to do what we've always done, which is turn them into good Americans. There's no reason to believe that the Mexicans, Guatemalans, Salvadorans and others arriving now are any less capable of that feat than were the Germans, Italians, or Poles of previous eras. Although these Latino newcomers arrive with very low education levels, their children quickly catch up with other Americans. Second-generation Latinos, those who parents were immigrants, complete high school at nearly the same rate as non-Hispanic whites, 86 percent compared to 92 percent. By the third generation, the overwhelming majority can't even speak Spanish. According to a recent study by Ruben Rumbaut, Douglas Massey, and Frank Bean, only 17 percent of third-generation Mexican Americans living in Southern California can still speak Spanish and 96 percent prefer to speak English at home. (On the assimilation of recent Latino immigrants, see also Linda Chavez's article, "The Realities of Immigration," in the July/August 2006 issue of *Commentary*.)

Defining "Assimilation"

I should note early on that a general defense of American values is beyond the scope of this testimony. Of course the members of this subcommittee agree with me that, in general, the American way of life is worth preserving. Others who disagree will of course see no reason to worry if that way of life is threatened, and will certainly see no reason to worry if many immigrants do not conform to it. To those people we have nothing to say; they will have to be educated elsewhere.

American culture is not perfect. But it is extremely successful in bringing freedom and prosperity to its millions of citizens. There is no call for junking it and starting from scratch. The improvements that need to be made can be made from within by those who choose to live here, and prior to changing it they should learn and understand what it is they are changing.

Assimilation is important not only for immigrants, but also for those who have been here for a generation or two – or more – but have never joined America's culture or have more recently rejected it.

Those of us who share the third vision discussed above have to grapple with the issue of how to encourage assimilation. If assimilation is unattainable, then the third vision is unrealistic.

To the left, we say that the process of assimilation requires the rejection of racial and ethnic preferences, as well as the mind-set that sees oneself as a member of a racial or ethnic group first and as an American only second. And to the right we say that, since in our view the process of assimilation has and can take place efficiently, effectively, and rather quickly, relatively high levels of immigration can be tolerated, even of non-Western, non-Anglo groups.

First, however, we have to define what we mean by assimilation. The correct definition, we think, will assure those on one side that we are not requiring the obliteration of all ethnic differences, while also assuring the other side that what is being required is what's needed to preserve the America we love.

Americans need not all eat the same food, listen to the same music, dance the same dances, or celebrate all the same holidays. But assimilation does mean that we must all aim to have certain things in common.

The Top Ten List

There are ten basic principles to which all Americans must subscribe. They are not outrageous, but they are irreducible (and they apply to *all* of us, native and immigrant alike):

1. Don't disparage anyone else's race or ethnicity;
2. Respect women;
3. Learn to speak English;
4. Be polite;
5. Don't break the law;
6. Don't have children out of wedlock;
7. Don't demand anything because of your race, ethnicity, or sex;
8. Don't view working and studying hard as "acting white";
9. Don't hold historical grudges; and
10. Be proud of being an American.

America has always been a multiracial and multiethnic country. But saying that it is, or should be, multicultural is very different. The ideal was, and still should be, that you can come to America from any country and become an American – but that means accepting some degree of assimilation. It is not diversity that we celebrate most, but what we hold in common. The same is also true for native-born Americans. All of us can claim equally to be Americans, but all must acknowledge a shared set of beliefs and mores.

America has always been diverse. But telling an elementary school that it cannot insist on teaching children standard English, or English at all; or telling a college that it cannot focus on Western Civilization; or insisting that an employer accommodate work habits it finds to be unproductive; or condemning social strictures as judgmental – well, all this may celebrate diversity, but it denigrates the common standards that a free society must have if it is to flourish. Still, it will not do simply to condemn diversity, any more than it will to embrace it indiscriminately. There is much diversity that is valuable or at worst harmless. Workers and students from all backgrounds have contributed enormously to our national life, and who cares what food they like? Some diversity is good, and some bad.

Accordingly, it makes sense to set out some rules essential for a multiracial, multiethnic America and that all Americans should follow – wherever they or their ancestors came from, whatever their skin color, whatever their favorite food or dance. Here, in more detail, are our ten, aimed as much at the native-born as the newly arrived.

1. *Don't disparage anyone else's race or ethnicity.* It may seem odd to begin the list with this one, but actually it's not. On the list of things we don't tolerate, intolerance deserves a prominent position. If we are to be one nation, we cannot criticize one another's skin color and ancestors.

2. *Respect women.* Just as we do not tolerate a lack of respect based on race or ancestry, we also demand respect regardless of sex. Some subcultures – foreign and domestic – put down women. That is not acceptable. This doesn't mean that men and women have no differences or that we all must be ardent feminists. But it does mean that women must be treated respectfully, and that where the law requires that they be treated equally – as it frequently does in this country – it be followed. If you come from a country or a culture where women are second-class citizens, you must leave that behind. And it doesn't matter if the roots are rap or religious, Tupac or the Taliban.

3. *Learn to speak English.* This doesn't mean that you can't learn other languages, too, or keep up a native language. But you and your children must learn English – standard English – as quickly as you can. And, if you expect to be accepted, you should avoid speaking another

language when you are with people who don't understand it. We have to be able to communicate with one another.

4. *Don't be rude.* Some people apparently view it as unmanly or uncool to be polite. But that is just adolescent sullenness. Customers, co-workers, fellow students, strangers – all expect to be treated courteously, and rightly so. Not every culture is a stickler for taking turns, queuing up, and following the rules (see next item), but Americans follow the British here.

5. *Don't break the law.* If you want to participate in this republic – if you want a say in making the rules and electing those who make them – you have to follow the laws yourself. That means, among other things, that you can't use illegal drugs, which is just as well since there is no surer way to stay at the bottom of the heap or to find yourself there in a hurry.

6. *Don't have children out of wedlock.* Moral issues aside, illegitimacy is a social disaster for women and children alike (especially boys). Here again, it is a sure way to stay poor and raise poor children. Perhaps in some countries it takes a village to raise a child, but in the United States it takes two parents. That said, the pathology of illegitimacy is more widespread among some native-born groups than among some immigrants.

7. *Don't demand anything because of your race, ethnicity, or sex.* You have the right not to be discriminated against because of these factors, and it follows that you also cannot demand discrimination in your favor. The sooner you can stop thinking of yourself first as a member of a particular demographic subset, and instead as a human being and an American, the better. This is true for both individuals and groups. The demagogues of identity politics promise nothing worthwhile.

8. *Working hard – in school and on the job – and saving money are not "acting white."* And, for whites, it is not being a nerd or a dweeb. America owes her success to a strong work ethic and to parents instilling that ethic in their children.

9. *Don't hold historical grudges.* There is not a single group in the United States that has not been discriminated against at one time or another. But we are all in the same boat now, and we have to live and work together. Your great-great grandfather may have tried to kill or enslave mine, but we are a forward-looking country and so we cannot afford to dwell on the past.

10. *Be proud of being an American.* You can hardly expect to be liked and accepted by other Americans if you don't love America. This is not a perfect country, and it does not have a perfect history. And there are lots of other countries that have good qualities. But there is no country better than the United States. If you disagree, then why are you here? Be a patriot.

One British expert, Lord Tebbitt, has suggested that successful assimilation can be measured by simply asking whether the new arrival roots for the British cricket team over all others. Conversely, many Americans were understandably angry in 1998 when large numbers of Mexican Americans turned out in Los Angeles to cheer for Mexico and jeer America at a soccer game.

How the Top Ten Are Intertwined

Think about it: If each ethnic group were to adopt these ten tenets, would high immigration levels be a problem, and would any racial or ethnic group – recently immigrated or not – be shunned?

Some of the ten items are closely related to one another. Indeed, four of them – regarding nondisparagement, not demanding preferences, respecting women, and not harboring historical grudges – all have to do with fully accepting one another as equally American. Two have to do with basic civility and communication, namely speaking English and being polite. Three are, among other things, simply good advice for success: working and studying hard, not getting in trouble with the law, and not having children before marriage (learning English can be put in this category, too). One commenter said that most of the rules were all about "getting along and getting ahead." Pride in being an American – being patriotic – perhaps belongs in a category of its own.

Another way to think about this issue – of objectionable versus unobjectionable immigrant customs – is to ask, In what respects have immigrants enriched American life, and in what respects have they not done so – or actually diminished it?

Certainly with respect to food, music, and dancing – for instance – immigrants have made American life richer. They have added particular words to our vocabulary. But in terms of politics, family structure, and economic organization, successful immigrants have been adapters rather than changers; the immigrants who have succeeded most and added most to American society have not been violent radicals, nor rejected conventional family structure, nor resisted capitalism. They have not brought Old World bigotries and conflicts with them, or insisted on special favors. They have been willing to become Americans and love America.

There is, perhaps, a categorical imperative here: Ask how an immigrant attitude or practice would affect the country if all Americans embraced it. If it wouldn't matter – eating empanadas – fine. If it would – refusing to accept the American capitalist ethos – then we have a problem.

Assimilation Helps Everyone

Although there is debate among scholars of immigration, interest groups, and some immigrants about the desirability of assimilation, we believe that immigrant assimilation should still be a national goal. All evidence indicates, first, that assimilation contributes to the success of immigrants in the U.S. and, second, that public support and acceptance of immigration is intimately tied to perceptions of immigrant assimilation. Only by encouraging assimilation among its immigrants can America maintain its proud history of welcoming immigrants from around the world.

Nor need a pro-assimilation policy be unpopular, with immigrants or nonimmigrants. Consider the issue of learning English. "Now That I'm Here: What America's Immigrants Have to Say about Life in the U.S. Today" reports the results of a survey taken by Public Agenda for the Carnegie Corporation of New York. Among the most striking findings of this study was that immigrants overwhelmingly believe it is their obligation to learn English. To be sure, there are major differences among immigrant groups, with 82 percent of European immigrants agreeing with the statement "The U.S. should expect all immigrants who don't speak English to learn it," while only 54 percent of Mexicans agreed with the statement and 43 percent said it "Should be left up to each individual" to decide. Still, even more than other Americans, immigrants in the survey also overwhelmingly endorsed teaching English immediately when children enter public schools, "even if this means they fall behind [in other subjects]," with some 73 percent of immigrants agreeing, compared to 67 percent of public school parents in general.

The events of September 11 vindicate the importance a pro-assimilation approach in every respect. First, our government must not encourage us to identify as members of racial and ethnic groups rather than as simply Americans. Second, it is essential that Congress embrace an immigration policy that serves the national interest. And, third, our society should encourage the assimilation of those who would live in America and claim its great privileges and boundless opportunities.

A Paradox?

There is an obvious paradox here. How can we have a policy of assimilation to American values when among the principal American values are individualism and freedom? Can we require adherence to a set of values, consistent with our notions of liberty?

The question is a fair one, but the answer is yes. The paradox is resolved in three ways.

Requiring people to learn about a culture cannot be called anti-freedom when ignorance of that culture itself threatens liberty. Robert Bork has remarked that the First Amendment's protection of the marketplace of ideas does not protect those who would destroy that very marketplace. It would be even odder, in any event, to refuse to transmit an appreciation of a love of freedom, when that transmission is essential for freedom's preservation, on the grounds that it is a threat to liberty.

Second, teaching American values need not be coercive or oppressive. There is a continuum in the manner that something is taught, with greater and lesser ratios of the descriptive to the normative, and less or more demand for acceptance of what is being taught at the end of the lesson. Hearing an explanation of American history and values is not the same thing as being forced to embrace some narrow ideology at gunpoint. Nor, indeed, is it likely to be necessary to force acceptance of American values once they have been explained: The product sells itself. In most instances, the only way that it won't be accepted is if it isn't taught. The immigrant audience, after all, *wants* to be in America – they came here for a reason.

Third, the assimilation process is not solely or even primarily an official, governmental one. There is, as discussed elsewhere, a great deal that is done by the little platoons. That, too, renders the process less coercive and lessens the tension with principles of freedom, individualism, and choice. This is not to say that private actors cannot be bullies, but social pressures do raise fewer libertarian concerns. Indeed, to prohibit such pressures would itself be an infringement of liberty.

How to Improve Assimilation: Some Fundamental Steps

If the ten values listed earlier ought to be accepted not only by immigrants but by all Americans, then how do we go about inculcating them?

For immigrants, naturalization should focus on assimilation or – as John J. Miller puts it in his 1998 book *The Unmaking of Americans: How Multiculturalism Has Undermined America's Assimilation Ethic,* and as many others used to put it – Americanization. When the reorganization of its Immigration and Naturalization Service was being discussed, the Justice Department suggested it would create a new "Bureau of Immigration Services" that would be aimed at improved "service" to its "customers" – i.e., immigrants. But as John Fonte of the Hudson Institute and Miller have pointed out, this is the wrong approach. It should be a "Bureau of Americanization," and it should be focused on creating citizens, not serving customers.[54] For the same reason, we should also make the naturalization process more rigorous. The standards in the past have been too often dumbed down and nonuniformly applied from region to region.

There is a step even prior to that, however. We should encourage those who plan to make America their home to become full-fledged citizens in the first place. For instance, it is ridiculous that citizens and noncitizens – even illegal aliens – receive equal weight in congressional reapportionment schemes.

Perhaps the most crucial part of the assimilation process – in naturalization, but also before and after, and even for some people whose families have been here for some time – is learning English. We simply have to be able to communicate with one another, and that means a common language, and that means English. So-called bilingual education – that is, teaching English to non-English speakers only slowly, in segregated classrooms, for only an hour or two a day – has proved to be nonlingual: Students never learn English, and their Spanish isn't so hot either.

That's why California, Arizona, and Massachusetts were so right to ban such programs in favor of English immersion. The importance of English fluency as a common civic bond also makes it outrageous that the federal government requires ballots to be presented in languages other than English in many neighborhoods. [link: http://article .nationalreview.com/?q=YTIzYTljNTgoMWEwMDA2ZjEzMjAwYz BkYTYxNGMxOWE=] Over six years into the Bush administration, it still remains to be seen whether its appointees will end the Education Department's coercion of school districts into adopting bilingual education, as well as the Equal Employment Opportunity Commission's war on companies that, for perfectly legitimate reasons, want employees to speak English when they're on the job. [link: http://alexander.senate .gov/index.cfm?FuseAction=PressReleases.Detail&PressRelease_id =1166&Month=5&Year=2007]

What the Government Should Not *Do*

One thing the government should do, if it does nothing else, is . . . no harm. But unfortunately the government now does a great deal to discourage assimilation.

Instead of creating incentives for immigrants to speak English, the government is instead removing them. The bilingual education and bilingual ballot policies discussed above are not the only problems: President Clinton signed Executive Order 13,166, requiring federal agencies and private entities receiving federal money to make their programs available in languages other than English – and President Bush has left it in place. This executive order is not only bad policy; it is also illegal, since it exceeds the president's statutory authority under Title VI of the 1964 Civil Rights Act; I discuss my objections to the executive order at greater length in a letter that I sent to the Justice Department early in the Bush administration, and which I include as an appendix to my testimony today. (A similar problem is the insistence of the Equal Employment Opportunity Commission on suing employers who make various English-language requirements of employees; my understanding is that

legislation is being prepared in the Senate to stop the EEOC from bringing such wrongheaded claims.)

Likewise, instead of encouraging immigrants – and everyone else –
to think of themselves as Americans first and to pay little attention to
where they or their neighbors came from, many government policies
encourage ethnic-consciousness and identity politics. Racial and ethnic
preferences in employment, contracting, and university admissions are
the most obvious example (I have suggested that immigration reform
explicitly provide that immigrants not be discriminated against *nor
given preference* on account of race, color, or national origin: http://
article.nationalreview.com/?q=NzQxZTc4NjkzMGFmMmQwMDI5
OWU5MDg0ZDM5OWMxNTk=]; federal voting law also requires
"affirmative action" in the form of racial and ethnic gerrymandering,
to guarantee racially and ethnically identifiable voting districts. Public
schools at the primary and secondary level, as well as public universities,
have embraced "multiculturalism," which emphasizes the differences
among Americans instead of what they have in common.

But we return as we must to the government program that manages
both to discourage English acquisition and to encourage ethnic sepa-
ratism: bilingual education. There is overwhelming empirical evidence
that this is an inferior way to teach English to schoolchildren, but it is
stubbornly defended. The real reason for this defense is not pedagogical
but ideological and political: It is multiculturalism on steroids, whereby
students are physically separated on the basis of national origin and then
given a different, ethnocentric curriculum.

Bad Government, Timid Politicians, Poisonous Elites

I hope by now that I've made it clear to the subcommittee that, when it
comes to assimilation, the federal government is not just failing to help
matters, it is frequently making them worse. Those of us who oppose one
government program or another are often cautioned by political experts
that it is not enough to be against something – one must also be in favor
of something. I always hate that: As Ward Connerly has asked, when a
doctor says he wants to remove your cancer, do you demand to know
what he's going to replace it with?

Thus, much of the preferred agenda in this area, at least in terms of government programs, is negative. That is, we would be satisfied in large part if the government stopped doing things to hinder assimilation, because it would in general take place naturally if the government played no worse than a neutral role.

We cannot pass a law that bans people from having children out of wedlock. But we were right to begin removing some of the incentives for doing so that existed pre-welfare reform. It also makes sense to remove other incentives for not working, and to keep in place disincentives for not working, whether it's in the workplace or the schoolroom. John McWhorter has argued persuasively that the progress of African Americans is retarded by affirmative action – "There is no such thing as a human being doing their very best when they are told they only have to do pretty darn well" – as well as by the sixties-originating mind-set that sees studying hard as "acting white."

We have plenty of laws on the books that prohibit racial and ethnic discrimination and harassment; unfortunately, we also have plenty of government actors that award preferences – in employment, college admissions, government contracting, and political districting – on the basis of race and ethnicity. In doing so, they send and reinforce the message that people ought to think of themselves in racial and ethnic terms, rather than simply as Americans. And they create a resentment that further divides us from one another.

Assimilation is accomplished not just through the law, of course. It is also a product of social pressures and, in particular, the attitudes of elites. And herein, of course, lies much of the rub in 2007. Once upon a time, the politicians and intellectuals believed in America enough to believe in assimilation; now they don't.

Linda Chavez wrote many years ago in *Out of the Barrio: Toward a New Politics of Hispanic Assimilation*, "Assimilation has become a dirty word in American politics," and Michael Barone concluded in his 2001 book *The New Americans: How the Melting Pot Can Work Again*, "The greatest obstacle to the interweaving of blacks, Latinos, and Asians into the fabric of American life is not so much the immigrants themselves or the great masses of the American people; it is the American elite."

Until very recently, neither major party was willing to talk about assimilation, for fear of being thought anti-immigrant or racist. And the academy seems to think multiculturalism is just a fine idea. Recently a number of studies have been published showing that some minority groups – especially blacks and, to a lesser extent, Hispanics – make up a disproportionate number of prison inmates. The instinct of the grievance elite has been to attack the police and laws as therefore biased. But this instinct is not only misguided; it reflects and encourages a rejection of civic solidarity between minorities and nonminorities.

Positive Steps: What Should Be Done

In addition to doing no harm, there are positive things the government can do. But it is important to bear in mind that other institutions besides the government have important roles in the assimilation process.

At the outset, it should be noted that there is a new Office of Citizenship in the U.S. Department of Homeland Security that recently published *Welcome to the United States: A Guide for New Immigrants* and held a conference in September 2004 on "Building a Common Civic Identity: A Symposium on the Civic Integration of Immigrants" ("civic integration" is the office's preferred phrase for "assimilation"). This new office is the logical place in the government for thought and action on improving our assimilation policies, and it is off to a promising start; likewise, and also to its credit, the administration has convened an "Assimilation Task Force."

The most straightforward task in assimilation is teaching immigrants to speak English. For children, this is done mostly by schools, but it is important not to neglect adults. Both the government (at the federal, state, and local levels) and private entities (companies, unions, churches, and so forth) can offer adult English-acquisition programs. Senator Lamar Alexander's "Strengthening American Citizenship Act" (S. 1393), which passed the Senate 91–1 in April 2006, provides education grants for English courses to legal immigrants intending to become American citizens and allows citizen applicants who speak fluent English to meet the residency requirement after four years of living in the U.S. instead of five; this year he has suggested a tax credit to companies who pay for employees to learn English and that English language proficiency be a requirement of green-card renewal (currently after 10 years). (S. 1393, by the way, includes many other good ideas for encouraging assimilation: providing grants to organizations that provide civics, history, and English courses, codifying the oath of allegiance, celebrating accomplishments by new citizens, and so forth. Likewise, Senator Alexander's suggestions this year are also valuable: for example, a GAO study on English acquisition, and presidential awards recognizing company efforts to improve assimilation. Newt Gingrich has proposed a National Program for English Instruction that is modeled after the "Ulpan Studies" program in Israel; this program would provide highly intensive English, American history, and civics instruction; successful participants would receive a stipend and have their naturalization periods shortened.)

And the government's role goes role goes much beyond simply ensuring that immigrants learn English. The naturalization process is, after all, about creating citizens, not simply residents who can speak a new language. John Fonte has written: "The citizenship naturalization process should be a life-altering experience, a rite of passage, such as a wedding, graduation, first communion, or bar mitzvah, which fosters emotional attachment to our nation and strengthens patriotism." It would make perfect sense (as many in an out of the government have suggested, and as the government is apparently now undertaking) to revamp the citizenship test that immigrants must take so that it more serious and less trivial – and, concurrently, to improve the classes that prepare immigrants for it and that teach them (or ought to teach them) American history and ideals. My son suggested that part of the process include a mandatory viewing of *Saving Private Ryan*. That's not a bad idea, and there may be better and additional movies – and books and songs – too. U.S. Citizenship and Immigration Services recently published *The Citizen's Almanac,* an anthology of patriotic anthems and symbols, speeches, founding documents, excerpts from landmark Supreme Court decisions – and a list of prominent foreign-born Americans. (Likewise, our public schools should teach an unabashedly pro-American version of U.S. history and civics, rather than the anti-American multiculturalism described earlier.)

As John Fonte pointed out in testimony before the House Judiciary Committee in 2002, current law requires the Attorney General to examine applicants for American citizenship to ensure, among other things, their "good moral character" and "understanding of and attachment to the fundamental principles of the Constitution of the Unites States," as well as their "ability to read, write and speak English."[55] Fonte stresses the importance of the word *attachment* to our constitutional principles – not just "understanding" them – and, later, the statute's discussion of "citizenship responsibilities." An oath is also set out by the statute, Fonte points out, and it requires that the new citizen "absolutely and entirely renounce" all "allegiance and fidelity" to any foreign state. (Taking this seriously, by the way, would require an end to dual citizenship.) Instead, the applicant must swear to "support and defend the Constitution and laws of the United States against all enemies, foreign and domestic" and to "bear arms on behalf of the United States when required by law."

Nor is there any reason why the citizenship process should stop with the administration of the oath, or be limited to those in naturalization classes. Follow-up programs would make sense, as would, for instance, public service advertisements. The former should be voluntary – citizenship is not probationary – and should be open to citizens and noncitizens alike; the idea is simply to provide resources and encouragement for those who are adapting to a new culture. The latter should likewise both provide information and send a positive message about the wonderful opportunities – large and small, exalted and quotidian – available in this great country. It's also easy to envision an ad for each of the ten essentials of assimilation listed earlier. It is likewise easy to envision an hour or half-hour class or video on each of the ten essentials. If the classes were not run or the videos not produced by the government, private actors could just as easily undertake them.

An important part of assimilation is simply learning what America has to offer. The government can teach this itself, or offer incentives to private entities that do so.

Consider just two possibilities: a tour of local historical and otherwise noteworthy sites, and a workshop for living in America. The former would include not just battlefields, old buildings, and the like, but public parks and libraries, the local sports complex, other ethnic neighborhoods – anything that would be interesting, enriching, and useful for an immigrant to know about. The latter would teach how to open a bank account, how public schools operate, what to do if your car won't start, how an emergency room works, how one chooses a college, and so forth.

Our politicians, military, intelligentsia, popular culture, and myriad "little platoons" (churches, unions, civic associations, etc.) also each have a role to play. Some are doing a good job now; others aren't. Our politicians should stop giving speeches in Spanish; we have few complaints about the military and nothing but complaints about the intelligentsia; the popular culture immerses everyone and provides a common denominator, albeit a very low one; and the little platoons are, as one would expect, an uneven lot, with some in some places helping much, and others in other places hurting even more, or doing nothing.

As discussed earlier, the government might offer economic incentives – tax credits, for instance, or favorable contracting terms – to companies or other private entities that offer assimilation programs. The most obvious such program would be English instruction, but there are others: outings to sporting events and national parks, for instance, or advice on housing and shopping – even special company picnics.

In the category of things that the government is doing now that are harmful but, if done correctly, could play an important positive role is: textbook selection. American history should not be sanitized, but neither should America be demonized. Too many textbooks are unremitting in an anti-American message that paints our history as nothing but racism, sexism, imperialism, and oppression. That is neither fair nor accurate, and it drives Americans apart rather than uniting them in patriotic pride.

Bienvenido a los Estados Unidos

For immigrants to become good Americans, they have to like America, which means liking Americans. And that means that the Americans already here must be welcoming toward the new arrivals.

There is a balance to be struck here. On the one hand, there should be social pressure to Americanize, certainly on the big things. Impatience at a lack of English fluency, and a raised eyebrow when languages other the English are spoken in public, are not a bad thing, for they express an expectation that English, the common currency of communication in this country, will be mastered. On the other hand, if immigrants sense they are unwelcome and disliked, it will be more difficult for them to become America-loving patriots than if they are met with smiles and support, even as they struggle to learn their new country's customs and ways, including its language. Every American should learn one Spanish phrase: *Bienvenido a los Estados Unidos* – Welcome to the United States.

In this regard, however, others have made the point that you don't get somebody to like you by doing them a favor, since that seems patronizing, but instead by asking that person to do *you* a favor. Part of assimilation includes learning a willingness to give something back to the American community that you have joined. Indeed, on one occasion when I was discussing the "Ten Requirements for Assimilation" list, a person in the audience suggested that doing some volunteer public service is important enough that it ought to be added as item number eleven. He has a point, and perhaps some community service ought to be an element of the naturalization program.

Note that the assimilation process is not just for immigrants, but also for their children and even their grandchildren. Indeed, in many respects all Americans – even those who have been here for generations – can stand substantial improvement with regard to one or more of the ten factors listed earlier. Some problems with immigrant assimilation are, really, that they are assimilating all too well, but to the wrong values or the wrong part of our culture. The inner city – with its high levels of crime, illegitimacy, and substance abuse, and lackluster academic and workplace performance – corrupts our immigrants, rather than vice versa.

Proud to Be an American

The last item on our list – pride in being an American – is much more critical now than when I first compiled the list in 2000. In obvious ways, wartime can dim the prospects for assimilation – but it can also strengthen them.

Patriotism is essential to bringing Americans of different races and ethnicities together. It is a neglected ingredient – even a secret weapon – in the continuing improvement of race relations in this country. Patriotism is important both for what it says to whites and nonimmigrants and for what it says to minorities and immigrants.

As to the former, patriotism requires adherence to the American creed, and an essential part of that is embracing one's fellow Americans, whatever their skin color or ancestry. Bigotry is un-American.

According to Gene Autry's ten-point "Cowboy Code," written in 1939 [link: http://www.geneautry.com/geneautry/geneautry_cowboycode .html], not only must "The Cowboy never shoot first, hit a smaller man, or take unfair advantage" (requirement #1), but "He must not advocate or possess racially or religiously intolerant ideas" (requirement #5). Requirement #10, by the way, is "The Cowboy is a patriot."

Recall the old war movies with a multiethnic roll call: Adams, Berkowitz, Callahan, Dubinski. . . . The point was, is, that we were, are, all on the same team. In *An American Dilemma*, Gunnar Myrdal concluded that, in the long run, America's founding ideals and the better angels of our nature would spell the doom of Jim Crow, and he was right.

We really are a nation of immigrants, and if someone comes here and learns our rules and plays by them, the bargain is that those already here must accept him as a brother, whatever his color, creed, or ancestry.

Theodore Roosevelt wrote:

> . . . [If] the immigrant who comes here in good faith becomes an American and assimilates himself to us, he shall be treated on an exact equality with everyone else, for it is an outrage to discriminate against any such man because of creed, or birthplace, or origin. But this is predicated upon the man's becoming an American, and nothing but an American. There can be no divided allegiance here. We have room for but one soul [sic] loyalty and that is loyalty to the American people.[56]

Thus, patriotism also requires everyone to embrace America – its ideals, history, and culture. That is the other side of the bargain. To be accepted, one must assimilate.

Assimilation doesn't mean you must forget your ancestors and your roots, eat nothing but hamburgers, listen only to country music, and give up polkas or tangos for square dancing. But English must become your and, especially, your children's primary language, the Fourth of July must be celebrated more loudly than Bastille Day or Cinco de Mayo, and you must bury your historical grudges against the foreign or domestic ancestors of your fellow Americans. You must work hard, follow the law, and join the bourgeoisie. All this, again, applies to native-born Americans as much as immigrants.

Consider this analogy: You find yourself living in an apartment building with many other tenants, some of whom are proud, long-time residents and some of whom are newly arrived like you. What is the likely reaction of the long-time residents if you never miss an opportunity to tell them what a lousy apartment building they have and what a lousy job they have done over the years in maintaining it? Remember: It's your home now, too. It's all right to make suggestions for how better to fix up the place now, but the present should be the focus rather than criticisms of the past.

Yet patriotism and assimilation are maligned today by the intelligentsia and, especially, the self-appointed spokesmen for racial and ethnic minorities in the grievance elite. By denigrating America, laughing at patriotism, and encouraging identity politics, these elites are ensuring balkanization and mistrust. America is multiracial and multiethnic, it is pluralistic, but it is not multicultural. *E pluribus unum:* out of many, one.

Patriotism and assimilation ought not to be dirty words, least of all for racial and ethnic minorities. To the contrary: Pride in being an American, and love for America and among Americans, is the best immigration and civil rights policy we could have.

Conclusion

In my testimony, I have mentioned a number of things that Congress should and shouldn't do to encourage rather than discourage successful assimilation. In conclusion, let me just emphasize some of the most important, which could be included in the immigration legislation you are now debating. First, you should declare English to be the official language of the United States, make clear that federal law does not require foreign languages to be used, and create incentives for the provision of English instruction. Second, you should make clear that no immigrant be discriminated against or given a preference on account of his or her race, color, or national origin. Third, greater civic literacy should be encouraged, both in the naturalization process and, again, in instruction provided by public and private entities besides the federal government.

NOTES

This chapter draws in part from testimony given by Roger Clegg and Linda Chavez to Congress on November 8, 2005, and May 4, 2006, and also on an article they co-wrote: *An Analysis of the Reauthorized Sections 5 and 203 of the Voting Rights Act of 1965: Bad Policy and Unconstitutional*, 5 Geo. J.L. & Pub. Pol'y 561 (2007).

Roger Clegg is president and general counsel of the Center for Equal Opportunity, located in Falls Church, Virginia. J.D. Yale, 1981, B.A. Rice, 1977. With special thanks for the assistance of Andrew Harrod; Allison Heiser; Kelsey Brudvig; and Sarah Aronhime, B.A. Christendom College, 2002, J.D. Brandeis School of Law, 2008.

1. See Pub. L. No. 109-246, § 7, 120 Stat. 577.

2. 42 USCS § 1973aa–1a (Aug. 6, 1965, Pub. L. No. 89-110, Title II, § 203, as added Aug. 6, 1975, Pub. L. No. 94-73, Title III, § 301, 89 Stat. 402; June 29, 1982, Pub. L. No. 97-205, §§ 2(d), 4 in part, 96 Stat. 134; Aug. 26, 1992, Pub. L. No. 102-344, § 2, 106 Stat. 921; July 27, 2006, Pub. L. No. 109-246, §§ 7, 8, 120 Stat. 581).

3. Compare HR 9, 109th Cong. (2006) (as reported by H. Comm. on the Judiciary) with Fannie Lou Hamer, Rosa Parks, and Coretta Scott King Voting Rights Act Reauthorization and Amendments Act of 2006, Pub. L. No. 109-246, 120 Stat. 577 (2006).

4. Jorge Ruiz-De-Velasco and Michael Fix, "Overlooked & Underserved: Immigrant Students in U.S. Secondary Schools" (2000), 2, available at http://www.urban institute.org/pdfs/overlooked.pdf ("Census data reveal that between 1980 and 1995, the share of immigrant children from homes where Spanish was spoken rose by 64 percent from 3.4 million to 5.6 million").

5. Voting Rights Act, 42 USCS 1973aa–1a (LexisNexis 2006).

6. See Roger Clegg, "Revise Before Reauthorizing: The Voting Rights Act @

40," National Review Online, August 4, 2005, http://www.nationalreview.com/ clegg/clegg200508040826.asp.

7. Stuart Taylor, Jr., "More Racial Gerrymanders," *National Journal*, May 16, 2006; "Incumbent Rights Act," *Wall Street Journal*, June 12, 2006.

8. Voting Rights Act, 42 USCS 1973aa–1a (LexisNexis 2006). For the most comprehensive criticism of Section 203 presented to Congress, see the testimony of Linda Chavez, chairman of the Center for Equal Opportunity, before the House Judiciary Committee's Subcommittee on the Constitution. *Voting Rights Act: Section 203–Bilingual Election Requirements (Part I)*, 109th Cong. 22–33 (2005). See also id. at 1339 (testimony of Jim Boulet, Jr., of English First); id. *(Part II)* at 63 (testimony of K. C. McAlpin of ProEnglish).

9. 42 USCS § 1973aa–1a.

10. Id. § 1973aa–1a(b)(2)(A)(i).

11. Id. § 1973aa–1a(e).

12. Id. § 1973aa–1a(c).

13. Id. § 1973aa–1a(a).

14. See Jose Enrique Idler, "En Ingles, Por Favor," National Review Online, March 8, 2006, http://www.nationalreview.com/ comment/idler200603080757.asp.

15. See John J. Miller, *The Unmaking of Americans: How Multiculturalism Has Undermined America's Assimilation Ethic* (New York: Simon & Schuster, 1998), 133.

16. Criminal Division, Public Integrity Section, U.S. Dept. of Justice, Election Fraud Prosecution and Convictions, Ballot Access & Voting Integrity Initiative, Oct. 2002–Sept. 2005, available at http:// cha.house.gov/media/pdfs/DOJdoc.pdf.

17. Linda Chavez, *Out of the Barrio: Toward a New Politics of Hispanic Assimilation* (New York: Basic Books, 1992), 133.

18. See Doug Bandow, "Lopez Losing," *American Spectator*, October 28, 2005 (Nativo Lopez's Hermandad Mexicana

Nacional "registered 364 non-citizens to vote in the 1996 congressional race in which Democrat Loretta Sanchez defeated incumbent Republican Bob Dornan."); Michael Kiefer and Elvia Diaz, "10 Charged with Fraud in Registering to Vote – All Legal Residents But Not Citizens," *Arizona Republic,* August 12, 2005, B1; Associated Press, "14 Illegal Aliens Reportedly Voted," KSL Newsradio 1160, August 8, 2005; Lisa Riley Roche, "Senators Target License Abuses," *Deseret Morning News,* February 10, 2005; Joe Stinebaker, "Loophole Lets Foreigners Illegally Vote," *Houston Chronicle,* January 16, 2005, B1; Associated Press, "Harris County Cracking Down on Voting by Non-U.S. Citizens," *Houston Chronicle,* January 16, 2005; Teresa Borden, "Scheme To Get Noncitizens on Rolls Alleged," *Atlanta Journal-Constitution,* October 28, 2004; Audrey Hudson, "Ineligible Voters May Have Cast a Number of Florida Ballots," *Washington Times,* November 29, 2000, A12 ("A sizable number of Florida votes may have been cast by ineligible felons, illegal immigrants and noncitizens, according to election observers. . . . This would not be the first time votes by illegal immigrants became an issue after Election Day. Former Republican Rep. Robert K. Dornan of California was defeated by Democrat Loretta Sanchez by 984 votes in the 1996 election. State officials found that at least 300 votes were cast illegally by noncitizens."); John Fund, "Phantom Voters: Ballot-box Fraud May Have Real Impact at the Polls," *Wall Street Journal,* October 23, 2000 (voter fraud a growing problem since "47 states don't require any proof of U.S. residence for enrollment."); Ishikawa Scott, "The Illegal Voters," *Honolulu Advertiser,* September 9, 2000, 1A; Kevin Dayton, "City Steps Up Search for Illegal Voters," *Honolulu Advertiser,* September 8, 2000, 1A.

19. Available at http://www.heritage.org/Research/LegalIssues/lm28.cfm. See also Hans von Spakovsky, "Why Is Obama Letting Non-Citizens Get Away with Voting?," Aug. 27, 2010 (article in *The Foundry: Conservative Policy News,* available at http://blog.heritage.org/2010/08/27/why-is-obama-letting-non-citizens-get-away-with-voting/); and statement of Colorado secretary of state Scott Gessler before the Committee on House Administration, U.S. House of Representatives, "The 2010 Election: A Look Back at What Went Right and Wrong" (March 31, 2011) (discussing noncitizen voting in Colorado), available at http://cha.house.gov/images/stories/documents/03312011gessler_testimony.pdf.

20. See, e.g., *Crawford v. Marion County Election Board,* 553 U.S. 181 (2008).

21. U.S. Gen. Accounting Office, Bilingual Voting Assistance: Assistance Provided and Costs, GAO/GGD-97-81, 20–21 (May 1997) [hereinafter GAO/GGD-97-81].

22. "30 States Have Bilingual Ballots," Associated Press, September 25, 2002.

23. See also John Miller, "English Is Broken Here," *Policy Review,* September–October 1996.

24. GAO/GGD-97-81, at 20–21.

25. See Miller, *The Unmaking of Americans,* 133; Amy Taxin, "o.c.'s Foreign-Language Ballots Might Be Lost in Translation: Phrasing Is Found to Differ by County, Leading to Multiple Interpretations and Possibly Confusion for Some Voters," *Orange County Register,* November 3, 2005; "Sample S.J. Ballot Contains Error: Spanish Translation Doesn't Make Sense," *Stockton Record,* February 27, 2003; Jim Boulet, "Bilingual Chaos," National Review Online, December 19, 2000; English First Foundation, "Bilingual Ballots: Election Fairness or Fraud?" (1997), English First Foundation Issue Brief, available at http://www.englishfirst.org/ballots/efbb.htm.

26. General Accounting Office, *Bilingual Voting Assistance: Costs of and Use During the November 1984 General Election,* GAO/GGD-86-134BR, September 1986, pp. 25, 32, 39.

27. See Miller, *The Unmaking of Americans*, 134.

28. See U.S. Commission on Civil Rights, DOJ Voting Rights Enforcement for the 2008 U.S. Presidential Election Briefing Report 26–27 (2009), available at http://www.usccr.gov/.

29. Miller, *The Unmaking of Americans*, 242–43.

30. Id. at 242.

31. See, e.g., U.S. Const. art. I, § 4, cl. 1; Michael J. Pitts, *Section 5 of the Voting Rights Act: A Once and Future Remedy?*, 81 Denv. U. L. Rev. 225, 265 (2003). I won't belabor the point that the framers were at some pains to ensure the proper allocation of powers between the federal and state governments, and while that allocation was obviously changed by the Civil War and the subsequent constitutional amendments (another point needless to belabor), it remains a central concern of the Constitution.

32. See 42 USCS § 1973c (2006).

33. For Section 5 as well as Section 203, the House of Representatives took the lead in the reauthorization process, establishing the record and holding the initial hearings to justify congressional action.

34. See *To Examine the Impact and Effectiveness of the Voting Rights Act: Hearing Before the Subcomm. on the Constitution of the H. Comm. on the Judiciary*, 109th Cong. 145 (2005).

35. S. Rep. No. 109-295, at 23–53 (2006) (Additional Views of Mr. Cornyn and Mr. Coburn).

36. See, e.g., *Fannie Lou Hamer, Rosa Parks, and Coretta Scott King Voting Rights Act Reauthorization and Amendments Act of 2006 (Part I): Hearing Before the Subcomm. on the Constitution of the H. Comm. on the Judiciary*, 109th Cong. (2006); *Voting Rights Act: Evidence of Continued Need: Hearing Before the Subcomm. on the Constitution of the H. Comm. on the Judiciary*, 109th Cong. (2006); *Voting Rights Act: Sections 6 and 8 – The Federal Examiner and Observer Program: Hearing Before the Subcomm. on the Constitution of the H. Comm. on the Judiciary*, 109th Cong. (2005); *Voting Rights Act: Section 5 of the Act – History, Scope, and Purpose: Hearing Before the Subcomm. on the Constitution of the H. Comm. on the Judiciary*, 109th Cong. (2005); *Voting Rights Act: The Continuing Need for Section 5: Hearing Before the Subcomm. on the Constitution of the H. Comm. on the Judiciary*, 109th Cong. (2005); *Voting Rights Act: An Examination of the Scope and Criteria for Coverage Under the Special Provisions of the Act: Hearing Before the Subcomm. on the Constitution of the H. Comm. on the Judiciary*, 109th Cong. (2005); *To Examine the Impact and Effectiveness of the Voting Rights Act: Hearing Before the Subcomm. on the Constitution of the H. Comm. on the Judiciary*, 109th Cong. (2005); *Voting Rights Act: Section 5 – Preclearance Standards: Hearing Before the Subcomm. on the Constitution of the H. Comm. on the Judiciary*, 109th Cong. (2005).

37. See, e.g., *Village of Arlington Heights v. Metro. Housing Development Corp.*, 429 U.S. 252, 264–65 (1977) ("Our decision last Term in *Washington v. Davis*, 426 U.S. 229 (1976), made it clear that official action will not be held unconstitutional solely because it results in a racially disproportionate impact.").

38. *Rogers v. Lodge*, 458 U.S. 613, 618 (1982); *City of Mobile v. Bolden*, 446 U.S. 55, 62–65 (1980) (plurality opinion) ("[The Fifteenth] Amendment prohibits only purposefully discriminatory denial or abridgment by government of the freedom to vote 'on account of race, color, or previous condition of servitude.'" (quoting the Fifteenth Amendment)).

39. *City of Boerne v. Flores*, 521 U.S. 507, 520 (1997).

40. See, e.g., *Bd. of Tr. of the Univ. of Ala. v. Garrett*, 531 U.S. 356 (2001).

41. *United States v. Lopez*, 514 U.S. 549, 552 (1995).

42. 129 S.Ct. 2504 (2009).

43. See, e.g., *City of Mobile v. Bolden,* 446 U.S. 55 (1980); *Washington v. Davis,* 426 U.S. 229 (1976); *Village of Arlington Heights v. Metro. Housing Development Corp.,* 429 U.S. 252 (1976).

44. *City of Boerne v. Flores,* 521 U.S. 507, 520 (1997); see also *United States v. Lopez,* 514 U.S. 549, 552 (1995). It is true that in the leading case *City of Boerne vs. Flores,* the Court explicitly distinguished the actions Congress had taken under the Voting Rights Act. On the other hand, however, in doing so it stressed Congress's careful findings, the act's limited duration, and its rifle-shot provisions. *Flores,* 521 U.S. at 532–33. And, of course, the Court's 2009 *Northwest Austin* decision (see footnote 42 *supra* and accompanying text) certainly did not treat the issue of the Voting Rights Act's continuing constitutionality as involving a simple application of *stare decisis.* Congress reauthorized Section 203 without ensuring its congruence and proportionality to the end of banning disparate treatment on the basis of race in voting, and the language in *Flores* could as easily be cited against the new statute's constitutionality as in its favor. Id. at 520 (holding that when Congress acts pursuant the Fourteenth Amendment, "[t]here must be a congruence and proportionality between the injury to be prevented or remedied and the means adopted to that end."). Likewise, the Court's decision in *Nevada Department of Human Resources v. Hibbs* – upholding Congress's abrogation of state immunity under the federal Family and Medical Leave Act – also stressed Congress's factual findings and the challenged statute's limited scope. *Nev. Dep't of Human Res. v. Hibbs,* 538 U.S. 721 (2003).

45. See, e.g., *Bd. of Tr. of the Univ. of Ala. v. Garrett,* 531 U.S. 356 (2001).

46. See Chavez, *Out of the Barrio,* 46; see also Abigail M. Thernstrom, *Whose Votes Count?: Affirmative Action and Minority Voting Rights* (Cambridge, Mass.: Harvard University Press, 1987), 57.

47. See discussion "Policy Objections to Section 203," *supra.*

48. 42 USCS § 1973aa–1a (LexisNexis 2006).

49. Chavez, *Out of the Barrio,* 39–59; *Hearing Before the Subcomm. On the Constitution of the H. Comm. On the Judiciary,* 109th Cong. (2005) (testimony of Linda Chavez, president, One Nation Indivisible). With regard to identity politics, by the way, note the irony here inasmuch as it is conservatives who have insisted most strongly that rapid English acquisition should be the paramount objective of public education for immigrants and their children; liberals, who have instead supported bilingual education as an element of identity politics, would now use the failure of public schools to teach English effectively as justification for requiring foreign-language ballots. See Chavez, *Out of the Barrio,* ch. 1.

50. Chavez, *Out of the Barrio,* 45–48; *Hearing Before the Subcomm. On the Constitution of the H. Comm. On the Judiciary,* 109th Cong. (2005) (testimony of Linda Chavez, president, One Nation Indivisible).

51. Chavez, *Out of the Barrio,* 47; Thernstrom, *Whose Votes Count?* ch. 3.

52. See Roger Clegg "The Future of the Voting Rights Act after *Bartlett* and *NAMUNDO,*" Cato Sup. Ct. Rev. 2008–2009, at 35.

53. See, e.g., *Crawford v. Marion County Election Bd.,* 472 F.3d 949 (7th Cir. 2001).

54. See http://www.nationalreview.com/nr_comment/nr_comment121801.shtml.

55. "Don't Forget about Citizenship When Overhauling the Federal Immigration Agency," quoting 8 USC 1443 (April 9, 2002).

56. Quoted in John Fonte, "How to Make an American," *American Enterprise,* September 2004.

PART THREE

Commentary

TEN

After NAMUDNO:
The Shape of Future Litigation

EDWARD BLUM

The most significant legal challenge in nearly three decades to Section 5 of the Voting Rights Act (VRA), *Northwest Austin Municipal Utility District Number One v. Holder*, 129 S.Ct. 2504 (2009) ("*NAMUDNO*"), was decided by the Supreme Court on June 22, 2009. In an 8-1 opinion, the justices overturned a lower court decision that had denied a small Travis County, Texas, suburban jurisdiction from seeking a "bailout" from the "preclearance" provision of the act. But it is what the justices did not do – strike down the act as unconstitutional – that matters most for the critics and defenders of this provision. Some have speculated that it is only a matter of time before the constitutional issue once again presents itself to the High Court, while others believe the issue has been dodged indefinitely. Who is right?

Some background on the case will be useful for understanding the court's opinion and what is likely to happen next. The 1965 Voting Rights Act was, as the Supreme Court recognized in this opinion, a "historic accomplishment" designed to end the official governmental barriers to voting that blacks faced in the Deep South by eliminating any type of literacy test, providing federal voting registrars, and criminalizing harassment of black voters. These objectives were enforced through two provisions: Section 4(b), which pinpointed the states and jurisdictions where black disenfranchisement was the most pernicious, and Section 5, the "preclearance" requirement, which was to end the never-ending gamesmanship by southern election officials that was used to prevent blacks from registering to vote.

Section 4(b) established the coverage formula for Section 5. In order to be swept into coverage by Section 4(b), a state or jurisdiction had to have two factors in place. The first was the use of a literacy test or other similar device as part of the jurisdiction's voter registration process. Although many jurisdictions throughout the country used literacy tests, southern registrars in particular used fraudulent ones specifically to keep blacks from registering to vote. Some required an applicant to interpret a complex section of the state's constitution, or read from a newspaper written in a foreign language; in any case, the results in most of the South were the same: blacks failed while whites passed. The second factor in determining which jurisdictions were covered were their voter registration rates as of November 1, 1964, and their election participation rates in the November 3, 1964, presidential election. Any state or political subdivision of a state in which fewer than 50 percent of persons of voting age were registered on November 1, 1964, or fewer than 50 percent of persons of voting age actually voted on November 3, 1964, were to be covered. In other words, if a jurisdiction used a literacy test and if registration or turnout was below 50 percent, then that jurisdiction or state was swept into coverage. Amendments to the act in 1970 and 1975 added new jurisdictions so that today Section 4(b) has resulted in all of nine states (mostly in the Deep South) and parts of seven others to be subject to Section 5.

Section 5 requires all of these targeted jurisdictions to seek approval from Washington before any new election procedures – such as redistricting or moving a polling place – can be made. No other statute in the legislative history of the nation has ever required a local jurisdiction to seek permission from the federal government before it can enact a law or procedure. Section 5 was wisely – but temporarily – put in place to prevent these recalcitrant southern jurisdictions from circumventing the new law to prevent blacks from participating in elections. It was originally scheduled to expire in 1970 but was extended to 1975, then again to 1982, when it was extended it to 2006. In 2006, Congress reauthorized it once again. It is now scheduled to expire in 2031, sixty-one years later than originally intended.

When the Texas utility district challenged the 2006 reauthorization, it asked the lower court to allow it to seek a bailout from these preclearance requirements, as a provision of the law allows; if it failed to achieve this exemption, it argued in the alternative the law was unconstitutional. A three-judge panel in the district court for the District of Columbia ruled against the district on both claims in 2008, finding that because the district did not register voters, it was not entitled to bailout. More significantly, it found that Congress had sufficient evidence of "second generation" racial discrimination in the states and jurisdictions covered by Section 5 to justify another twenty-five years of federal oversight, thus ensuring the act's constitutionality.

The Supreme Court disagreed – at least with one-half of the lower court's analysis. Writing for the Court, Chief Justice John Roberts noted, "Our usual practice is to avoid the unnecessary resolution of constitutional questions. We agree that the district is eligible under the Act to seek bailout. We therefore reverse, and do not reach the constitutionality of Section 5."

If, when, and how the justices will revisit the constitutionality of Section 5 is a matter of intense speculation among legal scholars. For many, such as Lyle Denniston writing for scotusblog.com, the opinion foretold of its impending doom: "The main opinion, in fact, provides what could easily be read as a roadmap for such a future constitutional complaint."[1] That judgment was echoed by Supreme Court advocate Tom Goldstein, who wrote, "If the statute remains the same by the time the next case arrives, the Court will invalidate the statute."[2] Yale Law's Heather Gerkin noted that the court "punted" but that "it's hard to read this decision and think that Section 5 is going to have an easy time for it the next time it is challenged in this Court."[3]

Yet there are skeptics such as Michael McDonald, a political scientist at George Mason University, who believe that the statute is so historically iconic that the High Court will continue to dodge the constitutionality question in the future: "In crafting this decision [allowing the jurisdiction to bail out rather than striking down the act], the Justices have effectively signaled that they will avoid ruling on future constitutional challenges."[4] In other words, McDonald and others believe that by opening up the bailout provision to approximately twelve thousand new jurisdictions covered by Section 5, the law is effectively immunized from constitutional review.

It may not be too long before this debate is resolved. There are three cases currently working through the federal courts in the District of Columbia that challenge these provisions: *Laroque v. Holder* (Civil Action No. 10-5433), *Shelby County, Ala. v. Holder* (Civil Action No. 10-0651), and *State of Arizona v. Holder* (Case No. 1:2011cv01559). If the Supreme Court eventually takes up one or all of these cases, most observers concur that the criticism at oral arguments in the *NAMUDNO* case by at least four justices suggests that the Court will find Sections 4(b) and 5 unconstitutional. Yet, even more important than the oral argument in *NAMUDNO*, eight justices agreed with Chief Justice Roberts's description of the state of the factual record and legal principles, and Justice Thomas, the lone dissenter, would have gone even further and struck the statute down immediately. Nevertheless, the Court's finding that all "political subdivisions" are eligible to file a bailout suit is problematic. Prior to oral argument and the Court's decision, this statutory argument was not considered likely to carry the day. That the Court adopted this argument may be taken as a suggestion that the Court wants to avoid deciding the constitutionality of Sections 4(b) and 5 where possible.

So how can a jurisdiction find a way to compel the High Court to address the constitutionality of Sections 4(b) and 5? There appears to be three litigation approaches to reaching the question of constitutionality.

GETTING TO THE CONSTITUTIONAL QUESTION

The Court's decision in *NAMUDNO* signaled that Section 5's bailout provision and Section 4(b)'s coverage formula should be "governed by a principle of symmetry"; i.e., if a unit of government is required to seek preclearance under Section 5, then it is eligible to seek bailout. And if a governmental unit is eligible for bailout, the Court appears unwilling to entertain a broader constitutional challenge to the statute. Even so, there are at least three potential plaintiffs that would be suitable for constitutional challenge: (1) a county, parish, or another larger political subdivision that encompasses other political subdivisions, one or more of which would not itself be eligible for bailout, which would make the county or parish ineligible for bailout; (2) a state or local political party;

and (3) a small political subdivision, such as a municipal utility district or newly incorporated city, that is less than ten years old, thereby making it facially unable to bail out. Each of these three potential actors for a constitutional challenge has strengths and weaknesses.

Who Gets to Bail Out?

The requirements for bailout are statutorily clear. Under Section 4(a), the first step in seeking bailout is to file a suit seeking a declaratory judgment in the U.S. District Court for the District of Columbia. In determining whether a covered jurisdiction is entitled to bail out of coverage, the district court must determine whether a number of factors have been satisfied for the ten years prior to the filing and during the pendency of the declaratory judgment action.

A consent decree cannot be issued unless:

· No test or device was used within the political subdivision for the purpose or with the effect of denying or abridging the right to vote on account of race, color, or language status;
· No final judgment of a court determining that denials or abridgements of right to vote on account of race, color, or language status has occurred "anywhere in the territory of" the state or political subdivision seeking bailout;
· No consent decree or settlement has been reached "in the territory of" the state or political subdivision seeking bailout that has resulted in the abandonment of voting practices challenged as a denial or abridgement of the right to vote on account of race, color, or language status;
· No federal examiners or observers have been assigned to the state or political subdivision seeking bailout;
· The state or political subdivision and "all governmental units within its territory" have followed Section 5's preclearance procedures and have repealed all changes to which the attorney general has objected or that have resulted in the denial of a preclearance declaratory judgment from the District Court for the District of Columbia;

· The attorney general has not objected to, and the District Court
  for the District of Columbia has not denied preclearance to, any
  submissions by the plaintiff "or any governmental unit within its
  territory";
· The state or political subdivision seeking bailout, as well as
  any government unit within its territory, has not engaged in
  violations of any provision of the Constitution or federal, state,
  or local law "with respect to discrimination in voting on account
  of race or color" or language status unless the jurisdiction can
  prove that violations were trivial or corrected immediately; and
· The state or political subdivision seeking bailout and "all
  governmental units within its territory" have (1) eliminated
  any voting procedures that inhibit or dilute equal access to the
  electoral process; (2) engaged in constructive efforts to eliminate
  intimidation and harassment of persons exercising their rights
  under the VRA; (3) engaged in other constructive efforts, such
  as expanding opportunity for convenient registration and the
  appointment of minority persons as election officials.
· A jurisdiction seeking bailout must provide detailed information
  on minority registration and voting and the disparities between
  minority and nonminority voting.

Avoiding the Bailout Cul-de-Sac: Three Hypothetical Plaintiffs –
A County, Parish, or Large Political Subdivision

A county or other larger political subdivision (such as a parish, township,
or other "political subdivision") with other governmental units within
its geographic territory is one potential party that could challenge the
constitutionality of Sections 4(b) and 5. A county in a covered state is
clearly subject to Section 5, so it would be entitled to file a bailout suit as
the law allows. But because many of the bailout criteria require that all
"governmental units" within the geographic expanse of the county also
meet the applicable criterion (regardless of whether the county can control that governmental unit's actions), even a county that has itself been
on its best behavior and has done everything it needs to do in order to

meet the bailout requirements will be stymied by a single governmental unit within its territory that had a preclearance submission denied or had not existed for the full ten-year period.

Thus, the ideal county to challenge the constitutionality of Sections 4(b) and 5 would be one that would itself meet the statutory bailout criteria but for the fact that a governmental unit, not under the county's control but within its territory, does not meet one or more of the bailout criteria. The plaintiff county would not be eligible for bailout on its face, but would not appear to be a "bad actor" under the statute. Shelby County, Alabama, the plaintiff in *Shelby Co. Ala. v. Holder,* fits this description because one of the towns within its borders failed to get preclearance from the attorney general for a series of land annexations in the late 1990s.

A county-sized government as plaintiff would have drawbacks, however. First, there is the risk that the suit could devolve into a question of whether it is proper for the county to be ineligible for bailout because of the actions of a governmental unit it cannot control; a court might be willing to find that the bailout provision is unconstitutional only to that extent and avoid dealing with the larger constitutional question. Second, a court may simply find that the statute could be read to allow a county to bail out regardless of the behavior of other governmental units within its territory, although such a holding would require an unnatural reading of the bailout provision. Third, there is the risk that there may be a fight over whether the governmental units within the county actually meet the bailout criteria themselves, and a court might be tempted to avoid the larger issues by finding that those governmental units have indeed met the criteria at issue.

Political Party

The Supreme Court's decision in *Morse v. Republican Party of Virginia,* 517 U.S. 186 (1996), established that Section 5 applies to political parties – at least under some circumstances. Morse was a splintered decision consisting of a two-justice opinion and a three-justice concurrence. Justice Stevens, writing for himself and Justice Ginsburg, found that

Section 5 applied to the Republican Party of Virginia's nominating convention practices because Virginia law guaranteed that the party's nominee would appear on the general election ballot, and consequently the party was exercising authority delegated by the state. The three-justice concurring opinion (Justices Breyer, O'Connor, and Souter) found that Court precedent had applied Section 5 to primaries and the political party's action in this instance was a substitute for a primary.

Because the Court has held that Section 5 applies to political party activities under certain circumstances, a political party is another potential plaintiff in a constitutional challenge to Section 5. A political party appears to be a promising plaintiff because, on the face of the bailout provision, it is not a "State" or a "political subdivision," which are the only entities that may file a bailout suit, and the lack of an ability to bring a bailout suit would help to avoid the bailout cul-de-sac. And because a political party, as a nongovernmental organization, does not contain any other governmental units, the scope and complexity of litigation would likely be less than would be required for a county or other large political subdivision.

Proceeding on this course, however, would involve many uncertainties. First, given the lack of a clear majority opinion in *Morse* and the failure of the lower courts to come to a consensus, the law is not settled regarding the circumstances under which political parties are actually covered by Section 5. It may very well be that they are only covered when they are exercising authority delegated by the state, which might tempt a court to say that the party is considered a "State" for bailout purposes since it is covered only to the extent that the state is covered. Such a result would appear to follow directly from the Court's statement in *NAMUDNO* that "[b]ailout and preclearance under Section 5 are governed by a principle of symmetry," as well as the fact that five justices did appear to find that a political party could be considered a "State or political subdivision" in *Morse*. The party would have a good argument, however, that it is not in fact entitled to seek bailout itself and that the state from which it received its delegated authority must seek bailout on its behalf, something that states have not expressed an interest in pursuing. If this argument were to win the day, or if a court were to find that the state is not itself eligible for bailout, the court could reach the substantive constitutional question. On the other hand, a court could decide that political parties, if covered by Sections 4(b) and 5, could seek bailout on their own in order to vindicate the symmetry principle in *NAMUDNO*. In the end, although there remains a risk of falling into the bailout cul-de-sac, proceeding with a political party as a plaintiff presents a good opportunity to obtain a decision on the merits of the constitutionality of these provisions.

"Young" Jurisdiction

Another potential Section 5 plaintiff would be a single political subdivision, like a municipal utility district or city, that has been in existence for less than ten years. Because several of the statutory criteria for bailout require a "clean record" for the ten years preceding the bailout suit, such a "young jurisdiction" would be precluded from obtaining bailout on the face of the statute. Since the young jurisdiction would, as a practical matter, be ineligible for bailout, a court is unlikely to direct it to seek bailout as a prerequisite to asserting a constitutional challenge, thus avoiding the bailout cul-de-sac.

The plaintiff could state up front that it is ineligible for bailout, and possibly seek a stipulation from the Department of Justice that this is the case. Given the mandatory nature of the language in the bailout statute, it would be difficult for the Court to read the bailout statute as permitting such a jurisdiction to bail out of coverage.

Even this strategy has risks, however. First, there is the risk that a court may find that the bailout regime is a permissible means of narrowing the reach of Section 5 and that ten years is a reasonable amount of time for a jurisdiction to wait before seeking bailout. Although this appears to be a very real possibility, there are counterarguments, including that even the burden of seeking bailout is impermissible where a jurisdiction has no history of Section 5 or constitutional violations. Also, a court might question whether the entity in which the young jurisdiction exists – e.g., a county – should be obligated to seek bailout before the young jurisdiction can attack Section 5 directly. But because it does not appear that a large jurisdiction can bail out the smaller jurisdiction within it, this does not seem to be a legitimate exhaustion requirement.

Moreover, because a large subdivision must show that its smaller units are compliant, it would seem that the young jurisdiction's inability to bail out would preclude bailout for the larger jurisdiction in which it exists as well.

In theory, a court could conclude that the "ten years" provision is not a de facto eligibility requirement and that it is only a yardstick against which compliance should be measured; a court reading the "ten years" in this manner might indicate that the "ten years" provision applies to a young jurisdiction in such a way that, in practice, it need only demonstrate its compliance for the time in which it existed. The counterargument would be that the practical result of such a reading is that all new jurisdictions are entitled to seek bailout from day one, and would thus obtain bailout immediately (no history means no history of noncompliance). This result would mean that no new jurisdictions would ever be covered by Section 5. It is unlikely a court would reach that result.

CONCLUSION

These three hypothetical plaintiffs are surely not the only ones that may surface during the next few years that have the potential to compel the Supreme Court to decide the constitutionality of Sections 4(b) and 5. Indeed, the plaintiffs in *Laroque v. Holder* argue that these provisions are unconstitutional. They are citizens of Kinston, North Carolina, who led a voter referendum to switch to a system of nonpartisan voting for city council members. Although the initiative passed by a wide margin, Attorney General Eric Holder denied preclearance under Section 5 because he believed the effects of nonpartisan elections would diminish the ability of black voters to elect their candidate of choice, even though Kinston is 64 percent African American. *Laroque* is currently on appeal after being dismissed for the lack of standing, but this case is far from settled.

Moreover, it has been suggested by a number of election law scholars that it is only necessary for the Supreme Court to find Section 4(b) unconstitutional for the entire preclearance mechanism to end. As Shelby County has argued in its briefs, while Section 5 may, in certain extreme circumstances, be a constitutional tool for safeguarding voting rights, the currently covered jurisdictions cannot be the same bad actors they were over forty years ago. As the Supreme Court noted in *NAMUDNO*, "[t]he evil that Section 5 is meant to address may no longer be concentrated in the jurisdictions singled out for preclearance. The statute's coverage formula is based on data that is now more than 35 years old, and there is considerable evidence that it fails to account of current political conditions."

Courts move slowly, so it may be 2012 or later before *Shelby Co., Laroque*, and *Arizona* are finally adjudicated. Until then, Sections 4(b) and 5, as they have since their initial passage in 1965, will remain controversial elements of our nation's election laws.

NOTES

1. Lyle Denniston, "Analysis: Is Section 5's Future Shaky?" SCOTUSblog.com. June 22, 2009, http://www.scotusblog.com/analysis-is-section-5s-future-shaky/.

2. Tom Goldstein, "Analysis: Supreme Court Invalidates Section 5's Coverage Scheme," SCOTUSblog, June 22, 2009, www.scotusblog.com/wp/analysis-supreme-court-invalidates'section-5-5%e2%80%99s-scheme-2.

3. Heather Gerken, "The Supreme Court Punts on Section 5," Balkinization, June 22, 2009, www.balkin.blogspot.com.

4. Michael McDonald, http://electionlawblog.org/archives/013943.html.

ELEVEN

Looking Backward to and Forward from the 2006 Voting Rights Act Reauthorization

DEBO P. ADEGBILE

In the America promised by our founders, every citizen is somebody, and every gen-eration has a responsibility to add its own chapter to the unfolding story of freedom. In the four decades since the Voting Rights Act was first passed, we've made progress toward equality, yet the work for a more perfect union is never ending.

PRESIDENT GEORGE BUSH, WHITE HOUSE STATEMENT
AT THE VOTING RIGHTS ACT REAUTHORIZATION
SIGNING CEREMONY, JULY 27, 2006

We shouldn't forget that better is not good enough.

SENATOR BARACK OBAMA, 42ND COMMEMORATION OF
BLOODY SUNDAY, SELMA, ALABAMA, MARCH 4, 2007

How much progress is enough?[1] Is voting discrimination tolerable in our democracy, and, when it occurs, how is it best remedied? As the chapters in this book make clear, these were the core questions that animated the 2006 reauthorization of key provisions of the Voting Rights Act of 1965 ("VRA") and that persist in its wake.[2] They are not small questions. The VRA is recognized not only as one of the most important civil rights laws ever passed, but also as one of the most important laws of any kind in the history of the United States. It is a rare statute, which merges our nation's past, present, and future; it bridges the cross-currents of the ugliest chapters of yesterday, today's challenges, and our aspirations for tomorrow. A survey of the history of the right to vote in America reveals just how difficult it has been to reach this stage in our progress. There was a period in which the Supreme Court severely undermined, if not essentially foreclosed, the possibility of voting equality.[3] For a long period Congress failed to confront flagrant and violent voting discrimination,[4] followed by belated responses that proved inadequate to meet the scale of the problem. Supported by a well-documented history of voting discrimination and enacted as a result of courageous resistance to entrenched discrimination, the Voting Rights Act drastically altered the pattern of exclusion. Although the act's special enforcement provisions have been extended four times, these provisions, which are central aspects of the VRA, continue to generate substantial debate, as the chapters in this book make clear.

Some ask why we still need a Voting Rights Act? The answer to this question lies in the rich and detailed sixteen-thousand-page legislative record that was before Congress prior to the 2006 re-enactment. The overwhelming congressional vote in support of reauthorization (98-0 in the Senate and 390-33 in the House of Representatives) reflected a consensus that the federal government needed to stay the course in its commitment to dislodge voting discrimination. The problems to which Congress addressed itself in the 2006 reauthorization are persistent and ongoing. Indeed, in a 2009 VRA case, the United States Supreme Court reaffirmed that "[m]uch remains to be done to ensure that citizens of all races have equal opportunity to share and participate in our democratic processes."[5] The Court recognized that the national effort to ensure voting equality and full voter inclusion, free from racial discrimination, is still evolving.

SECTION 5 PRECLEARANCE: THE
2006 REAUTHORIZATION

As Peyton McCrary's chapter explains (chapter 2), Section 5 of the VRA requires that covered jurisdictions – all or part of sixteen states with some of the most well-documented histories of voting discrimination – obtain federal approval (or "preclearance") from a three-judge federal court in the District of Columbia or administratively from the Department of Justice prior to implementing any voting-related changes. Re-

gardless of the venue in which preclearance is sought, the responsibility
of the jurisdiction seeking approval for voting changes is the same – it
must prove that the new rules do not worsen the position of minority
voters and that they are not intentionally discriminatory. In this way,
the preclearance provision operates as a democracy checkpoint of sorts
for covered jurisdictions, making equal and meaningful minority voter
access and political power achievable in many places where discrimination persists.

Prior to 2006, the Section 5 preclearance provision was last reauthorized in 1982 for a twenty-five-year period. The Congress that confronted the reauthorization of Section 5 in 2006 had passed few major
pieces of legislation and even fewer bipartisan pieces of legislation. Indeed, the 109th Congress was described at the time as "one of the most
partisan and polarized ever."[6] Set in that context, the VRA reauthorization stands out as particularly notable. In light of the unique bipartisan status of this congressional re-enactment, some have asserted that
the reauthorization was always certain. The serious legislative sticking
points along the way, however, tell a different story.[7] Some members
of Congress, commentators, and advocates hostile to the act wanted
to end the preclearance provision,[8] others sought to scale it back,[9] and
some even suggested expansion as a strategy, though doing so would
have weakened its viability.[10] These approaches were opposed by witnesses and members of Congress who recognized the continuing need
for preclearance.[11] Some of those witnesses sought to expand the act to
cure other forms of disenfranchisement.[12] Others underscored the necessity of restoring some of Section 5's vitality lost through the Supreme
Court's statutory interpretations following the 1982 reauthorization.[13]
Ultimately, the successful reauthorization of the preclearance provision, like that of the language-assistance provisions, was attributable to
the strong legislative record assembled by Congress, through the efforts
of the House Judiciary Committee and subcommittee leaders and membership,[14] and the experience inside and outside of Congress about the
"essentiality"[15] of Section 5 in ensuring progress and guarding against
backsliding.

A broader context shaped the legislative debate as well. By 2006, minority voters experienced significant gains with the aid of the VRA, and

some dramatic progress since the previous reauthorization in 1982. In the 1990s, African Americans were elected to Congress for the first time since the end of Reconstruction in five states covered in whole or in part by Section 5: Florida, Louisiana, North Carolina, South Carolina, and Virginia, as well as in rural Georgia, which had not elected an African American congressperson since 1890. By the time of the reauthorization, and in some cases before, voter registration and participation for African Americans and Latinos had risen dramatically.[16] The number of Latino elected officials in Arizona and Texas had risen from 232 and 1,466, respectively, in 1986,[17] to 369 and 2,075, respectively, by 2006.[18]

During the legislative reauthorization process Congress embraced that progress. Indeed, Congress acknowledged that much of the progress was attributable to the existence of the VRA itself.[19] Viewed through the lens of the long legislative and national experience with voting discrimination, Congress also heard testimony regarding ongoing and substantial voting discrimination and threats of retrenchment.[20] As noted voting historian Alexander Keyssar frames the subtitle of his engaging book, we have a "[c]ontested history of democracy in the United States."[21] Keyssar's point may seem counterintuitive when weighed against the "march-through-history" narrative marking the distance from slavery to the first elected African American president. It becomes less so, however, when we consider that racial justice in America has often been elusive, achieved gradually, and marked by both progress and retreat.[22] The expansions and contractions are part of this story. The VRA's preclearance provision operates to protect minority voters in the face of the historical tension and pattern. It tempers the power that threatens to trample minority voting rights.

THE CONGRESSIONAL RECORD
SUPPORTING REAUTHORIZATION

Some of the policy and legal analysis of the 2006 reauthorization of the preclearance provision described in the preceding chapters suggests a strong predisposition against its continuing necessity without regard to the record that Congress compiled demonstrating its ongoing importance. Arguably, one danger of a voluminous congressional record is that it becomes much easier to launch a theoretical and abstract critique of the Voting Rights Act's enforcement provisions than to take the time and effort to analyze the layered testimony, data, and reports that establish the substantial, empirical record.[23] The volume of the record, while noteworthy, is less important than the nature of the persisting discrimination that Congress found in it.

The voting discrimination considered by Congress included a pattern of repetitious voting rights violations, as well as violations that occurred when minority voters became positioned to assert greater political influence on state and local political systems from which they had been marginalized.[24] The record included statistics indicating that more preclearance objections – proposed voting changes blocked for their discriminatory attributes – occurred between 1982 and 2004 than between 1965 and 1982, and that approximately 60 percent of those objections contained indicia of intentional discrimination.[25] Moreover, in too many cases, discrimination in covered states like Louisiana and Texas could be traced through the decades. Since these states became covered by Section 5, every statehouse or assembly redistricting plan in Louisiana and Texas has drawn an initial objection in each redistricting cycle.[26] In addition, notwithstanding the existence of the preclearance provision, the congressional record revealed that there were more successful voting cases under Section 2 of the V R A in the covered areas than in other parts of the country.[27] Section 2 of the V R A is a key enforcement provision of the Fifteenth Amendment's guarantee of the right to vote free from racial discrimination which, in contrast to Section 5, applies nationwide, and provides protection against vote denial and vote dilution or weakening arrangements. Of all readily identifiable Section 2 suits since 1982, 57 percent of the cases with outcomes favorable to plaintiffs were filed in jurisdictions covered by Section 5, even though less than one-quarter of the nation's population lives in those jurisdictions.[28] Thus, covered jurisdictions were subject to more than twice their proportional share of successful Section 2 voting discrimination suits, which is all the more significant because Section 5 independently prevented covered jurisdictions from adopting (at least) an additional six hundred discriminatory voting changes in the places where it applied during that period. The existence of the preclearance provision deterred many other violations.

Collectively, these legislative facts reveal the significance and extent of voting discrimination in the Section 5–covered states in comparison to other parts of the country.

THE CONGRESSIONAL RECORD DOCUMENTS PERSISTENT DISCRIMINATION IN COVERED JURISDICTIONS

A close examination of the more than one thousand examples identified in the congressional record at the time of the 2006 reauthorization illustrates the difficulty of dislodging voting discrimination. The record before Congress in 2006 showed that Section 5 is necessary to protect against backsliding from remedies that follow successful litigation under other voter protection provisions. In the area of voting, a litigation victory standing alone does not ensure equal access for minority voters. Indeed, Section 5 was originally enacted because the case-by-case approach of vindicating the Fifteenth Amendment proved unsuccessful. Litigation victories were frequently followed by new roadblocks. To borrow the words of historian Alexander Keyssar, our democracy is contested.

Because the first unsuccessful constitutional challenge to the preclearance provision following the 2006 reauthorization arose out of Texas, it is particularly important to consider some of the reauthorization evidence that was before Congress involving threats to minority voting in that state. For example, in 2006 the Supreme Court found that the state diluted the voting strength of Latino voters in violation of Section 2 of the Voting Rights Act and in a way "that bears the mark of intentional discrimination."[29] In the 2006 *LULAC* opinion the Supreme Court explained:

> Texas has a long, well-documented history of discrimination that has touched upon the rights of African Americans and Hispanics to register, to vote, or to participate otherwise in the electoral process.... The history of official discrimination in the Texas election process – stretching back to Reconstruction – led to the inclusion of the State as a covered jurisdiction under Section 5 in the 1975 Amendments to the Voting Rights Act.[30]

Even following the ruling in favor of Latino voters, a Section 5 judicial preclearance action was necessary to prevent Texas from curtailing early voting in the special election held in the remedial district. The proposed modification to the early voting period appeared designed to aid the incumbent who owed his seat to the very same illegal congressional district that the Supreme Court had just invalidated, and to thwart the ability of the Latino voters to elect their candidate of choice in the fairly drawn district.[31]

Similarly, post-2000 Section 5 submissions prevented Texas counties such as Freeport, Haskell Consolidated Independent School District (covering three counties), and Waller from circumventing remedies to discriminatory voting practices in earlier case-by-case litigation.[32]

In another stark example of voting discrimination in Texas, African American college students in Prairie View A&M University faced decades of persistent efforts to bar them from voting in Waller County elections, including threats of criminal prosecution.[33] County officials repeatedly had taken steps to disenfranchise black students. First, in a 1978 decision affirmed by the Supreme Court, a federal court enjoined the Waller County registrar from requiring Prairie View students to demonstrate that their parents lived in the county or that they had secured a full-time job in the county as a prerequisite to registering to vote.[34] Even in the face of these successful Section 5 enforcement actions, the county continued its discriminatory practices. A 2002 Section 5 objection barred Waller County from eliminating the only majority-black district. In 2004, the timely intervention of the U.S. Department of Justice forced Waller County's district attorney to cease his threatened prosecution of any Prairie View student attempting to register to vote or to vote in county elections.[35]

The pattern in other covered states was similar. In 2004, South Carolina enacted a retrogressive method of election for the Charleston County School Board – the same method of election that, only months earlier, a court held violated Section 2 in Charleston County Council elections.[36] In 1994 and 1995, South Carolina also received consecutive Section 5 objections based upon evidence of discriminatory purpose when it attempted to circumvent a consent decree changing the method of election for the Spartanburg County Board of Education by abolishing the elected board.[37]

In 1993, the city of Millen, in Jenkins County, Georgia, drew a discriminatory purpose objection for delaying an election in a majority-black district that was drawn to remedy a Section 2 violation and would have created an opportunity for black voters to elect a majority on the city council for the first time. Two years later, Jenkins County drew another objection from the Justice Department due to evidence that it intentionally moved polling places to a remote, dangerous, and unfamiliar location outside the city.[38]

In 1997, Section 5 prevented Mississippi from returning to a new iteration of a Jim Crow–era dual registration system that was invalidated years earlier.[39] This voting change, which required voters to register separately for federal and state elections, was imposed with the purpose of erecting obstacles to minority participation.

In 2001, Section 5 preclearance blocked the boldly discriminatory attempted cancellation of an election in Kilmichael, Mississippi, by the white majority intended to thwart the growing black population from electing candidates of its choosing.[40]

What is the significance of these examples of voting discrimination – drawn from a congressional record that contained many, many more – and how did this type of evidence influence the decision to reauthorize Section 5? Taken together, the record of successive threats to minority voting rights blocked by preclearance, and other examples of intentional voting discrimination, demonstrate the continuing need for the preclearance protections. The record shows that absent Section 5's prophylactic preclearance remedy, continuing discrimination in various covered jurisdictions would leave minority voters to defend against successive incursions on their rights through slow, expensive, and, ultimately, ineffective case-by-case litigation. The congressional inquiry made clear not only that progress was incomplete, but also that many of the historic patterns and geographic overconcentration of voting discrimination had yet to be eradicated. Congress also heard evidence about the need for continuing the preclearance provision because of other repetitive violations in covered jurisdictions. Some of the evidence pointed to consecutive objections in short periods of time. For example, in Northampton County, Virginia, there were three straight objections for purposefully retrogressive districting plans adopted *after* the 2000 census.[41]

Selma, Alabama, provides another example of persistent discriminatory practices. Long after the violence of Bloody Sunday, The Department of Justice lodged two consecutive discriminatory purpose objections in the 1990s to stop Selma from attempting to prevent African Americans, a majority of the electorate, from electing a majority of the city council.

SECTION 5 RETURNS TO COURT

Minority voters invoked this extensive record of contemporary discrimination in a case filed by a small utility district in Texas, which was virtually unaffected by the preclearance requirement[42] but sought to have Section 5 declared unconstitutional barely a week after President Bush signed the reauthorization bill in 2006. During the Supreme Court oral argument in that case, *Northwest Austin Municipal Utility District Number One v. Holder,* counsel for the utility district argued that preclearance is unconstitutional because "we are in a different day."[43] Justice David Souter in particular was unpersuaded and pointedly inquired how counsel reconciled this assertion with the congressional record:

> Your argument is largely based on the assumption that things have significantly changed and that therefore Congress could not by whatever test we use extend . . . Section 5.
>
> But what we've got in the record in front of us . . . at the present time . . . a 16-point registration difference on Hispanic and non-Hispanic white voters in Texas. We've got a record of some 600 . . . section 5 objections, over a period of about 20 years. We got a record that about two-thirds of them were based on the Justice Department's view that it was intentional discrimination. We've got something like 600 section 2 lawsuits over the same period of time.
>
> The point that I'm getting at is I don't understand, with a record like that, how you can maintain as a basis for this suit that things have radically changed. They may be better. But to say that they have radically changed to the point that this becomes an unconstitutional . . . exercise within Congress's judgment just seems to me to . . . deny the empirical reality.[44]

Implicit in Justice Souter's observation is the idea that the Court should not take up the invitation to override the reasonable policy judgments of

Congress.[45] The unmistakable thrust of Justice Souter's question is that the congressional determination was amply supported by the record and entirely within its constitutional duty to enforce the Reconstruction Amendments to the Constitution. Indeed, six states covered by Section 5 – North Carolina, Louisiana, Mississippi, Arizona,[46] New York, and California – filed briefs urging the Court to uphold Section 5. Even these states acknowledged both the historical and contemporary importance of the preclearance provision expressed unequivocal support for its continuing necessity, and disclaimed the assertion that the provision was costly and burdensome:

> The Amici States recognize that Section 5 of the Voting Rights Act has allowed our Nation to make substantial progress toward eliminating voting discrimination. More, however, remains to be done. The Amici States urge this Court to uphold the constitutionality of the 2006 Reauthorization of the Voting Rights Act. Any assertion that Section 5 constitutes an undue intrusion on state sovereignty does not withstand scrutiny. Section 5 does not place an onerous burden on States. States have been able to comply with Section 5 without undue costs or expense. More importantly, Section 5 has produced substantial benefits within the Amici States and our Nation as a whole.[47]

The Supreme Court ultimately avoided the constitutional question in the Texas water district case challenging the 2006 reauthorization and declined the invitation of the small utility district to strike down Section 5.[48] Instead, the Court rested on the statutory claim and reinterpreted the preclearance provisions to permit every covered jurisdiction the opportunity to apply to be removed from federal preclearance oversight, or to "bail out" from coverage. The Court's ruling surprised many because it was contrary to the statutory definition and long-standing U.S. Justice Department interpretation.[49]

Within months of the Supreme Court's ruling, the district moved to dissolve itself as an entity.[50]

SECTION 5 OF THE VRA: BEYOND THE REAUTHORIZATION

How will Section 5 enforcement play out over the next several years? There are signs of persisting racial tensions in the places where Section 5 is focused. For example, in 2009, the elected Texas State Board of Education weighed a proposal by an expert that it retained to revamp the state's social studies curriculum by removing the discussion of Thurgood Marshall's contributions from the state's textbooks.[51] Thurgood Marshall, the first director-counsel of the NAACP Legal Defense and Educational Fund, Inc., successfully argued the case before the Supreme Court of the United States that ended the state's two-decade unconstitutional campaign to employ a discriminatory whites-only primary system as a method of intentional disfranchisement.[52] More famously, Marshall was lead counsel in *Brown v. Board of Education,* the landmark decision in which the Supreme Court unanimously reversed the "separate but equal" doctrine that allowed racial segregation in schools.[53] He was also the first African American to serve on our nation's highest court. It is hard to view Justice Marshall's proposed exclusion from the historical record in school books as something other than hostility to the equality principles that he embodied throughout his life and to which the VRA commits our nation. Fortunately, the Texas school board rejected the proposal to erase Justice Marshall from the state's history books.[54]

In 2010, some of the public acts by Virginia's highest elected official raised new questions about continuing barriers to racial equality in that state. In April of that year, Governor Bob McDonnell issued a proclamation recognizing Confederate History Month without making any reference whatsoever to the role that slavery played in the Civil War.[55] Initially, when Governor McDonnell was confronted about the offensive nature of this omission to many citizens of Virginia of all races, he defended it, dismissing slavery as not a "significant" issue to Virginia.[56] But "[a]fter a barrage of nationwide criticism for excluding slavery from his Confederate History Month proclamation, [the governor] conceded that it was 'a major omission' and amended the document to acknowledge the state's complicated past."[57] The apology did not end the criticism. As one Washington Post columnist pointed out:

> Although he acted only under severe pressure, Virginia Gov. Bob McDonnell was obviously right Wednesday afternoon to admit a major mistake, issue an apology and add a vital new paragraph clarifying his original proclamation of Confederate History Month.
>
> But the episode raises concerns about what McDonnell really believes . . .

> McDonnell . . . is still stuck with having made the astonishing blunder of
> issuing a formal statement Friday that effectively endorsed the South's cause in
> the Civil War.
>   He didn't quite say it explicitly. But there was no other way to interpret it.
>   The first paragraph said "the people of Virginia" joined the Confederacy in a
> war "for independence."[58]

Shortly after his apology, a new controversy with broader voting implications arose in Virginia when the media learned that McDonnell was revamping the vote restoration process for nonviolent felons by adding a new and subjective essay requirement to what had been an essentially automatic process.[59] Historically, subjective voting tests and poll taxes were the primary obstacle used to disfranchise African Americans before the passage of the VRA banned them.[60] Today, felon disfranchisement laws have a severe and disproportionate effect on African American and Latino populations.[61] Defending the governor's policy, a state official explained that "[i]t's an opportunity, not an obstacle."[62] Shortly thereafter, following additional national news stories, McDonnell downplayed the new requirement as a preliminary proposal that may not take effect.[63] Contrary to his statement, however, the media reported that the state had already informed at least two hundred affected citizens of the requirement in an official letter.[64] Notably, McDonnell had alluded to his intention to impose this new requirement during his campaign.[65] Governor McDonnell abandoned the proposal, and under his administration Virginians in the affected community have been re-enfranchised at a faster rate than under his predecessor. This change in course, however, followed the Lawyers' Committee for Civil Rights' invocation of the Section 5 preclearance requirement, and it may not have occurred without it.[66]

What do these recent experiences tell us as we look to the future? The facts on the ground are not solely indicative of steadfast progress; there are contrary indicators even as the 2010 census numbers bring a new redistricting and reapportionment cycle. The narrative is one of progress and ongoing challenges for minority voters simultaneously – one does not negate the other. Nevertheless, Justice Scalia focused on the progress that was evident in Virginia during the 2009 oral argument in the Texas utility district's challenge to Section 5:[67]

JUSTICE SCALIA: Wasn't Virginia the first State in the Union to elect a black governor?

MR. ADEGBILE: Yes, indeed it was.

JUSTICE SCALIA: And it has a black chief justice of the supreme court currently?

MR. ADEGBILE: Yes, Justice Scalia, I take the point. But I think it's not quite fair to say, and my predecessor at the podium made the point, that there have been African Americans to rise to high office throughout our history, but that the occasion of a single person sitting in a seat doesn't change the experience on the ground for everyday citizens. It is – it has an important salutary effect and it tells us something about the possibilities of our Constitution, but it doesn't mean that voters [who] are trying to vote in a school board election in Louisiana are going to have an easy time of it where racially polarized voting is as extreme as it is and when election officials manipulate the rules of the game to try and disadvantage the minority community.[68]

Even in the face of measurable progress, it is clear that Congress's predictive judgment that we have not yet irreversibly moved beyond the threats to our democracy was a reasonable one.

THE OBAMA FACTOR

Justice Scalia's questions during oral argument are a version of a question that others have asked, including some of the commentators in this book: Why do we need preclearance protection when the nation has moved from enslaving African Americans to electing an African American to the presidency? Inherent in the question is the idea that the nation has moved beyond both discrimination and the need to grapple with racial inequality. The utility district raised the question on the first page of its Supreme Court brief, invoking the crossover voting patterns during the 2008 presidential election as evidence of dramatic changes that allegedly undermine the need for preclearance.[69] The utility district's voting pattern argument brings a foundational element of minority voting-rights protection into view – racially polarized voting patterns.

Racially polarized voting exists where the race of the voters has a high correlation with their voting patterns and where white voters and minority voters prefer different candidates. These differences in voting choices along racial lines are significant because, in places where white voters will only rarely cross over to vote for minority-preferred candidates and white voters also make up a majority of the electorate, minority-preferred candidates are effectively shut out from the possibility of election. Election officials who are aware of these consistently polarized voting patterns can structure the voting rules in ways intended to exploit them. This is one reason why majority-minority districts have played an essential role in diversifying legislative bodies at every level of government: they create the opportunity for minority candidates to be elected where it would not otherwise exist.

Nevertheless some, like Abigail Thernstrom (see chapter 5), assert that majority-minority districts cause separation or division, but these claims are not borne out by the facts. Many of the majority-minority districts from which members of the Congressional Black Caucus are elected, for example, are among the most integrated districts in the nation. Moreover, two significant constraints in redistricting are housing patterns and population concentrations, because districts are drawn to encompass populations, and each must have roughly the same number of people to comply with the Constitution's one-person, one-vote requirement. Under this system, majority-minority districts are often a foreseeable by-product of generations of intentionally segregated housing patterns. Opposition to majority-minority districts, untethered to these real-world considerations, risks depriving minority communities of candidates of their choosing based upon unproven claims. Although certain racial cleavages persist in America, they have their roots in our history, and not in our legislative efforts to confront them. Thus we should carefully scrutinize arguments that suggest that the cart drags the horse when centuries of experience are to the contrary.

With this in mind, we can turn back to the 2008 presidential election and consider what it may indicate about the future. Although candidate Obama received 43 percent of the white vote, the narrative of a nationwide cross-racial coalition that elected President Barack Obama has substantial caveats. Indeed, in Section 5 covered jurisdictions, crossover voting was very limited. A closer look at the election results detailed in a friend of the court brief filed in the Texas Supreme Court case,[70] and in an NAACP LDF, Inc. report show that:

- · The six states with the lowest white voter percentage of support for candidate Obama are each fully covered by Section 5: Alabama, Mississippi, Louisiana, Georgia, South Carolina, and Texas;[71]
- · Candidate Obama's white voting percentage in Alabama, Mississippi, and Louisiana, respectively, was 10, 11, and 14 percent;[72]
- · Candidate Obama's victory resulted, among other things, from an increase in the share of white voters in the non–Section 5 covered states, and a nationwide increase in his share of votes cast by minority voters;[73]
- · Candidate Obama won just 26 percent of white voters in the covered states compared with 48 percent in noncovered states;[74]
- · Candidate Obama did poorly even among white Democrats in covered jurisdictions such as Alabama and Louisiana, where he did not carry a majority of his own party's white voters;[75]
- · Generally, white voters of every partisan affiliation in states covered by Section 5 were less likely to vote for President Obama than were their copartisans in the jurisdictions not covered by Section 5.[76]

Consequently, while President Obama's election as the first African American president is a significant marker in any assessment of racial progress and attitudes in America, a closer examination demonstrates the importance of retaining preclearance protections in covered jurisdictions. President Obama's election should be regarded as a new chapter in an evolving story, not as the end of the story itself. It will be important to examine the level of racial polarization in the covered jurisdictions in future years, not simply in federal elections but in more local elections as well.[77] That scrutiny will show whether the familiar pattern of racially polarized voting improves, thus removing a significant building block for voting discrimination and a significant predicate for the preclearance provision.

President Obama's electoral success was marred by reports of racial epithets etched on Obama campaign signs, cross burnings in at least two places, Obama figures hung in effigy, vandalism, active attempts to suppress the minority vote, and other similar incidents.[78] Just two weeks before the election, a man interviewed in a Mobile, Alabama, parking lot commented to a national news reporter that Barack Obama is "going to tear up the rose bushes and plant a watermelon patch."[79] More than two hundred hate-related threats were made toward President-elect Obama and African Americans in the three weeks following the 2008 election.[80]

LOOKING FORWARD

Over the next several years, and perhaps especially in connection with the post-2010 census redistricting cycle, important questions exist about how the Department of Justice will enforce Section 5 to block discriminatory voting changes. In light of stubborn racial attitudes that have persisted over time, rapidly changing demographic patterns, and continuing efforts by the Department of Justice to defend the constitutionality of Section 5 in court, enforcement activity will likely continue during the post-2010 redistricting cycle.

The Kilmichael, Mississippi, and Texas congressional redistricting examples – which present extreme facts in some respects – are nevertheless familiar in terms of the broader pattern that they represent: entrenched powers seeking to preserve their control through democracy-distorting practices as minority voters begin to achieve greater political access and participation. The 2010 census provides a good indication of potential hot spots for these types of efforts to thwart the rising minority political voices. For example, covered states like Texas and Arizona, with large and growing Latino populations, are already challenging Section 5.

Indeed Section 5 enforcement activity, consistent with the congressional prediction, has commenced. The United States and civil rights groups, including the Mexican American Legal Defense and Education Fund, invoking Section 5 preclearance, contested Texas's 2011 state house and congressional redistricting plans, citing e-mail evidence of intentional discrimination on the part of legislators as well as the allegedly discriminatory impact of the plans.[81] Following an oral argument in November 2011 the three-judge court denied Texas's request for summary judgment in its favor and noted that the state applied the wrong Section 5 preclearance standard.[82] Had Section 5 not been reauthorized, those plans would be the law of Texas today. As a result of the Section 5 ruling blocking Texas's state house and congressional redistricting maps, a federal court in Texas drew the district lines, and those lines are the subject of Supreme Court litigation.

This pattern persists beyond Texas in the 2010 redistricting cycle. For example, the Department of Justice has posed an objection to the redistricting plan of voting precincts proposed by East Feliciana Parish, Louisiana. In considering the impact that the proposed plan would have on a district that previously provided African Americans the opportunity to elect a candidate of their choice in the face of persisting racially polarized voting district, the DOJ determined that the decision, made by an all-white police juror governing body, to exclude a local prison population from the population process while concurrently adding a white population to that district that had never before been part of the district could not be deemed free of prohibited discriminatory intent.[83]

Similarly, the Department of Justice objected to the proposed redistricting plan for board of supervisor and election commissioner districts in Amite County, Mississippi. In that matter, the DOJ objected on the grounds that while the proposed plan maintained one of the two majority-minority districts in the county, it swapped out the second district for a new third, numerically majority–African American one.[84] While the state's position was that the plan thus maintained two majority-minority districts, the DOJ recognized the new district as illusory through stacking – that is, while the proposed plan succeeded in numerically creating a different majority–African American district, an analysis beyond census numbers alone showed that the proposed district would not operate as an opportunity-to-elect district because of lower voter turnout and reduced electoral cohesiveness in that area. Section 5, in each of these redistricting contexts, provided a direct impediment to plans that would otherwise have been passed, and that clearly – in some cases intentionally – would have diluted minority voting strength.

THE FUTURE OF PRECLEARANCE IN THE COURTS

As chapters in this collection and the discussion above make clear, the decision in the utility district's constitutional challenge to Section 5 does not finally settle the question of the law's status. Even as of this writing, there is an important case awaiting argument before a federal appellate court in Washington D.C., in which a constitutional challenge filed by Shelby County, Alabama, seeks to revisit the unsuccessful arguments against Section 5 advanced by the Texas utility district. The trial court judge in that case observed during the oral argument that both sides could find some support for their position in the Supreme Court's Texas utility district opinion. He then called for postargument briefing tightly focused on the state of the legislative record regarding Congress's decision to apply Section 5 preclearance to all or part of the same sixteen states covered under the 1982 reauthorization. Summarizing the weight of evidence supporting the congressional decision to maintain the existing coverage approach rather than modifying it, the NAACP Legal Defense Fund, Inc., explained on behalf of its African American Shelby County intervenor clients that:

> Whether to change or maintain [the geographic coverage approach for Section 5] was the subject of intense debate and careful assessment during the 2006 reauthorization. That debate included the consideration and rejection of a coverage amendment on the House floor, and intensified during the Senate Judiciary Committee hearings, where almost every witness appearing before the Committee offered testimony specifically about the coverage provision.... Read as a whole, the record demonstrates that Congress's decision to maintain the coverage provision was well supported in both theory and practice, and that it was consistent with the original enactment and subsequent reauthorizations of the VRA, all of which have been sustained against previous constitutional challenges.[85]

Plaintiffs attacked that legislative testimony as practically and theoretically flawed. The lower court ruled for the United States and intervenors who defended Section 5 in a thorough 151-page opinion mining the legislative record.[86] The case likely will be settled by the Supreme Court, and other pending cases raise similar claims.[87]

The constitutional attacks have not succeeded since 1965, but neither have they ceased. The Supreme Court's unwarranted skepticism about the continuing need for Section 5 and/or its geographic reach could signal its appetite for future rulings that narrow the act's effectiveness, but it would be an extraordinary judicial act, with far-reaching implications for voting rights, and likely for civil rights more broadly, if the Court were to cast aside the extensive record that Congress compiled and declare this watershed act unconstitutional. The Court seemed aware of these stakes in the Texas utility district case.

SECTION 203: THE 2006
REAUTHORIZATION AND BEYOND

The temporary language-assistance provisions of the VRA codified in Section 203 make it easier for voting-age citizens who are non-English-speaking or not proficient in English to surmount language obstacles to register and vote. The language groups covered by Section 203 are Alaskan Natives, American Indians, Asian Americans, and persons of Spanish heritage.[88] As some of the preceding chapters show, the context in Congress for the reauthorization of Section 203's language-assistance provisions posed its own challenges distinct from those posed by the preclearance provision.

Chief among the challenges posed by the language-assistance reauthorization was that opponents sought to conflate the protections that those provisions of the VRA afford to citizens seeking to vote with hotly contested immigration reform and enforcement issues. While Section 203 applies only to eligible voters who are citizens, that fact did not deter the opponents of immigration reform from seeking to couple the issues. The strategic purpose for joining the issues of immigration and voting language assistance was to block reauthorization. The debate over immigration had sharply divided the 109th Congress, and, as the strategy played out, injecting immigration issues into the Section 203 debate, if successful, could have destroyed bipartisan support for the entire VRA reauthorization bill.

In particular, House Judiciary Committee chairman James Sensenbrenner, Jr., who oversaw the VRA reauthorization bill in the House, squarely sided with more aggressive immigration enforcement in that very same legislative time frame. Rep. Sensenbrenner views illegal immigration as a core legislative priority.[89] But he was also a leader and strong supporter of the VRA reauthorization. Recognizing that immigration enforcement reform had been a signature issue for the Judiciary Committee Chairman, those who sought to link the immigration debate to Section 203[90] tried to embarrass Rep. Sensenbrenner with an apparent contradiction that would cause him to abandon the language-assistance provisions and possibly even the entire reauthorization. Rep. Sensenbrenner, however, did not take the bait. He remained a steadfast supporter of the bill with the language-assistance provisions intact. He viewed the VRA as a pillar of our modern democracy. During the legislative debates, Rep. Sensenbrenner expressed his view that "we are not dealing with illegal immigrants, we are dealing with United States citizens, and they are people who have either attained citizenship by reason of birth in the United States . . . or have been naturalized."[91]

As the VRA debates evolved, civil rights groups, and others advocating for reauthorization of the act, were thus forced to confront the reality captured in the adage that, in politics, "there are no permanent friends and no permanent enemies." Regardless of other policy differences, during the 2006 reauthorization, Rep. Sensenbrenner was a friend of VRA reauthorization proponents. Although many would play pivotal roles in the reauthorization, the bill would rise and fall in the Republican-controlled 109th Congress under his leadership – there was simply no way around his influence.

In some respects, the strategy of coupling immigration issues with the reauthorization of the language-assistance provisions made that aspect of the act more controversial in the prevailing political environment than the preclearance provision. The controversy played out in several ways and threatened, at critical points, to derail the entire reauthorization. Most notably, opponents of Section 203 attempted to use an appropriations bill for the Department of Justice to suspend funding for enforcement of the Section 203 language-assistance provisions.[92] Congressman Cliff Stearns sponsored the amendment.[93] Congressman Steve King made clear what VRA proponents knew at the time – that the funding amendment was a backdoor attempt to derail the reauthorization.[94] But both Republican and Democratic members of Congress rose in opposition.[95] As Congressman John Lewis explained, "[t]hese are our neighbors. They are taxpayers. They are Americans. We should be opening up the process to each and every American."[96] The amendment was defeated, but it was a very real test of the bipartisan commitment to reauthorization.

Congressman Lewis's statement in support of Section 203 and in opposition to the amendment also underscored the one aspect of the reauthorization that helped to cement support. Members of the Congressional Black Caucus and civil rights advocates understood that the democratic principles of open access that support the VRA must apply with equal vigor to *all* citizens.[97] Therefore they resisted any attempt to insert specious immigration concerns as a wedge issue during the reauthorization. Language-minority advocates also presented a strong case and built the record of need for the provisions.[98] Both the preclearance and language-assistance provisions were viewed as critical protections. The link between these two protections was underscored during the reauthorization hearings on legislative language of the proposed amendments to Section 5:

> MR. CONYERS . . . Let me go somewhere else here now. Section 203. Now, the notion that we're encouraging people who are newly sworn-in citizens not to continue to improve in English is an important consideration. And for me, it's a sensitive one because we've already heard from a number of Members of Congress on this who have some reservations. And we know that immigration is a huge issue.
>
> So I wanted to ask Mr. Adegbile whether or not we can get through this particular time situation and continue to have language assistance where needed, in view of the record that's been compiled that shows that it is not particularly expensive and doesn't seem to put out election workers at all.
>
> MR. ADEGBILE . . . Section 203 is a critical aspect of the Voting Rights Act. It was part of the evolution of Congress's understanding about our democracy and the barriers to that democracy. It's a provision that applies only to citizens – only citizens – and many people try to distort the record on that issue.
>
> People who receive 203 assistance at the polls are people who pay taxes, they are people who serve in wars, they are people in our communities, and they deserve a say in the political process. It is simply nonsensical to suggest that somebody is going to make a decision about whether or not they are able to learn to speak English because of a rule that allows them to have translated materials in voting. I don't think that anybody seriously posits that argument. And if folks say it, I think that it's a cynical argument.
>
> The NAACP Legal Defense and Educational Fund supports 203 language assistance because we recognize that barriers to voting affect many different types of citizens and that we don't enrich the democracy by saying some citizens can have access and others cannot."[99]

In the end, the preclearance provision and language-assistance provisions were linked for an up-or-down vote. There was a very high level of awareness during the reauthorization that a unified and disciplined coalition would create the best opportunity for legislative success in a difficult environment, and that approach proved successful.

THE NEXT TWO DECADES OF SECTION 203

Language assistance is provided based upon periodic assessments of where covered language-minority groups meet a population concentration and literacy threshold. The practical impact of this approach is that Section 203 reaches communities that shift and that there can be more regular expansions and contractions for coverage.[100] In this regard, the census plays a key role in future enforcement, and it is predictable that there will be changes in Section 203's scope, just as there were in 2002 when jurisdictions entered and exited coverage. With the advent of the American Community Survey data, which provides yearly census updates, coverage changes will become even more frequent, occurring every five years after the next Section 203 determinations are made.

Significantly, there is an underlying justification for voting language assistance that regrettably will be slow to change. As Jim Tucker's chapter 8 underscores, part of the rationale for Section 203 was that "[r]elief was needed from 'the current effect that past educational discrimination has on today's [language minority] adult population' and to overcome 'present barriers to equal educational opportunities.' Rather than attempting to 'correct the deficiencies of prior educational inequality,' a remedy was needed allowing 'persons disabled by such disparity to vote now.'"[101] Educational inequalities have proven particularly difficult to dislodge and are unlikely to be erased in the near future, despite the incentive that bailout provides to jurisdictions covered by Section 203 to improve English literacy for language minorities.[102] Unfortunately, the economic crisis that began in late 2008 has likely further eroded educational opportunities for many language minorities, as local school districts have eliminated billions of dollars from their budgets.

The temporary language-assistance provisions also differ from Section 5 because they have not come under consistent constitutional attack.[103] Despite the difficult legislative road, no case challenging the constitutionality of the language assistance has been filed since the 2006 reauthorization. While the past is often a good indicator about the future, it is possible that at some point a challenge to Section 203 will come and/or that litigation will be filed that seeks to narrow its effectiveness, as Jim Tucker describes in his thorough Section 203 chapter (chapter 8). Although any such challenge would likely fail, our democracy remains contested. For example, former congressman Tom Tancredo,[104] who supported the amendment offered by Congressman Stearns that was designed to effectively end Section 203,[105] caused a controversy in 2010 when he advocated that the long-repudiated literacy test has a place in our modern democracy. During opening remarks at a political convention in Tennessee, Tancredo reportedly said, "People who could not even spell the word 'vote' or say it in English put a committed socialist ideologue in the White House."[106] He also said Obama won because "we do not have a civics, literacy test before people can vote."[107] It is startling that forty-five years after the passage of the VRA and four decades after literacy tests were abolished nationwide, a former member of Congress and presidential candidate openly espouses such retrograde views.

More practical developments may ease some of the resistance to language assistance over the next twenty years. For example, innovations in technology have already begun to make access to translated ballot materials easier. The Help America Vote Act of 2002 provided billions of dollars in federal funds to states to purchase voting machines capable of supporting audio translations of voting instructions and ballots. In addition, jurisdictions that actively recruit community members as poll workers and election officials will begin to popularize best practices for Section 203 compliance. In the past, part of the difficulty with Section 203 compliance arose because of limited outreach to communities with language skills, denying bilingual voters equal opportunities to serve as poll workers. Use of such workers typically adds little or no cost to elections budgets. Continued Section 203 enforcement has remained fairly consistent under administrations of both parties, which, together with knowledge of cost efficiencies of better poll worker recruitment, will stimulate greater compliance. Indeed, the next legislative effort, which could occur before the temporary provisions of the act are scheduled to expire, may be to expand the reach of Section 203 to make assistance available to more Americans.

CONCLUSION

Our democracy is contested. A pattern of ebbs and flows is part of the civil rights and voting rights experience in the United States. Years ago, Thurgood Marshall expressed a similar idea:

> But to those of us who know that the struggle is far from over, history has another lesson. It tells us how deeply rooted habits of prejudice are, dominating the minds of men and all of our institutions for three centuries; and it cautions us to continue to move forward lest we fall back.[108]

At our best, we recognize that the genius of our Constitution lies not in the idea that our nation was formed perfectly – it was not – but rather in the framework that it provides to protect and improve our country. The preclearance and language-assistance provisions are effective tools operating within and validating this framework. During the 2006 reauthorization, Congress was faced with the question: is it possible to reconcile measurable voting progress with the need for still more progress? In response, Congress answered yes, and demanded more progress. It was the right choice. Congress determined that serious threats remain and that backsliding is possible, even likely. The record from the 2006 reauthorization supports that conclusion.

The American creed, fully expressed, encompasses the desire to strive for something as yet unrealized. As Congress recognized, we do not dishonor our progress by demanding more of it. Our progress in the area of voting has been neither easy nor inevitable, but it continues to be desirable and achievable. The VRA orients the nation toward progress and toward the "more perfect union" that we seek to become. And, if we remain vigilant and honor our Constitution's aspiration, it will continue to do so.

NOTES

1. Congress found that the progress made in combating racial discrimination in voting "is the direct result of the Voting Rights Act." Fannie Lou Hamer, Rosa Parks, and Coretta Scott King Voting Rights Act Reauthorization and Amend-

ments Act of 2006, Pub. L. No. 109-246, § 2(b)(1), 120 Stat. 577.

2. Congress also found that the progress made was incomplete. It enacted Section 5 in an effort "to rid the country of racial discrimination in voting," and not

"simply to reduce racial discrimination in voting to what some view as a tolerable level." *South Carolina v. Katzenbach,* 383 U.S. 301, 315 (1966); 152 *Cong. Rec.* S7976 (daily ed., July 20, 2006) (statement of Sen. Feingold).

3. Alexander Keyssar, *The Right to Vote: The Contested History of Democracy in the United States,* rev. ed. (New York: Basic Books, 2009), p. 135–36. See also *Giles v. Harris,* 189 U.S. 475, 482 (1903).

4. Richard Valelly, *The Two Reconstructions: The Struggle for Black Enfranchisement* (Chicago: University of Chicago Press, 2004), p. 243–46; see also Keyssar, *The Right to Vote,* p. 85–93; *South Carolina v. Katzenbach,* 383 U.S. 301, 314 (1966).

5. *Bartlett v. Strickland,* 129 S.Ct. 1231, 1249 (2009). For an analysis of the significance of the *Bartlett* ruling, see Ryan P. Haygood, *The Dim Side of the Bright Line: Minority Voting Opportunity After Bartlett v. Strickland,* Harv. C.R.-C.L. L. Rev. Amicus (2009), http://harvardcrcl.org/amicus/2009/10/22/minority-voting/.

6. Debra Rosenberg, et al., "Firmly in Control, Holding the Line: The Republicans Kept Their Lead In The Congress. But That Doesn't Mean Bush Will Have An Easy Time Of It," *Newsweek,* November 15, 2004, 30.

7. Carl Hulse, "Rebellion Stalls Extension of the Voting Rights Act," *New York Times,* June 22, 2006. For a discussion of the political hurdles to reauthorization, see James Thomas Tucker, *The Politics of Persuasion: Passage of the Voting Rights Act Reauthorization Act of 2006,* 33 J. Legis. 205 (2007).

8. *Understanding the Benefits and Costs of Section 5 Preclearance: Hearing Before the S. Comm. on the Judiciary,* 109th Cong., 7–9, 204–210 (May 17, 2006) (statement of Abigail Thernstrom).

9. H. Rep. 109-554, at 2, 4 (2006) (Rep. Lynn A. Westmoreland's and Rep. Charlie Norwood's House Amendments).

See Tucker, *The Politics of Persuasion,* 254, 257–58.

10. *Reauthorizing the Voting Rights Act's Temporary Provisions: Policy Perspectives and Views From the Field: Hearing Before the Subcomm. On the Constitution, Civil Rights & Property Rights of the S. Comm. on the Judiciary,* 109th Cong. 18–19, 267–308 (June 21, 2006) (testimony of Carol Swain) (urging nationwide extension of the preclearance provision notwithstanding the practical and constitutional problems her proposal raised).

11. *Renewing the Provisions of the Voting Rights Act: An Introduction to the Evidence: Hearing Before the S. Comm. On the Judiciary,* 109th Cong. 12–16, 25–29 (Apr. 27, 2006) (statements of Rep. John Conyers, Jr., and Rep. F. James Sensenbrenner, Jr.); *An Introduction to the Expiring Provisions of the Voting Rights Act and Legal Issues Relation to Reauthorization: Hearing Before the S. Comm. On the Judiciary,* 109th Cong. 201–13, 264–78 (May 9, 2006) (statements of Chandler Davidson and Theodore M. Shaw); *Understanding the Benefits and Costs of Section 5 Pre-clearance: Hearing Before the S. Comm. On the Judiciary,* 109th Cong. 163–73 (May 17, 2006) (statement of Drew S. Days III); *Renewing the Temporary Provisions of the Voting Rights Act: Legislative Options After Lulac v. Perry: Hearing Before the Subcomm. On the Constitution, Civil Rights & Property Rights of the S. Comm. on the Judiciary,* 109th Cong. 228–39 (July 13, 2006) (statement of Sherrilyn A. Ifill); *Voting Rights Act: Section 5 of the Act – History, Scope & Purpose: Hearing before the Subcomm. On the Constitution of the H. Comm. On the Judiciary,* 109th Cong. 86–90 (Oct. 25, 2005) (statement of Nina Perales); *The Continuing Need for Section 5: Hearing before the Subcomm. On the Constitution of the H. Comm. On the Judiciary,* 109th Cong. 4–15 (Oct. 25, 2005) (statement of Laughlin McDonald).

12. *To Examine the Impact and Effectiveness of the Voting Rights Act: Hearing Before the Subcomm. On the Constitution of the H. Comm. On the Judiciary,* 109th Cong. 4–14 (Oct. 18, 2005) (testimony of Jack Kemp) (embracing extension of the V R A to expressly reach felon disfranchisement).

13. *The Continuing Need for Section 5 Pre-clearance: Hearing Before the S. Comm. On the Judiciary,* 109th Cong. 174–93 (May 16, 2006) (statement of Pamela S. Karlan).

14. The bipartisan group of Congressmen Sensenbrenner, Conyers, Watt, and Chabot were responsible for organizing the hearings, crafting the text and scope of the reauthorization bill, and negotiating with those within their caucuses and constituencies who tried to fracture the coalition that supported passage.

15. During the oral argument in *Northwest Austin Municipal Utility District Number One* ("NAMUDNO") *v. Holder,* Justice Kennedy noted, "No one – no one questions the vitality, the urgency, the essentiality of [Section 5 of] the Voting Rights Act," even as he raised questions about the scope of its territorial reach. Transcript of Oral Argument at 35, NAMUDNO *v. Holder,* 129 S.Ct. 2504 (2009) (No. 08-322).

16. See *Quiet Revolution in the South: The Impact of the Voting Rights Act, 1965–1990,* ed. Chandler Davidson and Bernard Grofman (Princeton, N.J.: Princeton University Press, 1994).

17. National Association of Latino Elected and Appointed Officials, *National Roster of Hispanic Elected Officials* (1986), ix.

18. National Association of Latino Elected and Appointed Officials, *National Roster of Hispanic Elected Officials* (2004), 6, 116.

19. H.R. Rep. No. 109-478, at 2 (2006).

20. *Renewing the Temporary Provisions of the Voting Rights Act: Legislative Options After Lulac v. Perry: Hearing Before the Subcomm. On the Constitution, Civil Rights & Property Rights of the S. Comm. on the Judiciary,* 109th Cong. 242–29 (July 13, 2006) (statement of Alexander Keyssar).

21. Keyssar, *The Right to Vote.*

22. See generally Philip A. Klinkner and Rodgers Smith, *The Unsteady March* (Chicago: The University of Chicago Press, 1999).

23. For a careful analysis of the evidence underlying the 2006 congressional record, see *Nw. Austin Mun. Util. Dist. No. One v. Mukasey,* 573 F. Supp. 2d 221 (D. D.C. 2008) (Tatel, J., writing for the unanimous three-judge court); see also Kristen Clarke, *The Congressional Record Underlying the 2006 Voting Rights Act: How Much Discrimination Can the Constitution Tolerate?,* 43 Harv. C.R.-C.L. L. Rev. 385 (2008) (noting that the recently reauthorized Section 5 provision will withstand constitutional scrutiny because of the voluminous and extensive legislative record amassed during the 2005–2006 reauthorization process).

24. Brief of Intervenor-Appellees Rodney and Nicole Lewis et al. at 13–14, et seq., NAMUDNO *v. Holder,* 129 S.Ct. (2009) (No. 08-322) (noting more than six dozen examples from the congressional record of repetitious voting rights violations which are illustrative but not exhaustive of those found in the record).

25. *Voting Rights Act: Evidence of Continuing Need: Hearing before the Subcomm. On the Constitution of the H. Comm. On the Judiciary,* 109th Cong. 172 (Mar. 8, 2006); *Voting Rights Act: Section 5–Preclearance Standards: Hearing before the Subcomm. On the Constitution of the H. Comm. On the Judiciary,* 109th Cong. 180–81 (Nov. 1, 2005).

26. *Voting Rights Act: Section 5 of the Act – History, Scope & Purpose: Hearing before the Subcomm. On the Constitution of the H. Comm. On the Judiciary,* 109th Cong. 2177–80, 2319–23, 2518–23 (Oct. 25, 2005); *The Continuing Need for Section 5: Hearing before the Subcomm. On the Constitution of*

the H. Comm. On the Judiciary, 109th Cong. 16 (Oct. 25, 2005).

27. Shelby County, Ala. v. Holder, F. Supp. 2d, 2011 WL 4375001 *78 (D.D.C., Sep. 21, 2011). [Case no. 1:10-cv-00651-JDB, Mem. Op. pp. 147–48]

28. Id. at 125–26, 202–4. Indeed the actual statistics may skew more heavily toward the sixteen preclearance states because many cases brought there that settled before trial may not ever appear in any easily searchable electronic database.

29. League of United Latin Am. Citizens v. Perry, 548 U.S. 399, 440 (2006).

30. Id. at 439–40, quoting Vera v. Richards, 861 F. Supp. 1304, 1317 (S.D. Tex. 1994).

31. See League of United Latin Am. Citizens v. Texas, No. 06-1046 (W.D. Tex. Dec.1, 2006).

32. Voting Rights Act: Section 5 of the Act – History, Scope & Purpose: Hearing before the Subcomm. On the Constitution of the H. Comm. On the Judiciary, 109th Cong. 86, 2291–92, 2513–17, 2524–30 (Oct. 25, 2005).

33. Voting Rights Act: Evidence of Continued Need: Hearing before the Subcomm. On the Constitution of the H. Comm. On the Judiciary, 109th Cong. 185–86 (Mar. 8, 2006).

34. See United States v. Texas, 445 F. Supp. 1245 (S.D. Tex. 1978) (three-judge court), aff'd, Symm v. United States, 439 U.S. 1105 (1979).

35. See Nina Perales, Luis Figueroa, and Criselda G. Rivas, Voting Rights in Texas: 1982–2006, 17 S. Cal. Rev. L. & Soc. Just. 713, 733, 742–43 (2008).

36. See Voting Rights Act: Evidence of Continued Need: Hearing before the Subcomm. On the Constitution of the H. Comm. On the Judiciary, 109th Cong. 175–76 (Mar. 8, 2006).

37. See Voting Rights Act: Section 5 of the Act – History, Scope & Purpose: Hearing before the Subcomm. On the Constitution of the H. Comm. On the Judiciary, 109th Cong. 2041–43, 2049–52 (Oct. 25, 2005).

38. Voting Rights Act: Section 5 of the Act – History, Scope & Purpose: Hearing before the Subcomm. On the Constitution of the H. Comm. On the Judiciary, 109th Cong. 815–17 (Oct. 25, 2005).

39. See Voting Rights Act: Section 5 of the Act – History, Scope & Purpose: Hearing before the Subcomm. On the Constitution of the H. Comm. On the Judiciary, 109th Cong. 1599–1605 (Oct. 25, 2005).

40. Id. at 1616–19.

41. See Voting Rights Act: Section 5 of the Act – History, Scope & Purpose: Hearing before the Subcomm. On the Constitution of the H. Comm. On the Judiciary, 109th Cong. 2592–95 (Oct. 25, 2005).

42. The utility district submitted only eight voting changes in the twenty-two years of its existence and the evidence showed that the per-submission cost was $233.00. Brief for the Federal Appellee at 4, NAMUDNO v. Holder, 129 S.Ct. 2504 (2009) (No. 08-322).

43. NAMUDNO Transcript of Oral Argument at 15, NAMUDNO v. Holder, 129 S.Ct. 2504 (2009) (No. 08-322). The utility district was represented ably by Greg Coleman, the former solicitor general of Texas, who died tragically in an airplane crash in 2010.

44. NAMUDNO Transcript of Oral Argument at 15–16, NAMUDNO v. Holder, 129 S.Ct. 2504 (2009) (No. 08-322).

45. Modern Enforcement of the Voting Rights Act: Hearing Before the S. Comm. On the Judiciary, 109th Cong. 108–111 (May 10, 2006) (statement of Gregory S. Coleman).

46. The ebbs and flows in the area of voting rights are sometimes sudden. Although Arizona joined the states' brief defending the constitutionality of Section 5 in 2009 and explaining its important role in ensuring minority voter inclusion, in

2011 the state filed a constitutional challenge to Section 5 urging a federal court to declare Section 5 unconstitutional. See Complaint, *State of Arizona v. Holder,* No. 1:2011-cv-01559-JDB (D. D.C. 2011).

47. Brief for the States of North Carolina, Arizona, California, Louisiana, Mississippi, and New York as Amicus Curiae in Support of the Eric H. Holder, Jr., et al. at 1–2, *NAMUDNO v. Holder,* 129 S.Ct. 2504 (2009) (No. 08-322).

48. *NAMUDNO v. Holder,* 129 S.Ct. 2504 (2009).

49. Indeed, Congress received testimony calling for a change in law that would broaden access to bailout, but failed to act upon it. *Voting Rights Act: An Examination of the Scope and Criteria for Coverage under the Special Provisions of the Act: Hearing before the Subcomm. On the Constitution of the H. Comm. On the Judiciary,* 109th Congress, First Sess. at 91 (Oct. 20, 2005) (statement of Gerald Hebert).

50. See Minutes, Board of Directors, Northwest Austin Municipal Utility District No. 1, at 3 (February 2, 2010) available at http://www.nwamud.texas.gov/images/2/27/Minutes-2.2.10.draft.pdf (adopting resolution noting that the city of Austin intends to dissolve and abolish the Northwest Austin Municipal Utility District No. 1 by ordinance on or about February 4, 2010).

51. Stephanie Simon, "The Culture Wars' New Front: U.S. History Classes in Texas, A Closer Look," *Wall Street Journal,* July 14, 2009, A14.

52. *Smith v. Allwright,* 321 U.S. 649 (1944).

53. *Brown v. Bd. of Educ.,* 347 U.S. 483 (1954).

54. Russell Shorto, "How Christian Were the Founders?," *New York Times,* February 14, 2010, M32.

55. Anita Kumar and Rosalind S. Helderman, "McDonnell's Confederate History Month Proclamation Irks Civil Rights Leaders," *Washington Post,* April 7, 2010, A01.

56. Anita Kumar, "Virginia Governor Amends Confederate History Proclamation to Include Slavery," *Washington Post,* April 8, 2010, A01.

57. Id.

58. Robert McCartney, "McDonnell's Apology Raises Questions About What He Really Believes," *Washington Post,* April 8, 2010, B01.

59. Anita Kumar, "McDonnell In Hot Water Over Nonviolent Felons' Rights," *Washington Post,* April 11, 2010, C01.

60. See 42 USC § 1973aa (a) (prohibiting any citizen from being denied the right to vote in any federal, state, or local election "because of his failure to comply with any test or device").

61. The Sentencing Project & Human Rights Watch, *Losing the Vote: The Impact of Felony Disenfranchisement Laws in the United States* (1998), http://www.hrw.org/legacy/reports/reports98/vote/index.html.

62. Kumar, "McDonnell In Hot Water Over Nonviolent Felons' Rights," C01.

63. Anita Kumar, "McDonnell Spokesman Says Voting Rights Letter Sent to Felons 'Without Approval,'" *Washington Post,* April 14, 2010, B01.

64. Id.

65. Jim Nolan, "Kaine Urges Restoration of Voting Rights; He Tells Nonviolent Felons to Apply Before His Term Ends," *Richmond Times-Dispatch,* November 25, 2009, A01, available at http://www2.tricities.com/tri/news/state_regional/article/kaine_urges_restoration_of_voting_rights/36392/.

66. Lawyers Committee for Civil Rights Under Law to Virginia attorney general Kenneth T. Cuccinelli, II, Re: Section 5 of the Voting Rights Act and Restoration of Rights (Apr. 13, 2010).

67. *NAMUDNO* Transcript of Oral Argument at 55, *NAMUDNO v. Holder*, 129 S.Ct. 2504 (2009) (No. 08-322).

68. Id.

69. Appellant's Brief at 1, *NAMUDNO v. Holder*, 129 S.Ct. 2504 (2009) (No. 08-322) ("The country has its first African-American president, who received a larger percentage of the white vote than each of the previous two Democratic nominees.").

70. Brief of Nathaniel Persily, et al. as Amicus Curiae on Behalf of Neither Party, *NAMUDNO v. Holder*, 129 S.Ct. 2504 (2009) (No. 08-322) at 9–10.

71. Political Participation Group, NAACP Legal Defense and Educational Fund, Inc., *"Post-Racial America" America? Not Yet: Why the Fight for Voting Rights Continues After the Election of President Barack Obama* 10-11 (2009) (available at http://naacpldf.org/files/publications/Post-Racial-America-Not-Yet.pdf (last visited November 3, 2011)).

72. Id. at 13.

73. Id. at 11.

74. Id. at 12.

75. Id.

76. Id. at 12–13; see also Brief of Nathaniel Persily et al. as Amicus Curiae in Support of Neither Party, et al. at 1–2, *NAMUDNO v. Holder*, 129 S.Ct. 2504 (2009) (No. 08-322) at 18.

77. See Kristen Clarke, *The Obama Factor: The Impact of the 2008 Presidential Election on Future Voting Rights Act Litigation*, 3 Harv. L. & Pol'y Rev. 59, 203 (2009) (noting that despite President Obama's ultimate success in the 2008 presidential election cycle, courts must continue to make careful, case-by-case assessments and intensely localized appraisals about the level of racially polarized voting in those jurisdictions that may be subject to future Voting Rights Act claims).

78. James Thomas Tucker, "Electoral Access, Participation, and Voter Protection in the 2008 Election," in *America*

Votes! A Guide to Modern Election Law and Voting Rights, Supp. 2009, ed. Benjamin E. Griffith, 74–77 (American Bar Association, 2009).

79. Adam Nossiter, "For Some, Uncertainty Starts at Racial Identity," *New York Times*, October 15, 2008, 21.

80. Tucker, "Electoral Access, Participation, and Voter Protection in the 2008 Election," 74–77.

81. See United States' Statement of Genuine Issues, *Texas v. Holder*, No. 1:11-CV-1303-RMC-TBG-BAH (D.D.C. Oct. 25, 2011).

82. Order, *Texas v. Holder*, Civil action no. 11-1303-RMC-TBG-BAH (D.D.C. Nov. 8, 2011).

83. See Department of Justice letter to Nancy P. Jenson, Submission 2011-2055, East Feliciana, La., voting precincts (Oct. 3, 2011) (on file with the author).

84. See Department of Justice letter to Tommie S. Cardin, Submission 2011-1660, Amite County, Ms., Board of Supervisor and Election Commissioner districts (Oct. 4, 2011) (on file with the author).

85. Consolidated Supplemental Memorandum of Points and Authorities of Cunningham and Pierson Defendant-Intervenors In Support of Cross-Motions for Summary Judgment, No. 1:10-cv-00651-JDB (D. D.C. Feb. 16, 2011). The brief summarizes and cites the legislative record regarding the coverage question.

86. *Shelby County, Ala. v. Holder*, F. Supp. 2d, 2011 WL 4375001 (D.D.C., Sep. 21, 2011). [Case no. 1:10-CV-00651-JDB, Mem. Op.]

87. See Complaint, *LaRoque v. Holder*, No. 1:10-CV-00561-JDB (D.D.C., Apr. 7, 2010). Private citizens and candidates in North Carolina, where state officials in 2009 took the step of filing a brief urging the Supreme Court to uphold Section 5, have filed a constitutional challenge arising out of their dissatisfaction with a U.S. Justice Department objection under Sec-

tion 5 blocking an electoral reform that the department determined would disadvantage black voters.

88. See 42 USC §§ 1973l(c)(3), 1973aa–1a(e) (2006).

89. Congressman Jim Sensenbrenner, Issue Statement on Immigration, http://sensenbrenner.house.gov/Issues/Issue/?IssueID=5088 ("I put the issue of illegal immigration on the national agenda in 2005 with the introduction of the Border Protection, Antiterrorism, and Illegal Immigration Control Act, which passed the House of Representatives"). The Border Protection, Antiterrorism and Illegal Immigration Control Act sought to impose stiff penalties for illegal immigration and ratcheted up border enforcement. H.R. 4437, 109th Cong. (2005).

90. *Voting Rights Act: Section 203 – Bilingual Election Requirements: Hearing before the Subcomm. On the Constitution of the H. Comm. On the Judiciary,* 109th Cong. 45–59 (Nov. 8, 2005) (statement of Roger Clegg).

91. H.R. Rep. No. 109-478, at 135 (2006). See Tucker, *The Politics of Persuasion,* 207–210.

92. Tucker, *The Politics of Persuasion,* 205, 248.

93. Id.

94. Id.

95. Id.

96. 152 *Cong. Rec.* H4745 (daily ed., June 28, 2006) (statement of Rep. Lewis).

97. Of course, some CBC members depend on Latino voters or language-minority coalitions for election, so they may have a more direct experience understanding how Section 203 facilitates participation by limited-English-proficient voters. The same can be said for many Republicans as well. In 2004, President Bush received as much as 44 percent of the Latino vote. A majority of Filipino and Vietnamese voters tend to vote for Republicans, and language-minority voters of Japanese, Ko-

rean, and Pacific Islander ethnicity tend to split their vote evenly between Democrats and Republicans. Tucker, *The Politics of Persuasion,* 208.

98. *Continuing Need for Section 203's Provisions for Limited English Proficient Voters: Hearing Before the S. Comm. On the Judiciary,* 109th Cong. 346–53 (statement of John Trasviña); *Voting Rights Act: Section 203 – Bilingual Election Requirements: Hearing before the Subcomm. On the Constitution of the H. Comm. On the Judiciary,* 109th Cong. 12–21, 1378–1402, 1414–19 (Nov. 8, 2005) (statements of Margaret Fung, Karen K. Narasaki and John Lewis); *Modern Enforcement of the Voting Rights Act: Hearing Before the S. Comm. On the Judiciary,* 109th Cong. 14–16 (May 10, 2006) (statement of Juan Cartagena). See also Jim Tucker's chapter 8, supra.

99. *Fannie Lou Hamer, Rosa Parks, and Coretta Scott King Voting Rights Act Reauthorization and Amendments Act of 2006: Hearing before the Subcomm. On the Constitution of the H. Comm. On the Judiciary,* 109th Cong. 59–60 (May 4, 2006) (statement of Debo Adegbile).

100. Section 5 also permits expansion, through the so-called "pocket trigger" of Section 3 of the act, as well as contraction through the bailout provision. Because these changes in coverage require judicial action, the evolving scope of preclearance coverage is less predictable. That is especially true now following the Supreme Court's expansion of opportunities for bailout in the wake of the utility district case, as the pace of bailout has increased.

101. See Jim Tucker's chapter 8, at note 182–83.

102. See 42 USC § 1973aa–1a(d) (providing for bailout from Section 203 coverage for any jurisdiction establishing "that the illiteracy rate of the applicable language minority group . . . is equal to or less than the national illiteracy rate").

103. The only constitutional challenge brought to the V R A's language-assistance provisions was to Section 4(e) of the act, a permanent provision included in the original 1965 act which provides Spanish-language materials and assistance for Puerto Rican voters educated in Spanish. The Supreme Court rejected that challenge. See *Katzenbach v. Morgan,* 384 U.S. 641 (1966).

104. Rep. Tancredo did not run for re-election in 2008, choosing instead to run for the Republican nomination for president.

105. See 152 *Cong. Rec.* H 4664 (daily ed., June 27, 2006) (Roll Call vote no. 329) (reporting the vote on the Stearns amendment).

106. "Former Congressman Tom Tancredo Says Obama Won Because There is No Literacy Test Before Voting," Cleveland Leader, http://www.clevelandleader.com/node/12982.

107. Id.

108. "Thurgood Marshall: Justice for All," DVD (A&E Biography 1997) (on file with author).

Contributors

Debo P. Adegbile is the associate director–counsel/director of litigation of the NAACP Legal Defense and Educational Fund, Inc. (LDF). Adegbile's experience with LDF in the area of voting rights has encompassed constitutional cases and actions arising under the Voting Rights Act of 1965 (VRA), among other statutes. Adegbile successfully argued against a constitutional challenge to the core Section 5 federal preclearance provision of the VRA before a three-judge panel in federal court in Washington, D.C., in 2007 and subsequently before the U.S. Supreme Court in 2009. That case, *Northwest Austin Municipal Utility District No. One v. Holder,* followed a multiyear effort and collaboration with numerous local and national partners, which culminated in the reauthorization of several important provisions of the VRA.

Edward Blum is a visiting fellow at the American Enterprise Institute in Washington, D.C. He is also the director of the Project on Fair Representation, a not-for-profit legal defense foundation that supports litigation that challenges racial and ethnic preferences in state and federal courts. He is the author of *The Unintended Consequences of Section 5 of the Voting Rights Act* and dozens of articles for publications such as the *Wall Street Journal, Los Angeles Times, National Law Journal,* and *Legal Times.*

Roger Clegg is the president and general counsel of the Center for Equal Opportunity. He writes, speaks, and conducts research on legal issues raised by the civil rights laws. Clegg is also a contributing editor at *National Review Online* and writes frequently for a wide variety of popular periodicals and law journals. He has held a number of positions at the U.S. Department of Justice, including assistant to the solicitor general, where he argued three cases before the U.S. Supreme Court, and the number two official in the Civil Rights Division and Environment Division. He was vice president and general counsel of the National Legal Center for the Public Interest, where he wrote and edited a variety of publications on legal issues of interest to business.

Richard L. Engstrom is a visiting research fellow at the Center for the Study of Race, Ethnicity, and Gender in the Social Sciences at Duke University. He has extensive experience as a consulting and testifying expert on voting rights issues and has served as a special master and court-appointed expert in redistricting cases. He is author (with Mark Rush) of *Fair and Effective Representation? Debating Electoral Reform and Minority Rights*. His articles on voting rights and election systems have appeared in the *American Political Science Review, Journal of Politics, Electoral Studies, Legislative Studies Quarterly, Social Science Quarterly, Publius,* and *Journal of Law and Politics,* among other journals. Several of his articles have been cited by the U.S. Supreme Court.

Daniel McCool is professor of political science and director of the Environmental and Sustainability Studies Program at the University of Utah. His research focuses on Indian water rights and voting rights, water resource development, and public lands policy. He is author of *River Republic: The Fall and Rise of America's Rivers; Native Waters: Contemporary Indian Water Settlements and the Second Treaty Era;* and *Command of the Waters: Iron Triangles, Federal Water Development, and Indian Water.* He coauthored *Native Vote: American Indians, the Voting Rights Act, and Indian Voting; Staking Out the Terrain: Power and Performance among Natural Resource Agencies;* and *Public Policy Theories, Models and Concepts.* He edited two books with his students, *Waters of Zion: The Politics of Water in Utah* and *Contested Landscape: The Politics of Wilderness in Utah and the West.*

Peyton McCrary is a historian in the Civil Rights Division of the U.S. Department of Justice, and an adjunct professor at George Washington University Law School. Before joining the government, McCrary testified as an expert witness in fourteen voting rights cases, beginning in 1981 with *Bolden v. City of Mobile,* on remand from the Supreme Court. Over the past thirty years, he has published a prize-winning book, eight journal articles or book chapters, and six law review articles. His work for the Department of Justice focuses on the development of expert testimony in voting rights litigation. In 2011 Dr. McCrary received the Maceo Hubbard Award, the highest career recognition award a non-attorney can receive in the Civil Rights Division.

Laughlin McDonald is director of the Voting Rights Project of the American Civil Liberties Union in Atlanta. Prior to that he was in private practice and taught at the University of North Carolina Law School. He has represented minorities in scores of discrimination cases and specialized in the area of voting rights. He has argued cases before the U.S. Supreme Court and numerous federal appellate courts, testified frequently before Congress, and written for scholarly and popular publications on a variety of civil liberties issues. He is the author of several books, including *A Voting Rights Odyssey: Black Enfranchisement in Georgia* and *American Indians and the Fight for Equal Voting Rights.*

Chris Nelson is currently serving as one of three South Dakota Public Utilities Commissioners. Previously Nelson was secretary of state, state election supervisor in the secretary of state's office, and Uniform Commercial Code supervisor in the same office.

Bryan L. Sells is special litigation counsel in the Voting Section of the Civil Rights Division at the U.S. Department of Justice. Previously he was a staff attorney with the Voting Rights Project of the American Civil Liberties Union in Atlanta, where he specialized in Native American voting rights litigation under Section 2 and Section 5 of the Voting Rights Act and constitutional ballot-access litigation on behalf of alternative parties and independent candidates. He has represented the plaintiffs in numerous civil rights cases at the trial and appellate levels.

Abigail Thernstrom is vice chair of the U.S. Commission on Civil Rights and an adjunct scholar at the American Enterprise Institute. She is author, most recently, of *Voting Rights – and Wrongs: The Elusive Quest for Racially Fair Elections*. Her previous work on the subject, *Whose Votes Count? Affirmative Action and Minority Voting Rights* won four academic prizes, including one from the American Bar Association. She is author (with her husband Stephan Thernstrom) of *America in Black and White: One Nation, Indivisible* and *No Excuses: Closing the Racial Gap in Learning*. In 2007 she and her husband shared a prestigious Bradley Award for "outstanding intellectual achievement."

James Thomas Tucker is a partner with Lewis, Brisbois, Bisgaard & Smith LLP in Las Vegas, Nevada, and an adjunct professor at the University of Nevada-Las Vegas, where he teaches courses on voting rights and elections law. He is a former senior trial attorney with the Voting Section at the U.S. Department of Justice. In 2006, he worked for the National Association of Latino Elected and Appointed Officials (NALEO) to secure the twenty-five-year reauthorization of the Voting Rights Act (VRA), testifying before Congress three times in support of Section 203 of the VRA. Tucker served as co-counsel with the ACLU and Native American Rights Fund in *Nick v. Bethel, Alaska,* the first successful language-assistance case by Alaskan Natives under the VRA. The author of nearly two dozen journal articles and book chapters, most on the VRA, he recently published *The Battle over Bilingual Ballots: Language Minorities and Political Access under the Voting Rights Act.*

Index